Globalization and Gender

Globalization and Gender

Edited by
Sumita Sarkar
Manjari Srivastava

RAWAT PUBLICATIONS
Jaipur • New Delhi • Bangalore • Hyderabad • Guwahati

ISBN 978-81-316-0447-2

Published by
Prem Rawat for **Rawat Publications**
Satyam Apts, Sector 3, Jawahar Nagar, Jaipur 302 004 (India)
Phone: 0141 265 1748 / 7006 Fax: 0141 265 1748
E-mail: info@rawatbooks.com
Website: www.rawatbooks.com

New Delhi Office
4858/24, Ansari Road, Daryaganj, New Delhi 110 002
Phone: 011 2326 3290

Also at Bangalore, Hyderabad and Guwahati

Typeset by M & M Pre Press Consultants, Thiruvananthapuram
Printed at Chaman Enterprises, New Delhi

Contents

Preface ix
Acknowledgements xi

I
Women and Globalization

1. Globalization and Women at Work: A Feminist Discourse 3
Sumita Sarkar

2. Heteropatriarchy: Globalization, the Institution of Heterosexuality and Lesbians 23
Susan Hawthorne

3. Women's Empowerment Approach as a Means for Engendering the Development Process 39
Lovely Mamta Dhulia and Purnima Singh

II
Women in Formal and Informal Economy

4. Women in Industrial Sector: An Empirical Study 59
Debjani Mukherjee and Promila Singh

5. Stress and Coping among Women Managers in Indian Organizations 72
H.L. Kaila

6. The Employers' Role as Perceived by Mothers Working in Night Shifts 88
Jayanti Gokhale

7. Fair Gender Induction in the Armed Forces: Issues and Challenges 130
Nidhi Maheshwari and N.P. Singh

8. Status of Women Hawkers in New Economic Environment: A Case of Navi Mumbai 151
Manjari Srivastava and Sumita Sarkar

9. Women Labour Force in Unorganized Sector: A Study of Construction Workers in Navi Mumbai 170
Sumita Sarkar

10. Women Workers in Unorganized Sector and Brick Kiln Industry: A Case of Navi Mumbai 187
Sumita Sarkar

11. Exploitation and Harassment of Migrant Women and Girl Children Working as Domestic Assistant 200
Sibnath Deb

III
Women and Education

12. Globalization, Higher Education and Gender: An Appraisal of the Process of Reaching Out to Indian Women 227
Anjali Dewan

13. Reading Motivation in Primary School Girls: A Problem of Cognitive Mapping 236
Debdulal Dutta Roy

IV
Women and Identity

14. Discerning Whispers: Reflections on Self and Identity 251
Sujata Sharma

15. Gender Differentiation in Self-actualization and Personality Correlates of Professionals 305
Nishat Afroz and Ranjana Mittra

V
Women and Family

16. Psychological Fallout of Violence Against Women in the Family 327
Roomana N. Siddiqui

List of Contributors 336
Index 338

Preface

The term 'globalization' has gained increasing currency and is used with varying scope and significance. Clearly, globalization refers to something more than just the internationalization of the world economy. It is therefore necessary to define and characterize globalization and examine the qualitative changes that are likely to affect marginalized sections like women and the poor.

One of the major optimistic aspects of globalization as argued by their advocates is that it could provide vast opportunities for both women and the poor. For women, new jobs are likely to be created in areas that have not been traditionally male-dominated ones. Further, it may prove to be easier to redistribute access to knowledge and skills (which are increasingly important assets) than to redistribute more traditional assets, such as land or accumulated wealth. The challenge has thus emerged to consider the complex and multidimensional concepts of globalization and gender, to understand key relationships and implications of this changing process and then to grapple with them in the context of development.

Given the vast scope of globalization, this gamut of discourse on feminist agenda adopts a more specific approach to address various challenges that women are facing due to opening up of economy at global level and impacting at local parlance and women at large. These aspects of globalization, as feminists argue, are also affecting the negotiating power of women, particularly poor and working women and the institutions that mediate on their behalf. The moot agenda for the feminist critiques is to strive for widening opportunities for women, insuring against risks, spreading benefits, and to prevent the creation of new vulnerabilities. Thus, the feminist discourse should adhere to the broader patterns of change associated with globalization.

Research into the gender impact of globalization suggests that the process has had quite mixed consequences for women. On the one hand, we could point to the opening up of employment opportunities in the expanding service economy (for example, in global information and global communications businesses, global retail and tourism). Women also account for a large number of the jobs in globalized manufacturing industries, often working in the export-processing zones that are an essential component of transnational organized manufacturing production. The argument that is made is that such job opportunities have granted women access to a greater level of economic freedom, as they move out of the household and into the (global) market economy. However, what needs to be taken into account is the way women entering these globalized industries are overwhelmingly stratified into the lower rungs of the occupational health and positioning of their gender status. A consistent feature of these opportunities for employment in the global economy is the low economic value accorded to work performed primarily by women. The jobs that women are moving into like in the finance, information and communications industries, for example, have been characterized as work within "electronic sweatshops", low paid and highly Stressful, whilst those highly paid jobs within these industries remain male-dominated. Women dominate employment in export-oriented manufacturing industries such as electronics and garment manufacture. They are recruited as a low wage labour force in these light manufacturing industries. They are seen, and hence favoured, as a passive, flexible workforce that will accept low wages without demanding labour and human rights.

Gender inequality, therefore, is a fundamental component of global labour market. High level of gender inequality in globalized production lines is also to be linked to the deregulation of labour markets that has accompanied the global shift towards a more liberal market economy. A flexibilization of employment, associated with little or no protection for the worker, is thus also linked to the feminization of employment. Furthermore, on the issue of the flexibilization of female employment, the role that domestic workers play in globalized networks of production also needs to be considered.

In the above context, the present work includes a wider range of feminist discourses in various aspects of globalization and its changing status or positioning of 'gender'. It is thus a modest effort to put feminist concerns in the context of globalization.

Acknowledgements

The whole spillover of thought actually started from a 'Feminist Summit' that one of the editors Sumita Sarkar had attended at Townsville, East Australia in 2007. The ambience of active feminists' voice coming across several parts of the world was truly enriching and tempting to do something, which may not be at such a large scale but definitely may carry the similar agenda on 'voicing for women' in a globalized context. On a cosy evening sipping over a cup of coffee and *gappa* (chit-chat), the idea of writing on women-centric issues came up during a discussion between both of us, as we were trying to reason out the development of women and their positioning in the era of liberalization as an outcome of Sumita's post-summit effect! Changes are taking place in both economic and political world, but to what extent these changes have positively touched the lives of women? Have these liberalized policies induced in our postmodern socio-political structure truly empowered the women? How far are we today able to raise our voice when it comes to diversified walks of life and work situations that, needless to say, would not dare to ignore issues related to women exclusion, marginalization, inequality and power struggle across the globe and India is no exception!

To share our concerns with others as well as to present the thoughts of academia on gender issues, we decided to dialogue with various activists, researchers and academicians. The responses were overwhelming that culminated in the publication of this volume. The initiation for editing a book on 'Globalization and Gender' as we perceive it, is "a means to express our reaction towards gender issues that have been curbed and not much heeded by the policy makers, the lobbyists and the powerful!" The coining of the idea thus also includes the understanding towards development of a postmodern society and delineating the status of women in the context of globalized and liberalized modernity.

We convey our deepest gratitude towards the contributors who in our eyes are a significant voice and the carrier of feminist agenda. We were connected through Facebook, Orkut, g-mail and also on phone. This networking was truly not based on physical gathering/association of stereotype academic meeting, rather we would love to call it 'web space networking of women'. Dear readers, we look forward to your reactions towards several themes that these authors have addressed in this volume.

Our special thanks to Dr R.N. Sharma, Dean, School of Social Sciences, TISS for providing his critical views on some articles. We also want to thank Jayanti Gokhale for her contribution in working with manuscripts diligently and also providing her critical comments. Rajeev Garg and Debasish Sarkar always stood by us, and provided moral support and suggestions to take the work ahead successfully.

Finally, we specially thank Rawat Publications for their cooperation and accepting the manuscript for publication.

I

Women and Globalization

1

Globalization and Women at Work: A Feminist Discourse

Sumita Sarkar

Since last two decades the processes of globalization and the opening up of market economy have given rise to many philosophical and policy crisis (Eagan, 2005) especially in the context of developing economies. It is so because it provides a life-world, i.e., in the form of social reality as well as the world view which initiates several conceptual approaches and theoretical debates to understand globalization (Derrida, 2003; Egan, 2005; Jameson and Miyoshi, 1998). One of these theoretical approaches relates globalization with two broad macro processes, i.e., the globalization of trade and trade culture and the changing nature of labour and gender struggle in the transforming economy. The trend of debate is more towards dynamics of gender exploitation and social security aspects of labour force within a symbiotic post-war relation of "capital" and "labour". Against this backdrop, the present paper makes an attempt to explore the complex relation between the gender and the economic liberalization of trade and market policy that underpin globalization process. The paper analyses "gender" and "globalization" from macro as well as micro socio-economic postulates.

The Theoretical Discourse

The present content of theoretical proposition is that the impact of globalization on gender is explicit and geared to gender discrimination and inequalities in terms of access to and control over capital and resources. While some women have gained work opportunity in terms of newly emerging forms of employment, especially in the IT and service sectors the semi-skilled or the unskilled ones have lost the control over their natural resources (land etc.), resulting in the loss of traditional livelihood and sustainability. Under such climate of economic transition towards global economy, the moot issue remains "the status of women" in changing labour market and how the contemporary capital and labour operate in the context of globalization from a feminist perspective, more so, the dynamics of power and capital distribution exerting gender discrepancies that are otherwise left invisible in the "male stream of theoretical" discourse.

While probing the above issues, the underlying assumption is that women have never received equal treatment of homogenous category and, when united as gender, other factors like class, ethnicity, religion have further divided them in terms of the age, ideology and sexual preferences. One has to keep these differences in mind while talking about 'globalization and women' as indeed, one woman's forte might be another woman's loss. For instance, in the case of female migrant domestic helper in the countries like Middle East and Europe, an housewife gets service from a migrant domestic maid at the cost of exploiting 'her' wages and working hours or sex (Cecilia, 2000). Therefore, it remains an illusive concept of economic 'freedom' as described by the advocates of globalization and neo-liberalization who assert that women are expected to enter in many new job opportunities in new economic era, whereas the reality depicts that emerging new work opportunities laid out to them generate further exploitations and vulnerability.

The argument illuminates from several feminist critiques (Dex, 1985; Sanderson, 1990; Walby, 1990; Cecilia, 2000; Jain, 2000) that the globalization process is not necessarily integrating 'men' and 'women' into a homogenous entities in the sphere of economy, culture, technology and governance. On the contrary, many of these feminist writers consider that the globalization and neo-liberalization have geared the process of euphemism for ultra imperialism (Cecilia, 2000). Indeed, neo-liberalization and globalization have led to severe fragmentations and the emergence of divergent views and identity politics. In that sense, globalization certainly gets ambiguous to be entitled as esoteric, universal and equal. In the Second Global Knowledge Conference held in Kuala Lumpur (2000), two of the main themes of the conference were the 'indigenization of knowledge' and 'sovereignty'—a counter discourse to that of globalization (ibid.). The forces of globalization might have to contend with other forms of social and cultural resistance, thus making its spread a much more complex process. As Diana Wong (1990) puts it aptly: "the challenge of globality today may not lie in the attainment of convergence, but in the recognition and acceptance of difference".

One needs to consider that the debate on women labour force and globalization presents a much more complicated scenario as it places "gender dynamics" in all aspects of life, from family to the political spheres. But the essence of this moot debate remains live as whether globalization has chiselled away sexist structures, processes and attitudes? What would be the opportunities for future work and the preferences that can be rendered for women? It also raises the dilemmas, whether the oppression would continue to exist under induced patriarchic structure of gender discrimination and exploitation of women? As Ghosh (1999) has rightly observed ". . . structural adjustments in the labour market and massive lay offs (retrenchments) have the key to casualisation of workforce where women are disproportionately targeted and victimized". In India, for example, the laws of free trade of a number of commodities have threatened many industries like handloom, weaving, dairying and even dry land farming (for the coarse grains) which provide source of sustenance to millions of women, due to extinction of employment opportunities, if not erosion of the same (Jain, 2000). The critical issues of gender deprivation and discrimination revolve around the question of unequal wages, lack of maternity benefit, discrimination at workplace, lack of childcare facilities.

However, it is also to a large extent true that, through globalization, women have gained certain opportunities in terms of widening field of job options and also in terms of recognizing women's rights as a part of the human rights. Their empowerment (wherever applicable) has given considerable opportunities and possibilities of improving employment conditions through global solidarity and co-ordination. But, the argument here is that these gains have been made both 'as a result of and in spite of 'globalization'—within last three decades or so, through the momentum due to the international women's movements and through international discourses on women and exposition of their exploitation. Indeed these global debates and discourses have put forth the global governance on women's position and rights and in result, have made their impact on national governments to adapt their stance.

To understand the status of women at work under the globalized web of economic activity, feminist critiques have not only described the form of patriarchy superseding certain gender (females), but also tried to focus on how global capitalism or global imperialism affect all aspects of social relationship of "women" under different social and economic classes. As Hobsbawm (cited in Agnihotri, 1999: 7) points out: "Woman's assertion is a significant expression of democratic upsurge in developing countries and shall remain one of the largest contribution for the 20th century".

Under the above context, the following sections highlight few gender issues in relation to women's employment, their changing socio-economic status, opportunities and fringe benefits (maternity benefit, social security etc.) that they receive in the present era of globalization, at their work place, at their home and in society in general.

Feminization of Employment, Sub-Contracting and Flexibility of Labour Structure

The greater bargaining strength of internationally mobile capital has allowed both local and international capitalists to impose tough conditions on their workers. Such conditions not only reduce the power and rights of workers but also demean their working conditions. Women workers especially get the brunt of such exploitative, aggressive and capitalist policies of the global labour market. Under neo-liberalized global policies, corporates in competition make their own strategies in order to meet challenges for their own survival. One of such major strategies which deal with the labour can be seen from three major forms—labour flexibility, casualization and also feminization of labour. Consequently, two dual processes are emerging; first, the fragmentation of labour processes resulting in low skill and repetitive work, and the declining trend of regular work through various forms of non-regular, flexible employment, e.g., part-time, temporary, sub-contracted, and home-based work. The other process is upgrading the workers' skills in multitask jobs, using information communication technology (ICT). This results in an increasing demand for multi-skilled workers with hardware/software as well as business skills.

In the area of 'foreign trade sector' (FTS), both export and import policies have been restructured paying attention mainly to keep the capital productive and globally mobile both by national and international agencies. This severely affects the status of working women and their work situations. For example, export has boomed up in South-East and East Asia in the last quarter of the 20th century, as fuelled by the contribution in export related activities and through the remittances made by migrant workers. In Malaysia, electric and electronic products comprised about 60 per cent of the manufactured export and they generate one-third of the manufacturing employment in the country. A majority of the employees in such industries are Malay women. Thus, in the case of paid employees, mainly within the MNCs, women are employed to gain more flexible labour with much cheaper bargain on the part of employers. Hence, global capitalism makes use of existing patriarchal ideology whereby women are perceived to be more subservient to (male) managers' authority, less prone to organize unions, more willing to accept poor working conditions and easier to dismiss using lifecycle criteria such as marriage and child birth (Ghosh, 1999).

In India, there have been major changes since 1991 in implementing policies leading to reduction in the industrial licensing and opening up of the economy. The major thrust of the liberalization process has been wide-ranging trade reforms and restructuring custom duties with a gradual elimination of restrictions on trade. In the pre-reform regime the import duties in India were the highest in the world (NCAER, 2003). Since 1991, the tariff has been brought down from 60 per cent in 1994–95 to 45 per cent in 1997–98, and 40 per cent in 1999–2000 to 35 per cent in 2000–2001 (Chowdhury, 2004). Indian government is virtually compelled to protect the interests of the global corporates, otherwise it is argued that capital would go to Mayanmar, Bangladesh or other countries where wages are lower and workers have even fewer rights (Cecilia, 2000; Ghosh 1999).

The world of flexible labour, sub-contracting and the process of casualization raise many other complex issues in the context of "gender" exploitation in global economy. The informal sector is one of the most affected areas which even otherwise has been plagued by arbitrary gender discrimination, low wages and lack of job security. Then, there is a trend towards informalization of women's labour. For example, the export processing zones (EPZs) especially in the form of informal sector be it in the agro-based production or the manufacturing, is one area where exploitation is much higher. In India, EPZs consists of a majority of women workers as compared to any other areas of production. These women are lowly skilled, between the age 18 to 24, with no unionization and ready to work even at cheaper wage rates. They are exploited at job in many ways (Sharma and Sengupta in Hebsur, 1996).

In addition, the trend of extreme decentralization of production has given rise to sub-contracting or piecemeal work through small units employing informal workers. In India, for example, in places like Ghaziabad and Greater Noida, sitting at home, women are engaged in stitching buttons on T-shirts, which will be the final product of a company like Benetton or even smaller less famous manufacturers. The basic nature of contract here is the piecemeal job, with effective low rate of wages—which creates the need to earn more and eventually includes elder women and children—sometimes the whole family. A wide range of sub-contracting or piecemeal works include garment, luggage bag making, fancy items, food products and their processing, along with traditional sub-contracting like the 'pappad' or shoe laces making. These contract labourers are mainly the female labour force and are visible everywhere in Asia, especially in the countries like India. These women workers are fated to work under inferior employment conditions with no avenues to legal rights or voice against the employers. As a result, they succumb to low wages, overworking hours, and if they do not meet the demand of employers, termination of job contracts. Such work conditions reinforce traditional patriarchy, which colludes with global, national and local capital to maintain a system of gender relations that exploits and subordinates women—through sub-standard labour and low wages/income.

Gujarat is also another example (Chowdhary, 1996) in expanding fast growth informal sector and informalization of labour force. In last two decades, Gujarat has witnessed economic downturn by the decline of textile industry and also replaced by overall industrial development since 1987–97. Though a significant rise of working population indicates overall growth of employment and economy, the informalization or casualization of jobs in the formal sector have taken well advantage over the large number of displaced textile labour in Gujarat. A study (Chowdhury, 2004) shows a significant fall in the wage earning by former textile workers who are presently employed in the informal sector. Gujarat has established minimum wages in 53 activities in the informal sector where the wage varied from Rs 45 to Rs 53 in 1998. In the case of women, the wage is even lesser (i.e., less than Rs 37), with an increasing number of daily wage earners with approximately 33 per cent female workforce below the poverty line.

Thus, in general, the poor and the unskilled women workers class are the worst hit of the sub-contracting and casualization process, which squeezes profits at each level in favour of the employers. It involves low/minimum investment of capital input, with no risk or responsibility to labour force, void of social security and while maximizing the output.

Furthermore, the decline of trade unionism in the era of globalization is another trend that has severely affected working class movement in India. Unions appear to be unable to stem the tide of trade liberalization policies to protect labour interest. In fact, workers and their unions in India recently are on the receiving end due to growing influence of bigwig international organizations and corporates on Indian government. The result is that the 'regularity' and 'security' of industrial jobs are no more guaranteed. Moreover it has led to eroding women's right over work, and has also affected 'her' reproductive health and work status.

Breakdown of Traditional Family Structure and Kinship Network

Breaking down of extended or joint family structure and kinship ties is no more atypical to urban India. Rural India is also facing such a trend due to the gradual impact of globalization and changing economy in the country. Such a trend has severe impact on women both in rural and urban areas.

The era of globalization has accelerated the pace of migration more so in last 15 years. The pull-push factors have uprooted millions of

Asians especially the North-East Asians towards comparatively advanced countries to secure better means of livelihood. The trend of outsourcing and supply of cheap labour mainly from Asian labour market, is one of the major trends of advanced countries like America, Europe and Australia. In such context, India is of no exception in supplying cheap labour force to other countries. At global level, more than 120 million migrants have left their home countries in search of greener pastures abroad, leading to the warning by the United Nations as the 'human crisis of our age' (Celina, 2005).

In Asia, migration for economic reasons has denuded poor families leaving children to care for themselves with either father or mother away in a foreign land. The problems faced by female migrant workers have not received much attention by the researchers, activists or administrators. In India, such compulsive migration has multifaceted impact on women. For example, migration of rural men towards urban areas and later to outer countries has led to an increasing proportion of feminization of household, with a majority of them belonging to extreme poverty. For instance, 30–35 per cent of the rural households in India are female-headed households, compared to the 25 per cent in Cambodia, 15.75 in Korea and 21.4 per cent in Mongolia (Breman, 1996; Gulati, 1997).

However, moving out for rural men is not atypical in the history of migration in India, but the recent trend makes newly emerging phenomenon, which pushes thousands of rural women coming to cities and engaging themselves in unskilled labour (mainly in the construction and infrastructure-building projects) due to the lure of earning better livelihood. As a result of such intensifying pace of migration, the traditional joint or extended family is getting de-structured. Furthermore, globalization has also brought the philosophy of marketisation and consumerism in new era, which has led to erosion of traditional values, threatening the traditional kinship ties and bond of indigenous neighbourhood or communities. 'Cash and commodity' relation has replaced the earlier defined values, based on socio-economic relations; this in turn endangers social cohesion and kinship bond of rural India.

Thus, with the commercialization of agriculture, migration and breaking down of traditional value-laded social networks, poverty has taken a synonymous face of 'female' or female headed household. In indigenous rural areas, taking away of their customary land to make way for the building of dams and commercial crops (also cash crops) has led to a degeneration of the status of women, who once owned land; and cultivating their own lands was related to their higher status in the community.

Another reason of women migrating to urban areas is the gradual low productivity of agriculture. A research report (NCW, 2005) asserts that over 5–7 years there has been a steady decline of economic opportunity in rural India, ranging from 20 per cent to as much as 77 per cent. In such cases, traditional patriarchal ideology generally imposes the reproductive role on these women and also demands their productivity in terms of wage earning to meet the changing demand of economy and livelihood under globalization. These women usually are to carry their children with them due to lack of extended family support and poverty. Further, they are victimized in terms of exploitation of wages with no support of social security or health or medication, leading to malnutrition, increase in maternal mortality rate, jaundice, etc.

Migrating to comparatively advanced counties to earn better salary is another emerging phenomenon among urban women. These women are mostly hired on contracts both in skilled-organized and unskilled–unorganized sectors. Hiring their services is like domestic work, caretakers, homemakers etc. Though these women earn much better than they would have in their own country, by catering services to reproductive role like child rearing, cooking etc., there is a flip side. Housemaids in these foreign countries like US and Middle East often work in exploitative conditions. They are often paid lesser than agreed amount in the contract, overworked with domestic services and in many cases also sexually abused or used by the heads of households (Groots, 2005). Furthermore, in many cases, women workers who have migrated to another country often become severe victim of dislocation, uprooted from their native settlement, alienated from kith and kin. Subsequently, they even lose their traditional source of livelihood, leading to either feminization of poverty, or prostitution has become common phenomenon for female migrants in South-East Asia.

Furthermore, in urban India, for skilled expertise of women labour force, it has almost become a necessity to obtain a profession to support the family. Besides the trend of choice that modern women would like to see themselves as productive and successful like the traditional 'bread-earner' (men) especially when globalization has opened up various opportunity for women labour force, there is a trend among the couples to earn together to manage household across. The increasing cost of living, privatization of services, demanding quality of life and consumerism are a few factors that have created a forced situation for urban couples mainly living in cities to earn together. The impact of breaking down of joint or extended family is one of the major factors that have further initiated the necessity and compulsion for such forced situation of independent and individualized livelihood. In a globalized era as a result, the burden becomes double for these women for maintaining both—their family and the work front. In this context, the feminist critiques (Jain, 2000; Ghosh, 1999; Krishnaraj, 1989; Blanchard, 2003; Bernard, 1987; Kishwar and Vanita, 1984; Kumar, 1994) have been demanding more freedom and choice to reconsider the traditional gender role and gender relations. The fair demand of women to have shared responsibilities from their spouse in domestic chores and childcare tasks yet remains a neglected dimension by the patriarchal ideology. The emerging contradictions lead to marital disputes in family courts, resulting in divorce and separations.

Commodification of Women and Sexuality

The process of globalization has inflicted the philosophy of laissez-faire and neo-liberalization across the globe. The ideology enhances the concept of marketization and consumerism as interwoven factors ruling the new changing economy. The ideology of consumerism and marketization envisages world as market where individuals can access anything in the market what 'he' or 'she' wants to consume. It enhances the logic that everything in the world can be commercialized and commoditized. This rising trend of individualism and consumerism comes hand in hand with the neo-liberalized philosophy. In the same vein, the concept of woman as a commodity has been further reinforced through several service and entertainment sectors like the hotel industry, film industry, tourism, and so on.

The economic globalization in the form of market democracy has commoditized women and sexuality as never before. Women are commonly employed as models, films stars, telemarketers, servers and entertainers in bars and restaurants. This is because the service sector has always shared a very thin borderline with entertainment industries. As models, these women feature in advertisements falling into two categories: looking after the home and staying young, slim and beautiful. Articles in women's magazines are often written about looking beautiful through dieting, and how to get a 'man' and keep a 'man'. All of these images make women feel insecure about them because very few women look like supermodels on billboards, in magazines and on televisions (Jeong and Choi, 2005; Kumar, 1994).

Women are thus portrayed as ever-available sex objects in an endlessly repetitive male dominated world. These jobs are not only unstable, low waged and physically strenuous but also reinforce the use of feminity and sexuality to raise sales, making women more vulnerable to possibilities of sexual abuse and exploitation. The increasing rate of sex tourism, sex trafficking and violence against women are inevitable outcome of such commoditization of women and sexuality in Asian countries. A few data can be recalled in this regard:

The total number of reported rape cases in Malaysia increased from 879 in 1993 to 1,323 in 1997—a 50 per cent increase (AWAM, 2000). Rape of teenage girls rose from 604 in 1995 to 719 in 1996. Police reports that 67 per cent of the victims were the minor girls.

- Prostitution, forced prostitution, trafficking of women and children associated violence and harassment has become a major concern in South-East Asian region.
- Women migrant workers from the region engaged in tourism industry, service sector (domestic work) are increasingly becoming victim of sexual violence (Jeong and Choi, 2005).
- In India, in 1997, 14,000 women were raped and 27,513 were sexually assaulted (NCW Report, 2000).
- According to another report, 16 per cent cases of molestation of women, 785 cases of kidnapping/abduction (mainly used in sex trafficking), 68 per cent sexual harassment at work were reported during 1994–95 in the country (Crime in India, 2000).

These above data reflect on the growing malaise in so-called 'developing societies' more caused due to overriding of economic institutions over age-old community based societies, which confront new dimensions of exploitation and inequalities mainly in terms of gender. Feminist critiques like Jain, 2000; Gosh, 2005; Krishnaraj, 1989; Kumar, 1994; Celina, 2005 opine that though globalization in urban India projects modernity, egalitarian and secular world leading to changing female roles, in reality, the underlying truth is that globalization has reinforced the unequal gender relation in many folds. The pre-modern patriarchal ideology is far more active under the sleeves of modern fervour of globalization.

Market Liberalization in Agriculture and Status of Women

The shift in production towards cash crops from household subsistence production is one of the defining characteristics of commercialization in agriculture, associated with globalization. In many regions of sub-Saharan Africa, the introduction of cash crops has changed the gender division of labour and management of household resources. Women are increasingly put to manage the household food production while men's primary economic activity has become cash crop production (Tibaijuka, 1994). Women are still expected however to contribute to the men's cash crop production (especially in labour intensive operations), while taking over tasks that men customarily carried out before, such as land preparation and tilling for the household subsistence production. For example, Ibo women in Nigeria traditionally have had primary responsibility for household food production. While they engaged in planting, weeding, harvesting, animal husbandry and food processing, their menfolk were responsible for the soil preparation (Ezumah and Di Domenici, 1997). But with the men increasingly involved in cash crop production, non-farming activities and waged employment, the women have also become responsible for the work that was previously done by men (Karl, 1997). Most agricultural policies in developing countries generally tend to favour large farms, which are thought to have greater potential for achieving higher outputs.

In India, feminization of poverty has been atypical in the rural sector. About 94 per cent women workers are employed in the primary sector in India (ILO, 2002). In the rural informal sector, women usually engage themselves traditionally in agricultural and para-agricultural activities, like transplanting paddy seedling, by long hours of standing, bending in the slush of the field, winnowing and drying of grains, weeding and caring of cattle etc. All these farm activities are related to the subsistence of agriculture.

A study conducted by the National Council for Applied Economic Research (NCAER, 2003) has shown that there is a very large section of women workers (72.51%) in agriculture as compared to men (52.38%) and the share of casual workers belongs more to women than the men.

The emerging globalization and market liberalization policies (through WTO) in agriculture have severely impinged on the rural household economy, leaving women highly affected with several disadvantages. When agriculture takes a concept of commercialization, leading to mass production, it has its severe impact on health and economic status of women, and also their access over food production, seed keeping, hoeing, processing etc. As women have been the primary seed keepers and processors, WTO policies have made their impact throughout the food chain. The impact of WTO in agriculture has adversely affected women due to implementation of a few policies like AOA (Agreement on Agriculture), TRIP (Trade Related Property Rights), and the SPA (Sanitary and Phyto-sanitary Agreement).

Commercial farming, massive production of agricultural food and cash crop production are the growing trends among the rich farmers. In their large farms, the use of agro-chemicals like herbicides and weedicides are necessary for achieving higher yield. Normally, it is the women who are predominantly employed in such large farms and the use of chemicals has affected women's health, leading to serious health hazardous and gynecological illnesses like arthritis, intestinal and parasitic infections. Low affordability and inaccessibility to medication add to their woes. Furthermore, there is growing trend of using biotechnologies to develop high yielding varieties and tissue culture in the farming. Such high tech agro farmings are throwing women from their century old employment in subsistence agriculture. The trend might further worsen the employment situation for women in future, if practised to a large extent. There is also discrepancy in the wage structure of female workforce engaged in the farm activity. Differential wages in agriculture in relation to its degree of commercialization is another issue. It is reported by the NCW (National Commission for Women, 2005) that the average daily wage for a farm worker across India is as follows:

- Haryana: Male Rs 50–60; Female Rs 25–30
- Saharanpur (Uttar Pradesh): Male Rs 60; Female Rs 35–40
- North 24 Parganas (West Bengal): Male Rs 40 (6 hour work); Female Rs 25 (6 hour work)
- Andhra Pradesh: Male Rs 40–50; Female Rs 25–30

Thus, the discrimination is practised at two levels: across the region and along the gender lines.

Another study conducted by the Research Foundation of Science, Technology and Ecology, New Delhi for the National Commission of Women (NCW), in 2002, stated that the WTO is making a disastrous impact on the plantations sector. The report asserts that the tea plantation workers in Kerala, West Bengal and Tamil Nadu are virtually facing starvation due to the closure of several small and medium plantations. This is mainly caused due to the policies of WTO favouring the large-scale production and small farmers finding themselves unable to compete in the international market with the rich owned large plantations. Moreover, it also could be an outcome of unrestricted imports and a sharp decline of tea prices in the international market. This is evident from the export data for India with the sharp decline in the tea export from $542 million in 1998 to $209 million in 2003 (Shiva and Jafri, 2004).

In the case of coffee plantations, the average working days of the labour has reduced by 30 per cent (ILO Report, 2002). In the case of rubber plantation, the integration of Indian market to that of the international has led to accumulating huge surplus stocks, followed by the reduction of price. This has further intensified the problem and jeopardized the economic condition of the workforce, which is predominantly female (ibid.).

Thus, the traditional and central role of women in the food chain from seed keeping to food making is being broken with the onset of globalized food industry, led by multinational giants in the international market. Such a sad state of affairs is mainly caused due to international trade agreements where the vulnerable sections of populations, dependent on traditional sources of livelihood, stand threatened.

Another important issue is the 'trade related intellectual property rights' (TRIP). It has made adverse impact on women's traditional knowledge and control over seeds, by using the female workforce when required and taking over the control through mass production of agro-products. The end result is that a male dominated corporate-oriented food culture is being imposed in vulnerable societies including India. TRIP agreement is gradually transferring the control over knowledge of seed and biodiversity from rural women to global corporations engaged in agriculture. Under the SAP, Indian government's expenditure on the health services has been curtailed and women who traditionally used to take care of the family members are strained due to looking after the family and also due to rising expenses on health service.

Agreement on Agriculture (AOA), which is also a part of the WTO agreement has proved to be unequal and unfair in its application, which has allowed massive subsidies to rich farmers of the North leading to artificial dumping of cheap products on the poor South, thereby destroying livelihood and income of their rural populations. Furthermore, commercialization of agriculture is also destroying heritage of crop biodiversity and food diversity, which are traditionally maintained by rural women in societies, like India. In fact in subsistence economies, food security used to depend on women's knowledge and women's skills in varied operations like seed saving, agricultural production, food processing, local marketing and also the cooking.

Thus, in brief, globalization and WTO agreements have initiated the process of market liberalization and commercialization of agriculture in many developing societies like India. This has disturbed traditional community arrangements in agriculture and also brought new hardships to the womenfolk who stand more vulnerable today.

Concluding Observations

Traditionally, within Hindu culture dominated Indian society, women have been subservient to their male counterparts under the dominant institution of patriarchy. Though women being co-partners in traditional subsistent economies, never got the status of equal partnership in sharing the livelihood decision-making process, lest said about their sharing ancestral properties. Such inferior status to women has been challenged in free India, where a few highly educated women broke the traditional nexus of patriarchy and power and have come out openly in favour of gender equity and justice. It is also true that girl child today has a conducive environment to achieve educational and professional skills.

A more drastic and sensational change that is emerging on Indian scene is the process of liberalization and globalization, which are influencing traditional socio-economic institutions and the people in multiple ways. The above processes are happening under broader capitalist formations, and first time in India, capitalism is taking deep roots. The free economy and the above processes enhance marketization and consumerism as interwoven factors, ruling the new changing economy. The rising trend of consumerism comes hand in hand with new liberalized economic policies. In this changing Indian society, some view the concept of women as 'commodity' has further been reinforced through several services and entertainment sectors, like the hotel, film, tourism and media.

Amongst the most visible changes in economic institutions, is the status of labour, production processes and the work culture. While the dominance of 'trade union' movement is on decline due to onslaught of capitalist forces, the lowly skilled labourers are the worst victims of this change in 'industrial democracy' and the labour market. Labour flexibility, casualization of labour and feminization of labour are a few dangerous consequences of the processes of globalization and liberalization. The present paper dealt more with the impact of above processes on women workers. Various kinds of service sectors are emerging where employers are finding new methods of engaging female workers at low wages and insecure job conditions. Women are 'more flexible' labour with much cheap bargain on the part of their employer. 'Sub-contracting', 'home-based' and 'piecemeal' works are becoming rampant, where job security is temporary, with low wage and more working hours. Garments, luggage bag making, food products and several such other activities are thus de-skilling or de-casualizing the already vulnerable female workers. Export processing zones (EPZs) are another category where the 'nimble fingers' are engaged under similar work conditions, and where 'hire last and fire first' is the prevailing norm.

Migrating to comparative advanced countries has emerged as another phenomenon where skilled and even unskilled women are hired more on contractual basis, and many of them face new kind of challenges and exploitations. Along with more career-oriented opportunities for women in 'dynamic' 'globalized' economy—with their extending benefits to well educated career-oriented women, there is also a compulsion for couples to earn together to manage household across various strata of society. The increasing cost of living, privatization of services, demanding quality of life and consumerism are a few factors that have created a forced situation for urban couples to earn more.

Similar to the urban front, the situation in rural areas is equally alarming. Emerging globalization and liberalization policies (like, under the WTO) have severely impinged upon the traditional sustainability of vulnerable sections of rural India. Expectedly, the worse affected are the women. For instance, agriculture is being targeted with more and more commercialization and mass production. The marginalized families are pushing their females into contractual work for mass production. This has brought extra strain to their health and life-situations. They are losing access to traditional sources of livelihood, like seeds, common property resources and flexible working hours in the field. First of all, they have to pay more for two meals a day. Thus, there is a process of feminization of poverty, which though existed traditionally, now finds new forms and dimensions. Overall, economic globalization in the form of market democracies not only reinforces the patriarchy, it has commercialized women and their sexuality as never before.

To conclude, in the global tide of changing economy and labour market, 'women' have been highly exploited to suit to the new market economy in myriad ways. Dynamics of power distribution and gender discrepancies have taken the new forms of discrimination and victimization of women under the garb of economic empowerment. Hence, though globalization and new market democratization promise new employment opportunities, equal status, more freedom and choice to women's lives, in reality such economic vistas are the double edge sword rendering women to the onslaught of their productive and reproductive roles.

■ References

Agnihotri, Indu. "Globalisation and the State." Paper presented at DAWN Asia-Pacific Workshop on Political Restructuring and Social Transformation, Thailand, October 1999, 8–11.

All Women's Action Society (AWAM). Draft Report on Rape Research, 2000.

Asian Women Workers Newsletter, Committee for Asian Women (CAW). "Globalisation and Informalisation," International Women Workers Workshop, South Korea, October 2000, Korean Women Worker Association United, Committee for Asia Women and Women Working Worldwide.

Bernard, 1987, as cited in Mark, M., Gray, Miki, C. Cittilson and Wayne, S., "Women and Globalisation: A Study of 180 Countries, 1975–2000". International Organisational Conference, Ref. 42, p. 12, University of California, 2006, Research Working Papers, Funded by Centre for Global Peace and Conflict Studies, University of California.

Blanchard, Eric. "Gender, International Relations, and the Development of Feminist Security Theory." *Signs: Journal of Women in Culture and Society* 28, No. 4 (2003): 1289–1313.

Breman, J. *Footlose Labour: Working in India's Informal Economy*, New Delhi: Cambridge University Press, New Delhi, 1996.

Cecilia, N.G., 2000, Globalisation and Women, online article, a paper presented at a conference in October 2000 in Kuala Lumpur, Malaysia—Development and Liberation in the Third Millennium—organised by the Urban Rural Mission and Development and Service Desks of the Christian Conference of Asia (CCA).

Celina, K. Armbrust. Gender and Migration, Centre De Researche, METICES ULB, ENAR Fact Sheet-42, European Network against Racism, 2010.

Choi Jin-Sil and Jeong, Seon-hee. What Husband and Wife Live By? Television Show, South Korea, 2005

Chowdhury, S. Roy, 2004, "Globalisation and Labour", *EPW*, Vol. xxxiv, No.1, (2004): 105-108.

Christa Wichterich. *The Globalized Woman: Reports from a Future of Inequality.* New York: Zed Books, 2000.

Crime in India Report, 2000.

Derrida, J. "Autoimmunity: Real and Symbolic Suicide", *Dialogues with Habermas*, Translated by Naas, P.A., 2003, Chicago: University of Chicago Press.

Dex, S. *The Sexual Division of Work.* Harvester, 1985.

Dong-Sook S. Gills and Nicola Piper, *Women and Work in Globalizing Asia.* London: Routledge.

Dua, Enaskhi. "Beyond Diversity: Exploring Ways in which the Discourse of Race has Shaped the Institution of the Nuclear Family". In *Scratching the Surface: Canadian Anti-Feminist Thought*, edited by Enashki Dua and Angela Robertson. Toronto: Women's Press, (2005): 237-60. Quoted in Helene Moussa "Global Surge in Forced Migration Linked to Colonial Past."

Eagan, J. Globalisation: The Feminist Desire for a Primodial Place, or Why Feminist Philosophers Avoid the Issue of Globalisation, Working Research Paper, Department of Philosophy, University of California, East Bay, 2005.

Ezumah, N. and C.M. Di Domennici. "Enhancing the Role of Women in Crop Production: A Case Study of Igbo Women in Nigeria," *World Development Report*, Vol. 23, No. 10, October, (1997): 1731–1744.

Ghosh, J. "Globalisation and Economic Liberalisation." ISIS Women in Action.

Ghosh, J. 'Economic and Social Effects of Financial Liberlization', Paper for DESA Development Forum on Integrating Economic and Social Policies to Achieve the UN Development Agenda, New York, March 14–15, 2005.

Gulati, L. "Women Migrant Workers in Asia: A Review", *EPW*, Nov. 22, (1997): 3029–35.

Hebsur, R.K. (ed.). *Social Interaction for Justice.* Mumbai: Tata Institute of Social Sciences, Publications, 1996.

Hensmen, R. *Women in Black*. www.acme.journal (online), Vol. 2, 2000.

International Labour Organisation. Decent Work & the Informal Economy, 90th Session Report VI, Geneva, 2002.

Jain, D. "Feminisation and Globalisation." Synopsis Series: NCRW, Cuny and Japan Preparatory Committee Economic Dimension of Globalization Panel, 2000.

Jameson, F. and Miyoshi, M. (eds). *The Culture of Globalisation*, Duke University Press, Durham, 1998.

Jamieson, L. Lecture Series organised by the Gender Studies Unit, University Malaya, 2000.

Joice, Outshoorn, *The Politics of Prostitution: Women's Movements, Democratic States and the Globalisation.* Cambridge University Press.

Karl, M. *Women and Empowerment: Participation & Decision Making in Rural Environment for Women*, FAO, Rome, 1997.

Kishwar, M. and Vanita, R. "Pro-Woman or Anti-Muslim? The Shabhano Controversy". *Manushi* 32, 1987.

Kishwar, M. and Vanita, R. "The Burning of Roop Kanwar". *Manushi*: 42–43, 1987.

Kishwar, M. and Vanita, R., eds. *In Search of Answers: Indian Women's Voices from Manushi.* London: Zed Books, 1984.

Krishnaraj, M. "Globalisation and Women in India". *Development in Practice* Vol. 9, No. 5, 1989.

Kumar, R. "Identity Politics and the Contemporary Indian Feminist Movement." In *Identity Politics and Women: Cultural Reassertions and Feminisms in International Perspective*, edited by Moghadam, V.M. Boulder, CO: Westview Press, (1994): 274–92.

Maynard, M. *Dress and Globalisation.* Manchester University Press.

Maznah, Mohamad, Cecilia N.G. and Tan Beng Hui. *Feminism and the Women's Movement in Malaysia: A Unsung (R)evolution.* p. 226, London: Routledge, 2009.

Mithre, J. Sandrasagra, Third World Network, Online Bookstore.

National Commission of Women (NCW), Government of India, 2005.

National Council of Applied Economics Research (NCAER), Government of India, 2003.

Peterson, V.S. and Runyan, A. *Global Gender Issues.* USA: Westview Press Inc., 1993.

Price, Susan. "Democratic Socialist Party, Australia", Overview of Women and Globalisation, paper presented to the Asian Women's Workshop on Globalisation. Manila, November 22–24, 2001.

Richards, David L. *Women's Status and Economic Globalization,* University of Akron, International Studies Quarterly, Vol. 5, (2007): 855–76.

Sanderson, K. and Crompton, R. *Gendered Jobs and Social Change.* London: Unwin Hyman, 1990.

Sen, K. and Malia S. *Gender and Power in Afflient Asia.* UK: Routledge, 1998.

Shiva, V. and Jafri, A. Failure of BT Cotton in India, Research Foundation for Science, Technology and Ecology, Dehradun, 2002.

Shiva, Vandana. "The Effects of WTO on Women's Rights", Third World Network, Online Bookstore.

Tibaijuka, A. The Cost of Differential Gender Roles in African Agriculture, (A case study of Tanzania showed that reducing women's time burden in a community of smallholders would increase household income and labour productivity), *Journal of Agricultural Economics,* Vol. 45 (1), (1994): 68–89.

Tisdell, C. and Sen, R.K. *Economic Globalisation.* UK: Edward Elger Publishing, 2004.

Walby, S. *Theorising Patriarchy.* Oxford: Blackwell Publishers, 1990.

Women Workers in Asia: The Situation and Strategies for Fighting the Globalization, by Supawadee Petcharat, Bangkok, Thailand, INGN, Pub on Women and Gender.

Women's Development Collective. *Women's Agenda for Change,* 1999.

Wong, Diana. "Globalisation Reconsidered: Social and Cultural Aspects from an Asian Perspective", unpublished manuscript, 1999.

2

Heteropatriarchy: Globalization, the Institution of Heterosexuality and Lesbians

Susan Hawthorne

There have been many feminists' analyses of globalization in the last decade, including my own, but few have looked at the way in which heteropatriarchy and globalization intersect. Lesbians are said to be without culture or because it is a middle-class Western fad, lesbians are said to be free of the effects of globalization. But each generation of lesbians is denied knowledge of their history, and no one cares or notices. In countries throughout the "so-called" developing world, lesbians are chided for taking on Western fads. In other places, lesbians are arrested, raped and killed because as lesbians they are considered "less than human". Lesbians flee into exile, but what human rights campaign dare publicize their plight?

The core issue is that no one campaigns for the human rights of lesbians, even though lesbians fall into every group of dispossessed and marginalized peoples around the world. The indifference to the suffering of lesbians as lesbians—on top of racism, sexism, religious and ethnic hatred, and poverty—means that there are simply no campaigns, and no supporters for such campaigns—except other lesbians. Fear, silence, hatred and ignorance are the norm. I want to point to the strengths of radical lesbian feminist analyses.

Heteropatriarchy: Globalization, the Institution of Heterosexuality and Lesbians

There have been many analyses of globalization in the last decade or so, some, like my earlier work, has focused on women, and although that analysis included lesbians and critiques of heterosexuality as institutional power, I looked at it as one of several structural systems—including racism, classism, sexism, ableism, ageism, and marginalization based on religion, ethnicity or culture. I did not single out heteropatriarchy. I also note that when I make such analyses and do not mention the institution of heterosexuality or do not mention lesbians, no one seems to notice the absence of sexuality from the debate. But when I speak of sexuality as central to my analysis, people do say: what about class, race, disability, age, culture, religion, and ethnicity. I want to begin by saying that what follows does not exclude these factors, but it has to be possible to put sexuality and lesbians at the centre of our thinking if we really want to understand what is going on around us. That then has to be set alongside other analyses, discussed, synthesized and new theories developed.

Power

> . . . how few are willing to give up the power relationship. Even the powerless cling to the ideology, in the hope that as long as the idea exists they have hope of escaping powerlessness by achieving someway, somehow, powerfulness. Of course, as long as the conceptual framework of "power" itself is valued (especially, if valued by the Oppressed!) none of us has any hope (Atkinson, 1974: xxii).

One cannot speak of globalization without mentioning power. The superstructure of globalization is built upon excessive imbalances in power, although the rhetoric is all about level playing fields, transparency, choice and free trade. The reality is about impossible gradients, shifting targets and confusion, consolidation that reduces the range of products and often annihilates local assets and goods, and trade that is structured to benefit the powerful and the moneyed.

How does heteropatriarchy come into this? If we want a feminist analysis, is it enough to speak of men, whiteness, wealth and mobility? I do not believe so, for inside this grid is a fifth element that comes into play in relation to all of these and that is heterosexuality as an institution.

Let me take a moment to explain what I mean by an institution in relation to heterosexuality.

An institution formalizes relations between the people inside it, in this case the relations between women and men. In doing so, it controls and limits those relations.

Particular tasks and roles are allocated to people in the institution. In the case of heterosexuality it allocates not only by sex, but also by gender.[1] Attempts to challenge these roles have only succeeded in embedding them more deeply. The roles preserve the respective subordinate/dominant positions of women and men—and continue to do so even when challenged.

Institutions have authority over people in them. This authority extends to limiting men's behaviour and women's, and furthermore it affects people not involved in heterosexual relations because it carries such authority.[2]

The institution affects not only personal and intimate behaviour, it affects global behaviour. Think of the images from Abu Ghraib. They exemplify the heteroreality of militarism. Iraqi men are feminized, dominated, treated just like all the women in all the porn you have ever seen. But when it is pornography, it is not viewed as torture because those subjects (the women) are pre-feminised by their sex. The horror only occurs when men feminize "enemy" men, and or military women (even if under duress) feminize "enemy" men (Clarke, 2004; Hawthorne, 2006).

Unfair, says the liberal, war is always bad. Let us look at something that is marketed globally as good: development. Development is an interesting area and it is one that has changed its form significantly due mainly to appropriative moves by the big money spenders: the IMF, the World Bank, the UN and the on-ground workers, the women working in NGOs. There is now a recognition that women make development projects more successful, more cheaply than comparable projects with men. But when you look at the language of development it is premised on a woman being part of a family, whereas development projects focused on men put the men at the centre. And when women want aid, they are first contracepted when clean water, poverty alleviation and reduction of violence would help more.

Further, the woman is structured as part of a group. Now this is no bad thing, because, as I have argued elsewhere, relationships are central to human activity. But the relationship always assumed is that there is a man in the family—he may be kind, brutal, dependent, absent—but his symbolic presence is key to development thinking. Imagine if the development institutions thought instead of, say, communities of women—sisters, lovers, friends, aunts, mothers, grandmothers and daughters, with men at the semantic and symbolic margin. What if development institutions imagined single women? What if development institutions considered lesbians? Simply considering these questions creates a challenge. How would development projects look, if the assumed heteronormativity, which determines how money and resources are used, were removed from the development process (Bergeron, 2006)? How would the visibility of women's economic and social relationships change? Such shifts would change what we see—and it would affect heterosexual women and lesbians as well as those who do not want intimate relationships.

The "Purple September Staff" highlighted this in 1975 when they wrote about the normative status of heterosexuality and the very different effects of female and male conditioning. "In male conditioning, male heterosexuality is linked to male prerogative of a human identity; in female conditioning, female heterosexuality is linked to the denial of that same identity" (1975: 81). When I first read this in 1975, I thought that by 2007 it would no longer hold. But I look around and see girls wearing T-shirts with Porn Star, and heavy duty sexualization of girls at a younger and younger age (Caputi, 2004); and I see boys running about with pretend AK 47s under their arms (and in some places, real ones) and I see videos made by boys glorifying violence against and rape of girls. You might argue that I am seeing selectively. I will happily admit there are happy and fulfilled heterosexual couples, but they are overwhelmingly unrepresentative of the cultural trend.

The Phallus and the Penis

> The feminist aim is to render the phallus impotent, to sever its connection with the penis, and to ensure that the latter is reduced to nothing but anatomy (Thompson, 1991: 15).

Denise Thompson's distinction between the phallus and the penis is very important. Denise does go on to say that the "selective recognition towards women and away from men, does not have to be a permanent state of affairs" (p. 15). It is interesting to me that men of every generation can make statements over and over (i.e., permanently) that do direct attention away from women permanently and universally and it hardly raises an eyebrow. I believe that position of dominance that men hold—and that each person may hold in one or more parts of their lives—results in sloppy and uncritical thinking. And within the heterosexual world-view, it is easy to slide from lesbian to lesbianism (a state of illness), while heterosexual is a given, and an assimilationist view that is the prevailing one. Speaking of gay men recently, Jim Schembri wrote:

> Most of them are secure and comfortable and blend into mainstream society so well that they don't even worry about being referred to as "them", because they know that we straights consider them to be part of us (Schembri, 2007: 7, emphasis mine).

And when we are not assimilated—not part of them, we are afflicted with illness, criminality, and abnormality. It is fine so long as we shut up or play the exotic and erotic role of lipstick or SM lesbian.

And this is what a lesbian feminist reading of globalization can bring—another way of seeing the world. Indigenous women in many parts of the world are developing critiques of globalization that reflect the ways in which they are being recolonized by bioprospectors and drug companies. Lesbians are being recolonized in different ways in different countries.

For example, same-sex marriage. I did not join the women's liberation movement to fight for marriage, although I was furious when, in 2004, Liberal and Labour got together to create a new discriminatory law to prevent marriage.[3] But it is not something I am going to fight for because I see it as a new form of normative heterosexuality. If only we could quieten down those rabble raising lesbian feminists and pretend that they do not threaten the social structure. I believe that lesbian feminism is a threat, and should be, while simultaneously it is a positive and often joyous alternative.

Nor will I go to the barricades to get lesbians into In-Vitro Fertilization (IVF). The discrimination is wrong, but the outcome is not worth having. If we fight these battles for the privileges of heterosexuality, what energy remains for us to fight for those issues which put women and lesbians and lesbian feminism at the centre? How will it be possible for us to turn our attention for long enough to create change?

As Giti Thadani writes of India and the difficulty of what words to use to speak about lesbians, she writes "... one can be, but only if one remains nameless" (Thadani, 1996: 10). The same problem is raised by the use of overly inclusive language such as queer, LGBTI (QRS ...!), same sex, alternative sexualities, diverse sexuality, and minority sexualities. The symbolic meaning of these terms is to keep turning our attention towards the phallus which is a part of all these terms. I like the word lesbian. It has oomph. Many languages do have equivalents for the word lesbian, and those languages that do not are going to be the places where turning away from the phallus is particularly difficult.

In academia, any word except lesbian is preferable—because the lesbian, the lesbian feminist is unsafe ground for too many people in every department. We need a shift in the culture that recognizes the hatred at the root of this language. This is the result of globalized thinking that picks up the global and forgets the local, or to put it slightly differently, picks up the heterosexually acceptable language and ignores the intimate.

Origins and Violence

> It is crucial to remember ... that [many] "creation" myths are not about the origins of the world at all, but about the origins of patriarchy which has, nonetheless claimed itself as the world (Caputi, 1987: 9).

What is it that makes us feel real? Makes us feel like citizens? Jane Caputi's observation brings us back to basics. Who, in the mythology or the religion or the storytelling, gets the credit for creating meaning in the world? Most of the world's cultures have old stories that tell of times when women created the world, and went on to create social meaning. The vast majority of these stories have been steamrollered and steamcleaned, but they can be found in "mythologies" which are great repositories of women's knowledge. The Middle East, for example, is filled with ancient stories in which "goddesses" or as they were renamed "demons" populated the stories and were then torn to shreds, decapitated and violated. In Greece, the daughters of goddesses are raped, abducted and made hostage.[4] When the stories are retold they are reframed as origin stories. This is comparable to the discovery stories of Europeans—the first [white] man to cross the mountain, the river, the desert, and continent. They are stories of remaking reality in the framework of the group that won the latest battle.

In our contemporary global world, this is taking new forms. The area of conquest now is the immaterial, it is knowledge that is privatized and sold at great profit. One of those stories is the constant access to female bodies. So heterosexuality is ramped up to an ever greater pitch. Little girls are dressed in bras and panties before they have learned to run. They might not all wear pink, but the expectations of satisfying masculine sexual drive is happening at the age when girls have the developmental advantage over boys.

This is serious. How can a woman ever learn to move freely if she does not experience it in childhood? How can she sense the possibilities of her own power if adolescence gives no space for the girl within if it becomes instead a lesson in self-denial? The global advertising industry, the sex industry, the trafficking in girls and women industry are about the institutionalization of heterosexuality as dollars for tourism and a way of providing for that group of highly mobile, cashed up men who take for granted easy access to women's bodies.

The alternative, which could encompass female friendship, lesbian love, or solitary solutions, is simply not thinkable. They are not advertised on billboards or in movies or on TV soaps because within the heteropatriarchal world, they are a nonsense. The lesbian cannot have meaning. It is so far off the planet as to be out of this world.

"We are captive of Venus Martian in our sexual style our origins are Uranian our desires Plutonic our mood Saturnian to the point of lunacy truly we are interplanetary" (Hawthorne, 2005a: 103).

The violence carried out against lesbians is both symbolic and real. Lesbians are killed and tortured for whom they love. Men use rape both to punish and to convert. All she needs is a good . . . and that will do it. The symbolic violence can be seen in any porn magazine or website where "lesbian" eroticism becomes a turn on for voyeuristic viewers. The world rightly protests the destruction of the 2000-year-old Bamiyan Buddhist statues in Afghanistan. Giti Thadani (2004) in her research of ancient lesbian sites in India records the violence against 5000-year-old sacred stone sculptures. Why have we not heard about how the breasts of these statues have been cut off? Why is there no international protest? Is it because the statues are symbolic of lesbian existence, not just now, but back into ancient history? It is, as I have said before, impossible to get up a campaign that calls for an end to violence against lesbians. I have tried with Amnesty International and failed.

Nationalism and Exile

> On the one hand the lesbian is reduced to the Western other and declared not to be a citizen of the country within any socio-cultural-historical-cosmological context. But on the other hand the heterosexual business executive is very much the result of an economic order arising out of a 'Western' context, yet his Indianness is never called into question (Thadani, 1996: 87).

In the 1920s, a young woman named Grace McDonald travelled to England. She lived there for the rest of her life and the only photos of her are of her with another woman called Peg. Grace was my great aunt. We never met, but she sent gifts at Christmas. It is only in the last few years, after discovering the photographs of her and thinking about exile in relation to lesbians—and numerous discussions with Lara Fergus who is writing her Ph.D. on this subject—which I have come to see that it is more than likely that my Auntie Grace was a lesbian in exile. I have been an activist and writer in this field for thirty years and it took years and an accident of photographic preservation for me to see this.

It is an indication of the great losses we have of lesbian history. While heteropatriarchy is rewriting our histories, while it distorts and dismembers whatever we have, while it severs those crucial lines of inheritance, we are left floating without that matrix of connection that most people take for granted. For those who do not have the connections, there is usually some recognition—even if it comes late—that it has occurred. Here I am thinking of the Holocaust, of refugee displacement, of the Stolen Generations and dispossession of Indigenous peoples. These are all horrific events. Could we try to be horrified about what has happened to lesbians (Hawthorne, 2005b)?

> . . . no training session prepared me for this intense pain . . . my pain . . . the one I did not choose . . . all this alienation, this empty vacuum . . ., my body, my mind, my pain . . . this is not happening . . . I am a little speck in the universe . . . which universe? . . . the world is not anymore . . . I am . . . disintegrating . . . bit by bit . . . yell by yell . . . electrode by electrode. . . . The pain . . . all this pain here and there, down there in my vagina . . . the agony . . . where am I? Where is my I? (Rivera-Fuentes and Birke, 2001: 655)

"Where is my I?" asks Consuelo Rivera-Fuentes after her experience of torture. She is also asking where is my lesbian I? Where is the centrality of the experiences of lesbians recorded and recognized? Where is the recognition that the violation of lesbians goes on day after day and no one speaks of it (Hawthorne, 2006a)? She too, is writing in exile from England, not her native Chile.

Many a rural lesbian has made the move to the city, because it is simply too hard to live the way she wants in her own country town. Ask me. I grew up in the country in rural NSW. Do I live there? Do they know who I am? Hardly. So, like my great aunt, most of my life has been spent elsewhere. I am sure this applies to others in this room. Lesbians are a diasporic population. The connections zigzag down the generations, through maiden aunts.

Lesbian existence resists nationalism. And what could it mean for a lesbian to be patriotic (Hawthorne, 2006b)? I am sure that oxymoron exists, but as challengers to the symbolic and actual power of patriarchy and heterosexuality, "Like oil and water/lesbian life and patriotism don't mix" (Hawthorne, 2005a: 221).

The lesbian, as Monique Wittig so astutely pointed out in 1978, is "not a woman" because her "relation to a man" falls outside the heterosexual obligation that occurs inside the institution of heterosexuality. What does lesbian motherhood look like in this context? Is it possible to have the generational connection while remaining outside the "personal and . . . economic obligation" (Wittig, 1992: 20) of heterosexuality?

Just as lesbians are accused of disloyalty to family because we have left the places we come from, lesbians are also accused of disloyalty to their own culture. It is more than likely, that if we could find the connections, temples and statues and artworks as we can in India, we could begin to discover the ancient treasures that draw lesbians into focus. Would anyone support such a research project?

But, you know, when colonists first enter a country, they dispossess the people, not only of their land, but also of their culture. The colonists deny this possibility. They say "The natives have no culture." What could we know of the colonists through many thousands of years ago who, upon "discovery" of lesbians, have killed, raped, maimed and denied their existence? So many families have their own colonists inside them (Machida, 1996). How do we fight against this? And when our knowledge is digitized, who will use the word lesbian and in what context, and with what overtones?

Global Recolonization

> Making the nation-state safe for multinational corporations is commensurate with making it safe for heterosexuality, for both can be recodified as natural, even supernatural. Thus tourism and imperialism become as integral to the natural order as heterosexuality, and are indispensable in state strategies of recolonization (Alexander, 2005: 26).

Jacqui Alexander points to an interesting concept here, that of recolonization. It is particularly apt in the context of the Caribbean, where Western tourists flock, and where you can be imprisoned for being a lesbian. I think the important element here is that colonization is not a one-off event. Rather, it is a series of actions played out against those who challenge the stock knowledge of the dominant culture. It is like the movement of tectonic plates, simultaneously sliding across one another in several layers.

The land is taken and the colonized are killed, enslaved, violated and disconnected from their language and culture. Then the products of the land and the people are stolen: the land is mined, it is farmed wastefully, forests, rivers and seas are plundered, the land and seas bombed and used as dumps, the material goods and arts are commodified, made safe for tourists and people in other countries (they are watered down). More recently, the knowledge and the cell-lines of people are being stolen, but this too has happened in different ways over many years. All of these things continue to happen simultaneously.

In the context of lesbians, these days most lesbians have no land to plunder, indeed in too many instances that connection has been sacrificed. Lesbian bodies are violated in various ways: murder, torture, suicide, rape and most recently surgical violence. They are all justified as necessary. Gays and Lesbians of Zimbabwe (GALZ),[5] was the very first organization to be attacked for dissenting in 1995 (Tiripano, 2000). Now anyone in Zimbabwe with a dissenting voice is under attack. Many are fleeing into exile. In Sierra Leone, on September 29, 2004, FannyAnn Eddy[6] was found dead after being repeatedly raped. She had been working in the offices of the Sierra Leone Lesbian and Gay Association (Human Rights Watch, 4 October 2004, Morgan and Wieringa 2005: 20). And what of the lesbians who have died, for want of good medical treatment? Gloria Anzaldúa, dead at 61, because she could not afford the American health system. Lisa Bellear, who died far too young, at age 45, from a preventable illness. And what of the mostly young women who die in double suicides and whose deaths do not prompt families (like the Montagues and Capulets) to consider their part in their deaths (Gage 2007: 40; Thadani, 1996).

Surgical violence against lesbians can now be counted alongside the violence meted out to lesbians in the "mental health" system. Gender disorientation is a "medical tag". Interestingly, disorientation is a method of torture. Who, but lesbians (Jeffreys, 2005; Gage 2005; Janice Raymond 1980) even sees this as violence?

If we speak of these things, we are accused of harming the efforts of those trying to do something about the poverty, AIDS, and levels of violence in Africa, among Hispanic Americans and Indigenous Australians. Who will speak about it? Who will publicly defend the lesbians who step forward and make themselves visible? Who will want to give aid to help save the lesbians of Africa, of the Caribbean, in Taiwan, and across the Middle East?[7] Who will want to campaign for the lesbians who are the inmates of jails and mental institutions, who are over-medicated on anti-depressant and anti-psychotic drugs in our own countries? Who will defend lesbians against the charge of transsexual bashing, when the lesbian is trying to make visible the violence against lesbians?[8] The front has shifted. Lesbians are the invisible people whom no one wants to fight for. And when lesbians do become visible, new laws are brought into force, increasing the punishments (we saw it happen in Tasmania, although now happily reversed but only after an approach to the UN!). Lesbians in India are fighting this battle (Thadani, 1996; Sharma 2006; Hawthorne 2007), just as they are in many other places. Lesbians are either invisible and silent, or visible and illegal. The first represents an incapacity to imagine such a thing. The last a desire to punish for flouting patriarchal reality.

These are global realities. They are global issues and they are issues we should be taking back to our own communities. They are in fact the same issues that every group battling globalization confronts. There is a great deal of fear around the word "lesbian" and it is the reason I decided to speak about it today. As has been shown in Zimbabwe, if lesbians remain outside the scope of social justice reform, then everyone's civil and political rights remain in jeopardy. If we cannot create campaigns for the safety of lesbians—and many of us have borne the brunt of attacks from both our enemies and those we thought were our allies—then what are we fighting for when we take up any social justice issue? Are we wanting just partial freedom? Freedom for some, and not others? If this is so, what are we changing? Are we serious?

I want to finish on a note that is both joyful and sad with a few lines from a poem by Lisa Bellear:

> Three weeks have passed
> And tomorrow
> Three weeks and one
> Day will have passed
> Since we—you and I
> Held hands
> Sweet isn't it

Falling down across
Backwards sidewards
Totally totally totally
In love (Bellear, 1996: 23)

Notes

1. For critiques of the misuse of the word "gender" see Hawthorne, 2004c; Eisenstein 2007.
2. This is drawn from my essay, "In Defence of Separatism" (1976).
3. It is amazing what you can get away with saying in public about lesbians, and not be accused of discrimination or hate speech. In the lead-up to the federal elections in Australia in 2004, a Family First Party campaign worker made a joke about burning lesbians at the stake, and no media organization objected. If such a bad joke were made about anyone from a marginalized ethnic group, voices would be raised in protest. All that happened was that the worker was later stood aside. To speak out on behalf of lesbians is somehow seen as passé, boring, not relevant to the real political fight. To that extent lesbians have become—and perhaps in the coming years will become even more—difficult to centre a campaign around. See Hawthorne (2004a; 2004b).
4. Graham, Rawlings and Rigsby (1994) argue that women's social relationship with men suggests a form of societal Stockholm Syndrome, that is that the institution of heterosexuality and the individuals who patrol it – men and apologists of men's power—act as through women are *hostages* to men. The captive perceives the behaviour of the captors as ranging from extreme violence to kindness. The kindness creates a belief in safety in the midst of violence and abuse.
5. GALZ was established in 1990, and came to prominence in 1995 when it attempted to enter the Zimbabwe International Book Fair, which had as its theme, Human Rights and Justice. Permission was refused. For more information, see <http://www.galz.co.zw/cp_bookfair.html>
6. See her testimony, Eddy (2004) at the UN Commission on Human Rights just a few months before her death.
7. These are all countries where lesbians are punished harshly, ranging from jail to execution. See Hawthorne (2006a).
8. Frameline's San Francisco LGBT International Film Festival pulled a short science fiction film *The Gendercator* by lesbian filmmaker Catherine Crouch from its film festival programme in June 2007 because of its purported "transphobic" content. In a petition to the organizers, Lenn Keller, Max Dashu, Joey Brite and Martha Shelley, write:

> A lesbian voice is being silenced here. In the current climate of fear, we find it necessary to state that critiquing or asking questions about issues affecting our communities should not be confused with judgement or condemnation or, in this case, "transphobia".

Many have complained about the lack of lesbian content in the festival, and Frameline has chosen to silence one of the few voices. We think the LGBT community has been done a disservice. We, the undersigned stand for human dignity, rights, and freedom of expression for all.

References

Alexander, M. Jacqui. *Pedagogies of Crossing: Meditations on Feminism, Sexual Politics, Memory and the Sacred.* Durham and London: Duke University Press, 2005.

Atkinson, Ti-Grace. *Amazon Odyssey.* New York: Links Books, 1974.

Bellear, Lisa. *Dreaming in Urban Areas.* St Lucia: University of Queensland Press, 1996.

Bergeron, Suzanne. "Love, Sex and the World Bank: Queering Globalization and Development." Paper presented at National Women's Studies Conference, Oakland, CA, 16 June, 2006.

Caputi, Jane. *The Age of Sex Crime.* London: The Women's Press, 1987.

——. "The Pornography of Everyday Life." In *Goddesses and Monsters: Women, Myth, Power, and Popular Culture,* edited by Jane Caputi. Madison: University of Wisconsin Press, 2004.

Clarke, De. "Prostitution for Everyone: Feminism, Globalization and the 'Sex' Industry." In *Not for Sale: Feminists Resisting Prostitution and Pornography,* edited by Christine Starke and Rebecca Whisnant. Melbourne: Spinifex Press, 2004, pp. 149–205.

Eddy, Fanny Ann. "Testimony by FannyAnn Eddy at the U.N. Commission on Human Rights. Item 14. 60th Session, UN Commission on Human Rights." 2004, http://hrw.org/english/docs/2004/10/04/sierra9439.htm

Eisenstein, Zillah. *Sexual Decoys: Gender, Race and War in Imperial Democracy.* Melbourne: Spinifex Press, 2007.

Gage, Carolyn. "Teena Brandon: Gender Identity Disorder and Post-Traumatic Stress Syndrome." Paper presented at Maine Women's Studies Program, 2005.

——. "Shakespeare Got It Right". *Rain and Thunder: A Radical Feminist Journal of Discussion and Activism,* No. 34 (2007), Spring Equinox.

Graham, Dee L. R., Edna I. Rawlings and Roberta K. Rigsby. *Loving to Survive:*

Sexual Terror, Men's Violence and Women's Lives. New York: New York University Press, 1994.

Hawthorne, Susan. "In Defence of Separatism." Unpublished, 1976.

——. *Wild Politics: Feminism, Globalisation and Bio/diversity.* Melbourne: Spinifex Press, 2002.

——. "The Depoliticisation of Lesbian Culture." *Hecate* 29, No. 2 (2003): 235–47.

——. "A Family Fable." *Hecate* 30, No. 2: 127–128; *Rain and Thunder* (USA) No. 25 (Winter 2004a): 33.

——. "Post-Election Blues." *Arena Magazine*, no. 74 (Dec 2004/Jan 2005): 10.

——. "The Political Uses of Obscurantism: Gender Mainstreaming and Intersectionality." *Development Bulletin*, No. 89 (2004c): 875–91. Online at http://devnet.anu.edu.au/GenderPacific/pdfs/20_gen_mainstream_hawthorne.pdf

——. *The Butterfly Effect.* Melbourne: Spinifex Press, 2005a.

——. "Not on Anyone's Program: Lesbian Refugees and the Torture of Lesbians." Paper presented at the Conference "Hopes Fulfilled or Dreams Shattered." Centre for Refugee Research, UNSW, Sydney, 25 November 2005b.

——. "Ancient Hatred and its Contemporary Manifestations: The Torture of Lesbians." *The Journal of Hate Studies* 4: 33–58, http://guweb2.gonzaga.edu/againsthate/Journal4/04AncientHatred.pdf (2006a).

——. "Men's Patriotic Wars against Women's Intimate Lives: Patriarchy, the Institution of Heterosexuality and Patriotism." *African Safety Promotion: A Journal of Injury and Violence Prevention* 4, No. 2 (2006b): 20–31.

——."The Silences Between: Are Lesbians Irrelevant?" *Journal of International Women's Studies. Women's Bodies, Gender Analysis, and Feminist Politics at the Fórum Social Mundial* 8, No. 3: 125–38, http://www.bridgew.edu/SoAS/jiws/April07/Hawthorne1.pdf (April 2007).

Human Rights Watch, 4 October 2004.

Jeffreys, Sheila. *Beauty and Misogyny: Harmful Cultural Practices.* London: Routledge, 2005.

Keller, Lenn, Max Dashu, Joey Brite and Martha Shelley. "We Protest Frameline Censorship." *Petition.* Received 7 June 2007.

Machida, Tina. "Sisters of Mercy." pp. 118–29 in *Amazon to Zami: Toward a Global Lesbian Feminism*, edited by Reinfelder, Monika. London: Cassell, 1996.

Morgan, Ruth and Saskia Wieringa. *Tommy Boys, Lesbian Men and Ancestral Wives: Female Same-Sex Practices in Africa.* Johannesburg: Jacana, 2005.

"The Purple September Staff." In *Lesbianism and the Women's Movement*, edited by Myron, Nancy and Charlotte Bunch. Baltimore: Diana Press, 1975.

Raymond, Janice G. *The Transsexual Empire: The Making of the She-Male.* London: The Women's Press, 1980.

Rivera-Fuentes, Consuelo and Linda Birke. "Talking With/In Pain: Reflections on Bodies under Torture." *Women's Studies International Forum* 24, No. 6 (2001): 653–68.

Sharma, Maya. *Loving Women: Being Lesbian in Underprivileged India.* New Delhi: Yoda Press, 2006.

Shaw, Megan. "Labor Backs Ban on Gay Marriage." *The Age*, http://www.theage.com.au/articles/2004/08/04/1091557919497.html (5 August 2004).

Schembri, Jim. "You're Here. You're Queer. We're Used to it". *The Age* (2 June 2007): Insight 7.

Thadani, Giti. *Sakhiyani: Lesbian Desire in Ancient and Modern India.* London: Cassells, 1996.

——. *Moebius Trip: Digressions from India's Highways.* Melbourne: Spinifex Press, 2004.

Thompson, Denise. *Reading Between the Lines: A Lesbian Feminist Critique of Feminist Accounts of Sexuality.* Sydney: Gorgon Head Press, 1991.

Tiripano, Tsitsi. "Fighting for Lesbian and Gay Rights in Zimbabwe." *Off Our Backs* 30, No. 4 (April 1991): 1, 6–7.

Wittig, Monique. *The Straight Mind.* Boston: Beacon Press, 1992. First Published in Feminist Issue, 1981.

3

Women's Empowerment Approach as a Means for Engendering the Development Process

Lovely Mamta Dhulia and Purnima Singh

> Making women equal partners in the national development processes and equipping them to make informed choices in order to actualise their self-worth through empowerment are goals to which the government is committed. There is a long way to go but the endeavour is ceaseless.
>
> —India Country Report,
> Fourth World Conference on Women, Beijing, 1995

Few decades ago gender concern was conspicuous by its absence from the development agenda, and women almost invisible to the policy-makers and planners, were increasingly marginalized by the development process. It is only in the recent years that there has been a growing realization that human development is likely to make a quantum leap only if substantial investment is made in enhancing the status and elevating the role of women. Most of us are convinced now that human development is impossible without gender parity. As long as women are excluded from the development process, growth will remain weak and lopsided hence, there is a need to support the call for "women-centric" development. Sustained human development implies engendering the development paradigm. Looking at the massive global discrimination against women the Human Development Report (1995), concluded that "development if not engendered it is endangered." Consequently, the development initiatives today focus to a great extent on women all over the world.

Women and Development: Some Approaches

Unfortunately, for years development processes had neglected women as rightful beings and discriminately pushed them to states of mere survival. With changing times, however, their indispensable role in the development process has been globally recognized and all efforts are made to facilitate women's participation in the development process. Although, development over the decades has moved towards the same goal of improving the life of all human beings in general, yet, there have been some radical shifts in its specific priorities and emphasis as far as women are concerned. Moser (1989) reviewed gender planning in the third world and identified five broad approaches to development. The earliest was the *welfare approach*, which accorded women a central place in the family and focused on their homemaking and reproductive roles. This approach viewed women as a vulnerable group with special needs. Here, women were identified not just as beneficiaries of development but rather as passive recipients. In the 1960s as a consequence of strong feminist movements, issues of equity and social justice became an integral part of the development approach thus giving rise to the *equity approach* which during mid-1970s demanded equality for women in all spheres while at the same time argued for recognition of women as active participants in the development process. It focused both on their reproductive and productive roles where the latter was seen as a vital contributor to economic growth. The advocates of this approach strongly favoured the entry of women into the mainstream workforce and even sought equal rights for them at the work-place. Then, emerged another approach which considered women as the "poorest of the poor". This was known as the *anti-poverty approach.* It recognized the inequalities between men and women and linked these to lack of access to private ownership of land and capital for women, and gender discrimination in the labour market. Although, this approach did lead to some improvement in women's economic status yet, its implied impact was not visible. Hence, another more viable approach called *efficiency approach* was adopted that considered women as an important resource in developmental planning and recognized them as an underdeveloped capital. Later, the concern shifted towards capacity-building of women to develop their competencies and boost their self-reliance. This is referred to as the *empowerment approach.* Empowerment broadly implies "an increase in women's power to achieve equality with men, and recognition and cultivation of their latent capacities so that they can be treated as development agents with equal potential rather than mere beneficiaries." Like other developing countries in India too, within the framework of a democratic polity, from the fifth five-year plan onwards, there has been a marked shift in the approach related to women's issues from *welfare* to *development through empowerment.*

Concept of Empowerment: A Look from Gender Perspective

The notion of empowerment has originated from the theoretical postulations of Freire (1972), who put forth the notion of "conscientization", i.e., "awareness—generation approach" to enable members of marginalized groups to know and assert their needs but prior to which they had to be motivated to associate and organise together. It is a process that would encourage the marginalized and oppressed people to challenge the power imbalances in society and thereby seek their rights and gain control over their own lives. Although, Freire did not actually use the term empowerment yet, his notion of conscientization has much in common with the concept of empowerment. In the same vein, empowerment is defined by Bystydzienski (1992) as "a process by which oppressed persons gain some control over their lives by taking part with others in the development of activities and structures that allow people increased involvement in matters which affect them directly". Likewise, according to Batliwala (1993), the word "power" contained within the term empowerment signifies that it is about changing the balance of power in a given society, power being defined as control over resources and ideology, or in other words, it involves the process of challenging existing power relations and of gaining greater control over the sources of power. The primary concern of empowerment is changing the systemic forces to bring about a redistribution of power between nations, classes, castes, races, ethnic groups or genders. It implies that empowerment presupposes primacy of power over other aspects. Recent interpretations of empowerment have therefore, for this reason focused mainly on the notion of power (Sharma, 2000). Women's empowerment has been defined by Griffen (1989) as "adding to women's power". Similarly, Kabeer (1990) interprets it as a radical transformation of power relations between women and men "so that women have greater power over their own lives and men have less power over women's lives". Beteille (1999) observes that empowerment seeks to change society through rearrangement of power. Reflecting same line of thinking, Giddens (1984) views it as "transformative capacity". Viewing power itself as gendered, some feminists have sought to define empowerment as "power to" unlike men who define it as "power over" (Deutchman 1991). Wieringa (1994) refers to empowerment as a process of exposing the oppressive power of the existing gender (and social) relations, critically challenging them, and creatively trying to shape different social relations, i.e., trying to achieve gender equality.

Longwe (1991) in her "gender awareness" framework proposes gender equality at the following five levels: (i) welfare, (ii) access to resources and benefits, (iii) conscientization, (iv) participation in the decision-making process, and (v) control over one's life and levers of power. In the context of her work, women empowerment implies progressive elimination of gender disparities at each level. Karl (1995) views women's empowerment as a continuum of several interrelated and mutually reinforcing components including awareness building, capacity and skill development, control and decision-making power, and action towards gender equality.

Generally, empowerment of women is understood in terms of two different conceptions: (i) Unidimensional conception of empowerment that focuses on political empowerment and deals with the notion of power as command. There are at least three distinguishable usages of power as command—having command over one's own body and actions; over others actions; and over institutional resources such as decision-making bodies. (ii) Multidimensional conception of empowerment that incorporates dimensions like social, economic and psychological, besides, of course, political. In its broader conceptualization, empowerment refers to capacity building.

Recent researches have identified the different routes of empowerment commonly used by development agencies versus women's organizations and NGOs. The development agencies have adopted strategies of economic intervention and empowerment through integrated rural development programmes that deal with women's "practical" needs and interests, in order to improve their situation. Whereas, women's organizations and NGOs focus on the processes of awareness and capacity building aimed to transform unequal relationships and enable increased decision-making power. Their emphasis is on women's "strategic" interests aimed towards changing their "position" (Batliwala, 1993).

Women Empowerment: Global and National Initiatives

Empowerment is one of the recent policy agenda for women and has gained universal acceptance as a goal of development projects in the 1990s. The terms "women welfare", "women empowerment" and "gender justice" are an important feature of social and development programme of both developed and developing nations. The debate on "women empowerment" and "gender justice" was at the centre stage in the international arena in 1994 United Nation's (UN) Conference in Cairo, UN's Fourth International Conference on Women at Beijing in September 1995 and UN's Social Summit Conference at Copenhagen in March 1995. The Beijing declaration affirmed that national governments participating at the Conference including India were globally committed to "equal rights and inherent human dignity of women and men" enshrined in the Charter of the United Nations to the Universal Declaration of Human Rights. The various international and national conventions, constitutional mandates and directives, proclamation of "International Year of Women" and "Decade for Women", and various government plans and policies are indicative of global and national concerns for women's empowerment.

India as a signatory to the Universal Declaration has taken several measures, including legislations to enable development and advancement of women, for the purpose of guaranteeing exercise and enjoyment of human rights and fundamental freedom as available to men. At the time of independence when Indian Constitution was framed, it included the principle of gender equality as an integral part of its preamble and fundamental rights and at the same time empowered the state to adopt measures of positive discrimination in favour of women. The National Plan of

Action for Women, adopted in 1976 became a guiding document for the development of women till 1988 when a National Perspective Plan for Women (1988–2000) was drafted, which sought to integrate and coordinate the diverse schemes of women's development into a holistic perspective. It sought to project an image of women not merely as beneficiaries of development but also as equal partners in the development process. The commitments of the Ninth Plan (1997–2002) too have an objective of empowering women as agents of social change and development. However, the draft for the National Policy for the Empowerment of Women, 2001 accepts existence of "wide gap between the goals enunciated in the constitution, legislation, policies, plans, programmes, and related mechanisms on the one hand and the situational reality of the status of women in India, on the other".

The National Perspective Plan for women recommended not only social and civil rights for women but also positive action and proposed 33 per cent reservation for women in all local elected bodies. The Indian State took a significant step by passing the 73rd and 74th Constitution Amendment Acts of 1993 which provide for reservation of one-third of total seats for women in elected local bodies like panchayats and Municipal Corporations. Two attempts, once in 1966 and then again in 1998 were made to introduce Bill for Reservation of Women in the Indian Parliament and State Assemblies where their representation has never crossed the mark of 8.2 per cent and 11 per cent respectively, but both the times it had to face a setback. It was opposed because it is perceived to benefit women of forward castes to the neglect of women belonging to OBC, SC and ST community. However, the implicit reasons for the opposition of bill are different, the main being the feelings of insecurity about their political future on the part of the male MPs of the different parties. No matter, whatever the actual reasons may be for its opposition but one thing is certain that for balanced growth of the nation, political empowerment of women is really necessary which implies the importance of women's equality in power-sharing and active participation in the decision-making process at all levels of the power structure.

Several Acts have been enacted to provide for empowerment of women, including constitutional amendments, law, particularly social legislation; however, it is not always a very potent instrument of social transformation. Not surprisingly, much of the social legislation enacted for women's empowerment has produced little effect. Hence, much emphasis is laid on the conscientization of women, which holds the key to their empowerment. Conscientization refers to awareness about the structure of discrimination, exploitation and oppression in which one is situated. Sharma (2000) posits three aspects of conscientization in the context of women empowerment: (i) creating "awareness generation" among women about "gender gaps" in respect of material welfare such as food availability, nutritional inputs, mortality rate, sex ratio, etc.; access to resources and benefits such as education, wage, employment, land, credit and services; participation in decision-making process within the family as well as in public organizations, such as panchayats, legislative assembly, parliament, development projects, etc., (ii) inculcating beliefs that these gender gaps are man-made and therefore can be removed, and (iii) mobilizing women to assert for gender equality. Together with this, what is also needed is change in the attitude of men, as well as change in the social structures.

Major Challenges: Gender Inequality and Discrimination

Gender inequality became an issue in the early 1970s with Boserup's (1970) findings which revealed "gender gaps" in the distribution of work, resources and benefits. The Human Development Report (1995) estimated that women spend two-thirds of their working hours on unpaid work (men spend just a fourth), and most of these are for caring work. It is widely recognized that a large proportion of women's work still remains invisible in official data, because many women make a substantial economic contribution as home-based workers who are often counted as non-working housewives. In a traditional rural setting where a woman is expected to undertake all work relating to household and children, her economic activities are knitted into this 'other work' leading to its relative invisibility. If she is encouraged or enabled somehow to take up regular paid work, she indeed, becomes visible as a worker but then if there is no sharing of other responsibilities between men and women, she may land up being highly stressed and overworked. For women, the working hours are long and involve a great deal of drudgery, especially in rural areas of developing countries. For example, in Nepal, women work 21 hours more each week than men, and in India, 12 additional hours. In Kenya, 8 to

14 years old girls spend five hours more on household chores than boys. These inequalities in burden are the worse obstacles that women face in their life choices and opportunities.

Efforts to Make Women Economically Empowered

After independence, the question of bringing women in the forefront through opportunities and capabilities has been considered from time to time in our country. Economic empowerment as an approach to development and gender equality has acquired greater importance in India over the last decade. It is believed that economic empowerment of women can follow only if they are allowed a larger participatory role in the overall social scenario. Generally, economic empowerment is defined as an "economic change/material gain plus increased bargaining power and/or structural change which enables women to secure economic gains on an on-going and sustained basis". This definition emphasizes that employment is an essential but not adequate requirement for empowerment. It is equally important that structural changes that improve women's bargaining power and autonomy, accompany the process.

To understand the successes and limitations of the economic empowerment approach, it is instructive to look at the experience of the Self-Employed Women's Association (SEWA). It seeks primarily to empower women as income-generating workers. Generally, the women get a chance to work only, if they are able to seek the cooperation of other family members by justifying their earning as a gain in household income. Their experience is that over time, on account of this earning-role their bargaining position within the household improves (Rose, 1992). The SEWA strategy has the following steps:

(1) identification of groups of poor unorganized women workers, often invisible (mainly, home-based workers, street vendors, and the self-employed in various trades;
(2) organizing these groups and thus giving an identity to women workers;
(3) developing 'voice' or the ability to bargain for their rights;
(4) directly providing or facilitating the provision of necessary inputs and markets; and

(5) expected outcomes are more favourable and empowering both within work and family situations.

Women's economic roles are different from those of men, with the result that we find:

(a) lower participation of women in overall economic activity;
(b) greater concentration in the primary sector and only in a few industries and occupations; and
(c) greater concentration in unskilled and marginal work.

In other words, men and women are not found equally distributed across the various types of employment available in the country; and there is a male-female wage gap. As economic agents, the majority of women (an overwhelming 95 per cent as against 89 per cent of men) are employed in the unorganized sector, and most of women workers are found in rural India (90 per cent as against 75 per cent of men). And only 28.58 per cent of women (as against 71.43 per cent of men) are in the workforce (Census 1991). Although there have been important changes in the levels of women literacy, and more women are found in decision-making and managerial positions, but from a macro-perspective this description of women's employment has not changed enough over time. There are different reasons for this. One reason is that there is still an incumbent need for wider provision of education and skills. And the second reason for a less-speedy change in the structure of women's employment is the presence of many social and cultural constraints to women's work, including their reproductive responsibilities.

These characteristics of women's employment have influenced the governmental programmes designed to increase their economic participation, and thereby empower them economically. Especially, in rural areas governmental interventions attempt to increase women's employment directly as in the Integrated Rural Development Programme (IRDP). In 1997–98, the percentage share of women in IRDP and TRYSEM (Training Rural Youth for Self-Employment) was estimated at 35.75 per cent as compared to only 11.52 per cent during 1985–86. Schemes for skill training and the organization of women into groups for marketing and credit have been introduced, as in the Rashtriya Mahila Kosh and the Swa-Shakti programme. Rashtriya Mahila Kosh was created in 1993 to meet the micro-credit needs of poor and asset-less women in the informal sector. From its inception a total credit of Rs. 77.36 crore was sanctioned to benefit 350,000 women. It has expanded its institutional base at the grass-roots level through self-help groups for extending its credit services. In this process, it also started developing linkages with the existing women's groups of IMY (Indira Mahila Yojana) and DWACRA (Development of Women and Children in Rural Areas). Economic development would not be complete if access to resources is not ensured for women. A task force on women and children has been constituted to review the existing legislation and the government schemes for improving the asset base of women to enhance their social status.

The Women's Component Plan (WCP) introduced as a major strategy for the first time during the Ninth Five-Year Plan (1997–2002) was reviewed in August 2000. It took note of funds having been made available by a number of Ministries/Departments such as Health and Family Welfare, Human Resource Development, Labour, Agriculture, Rural Development, Social Justice and Empowerment, Tribal Affairs, etc., to benefit women. Some states such as Gujarat, Himachal Pradesh, Karnataka and Kerala had also earmarked funds under WCP. The Ministry of Rural Development has special components for women in all poverty alleviation programmes. In the Swarnajayanti Gram Swarozgar Yojana (SGSY), women are assisted through revolving fund, bank credit and subsidy thus providing opportunities for self-employment. The Jawahar Gram Samriddhi Yojana (JGSY) which aims at providing demand-driven community infrastructure and the generation of supplementary employment in the rural areas has 30 per cent of the employment opportunities reserved for women. DWACRA, which has been merged with SGSY, also works for organized participation of rural women in social development and economic self-reliance. SAWERA (Sustainable Agriculture and Women Employment through Rural Approach) is a new UNDP (United Nations Development Programme) supported on-going sub-programme in Uttar Pradesh and its target is empowerment of women farm-workers from landless and marginal farmer families. This sub-programme has identified already motivated, tenacious and strong groups of women farm-workers, who have been raised by the nominated NGOs (Non-Governmental Organizations), UP Mahila Samakhya and UP Bhumi Sudhar Nigam. These groups have almost taken-offbutneedacriticalsupporttoachieveasustainedexistence.Therefore, it is contemplated to link up these groups with Department of Agriculture and Agriculture Extension Services to gain access to productive assets like theland, micro-capital, credit, subsidies, appropriate technologies, training, knowledge of suitable agronomic practices, land and watershed development means and other inputs and services. Through this selective coordination, it is intended to make Department of Agriculture and Agriculture Extension Services, responsive to needs and priorities of women farmers, and handle gender issues more sensitively. Social employment schemes like the SGSY (Swarnajayanti Gram Swarozgar Yojana), the STEP (Support for Training and Employment Programme) and the NORAD (Norwegian Agency for Development Corporation) schemes give access to women in the employment field but numbers trained by them are still very less and need to be increased. Our present system does not adequately provide for imparting vocational skills, which alone can ensure a quick beginning of the earning. And women acquiring skills in traditional ways find no institutional arrangements for expanding or updating them. Investing in women's capabilities and empowering them to realize their potentialities is not only valuable in itself but is also a surest way to contribute to economic growth and overall development (Human Development Report, UNDP, 1996). Capacity-building and means for ensuring competence and commitment to the goal of mainstreaming gender into all walks of life must be made attainable at a more rapid pace both within the government and civil society.

Role of Education in Empowering Women

There is no doubt that years of neglect and discrimination against the females cannot be turned around in a day. However, careful planning on the part of the government to raise educational levels of women across the country with the cooperation of the civil society will result in their empowerment. It will raise their self-awareness and allow them to participate in decision-making process both at home and outside. Education is the key to making women self-reliant and giving them the confidence to pursue their goals. Women in India, in general, are not lacking in self-confidence but it is important for them to realize this individually as well as collectively. India needs to follow the example of countries such as South Korea,

Malaysia and Singapore which invested vast amount of resources in the education of their populace and advanced rapidly thereafter to never look back again.

In a report brought out by the United Nations called 'Women—Challenges to the Year 2000', it is remarked that, "Rural societies, which depend heavily on women for the survival, are especially resistant to educating them. Rural women tend to have more children, be poorer, and in their struggle to survive, have little or no time and energy to spare on adult literacy programmes. Survival needs aside; rural women are also more likely to encounter resistance from within the family to their pursuing an education: an educated woman might pose a threat to her husband and upset the family status quo". Moreover, in a patriarchal society such as India, education of a girl child is seen as a bad investment as she is bound to marry and leave home one day, to live with her husband's family. Thus, these are the mindsets, which need to be challenged and conquered if the country (India) wants to progress and fight centuries of backwardness. Empowerment of women also requires the participation and cooperation of men as they benefit by having educated mothers, wives, daughters and sisters. There is a saying that "if you educate a boy, you educate an individual but if you educate a girl, you educate a family".

India has taken several steps towards empowering of women through education. The National Policy of Education (1986) revised in 1992 and the Programme of Action (POA, 1992) reflects an unqualified priority to universal elementary education, total literacy and the ending of gender differentials. A fundamental mandate of the National Policy on education is to educate women for gender equality. Thus, it goes beyond merely eliminating gender gaps in educational attainments for it also seeks to alter the very process and content of education so that it changes people's attitudes. For the first time, it carried the message that along with expanding women's access to all kinds of education, the system, with all its institutions, had to shoulder a major responsibility for genuine empowerment of women. In the Total Literacy Mission of the government, which is in progress in 356 districts, women make up for over 62 per cent of adults enrolled in the programme. According to government figures, up to January 1995, out of a total enrolment of 74 million, 44 million were women. There are several other government initiatives such as Mahila Samakhya Programme in the four states—Uttar Pradesh, Karnataka, Gujarat and Andhra Pradesh which aims to bring about an "environment for women to seek knowledge and information in order to make informed choices" so that women are able to break out of their traditional mould; the Decentralized Planning for Elementary Education (DPEP) in seven states such as Assam, Haryana, Maharashtra, Karnataka, Tamil Nadu, Kerala and Madhya Pradesh aims to provide special gender focus to universal elementary education; 'Lok Jumbish'—a programme of universal elementary education in Rajasthan emphasizes on gender centrality, consensus building and partnerships. The Mahila Samakhya Programme launched in 1986 under the banner of 'Education for Women's Equality' by the Ministry of Human Resource Development is a government initiative implemented with the aim to build positive self-image, develop critical thinking, build group solidarity and collective decision-making, and action for social change. Participation in the programme has enabled the Sangha women to enhance their self-esteem, confidence and competence together termed as 'education for life skills' (in addition to information, knowledge and literacy) (Jain and Krishnamurthy 1996). Yet another noteworthy experiment is SARTHI (Social Action for Rural and Tribal Inhabitants of India)—an NGO based in the tribal area of Panchmahals in Gujarat. Through a community-based women-centred model of health, this programme has enabled women to define their problems and strategies, and organize to solve them collectively. Intensive training processes have been geared towards discussing and analysing participants' life situations and enabling them to overcome their powerlessness.

Within the country (India), however, wide variations exist, as mentioned in the report of UN CEDAW (United Nations, Convention on the Elimination of All Forms of Discrimination Against Women): "While Kerala has near universal literacy, female literacy in Rajasthan is only 20.8 per cent." These differences between states have to be reduced so that gender and educational disparities are minimized. Today, it is necessary that women are educated and sensitized to gender discrimination, for it helps them to perceive the inequities in their own surroundings and thus ask for change. The traditional pattern of socialization has been based on a patriarchal model and for the same reason has served as an instrument of perpetuation of patriarchy. What is needed is a qualitative change in the pattern of socialization from patriarchal to gender-egalitarian. For this a new kind of parenting, i.e., gender-sensitive parenting is required. This in turn calls for devising training programmes in gender-sensitive parenting. Both mother and father, but particularly the mother has to be initiated in the values and strategies of gender-sensitive socialization. The stress is laid on the training of mother because it is she who by all means plays a more significant role as an agent of socialization. It is, therefore, she who has to be especially prepared to socialize the new generation in a more sensitive manner towards the values of gender justice and equality (Sharma, 2000). This can happen when the entire society works towards such gender sensitization and makes a specific well-directed effort to eliminate gender discrimination. However, creating a new equitable environment is a major challenge. Realization has dawned in India that without gender equality in education women cannot be empowered. Education is seen as 'a potential equalizer' and it is generally believed that 'true education must liberate'.

Enforcement of Women's Rights through Legal Interventions

It is also essential that the school and college curriculum should contain modules on women's rights posited under the Indian Constitution and the Special Acts passed as measures of 'positive action' for them. The Department of Women and Child of the Central Government had in early 1990s published volumes in easy language explaining the rights of women under various laws and how they can get these rights through the implementing agencies. Even today, women are denied freedom of self-expression, as they end up being confined to domestic and related activities, and are denied education and economic power. It is because most of the women are ignorant of their legal rights and do not have the means to enforce their rights, and above all, social pulls and pressures prevent them from asserting these rights. Social attitudes have not changed sufficiently though laws have created a more enabling environment. What one must remember, however, is that unless laws create equality and fairness, there is no way of getting rid of discrimination. Far from having enough laws we still have a long way to go before we have equitable laws in the areas, which are traditionally of vital concern to women such as family laws that affect marital status, custody of children, a right to a home and its maintenance, inheritance and succession, adoption, and for the Hindus, rights in the joint family and its property.

A woman in India has inheritance rights in varying degrees under different Personal Laws. The law that has empowered women most in this respect is the Hindu Succession Act, 1956. The Act has revolutionized a women's right over property. A female has equal rights of succession as heirs along with the male heirs. While law is not an absolute instrument of empowerment, it cannot be denied that it does play a significant role. Legal literacy is necessary to make laws effective. In addition to legal interventions, socially, a change is seriously needed in attitudes towards daughters inheriting. Unless women's claims begin to be seen as socially legitimate, parents can use the right of testation to disinherit daughters by writing a will, even if the laws are made fully gender-equal. Measures to change attitudes, through conscientization require an emphasis that a women today needs to be economically independent for ensuring the welfare of herself and her family.

It is a fact that land continues to be a significant source of livelihood and social status for millions of rural families, and in some cases, it is also an important source of political power in rural India. However, most of the land is owned and controlled by men, thus depriving women of a critical means of economic well-being and empowerment. For majority of women who continue to depend on agriculture for their livelihood, access to land is the most important basis of economic security. Entitling women with land could empower them economically and strengthen their ability to challenge gender inequalities, both within and outside the home. For instance, where women got title they could now assert: "We had tongues but could not speak, we had feet but could not walk. Now that we have the land, we have the strength to speak and walk". This is the sense of empowerment more emphatically and openly being expressed by rural women as they feel it.

Empowering Women in the Political Sphere

In villages, panchayats can play a significant role in enforcing the land and property rights of women along with other rights related to employment opportunities, education, health, etc., since panchayats have been given the responsibility of preparing plans for economic development and social justice and implementing these plans and schemes with regard to a fairly comprehensive list of subjects (29 subjects as contained in Schedule XI). It also, affords to women who are elected as Panchayat members, an opportunity of personal growth and empowerment while at the same time creating an unique opportunity to change things in the village. All the provisions of the 73rd Constitution Amendment Act that seek to empower panchayats directly or indirectly serve to empower women. In many of the panchayats, which are headed by women not only has the participation and leadership of women made an impact on grass roots governance, it has also shattered many of the myths regarding their inability to handle power and responsibility outside their homes. The political empowerment of women in villages has had a favourable impact in two significant ways. There is, first of all, a visible improvement in the administration and delivery of services at the Gram Panchayat level, mainly because of greater focus on the felt needs of the people, greater transparency, greater reliance on horizontal linkages and greater participation of people particularly, women members of the village community. Second, the amendment has made possible the creation of political space for women, which in turn has enabled them to gain in social stature, confidence and to shake off age-old stranglehold of repressive tradition.

Some eyebrows are raised on the issue of reservation for women not only in contesting the elections and occupying political seats but also in admission to educational institutions or government services. It is enough to mention that the need for positive discrimination in favour of women was felt and provided for as long back as during the framing of Indian Constitution, but the provision is being implemented only now, and is therefore, totally justified. In the final stage, however, women's empowerment can be considered as 'complete' only when women as a collective group no longer require any positive discrimination or reservation. It is a happy sign that lot of young women have started expressing that they would prefer to come up in life on the basis of merit rather than through reservation. A right kind of 'seed' for empowerment is already sown and it will be necessary to nurture this.

Enlightening Optimism

By all means, it is a positive indication that women empowerment approach in our country appears quite promising in paving the way for attaining the goal of gender-balanced development, by highlighting the fact that all individuals whether men or women are equally capable of making choices and directing their own lives, and establishing that empowerment is innate to dignified human existence. It would be appropriate to refer to it as 'gender-empowerment approach', for it actually aims at overcoming gender inequality, discrimination and exploitation, to give rise to a gender-egalitarian society. Quite sensitively, it takes note of imbalance in gender relations and stresses the need for restoring the balance by transforming these gender relations from hierarchical to egalitarian plane rather than just dealing with women's power position only. It attempts at reworking of gender relations in a complementary rather than conflictual mode, i.e., by taking men along with women, and not by leaving them out or working against them. The time has come when both men and women need to transcend their gender identities and work together as equal partners. Ideally, the real fruits of empowerment can be reaped only within an environment of mutual respect, value, dignity and equality, and where women are able to share equal power with men. To achieve this, a greater emphasis is now laid on 'personal' or 'self-empowerment' of women, whereby they are assisted to enhance their skills and opportunities, to explore their world, to define their personal vision and to pursue their own goals. Today, for women, *power* has been redefined as the capacity to implement; which implies the implementation of abilities or capacities the women already have and as well as the new ones that they are developing. It is perhaps, assumed that women need the 'power' to develop and function as capable, strong and productive beings so that they turn out to be assets of society at par with men. The new upcoming gender ideology asserts that women too, must get equal space to breathe and grow, just as men do, for they are no less than them. The father of the nation, M. K. Gandhi, also advocated the same notion that—"between man and woman neither should be regarded as *superior* or *inferior.*" He reiterated that women empowerment is not only a moral imperative but a prerequisite for strengthening egalitarian values and fighting against injustice and oppression.

References

Batliwala, S. *Empowerment of Women in South Asia: Concepts and Practices.* New Delhi: FAO, 1993.

Beteille, A. "Empowerment." *Economic and Political Weekly* 34 (1999): 589–97.

Boserup, E. *Women's Role in Economic Development.* New York: St. Martin's Press, 1970.

Bystydzienski, J., ed. *Women Transforming Politics: Worldwide Strategies for Empowerment.* Indianapolis: Indiana University Press, 1992.

Deutchman, J. "The Politics of Empowerment." *Women and Politics* 11, No. 2 (1991): 1–18.

Freire, P. *Pedagogy of the Oppressed.* New York: Seabury Press, 1972.

Giddens, A. *The Constitution of Society.* Cambridge: Polity Press, 1984.

Griffen, V., ed. *Women, Development and Empowerment: A Pacific Feminist Perspective.* Kuala Lumpur: Asia and Pacific Development Centre, 1989.

Human Development Report. Published for the United Nations Development Programme (UNDP). Oxford: Oxford University Press, 1995.

Human Development Report. Published for the United Nations Development Programme (UNDP). Oxford: Oxford University Press, 1996.

Human Development Report. Published for the United Nations Development Programme (UNDP). Oxford: Oxford University Press, 2000.

Jain, S. and Krishnamurthy, L. *Empowerment through Mahila Samakhya Experience.* Jaipur: Sandhan Shodh Kendra, 1996.

Kabeer, N. "Gender, Development and Training: Raising Awareness in Development Planning." *GAADU Newspack,* No. 14 (1990).

Karl, M. *Women and Empowerment: Participation and Decision Making.* London: Zed Books, 1995.

Longwe, S. "Gender Awareness: The Missing Element in the Third World Development Project," in *Changing Perceptions: Writings on Gender Development.* Oxford: Oxfam, 1991.

Moser, C.O.N. Gender Planning in the Third World: Meeting Practical and Strategic Gender Needs. *World Development* 17, No. 11 (1989): 1799–1825.

Rose, K. *Where Women are Leaders: The SEWA Movement in India.* New Delhi: Vistaar Publications, 1992.

Sharma, S.L. "Empowerment without Antagonism: A Case for Reformulation of Women's Empowerment Approach." *Sociological Bulletin* 49, No. 1 (2000): 19–39.

Wieringa, S. "Women's Interests and Empowerment: Gender Planning Reconsidered." *Development and Change* 25 (1994): 829–48.

II

Women in Formal and Informal Economy

4

Women in Industrial Sector: An Empirical Study

Debjani Mukherjee and Promila Singh

The role and scope of Indian women in the industrial sector has evolved gradually after independence. In the early years, women were generally confined to their homes, the occasional working women being more of an exception to the rule. All it takes is a peek into the industries and top companies to realize that women still are not percolating into the upper echelons of industry.

In the sixties and seventies, more women started stepping out, but their work areas were limited to the jobs of teachers, doctors, nurses or lowly positions in offices and banks. In the last two decades of the 20th century, however, the floodgates opened up and women started entering fields hitherto unthinkable—engineering, computers, software, executive positions in the corporate world, etc. Even then, physically and mentally tough jobs were still not in their purview. However, this last bastion is also falling and in this first decade of the 21st century, there are hardly any jobs that they cannot hold just because she is a woman. Women are now working in "tough" sectors like coal, oil, steel, mining, aviation etc., shoulder to shoulder with men. Among these, the present study has attempted to explore the performance of women in the steel sector including the tough departments like coke ovens, blast furnaces, steel melting shops, etc.

Organizations around the world including India are facing the twin challenges of remaining viable and competitive. There is a premium on quality, innovativeness, uniqueness and cost-effectiveness. Meeting the stringent standards of respective industries coupled with complying with various legal, social, environmental requirements are forcing the organizations to utilize and exploit their resources to the greatest extent possible, prime among them being the skill, commitment and job involvement of the workforce. The resources being men, materials and finance, their availability of the required standards or quality and quantity is another daunting exercise. But with the improvement in the economic condition of the country, there has been a strengthening of financial institutions and in turn, their faith and confidence in the Indian customer.

Employee behaviour plays a crucial role in maximizing an organization's functioning irrespective of technological development. Job involvement in simple terms refers to the commitment that a person expresses to his job or work. It is devotion to duty in body and spirit. It is something intrinsic and vital to the individual that makes him consider work as the most important part of his life, and the major satisfaction that he could derive is from accomplishing his duty effectively. Lawler and Hall (1970) define job involvement as referring to psychological identification with one's work, as well as degree to which the job situation is central to person and his identity. Therefore, any effort to maximize organizational effectiveness depends on achieving the highest degree of job involvement among members of an organization.

Enhancing job involvement of the employees to their organization has emerged as one of the most important problems for the researchers. Though every employee in an organization works with similar tools, machines and materials, yet individual difference in their level of job involvement are quite evident. Organizations now-a-days struggle to retain their staff and draw commitment from the workforce to meet the organization's goals and attain their vision. The biggest of the above issues is job involvement as it actually translates into quality and productive output by the individual.

The 'hierarchy' or 'status' (designation) also affects work behaviour of the employee. Hierarchy of an employee plays an important part in large industrial houses. The Bhilai Steel Plant is the most profitable plant in the SAIL (Steel Authority of India Limited) family. Here, the shop incharges deal with thousands of subordinates and workers many of whom report directly to them. The power that these officers wield is tremendous. It will be of great interest to study the pattern of 'job involvement' of the executives according to their designations. In this research hierarchies have been studied at three levels, namely, frontline, middle ranking and senior ranking.

Gender stereotyping of the employee has an important role to play in the context of steel plant functioning, as working in hard shops is physically very strenuous as well as hazardous. Expected role of females would be to work for the service sectors than in the manufacturing sectors. It would be of great relevance to study the effect gender has on job involvement. The HRD section may rethink their placement policy if important differences are revealed. In various other field of work, like the IT sector, teaching, banks, etc., gender of the employee may not have the same kind of influence on his job involvement as in the case of steel sector, because physical hardships are not prevalent there. Will the so-called gender bias related with vocations, which plays on our mind, may actually turn out to be a necessity.

Keeping the above industrial requirements as a backdrop, it was interesting to do this study, investigating the work efficiency and involvement of Indian women employees in the steel sector and how they compete with their male counterparts. Does the fact that being male or female affect his/her job involvement? What is the impact of the rank or the official hierarchy of the executive in the process of his job involvement? These are queries that were explored and generally we can say that this study was undertaken to see the women functioning at all levels of hierarchies and how they are comparable with the males.

Methodology

The Sample

The sample for the present study was mainly confined to the executives of Bhilai Steel Plant which is a unit of the steel giant SAIL (Steel Authority of India Limited), a public sector unit. The population of the executives working in the steel plant is roughly 2,282, out of which 400 (17.5 per cent) was selected randomly for the study. As this study proposes to study the difference in the levels of job involvement (JI) among the two genders—males and females, it was seen that the sample had both in appropriate proportion. Executives of all status or ranks were taken. The grouping of the various ranks were done at three levels: (a) frontline (junior manager, assistant manager, deputy manager); (b) middle order (manager, senior manager, assistant general manager); and 3. topline (deputy general manager, general manager, executive director, managing director).

Design

This is an *ex-post facto* type of research. It is a systematic empirical enquiry in which independent variables are the demographic variables—gender and hierarchy. Each executive was tested to find out the level of his job involvement.

To see the significance of difference betwеen means f-ratios were computed in a two-way ANOVA (2 × 3) and mean JI of the various groups were also found.

Tools

To measure job involvement (JI) it was decided to use a 54-item scale developed by Singh (1984).

Data Analysis

It is obvious from Table 1 that the mean score of the entire sample (n=400) in JI was found to be 152.42. The standard deviation is 15.13. The mean

Table 1 *Descriptive Statistics*

	Mean	*Std. Deviation*	*N*
JI	152.4175 High JI	**15.1351**	**400**

Table 2 *Mean Table*

Gender	*Total (N)*	*Mean JI*	*Category*
Male	258	153.452	High
Female	142	149.020	Moderate

Figure A

Graph Showing Level of JI According to Gender

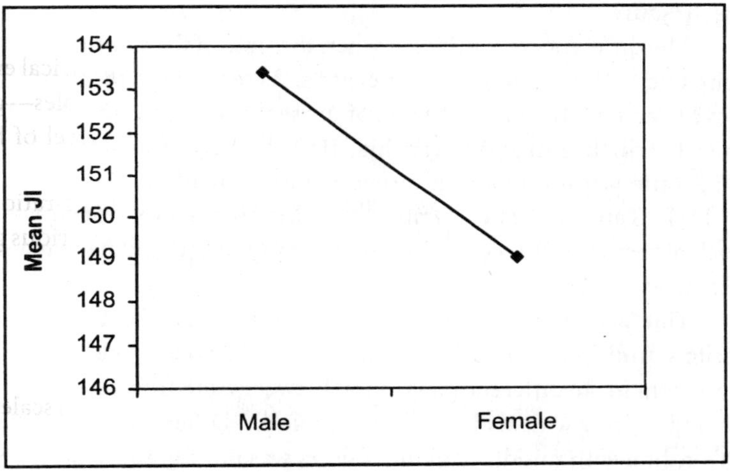

score reveals that the involvement level of the respondents towards their job is found to be above average i.e., they are highly involved in their job.

The mean JI score of the male executives was found to be (M=153.45) whereas the mean JI score of the female executives was (M=149.02). The difference between the two means reveal that JI level is different for different sex with males being in the high JI category and female being in the moderate JI category. F-Ratio was also found to be significant (F=5.03, p<.05) (Table 6). It indicates that male executives differ significantly from female executives with respect to their job involvement. This trend is obvious in the graph shown in Figure A.

Table 3 *Mean Table*

Hierarchy	*Total (N)*	*Mean (JI)*	*Category*
Frontline (1)	121	147.647	Moderate
Middle order (2)	182	147.919	Moderate
Top line (3)	97	158.670	High

The difference in the levels of JI among the frontline and middle-order executives was found to be almost nil with their mean JI scores being (M=147.64) and (M=147.91) respectively which is of moderate level. (Figure B).

The difference is significant when the state of the senior executives is compared with their junior counterparts. As seen in the mean table given above (Table 3), the mean JI score of the senior executives is (M=158.67), which falls in the category of very high JI level. Main effect of status was seen and F-ratio was found which turned out to be highly significant ($F=8.38$, $p<.001$) (Table 6). The findings revealed that senior executives have much higher JI level as compared to the frontline and middle management executives.

This fact is made all the more clear by the Tukey's Post Hoc Test done to show multiple comparisons between the various levels of hierarchy. Significant mean difference was found between both frontline and middle-ranking officers with senior officers (Table 4).. Difference between means of frontline with middle-ranking officers was not found to be significant. Research findings of Tannenbaum (1965), Mannheim (1975), Sharma and Kapoor (1978) also supplemented this result. They reported that individuals at higher ranks are found to be more involved with their jobs.

Figure B

Graph Showing the Level of JI According to the Hierarchy

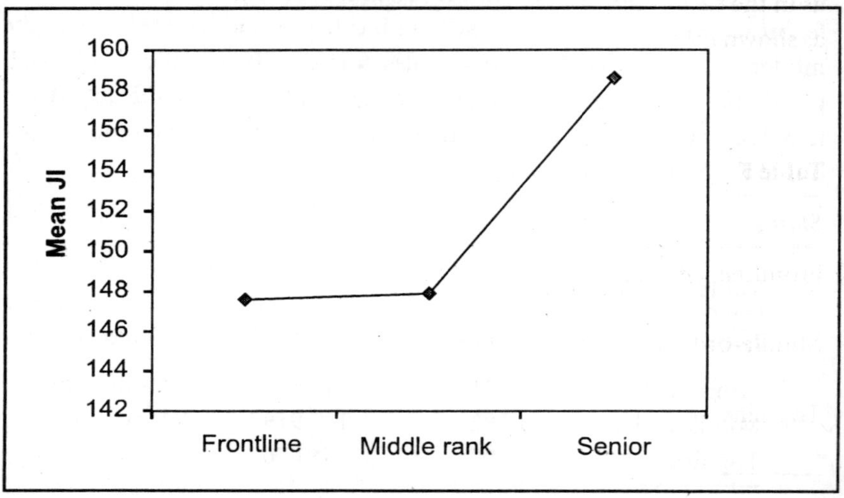

Table 4 *Post Hoc Test*

(Multiple Comparisons)

Hierarchy		*Mean Diff.*	*Std. Error*	*Sig.*
1.00	2.00	–1.6939	1.6358	.554
	3.00	–8.1729(*)	1.8497	.000
2.00	1.00	1.6939	1.6358	.554
	3.00	–6.4790(*)	1.6914	.000
3.00	1.00	8.1729(*)	1.8497	.000
	2.00	6.4790(*)	1.6914	.000

* The mean difference is significant at the.05 level.

Mean Table 5 shows that frontline and middle-order male executives have the same level of JI which of is high-moderate category. On the other hand frontline and middle-order female executives have low-moderate level of JI. However, there is a hike in the levels of JI of both males and females as they reach top line position. Females suddenly start expressing very high JI, which is a jump up straight from low-moderate JI in frontline and middle rank.

The increase in the JI level of the senior males is not that pronounced as in the case of senior females. This fact is supplemented by the bar chart as shown in Figure C.

Table 5 *Mean Table*

Status	*Gender*	*Mean JI*	*Category*
Frontline	Male	151.28	High-Moderate
	Female	144.00	Low-Moderate
Middle-order	Male	151.42	High-Moderate
	Female	144.41	Low-Moderate
Top Line	Male	156.30	High
	Female	161.03	Very High

Table 6 *Anova Summary*

Source	*F*	*Sig.*
Hierarchy	8.380	.001
Gender	5.03	.050
Hierarchy & Gender	2.493	.084

Figure C

Bars Showing Level of JI According to Gender and Hierarchy

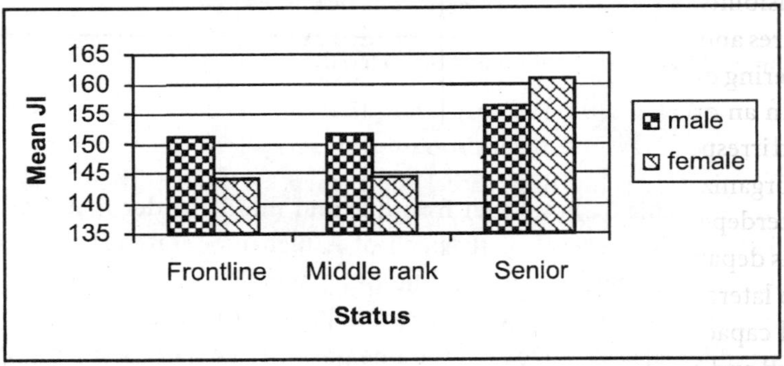

Anova Summary Table 6 shows that the effect of hierarchy on JI is significant (F=8.38, p<.001). The effect of gender on JI was found to be significant (F=5.03, p<.05). Interaction effect of both hierarchy and gender was not found to be significant, though it was found to be approaching (F=2.49, p<.08).

Discussion

As the aim of this research was to do a comparative study of the job-involvement level of the two genders, the results show women at the top to have emerged to be the most significant in this area.

The work culture in a steel plant though very demanding is extremely challenging, where work demands a lot of interaction with the co-workers and very long hours have to be put in. The normal office hours of 9 a.m. to 5 p.m. do not apply here. The males, who are go-getters in their work field and like to climb the hierarchical ladder in their work life, thrive on this kind of work culture. They put work higher on their priority list, than family and friends. In the steel plant non-stop production takes place throughout the year. Casualties and breakdown of machineries are common features and that means that the executives of that shop are on duty round the clock till that calamity is resolved. Each executive is answerable to his immediate superior and this ladder-wise reporting is done throughout the day and continues even after the executive comes home. The Indian females are generally more family oriented, and shoulder the dual job and responsibility of balancing work and life. They are not able to handle these pressures and cannot devote the time needed in these work areas, resulting in lowering of their JI

In an organization, it is important that the job needs to be accomplished irrespective of the specific roles and area of control of the employees. If the organization is like Bhilai Steel Plant where the various departments are interdependent, then to accomplish any task, coordination between various departments will form a vital part of functioning. This in turn will lead to lateral coordination on the part of the individuals. Here, the managerial capacity of the individuals comes into play. Males who are more inclined and equipped with the requisite skills for such an activity will find it easy to accomplish the tasks at hand than those who will stick to the predetermined roles. This kind of lateral coordination needs a lot of running around and handling numerous non-executives, workers and daily wagers. As working run in three shifts (morning, day and night), managing shift workers and taking reports at the beginning and end of every shift is part of the executive's daily job profile. Family responsibilities and other social obligations that a female is expected to execute probably incapacitates her on the work front.

Hierarchy seems to affect JI very significantly with senior executives above deputy general manager rank expressing very high JI as compared to their junior colleagues. The reasons that can be identified are numerous. Discussing this issue with the executives of various ranks revealed contradictory factors. The senior, both male and female executives talked about emotional bond with the steel plant getting cemented as the years went by. However, the frontline and middle-order executives expressed that the degree of democratic functioning is not appropriate and needs to be paid heed to. Delegating power and autonomy to the junior counterparts will definitely facilitate the degree of involvement in their jobs. Normally a positive correlation is there between hierarchy and age in public sectors, as mostly the promotions are time bound.

Frontline and middle-order female executives were found to express low JI but once they graduate to the senior ranks, they suddenly start expressing very high level of JI, even higher than the males. This can be explained by pointing out that frontline and middle order females are young and middle aged with family responsibilities paramount in their lives. Once they rise in status and are a little free from their family responsibilities, they find themselves in the tough world supposedly meant for males; hence they feel the need to perform better than the males.

An interesting paradox came to light in the present study—while women do not perform with work efficiency equal to that of men in the frontline and middle management, their job involvement and performance in the top level management is as efficient as, or rather more efficient than their male counterparts. The reasons for this turnaround may be manyfold, and as already explained, when a woman enters the work field, joining the organization at the lower or middle levels, she is likely to be at that stage in her own personal life when family commitments and domestic obligations make a much more pressing demand on her time and energy. Her energies are also dissipated in trying to get social and familial acceptance as a woman trying to gain a position of power in a man's world. As Henry and Washington (2001) say that, traditionally a man's performance is overrated in the light of positive expectations, while women's performance, regardless of quality is underrated. Even slight differences in evaluation lead to an accumulation of advantage for men over their careers and prevent women from advancing as far as they should.

Many executives expressed that gender barriers still impede women's progress in industry, but those "barriers are more subtle than they used. The overt stuff is gone", says Davis S., commercial development manager at Solutia. Many thought there still exists a fair amount of very subtle bias that shows up in the placement of women in particular types of jobs in industry. It can be seen that when women show up in very large numbers in staff positions instead of line positions, when the women are all going to the total quality jobs, the communications jobs, human resources, public relations, finance, they are never going to be business managers that way because they are never going to get the product line business experience that they need to ultimately be a business leader.

Some reactions were that as frontline and middle-management executives have to exert more stress on the balancing factors in work-life, the retention issues of the management go a long way to show how they are managing some of the unique issues for women, one such being finding ways of providing flexibility. When women need to take more time to manage their families at a certain point in their lives, the management should recognize that it is not forever and that it really is worth the investment to make it possible for them to do that. V. Valian, a psychologist at Hunter College of the City University of New York, in 1998, attributed much of the problem of slow advancement of women to 'gender schemas', a set of subconscious hypotheses about sex differences that both men and women hold. In these schemas, men are perceived as being better suited to professional success.

Once a woman reaches the higher echelons of the industrial world, she has reached that stage of life when her family responsibilities are discharged, children are on the way to being settled, and she can concentrate fully on her work area. As promotions in the public sector being mostly time-bound, she has now acquired an inner maturity, which helps her to focus and direct her energies to the optimum. She has now reached a stage where she can overcome the repercussions of generations of suppressions, which Indian women tend to internalize. The woman who has reached the top management line in industry is more secure and has a heightened sense of self-worth which gives her the confidence that she is at par with, if not superior to her male colleagues. A publication called Human Resource Planning (1 June 2004), reported that women have been repeatedly said to receive higher evaluation ratings than men, make better managers (supposedly because of superior interpersonal skills), and perform better because they are rated higher. It further reports that since 1993, they have collected 360 cases of performance, and potential data on men and women as individual contributors, managers and executives. Women may have to perform slightly better to get to the same level as men, and are more participative and attuned to others. This showcases the biases the women had to face.

U. Chowdhry (2001), a topline woman executive in Dupont comments that women's performance is observed closely, "through a 1,0003 magnifying glass." Chowdhry found the general attitude for women in the industry as "Give them yet one more experience and see how they perform before we give them any executive management responsibility. Let's give the women more experiences so we set them up for success." Women in general have to outperform themselves and their peers to be considered for opportunities with a high degree of responsibility. Women need to prove themselves repeatedly, despite their track record, Chowdhry emphasizes. She believes that these barriers are societal and can be found in all walks of life. She hopes that her generation will have "paved the way" for subsequent generations.

E. Piocos (2001), a senior scientist in Procter and Gamble, feels that to reach and sustain at the top level, the contribution to the company matters. She feels that top line promotion is because of the impact you have on the business not once but many times."

A. Niessen and S. Ruenzi (2007) report that gender research has typically found few real differences in performance.

After the initial struggle a woman goes through to balance her life and work, by the time she reaches the top levels, she has had the required experience in making her an expert multitasker. This multitasking, which becomes second nature to a lot of women, makes for a productive eight hours on the job.

Accelerated learning increases the productivity and contributions of women. People need to constantly look ahead to see what is the next skill or technology they will need to learn.

The status of women in Indian industry is evolving gradually and it is to be hoped that a time will come when Indian women in the frontline and middle management will also have more job involvement and work efficiency, like their counterparts in the top management. In keeping with the west where Niessen and Ruenzi (2007), found female and male managers not to differ in average performance in their work, there is room for much hope that Indian women in frontline and middle management too will achieve this distinction.

When that time comes, the findings of the present study will have to be researched and redefined. However, this study aims to provide a stepping-stone for further research in this area.

References

Chowdhry, U. As reported in Henry, C. and Washington, E. N. "Industry Women Speak Out: Setting Goals and Establishing Mentoring Networks are Key in Achieving Success." *Employment* 79, No. 27 (2001).

Davis, S. As reported in Henry, C. and Washington, E.N. "Industry Women Speak Out: Setting Goals and Establishing Mentoring Networks are Key in Achieving Success." *Employment* 79, No. 27 (2001).

Henry, C. and Washington, E.N. "Industry Women Speak Out: Setting Goals and Establishing Mentoring Networks are Key in Achieving Success." *Employment* 79, No. 27 (2001).

Lawler, E.E. and Hall, D.T. "Relationship of Job Characteristics to Job Involvement, Satisfaction, and Intrinsic Motivation." Journal of Applied Psychology 54 (1970): 305–12.

Mannheim, B. "A Comparative Study of Work Centrality, Job Rewards and Job Satisfaction." *Sociology of Work and Occupations* 2, (1975): 79–102.

Niessen, A. and Ruenzi, S. "Sex Matters: Gender Differences in a Professional Setting" (CFR-Working Paper No. 06-01, 2007).

Piocos, E. As reported in Henry, C. and Washington, E. N. "Industry Women Speak Out: Setting Goals and Establishing Mentoring Networks are Key in Achieving Success." *Employment* 79, No. 27 (2001).

Sharma, S. and Kapoor, V.K. "A Study of Job Involvement in Relation to Certain Demographic Variables among White-Collar Workers." *Indian Psychological Review* 16 (1978): 11–16.

Singh, A.P. *Construction and Standardization of Job Involvement Scale.* Varanasi: MPS Publications, 1984.

Tannenbaum, A.S. Unions. In *Handbook of Organizations,* edited by J. G. March, Chicago: Rand McNally, 1965.

Valian, V. *Why So Slow? The Advancement of Women.* Cambridge, MA: MIT Press, 1998.

5

Stress and Coping among Women Managers in Indian Organizations

H.L. Kaila

Though women workforce has risen to a greater extent, the old attitudes of men still exist in organizations. For example, a woman was not introduced while sharing a stage with men when everyone else was. Another woman was asked repeatedly by his boss whether she can work in shifts even though she happened to be a qualified engineer holding senior manager position. A senior man in the organization denied concession in work timings to a pregnant lady who requested so. Do these instances indicate that men lack sensitivity on women specific issues?

Women in offices quite often have to travel along with men as part of their duties or stay together during conferences. Men would readily agree to travel with a woman whereas a woman would face several questions from various fronts. She herself is in dilemma sometimes, whether should she accept this? How the family would react to it? How would organization address such gender issues? Whether this is an issue for young women working in MNCs?

In a study on stress coping styles among German managers (Kirkcaldy and Furnham, 1999), the abbreviated German version of Occupational Stress Indicator's Coping Scale was completed anonymously by over 160 managers. No difference in coping profiles of men and women was found, but different levels of management and educational status did influence preference for coping styles. More specifically, it was seen that at the most senior levels of management, delegation and maintaining stable relationships are considered the most useful forms of coping with stress.

A comparative study on managerial stress in Hong Kong and Taiwan: (Oi-ling, Luo and Cary, 1999) investigated occupational stress in managers in Hong Kong and Taiwan using the Occupational Stress Indicator-2 (OSI-2). The results showed that there were gender differences in managerial stress in Hong Kong: female managers scored higher in sources of stress and quitting intention; but had lower job satisfaction, worse mental and physical well-being than male managers. These differences could not be found in Taiwanese managers, yet Taiwanese female managers did report more stress related to "managerial role" than their male counterparts.

H.L. Kaila (2002) studied 120 managers in metropolitan Mumbai and found that 80 per cent of them experienced the most common workplace stresses and challenges such as: meeting deadlines, working in a competitive industry, managing finances, exhausting working hours, and rotation work in addition to handling regular tasks (such as sales, marketing, training, research and development, and accounts of core clients).

A Malaysian survey on occupational stress among managers (Taap, Fontaine and Chong Siong Choy, 2003) examined sources of stress among Malaysian managers working in multinational companies. A total of 440 managers participated in this survey. Data was collected through a questionnaire distributed to the managers in 34 multinational companies operating in Malaysia. It was found that workloads, working conditions and relationship at work were main concerns of the managers that lead to stress at the workplace. The results also indicated that certain demographic variables do influence the level of stress among managers.

Kasper, Meyer and Schmidt (2005) conducted an explorative analysis on managers dealing with work-family conflict. The sample was drawn largely according to the principles of theoretical sampling; family-work constellations provided the basis of selection. Thirty problem-focused interviews were content analysed. Results showed three distinct prototypes of dealing with work-family-tension: career as subject of social fascination, family as a factual task, the tradition of two worlds, double burden and the pressure of tasks. One outstanding result was that if both partners were professionally active, the family was increasingly dominated by merely functional requirements.

Armstrong-Stassen (2005) compared the reactions of executive-level and middle managers prior to a large-scale downsizing, during initial and final phases, and following the downsizing. Compared with executives, middle managers perceived greater job insecurity, were more likely to use escape coping, and reported lower job performance and higher levels of health symptoms. Over time, both executives and middle managers reported a decline in perceived threat of job loss but an increase in sense of powerlessness, a decrease in the use of control-oriented coping strategies, and reduced job performance in the initial phase of downsizing. Although less so, executive-level managers were also adversely affected by the downsizing, suggesting that this group should be included in stress management interventions.

The studies on managerial psychology recently as well as in the past depict that cross-culturally there are similarities and differences on managerial behaviours. Secondly, female managers report more stresses regardless of cultural background. Thirdly, the sources of managerial stress across cultures are similar. Moreover, the managerial researches so far have been based on quantitative methodologies. Hence, it is postulated that the use of qualitative and narrative methods on the study of managerial issues would broaden our understanding and provide us more depth in the field.

Method

A structured questionnaire using the following three open-ended questions was presented to individual managers in their respective organizations:

- What do you think was the greatest problem you faced in the past 12 months?
- Explain the ways it did affect you personally or professionally?
- Could you give a title or heading to this problem and how did you overcome this problem?

The managers were asked to narrate their experiences. The women managers took time out of their really busy and hectic schedule to share their problems and issues in organizations. Though managerial problems and coping have been researched using quantitative research techniques, the depth of understanding on managerial issues is lacking. Hence, a narrative approach was attempted in this study in order to enrich the managerial research.

Sample

The sample consisted of 140 female managers between 26 to 55 years of age in 81 organizations (including private and public sector, and MNCs) from different parts of India such as Mumbai, Bangalore, and Hyderabad, ranging from banks to IT, pharmaceutical companies to call centres. Data were collected from varied work backgrounds, different age groups and different levels of management: upper, middle, and lower working in various departments through in-depth personal interviews and e-mails in a few cases with the help of a structured questionnaire using open-ended questions.

Results and Discussion

The survey results have been presented under the following sections: problems faced by women managers, the ways in which the problems affect the women managers, and the coping strategies used by women managers to overcome their problems.

To the three questions asked, the women managers responded as under:

1. **Time Crisis:** The greatest problem I have faced during the last 12 months is time constraints to meet deadlines. At a managerial level, I am assigned with a lot of responsibilities and the expectation of the superiors from me is also high. Since I have a family to look after it is even more difficult to attend to my work responsibilities. Many a time it leads to an injustice on my part towards either the home responsibilities or work responsibilities.

   My problem has affected me positively and negatively. In a negative manner it brought about a lot of work pressure as I was falling short of time and I could not spend appropriate time on the assignments given to me by my superiors. Secondly, I found it difficult to maintain a balance between my home and work responsibilities also. But in a positive manner because of my constant efforts as well as correct planning I have become "immune to stress".

I overcame the problem by planning and prioritizing the tasks based on urgency, discussion with my colleagues and collectively resolving issues leading to lesser burden of work. Since, I cannot take long holidays, I take short breaks of 20 minutes from my work and listen to soothing music. I also watch plays in the theatre with my family to keep me in good spirits.

2. **Relocation Trauma:** During the recent times I faced the problem of relocation and shifting of archives because of the merger. Since we relocated from our old office to the current one, we had to physically shift more than 100 cartons of important documents and arrange it in the new location. Since there was very little time and less help I had to manually fill the boxes and arrange them in the new location.

   Manually shifting archives affected me personally and professionally. Personally, it caused physical discomfort and muscle pull due to manual shifting of archives. Professionally it affected because being a qualified professional I did not find it a pleasing task to do the work of shifting files and cartons by myself.

   I overcame the first problem of shifting by doing what was required i.e., shifted all the cartons manually with colleagues help and took proper medications for the muscle pull.

3. **Time Constraints to Meet Deadlines:** The greatest problem I have faced is the time constraint to cope up with multiple activities. Since I am a family woman I have to manage both the home as well as office. My responsibilities in office are also tremendous and I have to do multitasking but the time is so little that I sometime have difficulty in completing my assignments on time.

   The problem of coping with multiple activities in a limited time has affected me personally because I have to complete many assignments together I have to stay late in office which amounts to a lot of physical strain as well as neglect in my home responsibilities. I also tend to miss important events in my personal life. It affected me professionally as I find it difficult to finish projects on the given deadline because of the limited time available to me thus causing stress. It also leads to crashed expectation from my superiors as they expect a lot out of me. Therefore, I am constantly under pressure to prove myself in front of them.

I have managed to overcome my problem by prioritizing my work based on urgency of the tasks. I plan and organize my time so that multiple activities can lead to their goals. Sometimes I take a day or two off after hectic work schedules and go to resorts. When I return from there I feel recharged and like a new person altogether.

4. **Glass Ceiling/Competition:** The greatest problem was related to my upgradation. Despite performing well, year after year, I was not promoted to the higher cadre. I neglected a lot of areas of my life in the bid to get promoted but unfortunately I was never noticed when it came to promotion. Despite achieving all the goals on time, I saw that a higher number of males had risen to good posts and were the preferred candidates for promotion, resulting in humiliation.

   The problem affected me very badly personally. I started neglecting my personal life in the bargain to do well so that at least in the next appraisal I could get promoted. Similarly, I endured a lot of mental trauma and physical strain as I used to work till long hours in office and remain tensed about my promotion. Communication with my family decreased. My self-esteem took a huge blow as I started doubting myself. Professionally I did not let if affect my work; in fact I started working more so that I could do my best.

   I have not completely got over the problem as I am still struggling to understand why there was a bias towards the males and why hardworking deserving women like me were left out. But off late I have stopped thinking about it anymore, as it does not lead me anywhere. I constantly take support or spend time with my friends by going out for movies or dinner. I am doing my best but do not harbour the hopes of promotion any more. Volunteering or buying things for my nieces and nephews also helps me divert my attention from core problems.

5. **Job Insecurity/Uncertainty:** During the recent times I have faced the problem of insecurity and uncertainty in my job. This is due to the recent merger that took place between the two pharmaceutical companies. The merger changed the whole structure of our organization.

Many posts were declared unnecessary leading to ouster of many employees from the organization. I was constantly living under the fear of being asked to leave from the organization. With many new colleagues joining in there was uncertainty in what I was supposed to do and whether I was required by the organization or not.

Personally I felt lost. I felt stressed as I was constantly thinking about my work. For a short while I began to avoid pleasurable events. Professionally, I was very unclear as to where my job was leading me. For a while I was also contemplating to leave my current job and look for a new one. I was confused, as my role in the organization was not defined.

I have tried to overcome my problem with the support of my colleagues at work and seniors. Secondly, I started spending more time with my child and being with her itself was extremely de-stressing as for some time I would forget about my own problems. It has been nine months since the merger so I am now getting acquainted with the new structure and begun to understand my job responsibilities better. There have been constant talks with the Management and I have been assured that my job is secure hence I have stopped worrying about that aspect also.

6. **Clash with Superior:** The problem I suffered recently is altercation with my boss. He was not particularly happy with the way one of our core team members was performing. But instead of reprimanding him, my boss started to blame all the core team members. Since I am the project leader of the team I had a few altercations with my boss. I was aware of the performance deficiency of my teammate and the remaining team was compensating for that person. Instead of appreciating the good contacts and trust we were building with the customers/clients, he was getting upset about it. So in order to overcome this he started to mentally harass a few of us. He started to bad mouth about the team members against each other.

   This affected my social as well as professional life. Since my manager could not find any faults with my work he started criticizing me for my behaviour. This made me lose interest in my work and as a result I was not able to give my 100 per cent to my job. It also increased my stress level and I was not able to concentrate on my social life.

This problem can be solved if my boss handles this situation in a more mature and intelligent manner. Instead of harassing us to gain an upper hand he can make use of the good connections and trust that we have built up to get more business. Secondly, he can speak to our team member about his performance deficiency and guide him to perform better. In this way not only will our organization benefit but also all the team members will feel secure by having a good boss around us. I have not been able to overcome the problem but whenever I feel stressed out I go with my friends for a movie or have a good meal somewhere and then I feel better for sometime.

7. **Honesty is the Best Policy in Case of Fraud:** Due to bogus stamp papers distributed in the workplace and stolen National Savings Certificate issued through authorized vendors, my employees and I faced serious problems. We were accused of creating a fraud in the organization. The customers of my bank could not repay the amount within the stipulated period of time.

   Though there was no mistake on our part we as employees underwent serious problems. We were taken to court where enquiries were made. Professionally, it affected me because as a Manager I was under pressure to save the reputation of my organization. Secondly, it was my duty to support my subordinates and participate honestly in the enquiries made by legal authorities. Personally, I was under tremendous pressure and stress. I suffered from a mild heart attack because of the pressure I underwent. My family also underwent massive worries.

   If people were honest and did not commit such a crime then we would not have undergone such stress. Being an honest person, I participated in all the enquiries made on the organization and me, as I had nothing to fear. I fully supported my subordinates and stood by them. I was constantly in discussion with the top management regarding this scam. We won the court case and the culprits were arrested. Thus, we all stuck together like one family at the time of crisis. During stressful times I would either read books so that I could divert my attention from problematic issues or involve myself in making painting and handicrafts to get away from the problems.

8. **Uncooperative Subordinates:** The greatest problem I faced in the past 12 months was uncooperative attitude of my workers due to the

interference by the internal union. Some of my workers were a part of the internal union. For silly reasons they used to be instigated by their core members to suspend work at the drop of a hat.

The above problem affected me personally and professionally. Personally, because I used to be under constant stress because I was unable to understand why the workers were behaving so erratically and why they were not working. Professionally, it affected me because our daily production was affected as they were suspending work. Secondly, my superiors were under the impression that I was unable to handle the workers under my department.

I called the workers under my department in groups of fiveand advised them about the losses incurred because of suspending the work for some silly reason. I asked them the reason for suspending work and 50 per cent said that they did not know the reason and they were doing it because their fellow workers were doing it, 40 per cent said that they were doing it because their union head had asked them to do so. Whereas the remaining 10 per cent were among the one who were lazy and liked to drop work at the slightest reason. I looked into the matter with the help of our top management and as far as my workers were concerned I brought in an Industrial/Occupational Counsellor who gave them appropriate counselling regarding the disadvantages of being instigated by others to suspend work and generally made them aware of their contribution towards their organization so that they could work sincerely in the future. As far as my personal coping was concerned spending time with my baby was itself quite a stress buster and secondly since I am religious by nature, I would say my prayers and keep full faith in God.

9. **Loss of Communication:** The greatest problem I faced was loss of communication with colleagues in my prior organization. The merger brought about a whole lot of changes. One of them being—shifting the heads of all departments to the Head Office. This relocation led to loss of communication with my colleagues because a lot many of them were not at higher posts so they remained in the old office.

Loss of communication affected me personally by the way of setting in monotony and boredom. I was not in touch with many of my colleagues due to the merger so I was not aware of what was happening with them. In a way my social support system has broken down because with my job I rarely got the time to give them a call or keep in touch with them. In a professional way, less communication means I was not clearly aware of what was happening in different business areas because of the merger. Since I was new in the current organization and not well acquainted with my new colleagues there was ambiguity on the professional front.

I have not been able to overcome the second problem because I have completely lost touch with my old colleagues due to my hectic routine. I feel as if I have lost a backbone, as now I have no one to share my problems with. In the current organization there is still loss of communication as I am new here and not well acquainted with my new colleagues. So there is still ambiguity with respect to my job role also. In order to get away with tension I spend some time on my own "me time" so that I feel much better and relaxed.

10. **Shift Work Problem:** The greatest problem I face is working night shifts. Since I am in a call centre, night shifts are inevitable.

Working night shifts affected me personally and professionally. Personally, it becomes very difficult to manage my home and work together because at home I have to attend to my two-year-old baby and responsibilities in office are equally pressurizing. I felt guilty since I do not get time to spend with my family. Night shifts disrupt the whole schedule due to which I encountered a lot of health problems such as fatigue, headaches and a lot of stress. There is often a spillover of tensions from home to work and work to home. Professionally, my health problems decreased my productivity at work. As I was unable to handle my team, my appraisal rating from my superiors took a blow.

I have been able to overcome the problem with the support of my family. When I am not around my husband takes care of our baby. Secondly, I spend some of my time with my friends who are not from call centres, which take some load off. I am a member of an NGO named Aakansha and there is no other bigger pleasure than buying gifts for the needy children and seeing a smile on their faces. I plan and organize my schedule during night shifts so that I can spend adequate time with my child too.

The above responses revealed that majority of the women managers faced the problem of meeting deadlines due to time constraints. Many women managers combine their full time paid work with parenthood or household responsibilities. They tend to remain the primary caretakers on the home turf in spite of being assigned with a job which requires long hours of physically and mentally demanding work. Other main problems included getting work done from subordinates, relocation problems as well as feelings of job insecurity and uncertainity. It was also found that women managers find internal politics between their colleagues/subordinates as well as altercations, lack of communication with colleagues/friends and clashes with their superiors extremely stressful. The "glass ceiling effect" was also reported by one woman manager who said, "She felt that there was a bias against women who wanted to move up the ladder." Lastly, night shifts too posed a major hindrance for a woman manager who reported "Nights shifts are inevitable in call centres, but I feel guilty for not spending time with my family". According to a woman manager "The glass-ceiling effect and not being able to handle ones subordinate are problems that are very gender specific. In many organizations, in spite of working so hard, many women still face discrimination".

Women managers reported that their problems affected them personally as well as professionally.

Women managers who faced the problems of meeting deadlines due to time constraints, working night shifts and insecurity and uncertainty regarding ones job reported that personally overwork was causing a strain on their families and relationships as it robbed them of time, energy and attention needed to maintain healthy relationships with partners and children. They also reported missing out on important social events such as weddings or outings with families. According to one female manager "I have to complete many assignments together so I have to stay late in office which amounts neglect in my home responsibilities". Feelings of insecurity and uncertainty regarding ones job created a lot of anxiousness and stress in women managers because they were constantly bombarded with thoughts about their future in the organization. They also remained tensed, as they were unclear regarding their job function in the organization. Many of these women also reported a spillover of tensions about ones work to home and from home to work. This spillover resulted in conflicts between them and their spouses. Their problems are further compounded because they also tended to suffer from health problems due to long working hours or disruptions in shift hours. They complained of headaches, back pain, fatigue, weakness and other physical ailments. Their problems also brought along professional hazards for them in the form of dissatisfaction of superiors regarding their quality of work and low productivity in their performance in the organization.

Women managers who were concerned of interpersonal conflicts at work felt demotivated and stressed out seeing the conflicts between their colleagues. According to a woman manager "it's a challenge to remain neutral and listen to both sides of the story". As far as clashes with bosses were concerned managers felt demotivated to work especially when the clash was a result of misunderstandings or feelings of insecurity harboured by the superiors. A woman manager reported "Constant clash with my boss made me lose interest in my work and as a result I was not able to give my 100 per cent to my job". Uncooperative subordinates posed a problem for women managers because the attitude of the subordinates gave an impression to their superiors that the manager was unable to handle the subordinates. This problem also affected the productivity of the organization as the subordinates used to suspend work. Women managers reported a lot of confusion as they were unable to understand the real reason behind their subordinates' erratic behaviours. They also reported being under constant work pressure as they felt a need to prove themselves in front of their superiors.

Women managers who faced the problem of discrimination in the workplace reported "feeling humiliated" and left out because of unfair appraisals. Decrease in their self-esteem was another apparent effect due to the discrimination in the workplace. They also reported of neglecting their family life in a bid to do well, resulting in less communication with their family. Stress, feelings of anxiousness and work pressure were their chief problems.

Complaints of monotony, boredom and lack of social support were stated by women managers who reported the problem of communication. They also complained of feelings of ambiguity as they were unaware of the ongoings in different business areas due to restrictive communication. Health problems such as muscle pulls were the chief complaints of women managers who suffered from the problem of relocating from one office to another.

So far we saw the negative effects of problems faced by the women manager. But the results of this survey also revealed a welcome change. According to a few women managers, the stress, tension and anxiety caused to them because of work pressure and deadlines had made them "immune to stress" as a result of which they reported handling work pressure much better than before. This effect is called as eustress as it connotes a positive change in the behaviours with respect to handling of stressful situations.

Thus, it can be seen that the problems faced by women managers affected them personally and professionally and the effects of the problems they faced were positive as well as negative.

As far as coping with problems among women managers is concerned, it was seen that only a few managers were not able to overcome their problems. But overall, the responses towards coping with problems were positive.

Different individuals have different styles of coping with their problems. It was seen that many women managers worked actively towards eliminating their problems by meditating, going on holidays, taking short breaks and having appropriate medications. Other common coping strategies reported by women managers included, discussing problems with colleagues and seeking advise from superiors, spending time with friends, by going for movies and holidays, and planning and organizing ones schedule.

Many women managers were spiritually inclined as a result of which they participated in different kinds of religious activities to relax their minds such as singing bhajans, visiting temples or saying prayers. According to a woman manager "whenever I face a problem I send a small prayer up there so that things go well with me". Other interesting ways of coping with problems included pampering oneself by going for shopping or having a good meal. Many women managers joined NGOs where they generously donated gifts. One such manager exclaimed "There is no other pleasure than seeing a smile on children's face. It's very destressing". Many of them indulged in giving gifts to relatives and friends in order to feel better. But the unanimous votes went in the favour of spending time with one's family especially one's children. According to one manager, "It's extremely destressing to spend time with my child because for sometime I forget that I have a problem". Other indulged in activities like painting or watching plays in a theatre to keep their minds off work pressure.

Conclusion

When we observe International Women's Day on 8th March every year, we need to ponder over the gender issues in organizations. Male attitude is an issue to be addressed, attitudinal barriers from men trouble women. Though male dominance in organizations is changing a bit, still an issue remains to be addressed. Some suggestions can be considered to deal with these problems:

1. Successful women or women at higher positions should act as mentors to other women and make women-friendly organizations.
2. Women leadership training need to be emphasized so that they can tackle their issues more effectively.
3. The perspectives of international women's day need to go beyond gender and look at relationship building.
4. Include men in women's seminars and other programmes.
5. Gender sensitivity programmes at schools and organizations must be conducted on regular basis as a part of Human Resource Development.
6. Organizations need to develop women development cell for soft skills training and personality development programmes.
7. It is sexual harassment for some women and romance at work for others especially young people. These different sets of responses of women to the opposite gender need to be understood and addressed accordingly.
8. Essentially organizations have to take up work-family balance mechanisms such as pick-up facility, ATM machines, flextime, compressed week etc.
9. Women must come united, raise their voices on issues that haunt them, do not leave any single case of harassment unattended.
10. Introduce Employee Assistance Programme and counselling in organizations.
11. Psychosomatic ill-health of women working on computers is an issue to tackle. Yoga and health check-ups are necessary.
12. International women's day should be called as International Gender Day.

Though men and women are socialized differently, women are more rigorously trained for family and social roles; whereas men remain weak in these roles or opposite gender related responsibilities. Do men need to be re-socialized at the organizations for becoming gender-friendly or gender-just people? MNCs today are becoming inclusive organizations and open to people's issues (both male and female employees as equal partners).

A few common solutions are suggested to make a woman's life easier in organizations such as compressed working week, crèches at the workplace, employee counselling at workplaces, flexitime, compulsory periodical medical examinations, providing the facility of working from home, yoga for improved physical and mental health (Kaila, 2004; 2004a; 2005).

Notes

1. The present paper is extracted from a large study undertaken by the author at the SNDT Women's University, Mumbai.
2. The author of this article has worked on 15 women research projects involving 5000 women in Mumbai at the SNDT Women's University.

Further Reading

Armstrong-Stassen, Marjorie. "Coping with Downsizing: A Comparison of Executive-Level and Middle Managers." *International Journal of Stress Management* 12, No. 2 (2005): 117–41.

Coleman, D. and Iso-Ahola, S.E. "Leisure and Health: The Role of Social Support and Self-Determination." *Journal of Leisure Research* 25 (1993): 111–28.

Davidson, M.J. and Cooper, C.L. "Female Managers in Britain: A Comparative Review." *Human Resource Management* 26 (1987): 217–42.

Duncan, M. and Messner, M. "The Media Image of Sport and Gender." *Media Sport* 1, No. 1 (1998): 21–35.

Dworkin, S.L. and Wachs, F.L. *The Morality/Manhood Paradox: Masculinity, Sport, and the Media.* London: Kogan Page, 2000.

Hunsaker, Philip L. and Michael W. Coombs. "Mergers and Acquisitions: Managing the Emotional Issues." Personnel 6, No. 1 (1988): 56–63.

Kaila, H.L. "Stress is a Way of Life for Mumbai Workers." *Psychology International* 13, No. 3 (Fall 2002).

——. "Indian Women Managers: Their Stresses, Health and Coping Behaviour—A Survey in Mumbai." *Journal of Health Management* 6, No. 2 (2004): 147–61.

——. *Women of Mumbai towards New Millennium.* Mumbai: Himalaya Publishing House, 2004a.

——. *Women, Work and Family.* Jaipur: Rawat Publications, 2005.

Kasper, K., Meyer, M. and Schmidt, A. "Managers Dealing with Work-Family-Conflict: An Explorative Analysis." *Journal of Managerial Psychology* 20, No. 5 (2005): 440–61.

Kirkcaldy, B.D. and Furnham, A.F. "Stress Coping Styles among German Managers." *Journal of Workplace Learning* 11, No. 1 (1999): 22–26.

Oakeley, A. *The Sociology of Housework.* New York: Pantheon, 1974.

Oi-ling, S., Luo, L. and Cary, C. "Managerial Stress in Taiwan: A Comparative Study." *Journal of Managerial Psychology* 14, No. 1 (1999): 6–25.

Taap, A.M., Fontaine, R. and Chong Siong Choy. "Occupational Stress among Managers: A Malaysian Survey." *Journal of Managerial Psychology* 18, No. 6 (2003): 622–28.

6

The Employers' Role as Perceived by Mothers Working in Night Shifts

Jayanti Gokhale

Working in night shift is not a new phenomenon. Its history can be traced back to the early nomadic tribes, who required camp guards and shepherds to be awake and vigilant during normal sleeping hours. Later as civilization progressed, communication and transportation needs became more important, resulting in nightly mail deliveries, navigation and overland transportation. Security and law enforcement professions, bakeries and hospitals, required round-the-clock coverage for growing societies (Ede, 1983).

The organizations and or companies that now work shifts are law enforcement, hospitals, emergency services, food industry, computer industry, railroads, trucks, airlines, newspaper, printing and steel, petroleum and paper, military, auto plants, city state and federal government offices, fire protection, banks and more (White and Keith, 1990).

The kinds of organizations that need to work round-the-clock, meaning even at night, are the service organizations. And increasingly women dominate this sector, thus working at non-standard or atypical hours.

In India, out of the total working population in urban areas, less than 10 per cent are employed in the organized sector and only about 15 per cent are in the regular salaried employment. Out of the total employed in the organized sector, about 55 per cent are in the service sector and less than 30 per cent in the manufacturing sector (CMIE, 1996). Increasing number of women joining the IT-BPO industry is a pertinent feature as these women have night shifts. Today, the IT-industry has 28 per cent women in its workforce compared to 24 per cent in 2005–2006 (NASSCOM, 2008).

The data, in the nursing profession as per government statistics (Registrar General, 1998), shows women as nurses constituting as 89 per cent (2,44,000) compared to 11 per cent (30,600) men in the same occupation. Also, 84 per cent (1,13,100) are women as "ayahs", nurses and maids, with men only 16 per cent (21,000). Men as health visitors are 40 per cent (24,200) whereas women again dominate at 60 per cent (35,900). In all, women as health care personnel are thus 3,93,000 and this figure is likely to increase. The occupation of nurses maintains highest number of women (89 per cent) compared to the men (11) per cent.

Similar trends are observed in developed countries. For instance, jobs of nursing aides, orderlies and attendants are among the ten occupations projected to account for the largest number of new jobs between 1992 and 2005 in the United States (Wallace, 1998: 26).

Typically, in Maharashtra, female personnel vary in the age from 21 to over 55 years who predominantly carry out the nursing care. Their duties are performed according to the shift system. The various chores, which constitute patient care and hospital, deal with human, emotional and psychological problems apart from the obvious health or medical problem under treatment. On an average, nursing duties can be more taxing than similar work at a desk in an office or in other business or industrial establishments. The work conditions or duty obligations make the nurse's role very different from other working women not only in the place of work but also in the social and domestic sphere (Rustamfram, 1999: 31). Few efforts are observed in the Indian context on providing a family-friendly workplace by employers especially for women in night shift duties. Menon (1999) argues that transportation of women workers must be provided by employers. Further childcare at night is a serious concern especially with mothers working night shifts (Bhave, 1994). Recent literature suggests an increased effort from employers to help employees meet childcare management at night (Nausbaum, 1995). In many workplaces or communities, the need for non-standard hours childcare is still a "sleeper" issue unknown or ignored till it becomes a crisis. In India childcare challenge in non-standard or atypical hours is yet to gain recognition from employers and or government bodies; the growing mismatch between worker's changing schedules and available childcare services is still a dormant issue.

On the whole, women working in night shifts and the role of employers in providing a family-friendly workplace with a special focus on childcare remain an unexplored area of research. Family-friendly workplace here is implied as meals, accommodation provision, transportation and crèches.

It is a well-established fact that the industrial world is moving towards a day and night work economy. More so, employment during night hours is becoming common in industrial societies.

Review of Literature

With women employed at night hours, literature suggests some investigations on nurses as the shift duty workers (Gadbois, 1991; Alward, 1992; Tasto et al., 1978). In other occupations that demand working hours at night, like telephone operators, receptionists in hotels, ground staff in aviation industry, attempts have been limited in exploring their personal and professional situation.

Some researchers have studied the need for accommodation and transportation (ASSOCHAM, 2008) that makes commuting easier and the workplace favourable, thereby reducing travelling time. Research suggests that though these provisions make work life favourable it is more often denied rather than provided or provided in an unsuitable manner (ibid.). Few researchers (Bhave, 1994; Nausbaum, 1995) have explored childcare at night as a facility for mothers working night shifts. Though, there is a limited and a lack of systematic effort to explore the role of employers vis-à-vis the night shift employees.

House Size and Rest

The inquiry carried out by Calliot (in Carpentier, 1977) ascertained the effect of housing and family size on perceived shift difficulties. Those employees who were living in small houses and had a big family found it very difficult to take rest during day time. The family members also experienced inconvenience because they had to restrict their activities.

A study reported by Brown (1975) concluded that the night workers who slept by day were disrupted by the activities of the family members. The disruption was caused in the activities of family members also. Need to sleep during day time curtail many activities, which may be part of the household. The trend increased with the number of children in the family. Further, the lack of freedom tended to affect adversely the relationship within the family.

Accommodation and Transportation

Accommodation to employees is a concern of working mothers. In a metropolis, housing needs are often difficult to meet. Especially with shift duties, the requirement to have accommodation near the workplace increases considerably. Childcare can then be managed with lesser constraints.

Provisions as accommodation and transportation are also important facilities that help employees to balance their work and family lives. Transportation can help working mothers to meet the childcare challenge. For instance, mothers can consider bringing children to the workplace if a transport service is provided with regards to night shift. Menon (1999) urges that transportation of women workers must be provided by employers to ensure their safety, in night hours.

With the increase in IT-BPO sector where women employees form a significant part of the workforce, it is now putting employee safety as a priority. A survey on workers in nightshifts in several industries (textiles, leather, hospital, BPO) asserts the women working in BPOs only felt safe. And, also safety was ensured for those who worked for big, well-known firms and those who were in skilled jobs. However, a large percentage of women in night shifts feel unsafe (ASSOCHAM, 2008).

Crèches at Workplace

Many women's work analysts (Myers and Indriso, 1987; Government of India, 1988) have argued for provision of a crèche at the workplace to help mothers balance employment and childcare. Also, the need for maintaining quality of crèche is reiterated by many researchers.

The lack of quality childcare not only affects the personal lives of millions of workers each day, but also impact of childcare problems is also felt in the workplace. Employers may notice it in terms of days missed from work tardiness and low employee morale. According to an estimate, in the United States, the cost to business of childcare related to absenteeism was US $3 billion annually. Employees also lose time at work by worrying. They worry about a sick child, taking children to health care appointments, going to school, events, and having to replace a regular caregiver or about where their child is, what he or she may be doing after school. In a recent ILO Conference Preview (1995: 10), labour experts affirm that attention needs to be paid to needs of women workers during pregnancy and nursing period. A mother should have a provision to feed child at workplace (Ntombela, 1995).

Millions of school-age children spend hours before or after school neither in an organized programme nor are supervised by an adult at home. Seppanen et al. (1993) have examined before and after school programmes in depth. Because of their low income, poor families have fewer choices available in before and after school programmes. In many areas the demand for publicly sponsored before and after school programmes outstrip availability (for details, see Sen and Snow, 1994: 46–47, Table 3-1).

Workers at or below poverty line are far more likely than those in the middle and upper class to have work on weekends when traditional day care and after school programmes are available, making childcare harder to obtain (Hoefferth, 1992). Irregular work shifts make even informal, quality childcare difficult to arrange.

In the Indian context, legislation has played a prominent role in making a provision for crèches at workplace (Factories Act, 1948: Section 48; Plantations Labour Act, 1951; Beedi and Cigar Workers (Condition and Employment) Act; Contract Labour (Regulation and Abolition) Central Rules, 1971). Though progressive law has backfired on women resulting in employers not hiring women or hiring one woman worker less to escape the legislation (Rane, 1978).

In organizations that have made provision for crèches at workplace, quality continues to be a dominant and many a times neglected dimension (Khallar, 1991). In a recent study by Associated Chambers of Commerce and Industry of India (2008) reveals that though childcare facilities existed in some organizations that has shift duties, they were far from satisfactory and hence underutilized.

Employers' concern for childcare at night has received scant attention from labour officials, employers or government bodies. Reese (1996) maintains that the number of employees working non-standard hours is increasing but the availability of night time care is not catching up. According to the Women's Bureau of the U.S. Labour Department, over 14 million Americans worked non-traditional hours in 1991 and in 1990 approximately 7.2 million women with 11.7 million children under age of 15 worked full or part time jobs with non-standard hours. However, Women's Bureau estimates that there are only about a dozen 24-hour crèche care centres offered by private employers, employer consortiums and employer community partnerships. According to Marguerite Sallee, president and CEO of Corporate Family Solutions, for many companies, low utilization at night makes 24-hour care unfeasible from a business standpoint. She adds that it may take strong incentives, such as tax breaks, to encourage companies to gear up for the increasing number of shift workers requiring night time childcare.

Although in times of emergency, the workplace has responded speedily in meeting childcare needs of nurses. Baverman and Chowers (1992) revealed that childcare was a prominent factor in determining response to emergency call-up because civilians were likely to be targeted. The hospital's administration immediately responded by providing hospital based childcare for two days before the 'first scud missile' fell.

Recent literature suggests some effort from employers to help employees meet childcare management at night (Nausbaum, 1995). In many workplaces or communities, the need for non-standard hours childcare is still a "sleeper" issue unknown or ignored till it becomes a crisis.

Scope and Objectives

The above observations repeatedly put forth the fact that the workplace as a family friendly environment is necessary in contemporary society especially when working hours are at night and the employees are women, mainly mothers working nightshifts. For the workplace to become a family friendly environment the role of employers is crucial in making provisions for the same.

Till date, literature on the role of employers and the workplace as a family friendly environment lacks a systematic analysis. This is more so in the case of women who work night shifts, in particular in the Indian context. There is a paucity of data on issues like provisions at the workplace like meals, transportation, accommodation and creches at night.

The present paper thus attempts to explore the role of employers in providing a family-friendly workplace with a special focus on childcare facilities at night.

To make modest contribution towards filling such gaps in the area of research, the present study focuses on the following:

Objectives of the Study

1. To examine the childcare management by night shift women workers as mothers.
2. To explore the role of family and community in early childcare management of night shift working mothers.
3. To explore the role of employers in early childcare of night shift working mothers.
4. To understand the implications for policy on childcare for night shift working mothers.

Methodology

The present study is exploratory in nature to the extent that it deals with the hitherto unexplored phenomenon of working mothers perception of the role of the employers in providing a family friendly environment at the workplace like meals, accommodation, transportation, crèches, etc. in the Indian context.

Survey design has mainly been used as a method of investigation and is supported by secondary data along with the expert view of other actors like employers, caretakers and supervisors of the respondents—staff nurses.

There are 17 Municipal hospitals in Mumbai employing about 3,000 staff nurses. For the present study I considered seven main Municipal hospitals that maintained homogeneity in the working conditions of nurses employed by them. The significance of staff nurses in such hospitals, as a large workforce, was another criteria while selecting the sample. Of the 3,000 staff nurses, 20 per cent, that is, 600 staff nurses were initially considered as the sample from among the seven hospitals. However, this representation sample of 600 nurses could not meet the criteria of having one child at least less than six years of age and working nightshifts as part of their regular work schedule. Moreover, the sample size of 600 was found to be very difficult to operationalize given the geographical location of the hospitals in the city. Accordingly, out of the 600 staff nurses, the sample was limited to 250.

The main sample was supported by a sub-sample (50) of caretakers who looked after the children of respondents of staff nurses. Further more, 11 personnel administrative staff heads, like matrons, assistant matrons and sisters-in-charge were also included in the formal interviews, in order to collect their views on related issues. The data was collected from April–September 1999.

Findings

The role of the employers is examined with a special focus on provision of childcare at night.

At the onset, the respondent's perception on provisions by the employer for housing, meals, accommodation and transportation concerns are discussed.

Congested Living Conditions

Rest after a night shift though necessary was difficult for respondents. House size was a serious constraint for several staff nurses. Similarly in an enquiry carried out by Calliot (in Carpentire, 1977) revealed the effect of housing and family size on perceived shift difficulties.

The data in Table 1 suggests that 41.6 per cent of the respondents live in congested houses with less than 300 sq. ft. area. Another 42.4 per cent of them live in a house size between 300 to 500 sq. ft. The remaining 16 per cent of the nurses live in relatively larger area (more than 500 sq. ft.) houses.

Table 1 *House Size and Number of Family Members*

House Size	*Number of Family Members*			*Total*
	< 4	*4–8*	*> 8*	
< 300 sq. ft.	77	27	–	104 (41.6)
300–500 sq. ft.	73	25	8	106 (42.4)
500–700 sq. ft.	14	15	4	33 (13.2)
> 700 sq. ft.	4	2	1	7 (2.8)
Total	168 (67.2)	69 (27.6)	13 (5.2)	250 (100)

Figures in brackets indicate percentages.
Chi-square = 21.627, df = 12, p value = 0.042, significant

The data further suggests that over one-fourth of the respondents live in less than a house size of 300 sq. ft., with 4 to 8 family member, and 25 respondents in the subsequent house size interval range of 300–500 sq. ft. with the same number of family members. Eight respondents live in the same house size interval range but with more than eight family members. This association is confirmed by the significant chi square value.

The discussion here mainly addresses those sixty respondents (24 per cent), who have four or more members in the family but live in congested houses.

For the remaining respondents, the living conditions are not crammed, although area of house size may be less, but then so are the number of family members.

When it comes to the sleep during daytime for women, there are social and structural aspects that need attention. One is the routine tasks and activities of other family members for which she (the respondent) is responsible. The other is, with elderly or other male members in the house (such as father-in-law or brother-in-law), it is difficult for a woman to sleep in the house during the day, particularly when space is the constraint. The pressing need of sleep can be met only after completing routine tasks and when other elderly members of the house are asleep, i.e., after the noon meal. "I live in a joint family. The family members rest only in the afternoon. My father-in-law is retired. It is not possible to catch a few hours of sleep at any time as there is little space in the house and I cannot sleep anywhere", stated one respondent. Unlike men, women get few hours of sleep to recoup from the previous night, as domestic work predominates.

Another point to be noted is that if the subsequent day (after the night shift) is a holiday (as Sunday or any other public holiday), then children, spouse and/or other family members are in the house and thus getting rest and sleep is more difficult.

One respondent complained, "If the next day after night duty is a Sunday, then the work is even more. My children and husband are at home. When I try to catch a few hours of sleep, there is constant noise of children shouting and fighting. Neither is my husband considerate. He does not pay attention to the children nor he does housework".

Similarly, for male workers, as reported by Brown (1975), the night worker's sleep by day is disrupted by the activities of family members also. His need to sleep during day time curtail many activities which may be part of the household. This trend increases with number of children in the family. Further, the lack of freedom tends to adversely affect the relationships within the family.

As the night shift is burdensome compared to other shift duties, for all, there is no exemption from the night shift. A nurse can choose to do morning or evening shift, but it is compulsory to do the night shift.

Table 2 *Respondents' Perception of Need for Accommodation from Employers*

Need for Accommodation	*Frequency*	*Percentage*
Yes	235	94
No	15	6
Total	250	100

Table 2 suggests that almost all the respondents felt that residential accommodation would be a very useful provision if such a facility is extended by the hospitals.

Of the total sample of 250 nurses, only a very few (6 per cent) were staying in the government staff quarters provided by the Brihanmumbai Municipal Corporation (BMC).

The staff quarters and workplace were not necessarily within the hospital premises or geographically proximate but spread across the city.

The type of accommodation varied from the family type to a single or unmarried quarters type.

Nurses living in government quarters have felt that it did not necessarily meet their family needs. For example, a staff nurse staying in a single room accommodation, as she did not get a family type, stated: "My husband and son live in Kerala; my mother-in-law looks after my son. My husband prefers to stay in Kerala, as in metropolis there is no proper place to stay. I feel extremely disturbed with this living arrangement. I often take leave and visit them".

Respondents further expressed concern that getting a government accommodation from the workplace was not easy and a cumbersome procedure:

> "Accommodation is not made available on need. It is on seniority. So, the queue is very long. I have had to wait for eight years till I was able to get a staff quarters. My children are now 6 and 8 years old. The need is more in earlier years when the childcare and domestic responsibilities dominate", remarked a nurse.

A nurse, living as a single parent due to her spouse staying overseas for job, recalled: "I have two daughters. I cannot leave them alone. I have to leave them with the caretaker for the night. They go to school from there the next day and return home after school is over. I live 1½ hours away from my workplace. I want to move close to the hospital but the costs of houses are prohibitive. If I had a government quarters, it would have reduced my worry of childcare at night. My mother and sister-in-law were here but had to leave for domestic and health reasons".

Employees also mentioned that administrative heads have been considerate in several cases to meet their housing needs.

To illustrate, a nurse, who is also a single parent, stated: "I have separated from my husband. I requested the in-charge to consider my case. Today, I live in the staff quarters of the hospital that is within the premises. My four-year-old daughter sleeps at night with my neighbour during the night shift. My problems of safety and childcare are solved. I am grateful to the authorities for considering my case favourably.

Since the waiting to get housing facilities is long, nurses take a housing loan and try to purchase a house.[1]

It may be further added that the municipal authorities have been sensitive to employees housing needs in various situations. "I lived under a leave and license arrangement. During the Mumbai riots, I lost all my belongings", revealed a Muslim nurse. There was a lot of communal tension and destruction of property. I appealed to the matron. She considered my case favourably. I now live in the government quarters".

Accommodation available from the Brihanmumbai Municipal Corporation is not necessarily in liveable conditions. Houses needed repairs. This in fact has been one of the reasons for some of the respondents not being keen for the official residences.

One respondent informed: "I got accommodation for a different reason". "A staff quarters was available but nobody was ready to occupy it as it had a leaking roof. I accepted it and moved in with my family. I spent a considerable amount on repairing it".

According to the present study, 69.2 per cent respondents had taken a loan for buying a house from the BMC; in comparison only 10 per cent of the spouses had taken a loan from their organizations. Other spouses did not have a house loan facility as their jobs were contractual rather than permanent.

The data when further analysed shows that a large majority (69.2 per cent) of the respondents lived in ownership, 22.4 per cent in rental houses and 7.6 per cent in the government staff quarters.

Due to the housing loan, nurses were bound to continue their service with the BMC for the next 8 to 10 years or so. Other sources of loan were the private loans from banks or other state agencies, like the co-operatives.

Among those respondents staying on a rental basis, over a half had the illegal arrangement of 'leave and license'. It means that the nurse and her family can stay there for a period of 11 months only. One has to shift thereafter. A deposit of Rs. 20,000 or so is also to be paid which is refundable. "I have shifted three times in the past 3 years. It feels like a refugee with no permanent place to go. One has to vacate the house after every 11 months. Everything gets disrupted," stated a helpless respondent.

Frequent changing of place causes disruption in the family routine, access to childcare, schooling, and or workplace. It means reorganizing a whole series of tasks or making arrangements for routine tasks as picking and dropping children to school or crèche, maid help, etc.

As stated by a nurse, "I have recently shifted to a house under new leave and license arrangement. Now my baby-sitter is far off. I have to travel for 40 mts., leave my child there and then come for work. Night and evening shifts are most inconvenient. When I return from evening shift its almost 10.00 p.m. The baby-sitter is reluctant to keep the child for so long. At night shift, I leave the child at baby sitters' place at 8.00 p.m. or so. My husband picks her up at 11.00 p.m. This cannot continue for long".

A very few of the respondents (6 per cent) (Table 2) did not feel the need for an accommodation from employers because they did not want to stay with the working colleagues as neighbours. In addition, they had ownership houses that they were satisfied with.

Transportation

Table 3 *Respondents' Perception of Need for Transport Service Provided by Employers*

Need for a Transport System	*Frequency*	*Percentage*
Yes	239	95.6
No	11	4.4
Total	250	100

Table 3 suggests that almost all (95.6 per cent) of the employees (respondents) emphasized the need for a transport service from the organization.

At the time of present study, nurses used local trains (67.2 per cent), bus (43.6 per cent) and autos (13.6 per cent) to reach the workplace. Respondents reached local stations or bus stops and waited at least 10 to 15 minutes for the transport for reaching their destination; another 15 minutes at least were required to reach the hospital by foot. The time required was even more when children had to be dropped at a crèche and then the respondent would come to the workplace. Staff nurses had train or bus pass that made travel costs cheaper. Travelling by auto was considered expensive.

Employees receive a conveyance allowance of Rs. 85 per month. It meagrely helped in meeting the travel costs. A transport service would be a better option for respondents to reach the workplace as against the local transport.

A lot of time is spent on waiting for transport and far reaching the bus stop or station. The bus and trains were very crowded that made travel difficult.

Nurses travelling by autos felt that it was expensive to do so, on a regular basis though a lot of time was saved.

One respondent who used the auto to travel narrated her experience as: "I travel by auto as I have a leg problem. I cannot travel in crowded trains. It is impossible for me to get in and out. Autorickshaws are very expensive. I also have to leave my daughter at the crèche before I come for work. A transport service will be of immense help".

Table 4 *Respondent's Perception of Transport Service from the Workplace and Travel Time from Workplace to Home*

Need for Transport Service from the Workplace	*Travel Time from Workplace to Home*			*Total*
	< 1 hour	*1–2 hours*	*> 2 hours*	
Yes	130	105	4	239 (95.6)
No	11	—	—	11 (4.4)
Total	141 (56.4)	105 (42.0)	4 (1.6)	250 (100)

* Figures in brackets indicate percentage.

Table 4 suggests that 56 per cent of the respondents reached the workplace in 1 hour time, 42 per cent took about 2 hours and a very few travelled for over 2 hours to reach the hospital. Nurses who were keen that a transport service from the organization should be provided required at least an hour or more to travel to the hospital.

"A transport service will be very useful. It will save a lot of our time and energy. At present, I leave at 7.00 p.m. for night shift duty. Drop my children at the other side of the station to their caretaker by auto, then catch the local train to the hospital that takes an hour and quarter" explained one nurse. While nurses felt the need for a transport service, they also admitted the fact that getting a door-to-door service would be difficult.

"It is not possible to be picked up from the doorstep, since we live in different directions. But something like a common destination/route can be worked out. A convenient time for each shift can be decided. Employees can be dropped and picked up from one point that is suitable for many nurses. It will save a lot of time of walking from the railway station and or bus stop to hospitals", suggested a nurse.

Another respondent stated, "One is totally dependent on the local transport system. At times when the trains are late there is no consideration from the hospital authorities. We are marked absent for no fault of ours. If a transport service is provided, we would not have to depend on local transport".

A crèche at the workplace is another service that is desired by a large majority (70.4 per cent) of the respondents (see Table 6).

When a transport service is provided, it can further assist women to travel with children to the workplace. "The trains are crowded; with a transport service I can think of bringing my child to the hospital", stated a nurse.

Another concern expressed by nurses was the timings of the evening shift. The evening shift extended to 9.00 p.m. It gets late by the time nurses reach home after travelling for over an hour and a half, thus causing a threat to personal safety. As stated by one of the respondents: "I finish my evening shift at 9.00 p.m. By the time I reach home it is 11.15 p.m. It does not feel very safe to travel that late at night. Also, my maid and children are alone at home. My husband expired 4 years ago. If there is a transport service it will be very useful. At least my safety can be ensured".

Some nurses mentioned that they had applied to the head office for a transfer to a hospital located near their residence, but were denied. As a result, employees spend a couple of hours travelling to and fro from the workplace, compounded with other constraints of childcare, personal safety, etc.

In contrast, a few of the respondents (Table 4) stated that a transport service from the workplace would not be of use. For these respondents, the data further suggests that they reached the hospital within half an hour or so.

Meals

Table 5 *Respondents Perception of Provision of Meals in Shift Duty Hours*

Need for Meals	*Frequency*	*Percentage*
Yes	222	88.8
No	28	11.2
Total	250	100

Table 5 suggests that an overwhelming (88.8 per cent) of the respondents emphasized the need for provision of meals in shift duty hours.

A respondent stated, "I leave my house at 7.00 p.m. to reach here at 9.00 p.m. By 11.00 p.m. I feel hungry. But the canteen is closed by then. I usually have tea and bread or biscuits. I can have a meal if there is a canteen facility available at that hour. The present one closes by 10.00 p.m. Also the quality of meals needs to be improved".

Thus, the nurses asserted the need for a canteen especially on morning and evening shift. The morning shift begins at 7.00 a.m.; so, respondents have to leave their house by 6.00 a.m. Even if they cooked or bought the previous days dinner as a packed meal, the food would spoil by afternoon, more so in the summer season.

All hospitals have a canteen attached to it. But nurses did not feel comfortable to go and eat there. It was open for doctors, students, interns and other hospital staffs. In their own words:

> "Even if a canteen is there, it is not accessible to nurses. There are doctors and other senior staff there. I order my food through the peon from there."

Even though nurses had some access to get food from the canteen, it was not necessarily utilized by all, as quality was another constraint: "The food is available in the canteen here. But we hardly use it. The costs are subsidized along with the quality. Food is of poor quality. The peon brings us food from an Udipi restaurant across the street".

In the afternoon shift respondents felt that the canteen would help them to have a meal or snack and tea. The availability of a canteen for provision of meals was also expressed with similar constraints as the quality and accessibility.

Those few (11.2 per cent) nurses, who did not feel the need for a meal service, were against it because they never ate from outside and always carried food from home. Even if the meal was available, they felt that they could never be sure of the quality.

It may be argued that a canteen service may have little relevance to the childcare. But the researcher has considered it as a part of her (respondents) workload. When the option of having meals at the workplace exists, nurses can then avail of meals which she otherwise has to prepare and bring from her home.

Need for a Crèche for Childcare at Night

By now, as expected, a large majority (70.4 per cent) of the respondents expressed the need for a crèche service at night. Crèche service during the day is at least available in some form or the other. But at night childcare is almost non-existent.

As mentioned earlier, childcare at night was with the help of neighbours, friends or relatives primarily on personal requests.

Table 6 *Respondents' Perception of Need for a Crèche at Workplace*

Need for a Crèche at Workplace	*Frequency*	*Percentage*
Yes	176	70.4
No	74	29.6
Total	250	100

Interestingly, data in Table 6 indicates that over one-fourth of respondents negated the need for crèche care at night. The reason stated was that only the family members should look after children and that outside family help was not acceptable.

A number of studies in the Third World countries suggest that women overwhelmingly prefer to have their children cared for by a trusted relative or neighbour rather than by an institution (Rivera, 1979; Engle,

1986). This provides one explanation for the underutilization of both types of childcare facilities. It also provides a rationale to some employers for not providing childcare centres. But the issue is not so simple. Preferences may be a reflection of the lack of acceptable alternatives rather than a confirmation of contentment with family caretaker arrangements.

A six-country study of Asia and Latin America (OEF, 1979) illustrates the importance of providing adequate care. Most of the women in that study believed that persons other than the family are not particularly capable or motivated to provide quality childcare. However, it was found that in areas where families are aware of the existence of childcare facilities which offer quality care, they were anxious to have access to such services.

Another related concern was safety of children at night.

"I am not sure if my child will be safe at night. I cannot risk keeping my child in the crèche. I have sent my child to the village with my mother. Child may be distanced but is safe", revealed one respondent.

Not all respondents felt that the crèche at night should be at their workplace. Several issues were raised by staff nurses that were commonly overlooked by employers, in their meagre attempts, if any, to start crèches at the hospital. A few nurse-mothers referred to a crèche at one of the hospitals as an example to illustrate their apprehension:

> "In our hospital the crèche is located near the public bathroom". It's so unhygienic. The stink is unbearable", complained a nurse. "I also feel that it is very close to the wards. Infection can easily spread and children can fall ill. I cannot think of keeping my child there."

> "A crèche was started in our hospital", informed a staff nurse from another hospital: "But children were not treated well. They were beaten often. Caretaker was rough in handling children. The location was not carefully thought of", she added. As the quality was poor, it was underutilized, that was used as a good reason to stop the crèche from functioning.

> "There is a good crèche in one municipal hospital", mentioned another nurse. "The children are looked after well. I have a friend whose child is in that crèche. When children are sick, a

Paediatrician from the same hospital also visits the crèche and attends to the patient", she stated.

A commonly cited reason for negating a crèche at workplace was the distance travelled from home to hospital. "It's impossible to travel with child in crowded local trains and buses with the child. I feel a crèche near the house will be more accessible" suggested another nurse.

The researcher encountered one crèche in a hospital during the data collection. The crèche was located near the bathroom. There were 13 children in the age range 6 months to 13 years, and one attended by a caretaker. Crèche was open from 7.00 a.m. to 8.00 p.m. The caretaker said, "As schools are closed for summer, staff nurses bring their older school children also". The crèche is used by several personnel like doctors, administrative staff, clerical staff, staff nurse, etc. Some staff, like resident doctors that lived on campus also used the crèche-facility as their spouses were away for some reason", she added. The crèche was managed by a local body, the Rotract Club. Milk for children was provided by the hospital management.

There was no other crèche in any other municipal hospital where interviews with nurses were conducted. During the interviews nurses often made a reference to a crèche in another municipal hospital that had a quality service, like a good caretaker, a systematic routine, medical care by a Paediatrician from the same hospital, etc. though this crèche was not opened at night.

Further investigations revealed that sporadic attempts to start a crèche in four other hospitals in this study were made. The attempts did not materialize due to lack of a proper follow-up; even if they did function for sometime, poor quality was a complaint from respondents, hence underutilized and therefore regarded as unnecessary.

Uniformly poor conditions in crèches provided by a few industrial organizations (during the day) are documented in a study by Swaminathan (1985). The researcher noted that the finances were available, but little thought had been given to their proper utilization. All facilities were missing like organized child development activity (children sit idle and aimlessly all day), appropriate equipment (few or no toys), and appropriate interaction with an adult. Further, reasons cited in this study for under-utilization were the neglect of children, harsh or rude behaviour by attendants, and untrained staff. The poor quality felt by the mothers leads to their underutilization. But few employers relate this underutilization with the quality or nature of their services provided; crèches are seen as unnecessary by many employers precisely because they are underutilized. A vicious circle is thus perpetuated (ibid.).

Table 7 *Respondents' Perception of Location of Crèche at Night*

Location	*Frequency*	*Percentage*
Workplace	109	43.6
Near home	64	25.6
Not applicable	74	29.6
Total	250	100

As regards respondents' perception about the location of a crèche, Table 7 suggests that 43.6 per cent of the respondents maintained the need for a crèche at the workplace (i.e., hospitals).

Nurses with infants felt that they could bring children to hospitals when on night shift. Nursing mothers can breastfeed their children.

For mothers with pre-school children, crèche at workplace was a suitable option than a childcare arrangement. However, quality must be addressed adequately while setting up a crèche, a majority of the nurses felt.

Not all felt that the crèche could be used on a regular basis: "I may not bring my child every night whenever I have a night shift but at least do not have to resort to leave when other arrangements fail" remarked a nurse.

"Crèche at night at the workplace is necessary. Crèche services need not be restricted to night time alone. Crèches should be available according to shift duties of nurses" another respondent opined.

The dual system theory (or socialist feminist) (Walby, 1992) maintains that fundamental changes are required in the institutions for the economy and family if women's equality is to be achieved. Here, the need for a crèche is extensively discussed that emphasized a fundamental change in institution as the workplace (that is part of an economic system).

About one-fourth of the nurses felt that crèches at night need to be near the home rather than at the workplace. One of the most common reasons cited was the distance from the workplace. Mothers felt it extremely inconvenient to carry their children in crowded locals or buses with their water, tiffins and a pair of clothes. As some observed:

> "The trains are so crowded. It is just about possible for me to get into the local train. I cannot bring my child to the workplace. It is most inconvenient. A crèche near the home will be suitable. Distances are prohibitive".

Whether it is care during the day or the night, one of the most important characteristics of a successful childcare programme is felt, by the parents, to be its community basis, both in terms of the location and the participation (OEF, 1979; Schmink, 1982). In the Dominican Republic, the overwhelming majority of women (90 per cent) preferred neighbourhood locations (as opposed to the workplace) for day care centres to avoid transportation problems. Similar preference has been expressed by working women in several other developing countries, like India, Colombia and Brazil (OEF, 1979; Rivera, 1979; Schmink, 1982; Swaminathan, 1985), although these studies have not indicated the type of work in which these mothers are engaged. Here, once again, the interlink between two systems (transport and crèche) is reiterated.

Table 8 *Amount Willing to Pay for a Crèche Facility*

Amount Per Month	*Frequency*	*Percentage*
Rs. 200–Rs. 400	9	3.6
Rs. 400–Rs. 500	15	6.0
> Rs. 500	152	60.8
Not applicable	74	29.6
Total	250	100

Table 8 suggests that a majority (60.8 per cent) of the respondents profess that they are willing to pay more than Rs. 500 per month as charges towards the crèche care at night. All the respondents time and again emphasized the need for quality in such crèches.

"We do not mind paying even Rs. 700 to Rs. 1000 per month but need to be assured that our children are looked after at night; only then can our mind be at peace", stated one of the respondents emphatically.

Flexibility in Working Hours

Data in Table 9 suggests that a large majority (71.6 per cent) of the respondents sought flexibility in working hours of reaching late to hospital.

Nurses mentioned that the rule was of three late marks (half an hour) are allowed in a month. If it exceeds three, they are marked as absent, and a days pay is cut thereafter.

"If the locals are running late there is no consideration", complained a nurse. "We are marked as late on the day. At least, some consideration needs to be shown if the local transport system is disrupted", she concluded.

Table 9 *Respondents' Perception of Flexible Working Hours for Childcare*

Flexible Working Hours	*Frequency*	*Percentage*
Considerations to reach late	179	71.6
Considerations to leave early	184	73.6
Considerations to adjust shift duty	163	65.2
Total*	250	100

* Total is more than 250 due to multiple responses.

About three-fourths of respondents mentioned that, in emergency, leaving the hospital half an hour early than the scheduled shift duty timings helps them balance childcare and employment requirements.

"I have shifted to my mothers' place as my daughter is not well. I requested the sister-in-charge of the ward to relieve me half an hour early. Such considerations are better options than taking leave for the whole day", revealed a respondent.

Three chances to reach late or leave early in a month were felt inadequate by many respondents. Nurses mentioned that in case of emergencies matron should be considerate towards genuine reasons such as child's health, childcare or health of the nurse herself.

A majority of respondents also sought considerations to adjust shift duty in order to enable them to balance employment and the childcare.

It may be noted that respondents did not have an option of doing the night shift. It was compulsory. They could choose only between the morning and the evening shifts. That means, either respondents did all three shifts: morning, evening and night, or only the night shift and either morning or evening shift.

Very few respondents in the study had opted for the evening and night shifts for childcare reasons. Nurses confirmed that choice for a specific shift duty was solely due to childcare reasons—thus only after the childbirth.

"Morning shift is very inconvenient for me", reported a nurse. "In the afternoon shift, I get the morning time to complete domestic work and childcare tasks. My husband cannot manage to bathe the child, pack her tiffin and leave for office. So I have opted for the evening and the night shifts", she added further.

Despite altering shift duty schedule, it may not necessarily match with children's school timings, thus some problems may prevail.

"I leave for the afternoon shift at 1.00 p.m. My eight year old daughter returns from school at 2.00 p.m.; My husband returns at 6.00 p.m. or so. Till then she is a latch-key child", stated an anxious nurse.

In a similar vein, another mother narrated: "When I have night shift at 7.40 p.m., my children (4 years and 8 years) are in latch-key. My husband also has the shift duty. He returns sometimes at 9.00 p.m. Till then children are alone".

In a study on women and shift work, Barton et al. (1993) reported that some permanent night shift nurses had specifically chosen to work at night for domestic reasons.

Walker (1985) observed that the fixed night shifts for mothers were incompatible with their child rearing responsibilities. Constant tiredness because of reduced sleep may be the cost to pay for such work.

To illustrate, a nurse exclaimed: "I had opted for the permanent night shift due to childcare concerns. But my health got severely affected due to lack of sleep and fatigue. I then again shifted to the evening and the night duties".

It is therefore rightly observed by Biebly and Biebly (1984) and

Duncan and Perucci (1976) that women more than men take family obligations into account when making labour force decisions.

To explain further, narrating her plight in childcare a respondent reported: "When I had morning shift and my husband had night shift—that got over by 8.00 a.m. or so—I used to carry my one year old child to the station. My husband would take time off and come to the station from his workplace and take the child back to his workplace. Father and child will return home after his night duty got over. I thus changed my duty to evening and night shifts."

In all, 15 respondents had changed their shift to a continuous afternoon and night shift. Among these, 4 respondents had spouses with the shift duty whereas 9 spouses worked in the standard hours.

Nurses agreed that the flexibility in reaching late helped them particularly when child had to be dropped to the crèche and then come to the (workplace) hospital. Many a times the next caretaker of child was yet to come. Mothers then wait till the caretaker (the spouse, maid or relative) come to the house—then only the nurses leave for work. As stated by a respondent: "It is better than taking leave. My husband is employed during the standard work hours. It happens that due to traffic or other reasons he reaches a bit late, then the flexibility in reaching late is at least of advantage."

The flexibility for reaching half an hour late is useful on all three shifts and it is not dominantly used in a particular shift.

So far the discussion extensively focused on the role of family members and employers in childcare management at night by mothers in nightshifts. After examining respondents perception on need for a favourable system like transport, accommodation, crèche, flexible working hours at the workplace etc., the researcher puts forth consequences of unsuitable childcare alternative.

Leave of Absence

A majority of the administrative heads maintained that the leave of absence was sanctioned according to rules and regulations. At times they were considerate towards the emergencies.

Similarly, leave was not sanctioned if there was no leave left for the staff nurse. Also, if the reason felt was not genuine, leave was not sanctioned, like in the case of abortions—if an authorized certificate from the BMC hospital is not produced.

Childcare was the most common reason cited by staff nurses for taking the leave, closely followed by child's illness. Other reasons were their own sickness or domestic concerns.

Workplace Environment

Administrative-in-charges of four hospitals maintained that staff nurses did not get a break of 20 to 30 minutes at night, whereas in other three hospitals it was unofficially permitted. Though a majority of the administrative heads agreed that a break of 20 to 30 minutes in the night shift was necessary for staff nurses as the workload at night shift was not necessarily heavy but it again depended on the ward.

Matrons, assistant matrons and sister-in-charge unanimously felt the need for a crèche at the workplace, when staff nurses are on night duty. They further added that it would improve their job performance, as one major domestic responsibility they (staff nurses) would be relieved of.

They also agreed that a transport facility would help the staff nurses to cut their travel time and devote it to the childcare.

Two administrative heads who negated need for a transport system maintained that the local transport system was sufficient and efficient for employees. According to them, trains and buses in the metropolis are well connected.

All administrative heads expressed accommodation as a common need for employees. They felt that it needed to be close to the workplace and not widespread across the metropolis. As earlier expressed by (employees) the staff nurses, matrons and sister-in-charge reiterate need for staff quarters especially when the children of employees are small and need utmost care.

Meal service was also considered as an important part of the workplace that can be of help to staff nurses, according to the administrative heads.

Matrons and sister-in-charges maintained that the duty hours can be adjusted depending on the availability of staff nurses in the ward. Similar was their attitude towards the staff nurses coming late or leaving early due to certain urgencies. While being considerate to the staff-nurses, the sister-in-charge, assistant matrons and matrons also made it clear that they were answerable to their seniors towards efficient services of the staff nurses.

Implications for Policy

So far the focus was on the experiences incurred by the nurses employed in seven hospitals run by Brihamumbai Municipal Corporation. The discussions in previous chapters also highlighted the role of family, the community and the employers in helping the staff nurses in childcare and thus making them, if not comfortable, at least adjusted in their job setting. During the discussion, several adequacies and inadequacies emerged regarding these roles.

The obvious question would emerge: "What could be the policy implications which create a conducive environment for working women in night shifts (in the present context staff nurses employed in hospitals) such that they can take care of their dependent children satisfactorily and also perform their duties at the workplace?". The present chapter highlights policy implications in the context of the employers, the community and the family.

Data emphatically points towards respondents' perception of asserting the need for residential accommodation, transport, meals, childcare at night, flexible working hours and leave of absence provisions, all of which enable them to balance their employment with the childcare.

The needs are interlinked; one meshing into another, or helping another, e.g., the crèche at workplace and transport service to the workplace supporting each other. Mothers can bring children to the workplace where there is a crèche and take them back after the duty hours.

Accessibility is important in all respects. Whether it is a crèche or a housing provision, geographic proximity to the workplace is necessary to minimize the growing mismatch between the family and the work.

Some suggestions for meeting employee needs towards housing, transport, canteen facilities and crèches as childcare centres are discussed.

Housing Needs of Employees

Housing concerns are basic among welfare needs and warrant considerable attention where accommodation is one of the biggest concerns of the labour force. A majority of the staff nurses under present focus are from smaller townships or interior regions, thus needing a place to stay in a costly metropolitan setting.

Being employed in rotating shifts implies reporting and returning from duty at varied hours, standard and non-standard. Housing provision in such instances especially if near the workplace can save a lot of travel time and ensure safety and perhaps have better access to childcare (if the workplace makes such a provision).

Nurses are the main service workforce of any hospital that enables its functioning round-the-clock. Staff nurses are often required to do double duties, called on for emergencies, etc., that demands working at all and odd hours. Staff nurses also opt for the evening and the night shifts for childcare reasons.

The constraints regarding accommodation for staff nurses are as follows:

Limited Staff Quarters Available

The vast workforce of the municipality stresses more demand by employees on employer to meet their housing needs.

Nurses have a limited number of staff quarters allocated to them. Administrative staff, clerical personnel and doctors get a preference over nurses on the availability of accommodation by municipality.

Nurses, in this regard, argued: "The administrative personnel as head clerk, telephone operators, etc. working in the hospital are provided with staff quarters on campus, why not us?" They further added: ". . . even resident doctors, who are here only for internship are provided with accommodation. Resident doctors are a floating workforce, whereas the nurses are permanent".

As mentioned earlier 70 per cent of the staff nurses reside in the ownership houses, 22.4 per cent in a rental basis and only 7.6 per cent in government quarters.

Data in Table 10 informs that respondents living in ownership houses have also affirmed the need for accommodation near the workplace.

The plight of nurses needing accommodation is further heightened by those staying illegally on a leave and license basis (as narrated in the previous chapter). Understandably, respondents living on a rental basis have also maintained the need for accommodation.

Table 10 *Respondents' Perception on Need for Accommodation and House Type*

House Type	*Respondents' Perception on Need for Accommodation*		
	Yes	*No*	*Total*
Ownership	163	12	175 (70.0)
Rent	54	2	56 (22.4)
Government	18	1	19 (7.6)
Total	235	15	250 (100)

Staff Quarters Available on Seniority

As staff quarters are limited, availability is on the basis of seniority. Staff nurses have to wait at least for a period of two years or more before a staff quarters is allotted to them. Meanwhile, they try for ownership housing.

"I have opted for a housing loan as there are 6 nurses ahead of me for the residential accommodation. By the time I get a staff quarters, at least four years will pass by. Children will grow up. The need is felt more in the early years, when children are small", illustrated one nurse.

Lack of Proximity to Workplace

The staff quarters provided to nurses are all not necessarily within hospital premises or near the hospital. Some are located at distant locations from hospitals. Accessibility to the workplace then gets limited.

Some staff nurses had applied for a transfer to nearby hospital from their residence. But, permission was not necessarily granted. Hence, they have to travel long distances spending more money and time on commuting.

Suggestions to Meet Housing Needs of Employees

At the onset, it is necessary to acknowledge the benefit of housing loans available to employees. It helps them to purchase a house in the metropolis.

Also, there have been distinct efforts to provide accommodation to staff nurses, however, the fact remains that a majority of the staff nurses do not have access to government accommodation.

It is evident that priority is given to other government staff (doctors, administrative and managerial staff, etc.).

It is therefore imperative that for efficient working by staff nurses, residential accommodation is necessary so that the burden of childcare could be lessened.

Increasing Availability of Staff Quarters

Often, new buildings are constructed within hospital premises for resident doctors, for increasing accessibility to workplace. Similar considerations should apply for the staff nurses.

The available houses are also not in good condition; with very poor maintenance houses need repairs for leaking roof, plumbing, and sanitation.

Transport Service

As discussed in previous chapter, respondents use local trains predominantly to travel to the workplace. Buses as a mode of transport are also used frequently.

The conveyance allowance of Rs 85 per month for nurses is frugal considering the distance and rising prices of goods and services. The need for a transport system has been opined by an overwhelming 95.6 per cent of the respondents though.

A transport service to and fro from the workplace will be a convenient proposition for employees to have an alternative to the crowded local train system. Though it is also true that the respondents live at widespread geographic distances, it would be unviable to provide a door-to-door transport service.

Alternatively, a common pick-up centre point can be worked out, that is central to their movement.

The transport service can cater to all employees at the workplace.

As mentioned earlier the provision or support systems are interlinked; employees can then bring children by the staff-bus to the hospital, where there is provision for proper crèche facility.

As the staff nurses find commuting to hospitals difficult, so is the case with women in other professions. Spouse employment, absence of crèche near the workplace, non-availability of school in/near their organizations, low salary, lack of accommodation, health and transport facilities etc., are revealed as chief causes for these women quitting their jobs.

Recently, National Commission for Women (NCW) has recommended agricultural universities and development departments to give special consideration to provision of transport, accommodation, spouse employment, etc. (Aneeja, 2001).

In lieu of distances being far off from the workplace, the management authorities can consider transferring the staff nurses to other municipal hospitals that are within their commutable distance.

This may not always be possible as the staffing needs of one hospital may vary from another, yet a concerted effort can help to meet needs of employees and serve interests of employers as well.

Canteen Facilities

There are three issues regarding canteen facilities that were raised by respondents:

Access to Canteen Facilities

Going to the canteen and eating there is restricted due to organizational hierarchy. As a result, respondents did not go to the canteen and eat there, but asked for food to be brought to the common room by the ward boys. The canteen was thus underutilized by the respondents.

Quality of Food

Nurses complained that quality of food in the canteens was barely satisfactory. Thus, respondents relied on snacks like "idlis', dosa's, etc." from a nearby restaurant as meals. Nurses further mentioned that the problem was dominant during morning shifts, when they had to leave their houses as early as 5.30 a.m. to 6.00 a.m.

As quality suffers, respondents refrain from eating canteen food, resulting in its underutilization.

Timings of Canteen

An overwhelming majority of nurses used the canteen during morning shift for their meals. In the evening shift, they needed tea and snacks, and at night shift the beverages (tea or coffee) and snacks.

Canteens in municipal hospitals close between 10.30 p.m. to 11.00 p.m. thus, being inconvenient for the night shift staff.

Some Suggestions

Underutilizations of the canteen facility due to lack of accessibility and quality are the main concerns of nurses.

Quality of food needs to be improved to certified standards. Canteens should be supervised regularly. Stringent standards need to be followed that improve quality of food and related aspects like cooking procedures, customer service, prices, etc. It would benefit not only the nurses but also all other users.

When nurses are assured that they can have a meal at the workplace, it also means some workload reduced at home where otherwise they have to cook a meal, especially during the morning shift, thus reducing their double burden.

The issue of accessibility to canteen is a larger issue that is closely linked to occupational hierarchies at the workplace.

Nurses are subordinates to doctors, whether they work as staff nurses or matrons. The hierarchy perpetuates in up-down order, thus keeping occupational distance.

It will definitely be useful if nurses have "equal access" to canteen facilities.

Such matters are rarely represented in the labour union meetings, as these are specific to nurses alone; due to sex typing of nursing as an occupation, the matters further become a gender-specific concern.

Suggested Models in Childcare

Respondents in this study have reiterated the need for childcare.

The following text explores childcare models in non-standard hours and then suggests a model for childcare, in the context of the present study, as a means for the women workers to balance their employment and the early childcare.

Pioneering efforts in non-standard hours childcare reflect heightened interests from employers at various levels of involvement.

Models in Childcare

Literature suggests three types of models in the non-standard hours childcare that are based on participation and responsibility of various stakeholders ranging from parents, child development specialists to employers. These models are mainly adopted in Western countries.

They are the single employer, employer consortium and community partnership models. Each of these is discussed below.

Single Employer Model

As compared to their day care models in USA, a distinct interest by employers is observed for the night care of childcare. In fact, initiatives and resources of employers are key determinants to this facility provided.

The single employer models are most common in manufacturing and service sectors, and they exist in both public and private sector workplaces in the USA (Nausbaum, 1995).

For example, the Toyota Child Development Centre provides on site facility round-the-clock for 230 children from ages 6 weeks to 13 years. The programme is designed to meet needs of Toyota team workers who work on shifts as well as overtime.

The children receive assistance with homework, eat dinner and go to bed. Children are picked up by their parents after the shift ends at 2.15 a.m. To ensure quality, Toyota selected a consultancy group—Corporate Child Management Services—for childcare in non-standard hours. It also helps parents to pay subsidized rates as compared to the local markets.

The Massachusetts Bay Transport Agency (MBTA) has a contract with 32 licensed childcare centres. A childcare committee of MBTA employers worked through a formal public process to identify providers and evaluate them considering licensing, geographic location, homes of operation, ages of children served, and the overall interest in the programme. It is important to note that although the MBTA provides employees with information and material about eligible childcare providers, it does not recommend particular providers; MBTA subsidy is paid directly to the childcare provider.

One reason for the interest in non-standard hours childcare by employers was the growing need to employ workers for their multi-shift manufacturing site to operate plant on a round-the-clock basis.

Also, expenses from other manufacturing firms reiterated a significant turnover among employees, as childcare in non-standard hours was a problem. The provision boosted employee morale especially when it was quality contracted and provided a subsidy.

The Employer Consortium Model

Unlike the single employer consortium, the employer consortium involves several companies joining together to discuss common needs and explore funding strategies. The local consortia, industry consortia and cross country consortia are examples of employer consortium (ibid.).

In the close to home project in USA, a local consortium business forms a particular geographic area—came together and maximized the use of resources in the community. New providers were offered support services. Free workshops were conducted for providers of childcare (old and new) including information on how to accommodate non-standard schedules. The businesses partly manage and finance the childcare centres.

Contrastingly, in an industry consortia, employers who are part of a particular service or industrial sector come together to address common childcare issues that arise from their employées' similar needs and schedules.

Several of the major hotels in downtown Atlanta, Georgia-Marriot, OMNI and Hyuatta—joined together to address the unique childcare difficulties facing hospitality industry employees.

The Children's Inn, a 24 hours childcare centre was opened on site with the help of a local company specializing in childcare. The costs were subsidized for plants due to financial support provided by employers.

In the National Cross Industry Consortia in USA, companies pool resources and contribute funds to the development of community based programmes. Though this is the most ambitious and most difficult type of consortium to coordinate, it is potentially the most effective. The American Business Collaboration (ABC) for quality Dependent Care founded in 1991 is the only example. It is important to note that most of the work of ABC partners is actually done at the local level.

The local consortium example cited above is similar to the national cross country consortia. However, the national cross industry consortia is on a wider scale.

The community partnership model is different from employer consortium or single employer model.

Employers, parents, childcare experts, and community members come together and work out a viable partnership for childcare in non-standard hours. It is difficult and thus needs considerable coordination and cooperation from various stakeholders.

A Childcare Model in the Context of Present Study

With growing family trend towards nuclear type and decreased availability of family members as relatives for childcare, respondents in this study have pronounced the need for a crèche not only while on nightshift but also on morning and evening shifts. Though there is a wide consensus on the need for a crèche at night, there is some debate on its location—whether at the workplace or near the home.

One of the attempts in this study has been to investigate means for the working mothers to balance employment and early childcare. The findings maintain that staff nurses do not necessarily live near the workplace/hospitals but are distanced by a travel time of one to two hours or more. Given the geographic distance of residences of staff nurses and the hospitals, the researcher finds it difficult to discuss the feasibility of a crèche either only at the hospital or near the residence, but rather the facility to be made available both near the residence and also the workplace (hospital).

To begin with, the provision of a crèche at the hospital is discussed. While asserting the need for a crèche at the workplace and near the home, pertinent aspects of programme service, location finance and management constraints are mentioned.

The workplace in this study is the hospital that, like manufacturing and other service industries, operates round the clock. Staff on rotating shifts, especially the nurses, doctors, and ward assistants (predominantly females) form an important and substantial part of the hospital workforce.

The need for a crèche at the hospital has been reiterated by respondents time and again in this social inquiry. Considering the rotating shifts at workforce and the increasing mismatch between childcare and work schedules, it is felt that a 24-hour childcare centre at the hospital would help both employees and the employers. Referring to the literature on childcare in non-standard hours, a single employer model can be used as a guideline to provide childcare for the hospital employees.

Programme Service

Due to its 24-hour operation, users can avail the crèche facility depending on the need and according to their duty hours, i.e., morning, evening or night duty.

Age range (of child) can vary from three months to the school age. Programme routine of feeding, sleeping, studying, etc., will vary depending on time of the day and night.

Caretakers can be given training through a childcare consultancy organization. The shifts of caretakers also can change after a stipulated time period.

The use of this service can be opened to all employees and employers ranging from the health care personnel to the administrative staff.

Provision can also be made for sick children and cared for by regular visits of paediatrician doctors who are attached to the hospital.

Location

The location for childcare centre can be worked out in collaboration with the management of the hospital and the users. The place must be safe, not congested and properly ventilated. Safety of children must be ensured for all times. Also, whether the crèche can be used by other parents in the neighbourhood can be decided by the management authorities.

It is important to recall that there are several hospitals in the city commonly administered and managed by the municipality authorities. Thus, all municipal hospitals are homogenous in rules and regulations.

If a crèche is opened in each municipal hospital, there can be a variation among the users and the location. For instance, as distance is a problem, nurses could use other municipal hospital childcare centres while they work in another municipal hospital. Another option could be, if two to three municipal hospitals are located nearby, they would have a common childcare centre. The central argument is to make the facility as much accessible to the users as possible.

Finance and Management

Cost of childcare can be subsidized with the hospital largely sharing the cost.

Till date, prior experiences have reiterated a general disinterest among the employers especially in the day care; whereas the literature on non-standard hours childcare has pronounced onus and participation on the side of employers. Similarly, in the present case, the onus and initiative from municipal authorities would be crucial. Their role in childcare centre management and financing will largely determine success of the programme. Provision of food, medicines, etc., can be a part of the service.

Constraints Envisaged

A crèche in the hospital is often misunderstood to be a women's issue and thus under-represented in union matters, which are male-dominated. Staff nurses revealed that they hardly attended union meetings, when they did, they were under-represented. If they spoke or expressed their need for a crèche, it was often brushed aside as a typical women's problem. Other concerns like the need for breastfeeding child by a nursing mother are not even expressed. "It is humiliating for a woman to talk about her specific needs in front of so many men. The union members are ruffians and intimidating. They laugh at us. It's very awkward to be there", emerges the main concern of respondents. The cycle is vicious. Women do not express themselves due to inhibitions and the union members allege women's lack of representation in union deliberations. Childcare need has to be mandated in meetings through a better representation from various quarters. It is by now evident that nurses avoid bringing their children to the workplace due to long distance of travel and absence of crèche facility. It must be considered that employees staying within commutable limits have the access to childcare. Also, nurses living at long distances mentioned that, if there was no better choice, they would bring their child to the hospital provided there was a crèche available and of good quality. This will prevent mothers from being forced to take the leave of absence often.

Further, children need not be left as latchkey or in custody of unsatisfactory caretakers. Staff nurses have commonly mentioned that hospital as a workplace is prone to infection due to diseases and ailing patients in wards; thus, making environment unsuitable for the childcare. However, a safe location for a crèche can be identified that is at a distance from infectious wards. The crèche can also be located in the administrative block of a hospital.

Time and again, space constraints are a common excuse to avoid providing crèche at the workplace. It may be noted that municipal hospitals occupy large areas of the city and are the property of government. It is not the lack of space, money or staff; it is the lack of a will to see childcare as a need rather than an option.

Quality of services is another reason commonly cited for under-utilization of such facilities. Quality can be maintained through close monitoring and supervision. Also, childcare organizations can be consulted to have inputs for a better childcare management.

Round-the-Clock Childcare Centres in Community

Like the workplace, similar efforts need to be directed towards setting up childcare centres at the community level for the non-standard and standard hours.

The community partnership model can serve as a guideline to initiate round the clock crèche service at the local level. It implies involvement from various quarters like parents, employers, local government, community groups etc.

Though some private and informal initiatives are observed, only a few crèches are available during non-standard hours. Also for those that exist, quality is a distant reality.

Till date the role of employers and government has not only been dormant but detrimental in promoting childcare services for urban women in cities and towns.

For initiating childcare in the non-standard hours, role of government and employers needs to be in the forefront as much as parents and childcare professionals taking the responsibility.

It needs to be noted that as the location of a community based crèche is not within a premise (like a hospital), it warrants security and safety of children even more.

Like the example cited in the case of Palcare, crèches can be located near the local station where parents frequently use local trains as transport to reach the workplace (Nausbaum, 1995).

Conclusion

It is well established that an increasing number in the workforce particularly women are to be a significant part of the 24-hour economy and therefore the issue of employee welfare measures can no longer be ignored. More so, when the employees are mothers working nightshifts with dependent children the issue of childcare comes to the forefront, along with the other concerns of transportation, accommodations meals, etc.

It may be pertinent to mention that recently the 6th Pay Commission (2008) has made some significant considerations for working mothers. It provides a two-year job protected leave as maternity leave. In case a mother has adopted a child, a similar provision is given depending on the age of the child. Fathers are also entitled for paternity leave. This is a move by the government enabling women to be in a favourable situation. Government has further extended leave by recognizing women's responsibility in childcare as Child Care Leave (see Annexure for details).

Further, this regulation comes more into light and gains prominence in the midst of a dwindling economy characterized by recession. Though childcare still remains a mother's concern, as the paper discusses it only in the context of mother's working nightshifts. According to me childcare should be a parent concern and a provision in all organizations where there are employees (men or women). And there should be a regulation on the quality of crèches that are provided at the workplace or otherwise that will reduce considerable anxiety in the minds of parents while at work thereby providing a family friendly environment for workers. Further, absenteeism is likely to reduce and productivity thus will increase with these family friendly measures.

Annexure

(Source: http://invest-n-trade.blogspot.com/2008/09/maternity-leave-child-care-leave-sixth.html/)
Some more good news for the central government employees, especially the female employees. The Central Government has decided to increase the period of **Maternity Leave** for women employees and also introduce the concept of **Child Care Leave**. Though this recommendation by **Sixth Central Pay Commission** will be beneficial for female employees, it will equally be beneficial for male employees as the entire family life would benefit. Below we present the text as it appears on the Office Memorandum concerning the subject.

(a) The existing ceiling of 135 days **Maternity Leave** provided in Rule 43(1) of Central Civil Services (Leave) Rules, 1972 shall be enhanced to 180 days.
(b) Leave of the kind due and admissible (including commuted leave for a period not exceeding 60 days and leave not due) that can be granted in continuation with **Maternity Leave** provided in Rule 43(4)(b) shall be increased to two years.
(c) Women employees having minor children may be granted **Child Care Leave** by an authority competent to grant leave, for a maximum period of two years (i.e., 730 days) during their entire service for taking care of up to two children whether for rearing or to look after any of their needs like examination, sickness etc. **Child Care Leave** shall not be admissible if the child is 18 years of age or older. During the period of such leave, the women employees shall be paid leave salary equal to the pay drawn immediately before proceeding on leave. It may be availed of in more than one spell. Child Care Leave shall not be debited against the leave account. Child Care Leave may also be allowed for the third year as leave not due (without production of medical certificate). It may be combined with leave of the kind due and admissible.

1. These orders shall take effect from 1st September, 2008.
2. In view of paragraph 2 above, a women employee in whose case the period of 135 days of maternity leave has not expired on the said date shall also be entitled to the maternity leave of 180 days.
3. Formal amendments to the Central Civil Services (Leave) Rules, 1972 are being issued separately.
4. In so far as persons serving in the Indian Audit and Accounts Departments are concerned, these orders are issued in consultation with the Comptroller and Auditor General of India.

References

Alward, R. *The Nurses Shift Work. Handbook.* American Hospital Association (AHA), 1992.

Aneeja, G. "Women On and Off Farms: Building Links" in *Economic and Political Weekly,* Vol. XXXVI (January 13, 2001): 103–104.

ASSOCHAM (The Associated Chambers of Commerce and Industry of India). "Night Shift for Women: Growth and Opportunities." (A research study. Sponsored by National Commission for Women [NCW], 2008).

Barton, J., Smith, L., Totterdell, P., Espelten, and Folkard, S. "Does Individual Choice Determine Shift System Acceptability?" *Ergonomics* 36 (1993): 93–99.

Baverman and Chowers. "Would Provision of Childcare for Nurses with Young Children Ensure Response to Call-up during a Wartime Disaster? An Israeli Hospital Nursing Survey." *Journal of Emergency Nursing* 18, No. 2 (1992): 132–34.

Bhave, J. "Crèche Care at Night." *Social Welfare* 41, No. 6 (September 1994): 15–18.

Biebly and Biebly. "Work Commitment, Sex-Role Attitude and Women's Employment." *American Sociological Review* 49 (1984): 234–47.

Brown, D. "Shiftwork: A Survey of the Sociological Implications of Studies on Male Shift Workers." *Journal of Occupational Psychology* 48 (1975): 23–24.

Calliot, R. Consequences Sociales du Travail a feu Continu in Economie et Humanisme 122 (1959): 62–72 in Carpentire, J. and Cazamian, P. *Night Work: Its Effect on the Health and Welfare of the Worker.* Geneva: ILO, 1977.

Central Rules. Contract Labour (Regulation and Abolition) Government of NCT. Delhi Construction and Maintenance of Crèches, 1971.

CMIE. *Economic Intelligence Service: Monthly Review of the Indian Economy/CMIE.* Mumbai: Centre for Monitoring Indian Economy Pvt. Ltd, 1996.

Duncan and Perucci. "Dual Occupation Families and Migration." *American Sociological Review* 41 (1976): 252–61.

Ede, M.M. "Shift Work and Your Health." Ph.D. Thesis, Source—Interface: Work/Family, Shoreview, M.N., 1983.

Engle, Patrica. "Child Care Strategies of Income Earning and Home Production Mothers in Rural and Urbanizing Guatemala." Paper presented at the Panel on Women's Work and Child Welfare in the Third World, American Association for the Advancement of Science Meetings, Pa, May 1986.

Gadbois. "Round the Clock Operations in Hospitals: Shift Scheduling, Task Demands and Work Organization." Abstracts: International Symposium "Shiftwork and Job Demands," Paris, 11–12 July 1991.

Government of India. "Shramashakti." Report of the National Commission on Self-Employed Women and Women in the Informal Sector, 1988.

Hoefferth, S.L. "At the Margin: Managing Work and Family Life at the Poverty Line." Paper presented at the Annual Meeting of the American Sociological Association, 1992.

International Labour Organization Conference Preview. *World of Work*, No. 29 (1995): 10.

Khallar, M. Whitter Child Care Services. "Child Case as an Essential Input in Women's Development," Centre for Women's Studies and UNICEF, 1991.

Menon, S. "Work at Night . . . In the Day Intensification of Women's Labour." *Labour File* (May 1999): 9–16.

Myers, R. and Indriso, C. "Women's Work and Child Care." Supporting the Integration of Women's Productive and Reproductive Roles in Resource Poor Households in Developing Countries. Paper prepared for a Workshop at the Rockfeller Foundation in February on Issues Related to Gender, Technology and Development, 1987.

NASSCOM. Nasscom for better security for BPO women BPO staff, copyright 2008 Indian Syndicate.com Pvt.Ltd <http://www.bpowatchindia.com/bpo_news/nasscom_gender/september-17-2008/nasscom_security_measures.html> (November 17, 2008).

Nausbaum, K. "Child Care Before Nine and After Five: An Emerging Issue Care Around the Clock NCCIC." Women's Bureau, 1995.

Ntombela, N. *Women, Work and Breast-feeding in Dialogue on Diarrhea*, no. 59 (December 1994–February 1995) published by Appropriate Health Resources and Technology Action Group.

Overseas Education Fund (OEF). Child Care Needs of Low Income Mothers in Less Developed Countries: A Summary Report of Research in Six Countries in Asia and Latin America (Korea, Malaysia, Sri Lanka, Brazil, Dominican Republic, Peru), Washington, D.C.: Overseas Education Fund of the League of Women Voters, 1979.

Rane, A.J. "A New Look at Factory Crèches." *Eklavyya*. Mobile Crèches Annual Report, 1978.

Reese, S. "Moonlight and Childcare." *American Demographics* V (18 August 1996): 20–22.

Registrar General of India, Census of India. *Statistical Profile in Women Labour*, No. 5 (1998). Labour Bureau, Ministry of Labour, Government of India, 1981.

Rivera, C. "Labour Force Participation and Day Care Utilization by Low-Income Mothers in Bogota, Columbia." A Ph.D. Dissertation, Brandeis University, May 1979, Unpublished.

Rustamfram, N. "Job Satisfaction of Staff Nurses in Medium Sized Private and Public Hospitals." Unpublished Doctoral Dissertation. Tata Institute of Social Sciences, p. 95.

Schmink. "Women in the Urban Economy in Latin America." Working Paper No. 1, New York: The Population Council 1982.

Sen and Snow. "Power and Decision." *The Social Control of Reproduction*. Harvard University Press, 1994, pp. 46–47.

Seppanen, P.S., Love, J. M., De Vries, D.K. and Berstein, L. *National Study of Before and After School Programs*. Portsmonth: REC Research Corporation, 1993.

Sixth Central Pay Commission. <http://invest-n-trade.blogspot.com/2008/09/maternity-leave-child-care-leave-sixth.html> (2008).

Swaminathan, M.C. *Who Cares? A Study of Child Care Facilities for Low Income Women in India*, New Delhi: Centre for Women's Development Studies, 1985.

Tasto, D.L., Colligan, M.J., Skjei, E.W. and Polly, S.J. "Health Consequences of Shift Work." Final Report, SRI Project URU-4426. Cincinnati: Taft Laboratories, National Institute for Occupational Safety and Health, 1978.

Walby, S. *Theorizing Patriarchy*. UK: Blackwell Publishers, 1992.

Walker. "Social Problems of Shift Work." In, *Hours of Work: Temporal Factors in Work-Scheduling*, edited by S. Folkard and T. Monk, Chichester: Wiley, 1985.

Wallace. "Downsizing the American Dream: Work and Family at Century's End." Pp. 23–28 in *Challenges for Work and Family*, edited by Vannoy, D. and Dubeck, P., NY: Walter de Grugter Inc., 1998.

White and Keith. "The Effect of Shift Work on the Quality and Stability of Marital Relations." in *Journal of Marriage and the Family* 52 (May 1990).

7

Fair Gender Induction in the Armed Forces: Issues and Challenges

Nidhi Maheshwari and N.P. Singh

> The test of whether or not you can hold a job should not be the arrangement of your chromosomes.
>
> —Bella Abzug, First Jewish Lady Congressman in Washington (as cited in Ziegler, 1972)

"Do you have it in you?" . . . The popular question send shivers down the spine of many young aspirants, including females, who wish to serve the nation through Indian armed forces. The zest to perform for the country by safeguarding the frontiers is a sacred dream to cherish. Nation owes a lot to those women who literally broke ground, opened doors, and made the choice of a military career easier for those who followed. It is evident that there are certain prompts for the female aspirants to join the services like: an exciting/hands-on, atypical (not a 9 to 5 job) career with a strong sense of camaraderie, high status indicative of a sense of national pride etc. However, the entry of females to the services and challenges thereon, has raised questions on such a non-conventional role of Indian females. Hence, it is the need of the hour to focus on the issue through various perspectives.

Demographic Perspective

Although women are recruited to serve in military in most countries, only a few countries permit women to fill active combat roles. Countries that allow this include New Zealand, Canada, Denmark, Finland, France, Germany, Norway, Israel and Switzerland. Other nations allow female soldiers to serve in certain combat arms positions, such as the United Kingdom, which allows women to serve in Artillery roles, while still excluding them from units with a dedicated Infantry role. The United States allows women in most combat flying positions. Following is the global participation of women in the armed forces (Wikipedia, 2009):

Australia

Women make up 12.8 per cent of the Australian defence forces (with 15.1 per cent in the Royal Australian Air Force, 14.6 per cent in the Royal Australian Navy and 10.5 per cent in the Australian Army) and 17.5 per cent of the reserves. However, only 74 per cent of the total number of available roles in the Australian armed forces is available to women. Despite this, using 1998–99 figures, the ADF had the highest percentage of women employed in the world. Also in 1998, Australia became the second nation in the world to allow women to serve on its submarines.

Britain

In 1949, women were officially recognized as a permanent part of British armed forces, though full combat roles were still available only to men. The seizure of Royal Navy sailor Faye Turney in 2007 by the naval forces of the Iranian Revolutionary Guard led to some media comment on the role of women and mothers in the armed forces. Female personnel currently make up around 9 per cent of the British armed forces. Most importantly, the Commander-in-Chief of the British armed forces is a woman (Queen Elizabeth II) though her position is only nominal.

Denmark

Currently, 5 per cent (862) women including 98 officers, 191 NCOs, and 571 privates are present in the Danish armed forces. NATO's report indicates that the Danish military does not promote women to positions of leadership. As of 2002, the highest rank reached by a woman in the Danish armed forces was Lieutenant Colonel. Also, recent recruitment of women has been low in Denmark due to rising job opportunities elsewhere.

Eritrea

Female soldiers make up more than 25 per cent of the Eritrean military and thus, played a large role in both the Eritrean civil war and the border dispute with Ethiopia.

Finland

The Finnish defence forces do not conscript women. However, since 1995, women between 18 and 30 years of age have the possibility of voluntarily undertake military service in the defence forces or in the border guard. All services and units in the Finnish defence forces and the Finnish border guard accept females. Yearly, some 500 women complete the voluntary military service, while some 30,000 men complete the obligatory conscription. The women who have completed the voluntary military service are eligible for further military employment. If they have at least NCO training, they can apply for career NCO positions or for officer training. These career paths have been open since 1996, when the first women completed the military service. In 2005, 32 female career officers were in service. The number of female warrant officers was 16 and the number of female specialist officers was seven. The women made up about 16 per cent of the total career NCO cadre.

France

Women represent 19 per cent of all French military personnel. They are allowed to serve in all posts (including combat infantry), except submarines and riot control gendarmerie. However, they still represent a small part of the personnel in the following specialties: combat, security, mechanics, especially within the infantry and marines (only 337–1.7 per cent—combat infantry soldiers and 9–0.4 per cent—marines are female).

Germany

As of April 2008, about 15,200 female soldiers serve in the Bundeswehr, representing a share of 8 per cent of all troops except conscripted soldiers. The German Bundeswehr now expects the percentage of all female personnel to rise to about 15 per cent in the middle-term future.

Libya

Libya is one of only two Islamic nations to have women in their military, the other being Pakistan. The 200-strong unit is Colonel Gaddaffi's personal bodyguard and is called variously the "Green Nuns" and "The Amazonian Guard" or more commonly in Libya "The Revolutionary Nuns".

Nepal

It is worth noting that Peoples Liberation Army, the armed forces of the Communist Party of Nepal (Maoist) have a 30 per cent female participation quota for their combat forces, and frequently claims 40 per cent actual participation. A proposal of a 40 per cent female combat troop quota in the future Nepal Army has been frequently forwarded publicly by Maoist leaders during their peace negotiations with the current government.

Norway

As of 2006, women comprised only 6.6 per cent of the total strength of armed forces—Army 132, Navy 115, Air Force 83, Home Guard 13 and Logistics 111. However, the Norwegian government has set a target of 15 per cent of their armed forces to consist of women by 2008, from the 2006 value of 6.6 per cent. This aim is accompanied by efforts to increase the awareness of sexual exploitation and gender issues within the armed forces. All women between 18 and 20 years are given the opportunity to attend national conscription selection.

Poland

In present Poland a law passed on April 6, 2004 requires all women with college nursing or veterinary degrees to register for compulsory service. In addition it allows women to volunteer and serve as professional personnel in all services of the army. As of June 30, 2007 there are 800 women in the army, of which 471 are officers, 308 non-commissioned officers and 21 other ranks, in addition 225 are in military training schools.

Russia

By the early 1990s, 100,000 women made up 3 per cent of the Russian armed forces, with the current tally standing at around 115,000 to 160,000, representing 10 per cent of Russia's military strength.

Sri Lanka

The Sri Lanka Civil Defence Force, formerly the Sri Lanka Home Guard, has been open to women recruits since 1988. In 1993, these guardswomen were issued firearms and deployed to protect their home towns and villages against attacks by LTTE. As a result, there have been many casualties (including fatalities) from attacks. Currently, female personnel of all three services play an active part in ongoing operations. As of 2008, there were three female officers of the rank of Major General and one Commodore.

Sweden

Since 1989, there are no gender restrictions in the Swedish military on access to military training or positions. Women are allowed to serve in all parts of the military and in all positions, including combat. However, there current strength is not known.

Thailand

Thailand has recently begun recruiting and training women to conduct counter-insurgency operations. A ranger commander said that when women are protesting, "It is better for women to do the talking. Male soldiers look tough and aggressive. When women go and talk, people tend to be more relaxed."

Turkey

The women participation in Turkish armed forces in terms of figures is not known but a Turkish woman needs special mention. Sabiha Gökçen

(March 22, 1913, Bursa—March 22, 2001, Ankara) was the first female combat pilot in the world, as well as the first Turkish female aviator. Throughout her career in the Turkish Air Force, Gökçen flew 22 different types of aircraft for more than 8000 hours, 32 hours of which were active combat and bombardment missions. She was selected as the only female pilot for the poster of "20 Greatest Aviators in History" published by the United States Air Force in 1996.

United States

From 2005, the first all female C-130 Hercules crew was initiated to serve a combat mission for the US Air Force. So far the position closest to combat open to women in the US Army is in the Military Police, where women man machine-guns on armoured Humvees, guarding truck convoys. Currently, there are 50,000 females serving in Afghanistan and Iraq. Females make up about 15 per cent of the Army. As of November 2008, Sgt. Leigh Ann Hester became the first woman to receive the Silver Star, the third-highest US decoration for valour, for direct participation in combat. And, Ann E. Dunwoody became the only woman with the rank of four-star General in US Army.

India

Initially, the role of women in the armed forces was limited to the medical profession, i.e., doctors and nurses. In 1992, the doors were thrown open for entry of women as regular officers in aviation, logistics, law, engineering and executive cadres under the Women's Special Entry Scheme (WSES). Currently, women in the medical branch, i.e., doctors and nurses can serve as Permanent Commissioned (PC) officers and are eligible for pension after retirement. They also have the option to serve as Short Service Commissioned officers. Women in the non-medical cadre, serve as Short Service Commissioned (SSC) officers. Under this type of commission, eligible women who qualify various tests successfully, serve as Short Service Commissioned officers in the following branches of the armed forces for a period ranging from 5 to 14 years:

Army: EME, Signals, Engineers, Army Education Corps, Army Ordnance Corps, Army Service Corps, Intelligence and Judge-Advocate General's branch.
Navy: All branches of the Navy (except submariners and divers).
Air Force: Flying (AN-32, Avro and Dornier transport aircraft and helicopters), Technical and Administration branches.
Coast Guard: All branches of the Coast Guard.

Most recently, announcement of Permanent Commission to Women Officers in the executive cadre, is a proof of their established ability as efficient and effective officers in the defence services.

There are currently 1,072 women officers in the Indian Army, excluding those in the Army Medical Corps. The strength of women officers in the IAF, including medical services, is 793. Of these, 63 are in the flying branch, 132 are in the technical branch, 126 are in the medical and dental branches and the remaining are in the non-technical ground duty branches. There are 258 women officers in the Indian Navy. The Armed Forces Medical Services have 752 women medical officers, 86 women dental officers and 2,834 members of the all-women Military Nursing Service (MNS). Of the 752 women medical officers, 490 hold permanent commissions. Similarly, 38 per cent of women dental officers and 90 per cent of the MNS officers hold permanent commissions.

Evolutionary Perspective

Long black hairs falling down the well-nigh transparent nape with characteristic curves in the body draped in a chiffon sari and a delicate voice full of charm, projects the image of an Indian female. While, thick moustache on an oval face with bright eyes guarded by intense eyebrows, sturdy-muscular body and heavy voice gives an impression of an Indian male. This mental script has an evolutionary basis. In pre-historic times, men go out to hunt and gather food for family while women remain in the caves to look after their children and do the cooking. Men became physically sturdier, sharper in analytical/mapping abilities and pattern recognition skills, while women became more caring, nurturing and empathic. Simultaneously, psychological attributes of assertiveness, dominance and hardiness came to be associated with masculinity; while those of empathy, passivity, submissiveness and compliance were allied with feminity. Thus, either gender developed certain skills more than the other or gradually job allocation also took place on similar lines. It clearly specifies why women had to wait for long to be inducted into the armed forces, which was presumed to be an all-male bastion.

Historical Perspective

While it is true that women have been the cause of many a war, but, it is equally true that when they did get into the thick of action, they also proved themselves to be amongst the grittiest of leaders and fighting machines. Indian literature eulogizes innumerable stories of fighting women. The greatest of them was Goddess Durga who vanquished the demon king Mahishasura, an event celebrated during Dusshehra. Other shining examples come from our medieval and modern history namely Razia Sultan, Rani Laxmi Bai, Chaand Bibi, Kittur Chennamma and so on. The administrative skills and chivalry exhibited by these warriors is beyond doubt. Also, in the list one cannot forget the eminent name of Capt. Laxmi Sehgal of Indian National Army. None can be a better woman in shining armour than her. And most recently, nation salutes to Lt. General Puneeta Arora as the First Woman General of India. Thus, the gallant role of women is not avant-garde but it has come to the fore with the entry of women to the Services.

Neuro-biological Perspective

Biologically, women have a weaker upper torso and muscular built than men. And, the periodic cycle with associated hormonal changes, mood disturbances and hot flashes adds to the agony and feelings of distress. According to Cline (2004), average female soldiers do not possess as much physical strength as their male counterparts. The female skeletal system is less dense, and more prone to breakages. The Centre for Military Readiness (2004) reported that, "Female soldiers are shorter and smaller than men, with 45–50 per cent less upper body strength and 25–30 per cent less aerobic capacity, which is essential for endurance". Also, their levels of stress tolerance differ from men in terms of magnitude and intensity, both. According to the National Institute of Mental Health (2008), women suffer from Post-Traumatic Stress Disorder (PTSD) at almost twice the rate as men do. PTSD is a condition that develops after a distressing ordeal that involved physical harm or the threat of physical harm. People with PTSD may suffer flashbacks to the traumatic event, become aggressive or withdrawn, have nightmares, or become emotionally numb or even violent. As per Kessler, Chiu, Demler, Merikangas and Walters (2005), women ruminate over non-traumatic negative events more than men, who tend to use more distraction-based coping techniques. While these behaviours may pose evolutionary advantages for each sex, they may also contribute to the increased incidence of PTSD in women. In another study, Taylor et al. (2000) discovered that there are neuro-endocrine differences between men and women that may produce different responses to stress. Oxytocin, which promotes care giving behaviour, is secreted in greater amounts by women. Women, in times of stress, exhibit a 'tend and befriend' response i.e., they respond to stressful situations by protecting themselves and others through nurturing behaviours and forming relationships with others. Thus, they seek out and benefit from support.

However, notwithstanding the biological confines and neurological differences, the perceptual skills, psycho-motor coordination, acute sensitivity, mental flexibility, sustained attention and memory efficiency in women reinforces their claim to the glorious forces. In the services, they have been able to actualize their potentials to the fullest. They have done extremely well as candidates in the Services Selection Boards and as cadets at the armed forces training academies. Women displayed more endurance and some even outran their male counterparts in cross-country runs and long distance marches. Cognitive, emotional and social competence of women had well been exhibited in the services like Signals, EME, ASC, Aviation, Ordnance, Submarines etc. where they are supposed to encode and decode the information, lay land mines, track aircrafts, control air-traffic, keep vigil over the enemy targets, estimate the threat frequency and intensity, supervise transportation of ration and services to the forward areas, maintain records, construct makeshift bridges to facilitate troops' movement and also organize sport events and parties to relieve the stress of officers and jawans with whom they work. Overall, they are thoroughly involved in the '*Risk Management of the Armed Forces*'.

Psycho-social Perspective

Combating Sex-Role Stereotype

Socialization process reinforces sex-role stereotype where the role of men and women are fixed by the society. Society demands the possession and practice of dominance, aggression, hardiness and competitiveness by males; and empathy, compassion, flexibility, compliance and submissiveness by females, exclusively. According to Bem (1974), when an individual displays behaviours that coincide with the stereotypes of their gender, they tend to be evaluated positively. When their behaviour contradicts commonly held stereotypes, they may be viewed negatively. In the book *Beyond the Double Bind: Women and Leadership* (Jamieson, 1995) presented a classic and fitting example of the double bind: a test of whether a woman was a witch. "The suspected witch was submerged in a pond. If she drowned, she deserved to; if she didn't, she was a witch. In the first case, God was revealing her nature; in the second, the devil. Under torture, women either did or did not admit to complicity with Satan. If they did, they were executed for their crime. If they didn't, their silence was attributed to solidarity with Satan and they too were marched off to the stake". Jamieson's book (which opened with the chapter "Hillary Clinton as a Rorschach Test") marshalled research and observation of contemporary and historic women to argue that women often find themselves in a "damned if you do and damned if you don't" situation. Jamieson observed that the climate pushes women to transcend the traditional bind of femininity, in which women who follow male-coded leadership models risk being perceived as too "masculine," "hard," and "unlikeable," while "feminine" women risk the charge that they lack the appropriate characteristics for leadership. Further, Jamieson has given the following five *binds* that shape contemporary culture and its view of sex-stereotypes:

1. Women can exercise either wombs or their brains, but not both.
2. Women who speak out are immodest and will be shamed; women who are silent will be ignored.
3. Women are subordinate, whether they claim to be different from or the same as men.

4. Women who are considered feminine will be seen as incompetent; women who are considered competent will be seen as unfeminine.
5. As men age, they become wise and powerful; as women age, they become wrinkled and superfluous.

Prevalent sex-role stereotype is further established by a published report titled "The Double-Bind Dilemma for Women in Leadership: Damned if You Do, Doomed if You Don't," based on surveys of men and women in corporate leadership (*Catalyst*, 2007). This report indicated that women face extreme stereotyping that leaves them a narrow path to tread as leaders. Women leaders who seem to conform to feminine stereotypes are likely to face the perception that they are "too soft," while women who seem to conform to masculine stereotypes likewise risk seeming—"too tough". Moreover, women must meet higher standards of competency than men, and they find it more difficult than men to gain their peers' regard as both competent and likeable (while men find it possible to be both).

Armed forces as a professional choice, is associated with the exhibition of masculine traits, viz. vigour, strength, chivalry, courage, robustness etc. which is at crossroads to societal expectations, thus, awarding it the status of an all-male profession. According to Eagly and Karau (2002), gendering of leadership roles does occur within organizations. Leaders of each sex are more effective when they are in a leadership role congruent with their gender or numerically dominated by their gender. Women fare less well in situations in which leadership is defined in masculine terms, such as in military. Men fare less well where leadership is defined in less masculine terms, such as in educational and social service organizations. However, both past and present stands witness to the fact that females are consistently shining out in armed forces as a vocation and accomplishing the Herculean task of breaking this sex-role stereotype.

Overcoming the Fear of Success

Women leaders' behaviour repertoire is limited, both at the organizational as well as societal level, because they pay a heavy price in terms of negative evaluations for adopting stereotypically male behaviours (Heilman, Wallen, Fuchs and Tamkins, 2004). Thus, they have a fear and anxiety associated with their success.

At organizational level, there is a very narrow band of acceptable behaviour for women leaders, and women walk a tightrope in trying to stay within this narrow band. The organizational demands are at crossroads to the societal expectations. Women leaders from large traditional corporations are expected to be tough, but not too macho; to be ambitious, but recognize that they would not receive equal opportunities; to be independent, but follow the advice of others; and to take risks, but avoid failure (Morrison, White and Velsor, 1992). Clearly, women have less freedom than do men to display a wider range of leadership styles without facing criticism.

At individual level, when female applies for the defence forces, it is more a sort of venture into the unknown field than exercise of a good initial choice by her. Parents at that stage are least bothered because they postpone their apprehensions to the day she will be selected. Society, however, consistently has its reservations on the approach of girls to the armed forces. After going through the Services Selection Board (SSB) during selection, she has a feel of what she is venturing into and she starts mustering the preferences of a much more comfortable life or carrying on with the same adventure. Getting selected, stirs a mixed feeling in her—a feeling of joyous fear and anxiety for the future. More so, parents get into a dilemma of fulfilling the daughter's wishes or societal expectations. The grand old generation of society states the decision as, "Daughter is going out of hands, who's going to marry her?" Their notion of 'settlement' focuses primarily on marriage and rearing of kids. The middle generation says, "Let's see what happens, now-a-days, youngsters don't listen." And the younger generation says, "Why one wants to get out of luxury and venture the forbidden areas?" Hence, society judges the decision ambivalently, putting both the aspirant as well as her parents into a state of dilemma. Fear of failure is mixed with the impending fear of success also, as it may threat her image as a woman. It may project her as a rough, tomboyish and a rude individual with killer instinct. Thus, making armed forces a final choice becomes an Achilles' heel for her and brave are the ones who overcome the fear of success and become an officer into the Forces.

Breaking the Glass Ceiling and Maternal Walls

The 'glass ceiling' is a metaphorical transparent barrier that keeps women away from rising above a certain level in organizations (Morrison and

Glinow, 1990). One explanation to this is discrimination, which often occurs in such subtle forms as increasing women's probability of failure, denying them access to developmental opportunities, or presenting only stereotypical challenges (Nelson and Burke, 2000). Related to this glass ceiling is the idea of 'glass walls', which are barriers that constrain women in support positions rather than allowing them to move to positions of responsibility that are perceived to be directly contributing to the success of an organization (Heilman, 2001). Another point in the issue is the 'maternal walls' where women are assumed to carry on maternal roles after a certain stage and this may cause a hurdle in organization's progress. So, they are assumed to rise only up to a certain level in their career. Much of these facts may be true in armed forces, which might be mistakenly disguised under the name of operational constraints and may prove to be an obstacle for women officers in deriving job satisfaction.

Enhancing Personal Effectiveness and Purposefulness

Modern feminist theory proposes that women lead differently than men and has a 'feminine advantage' with them. Women have the attributes and skills necessary for more effective leadership including a more interactional leadership style, the ability to build consensus, a tendency to empower others and a greater ability to nurture others. They operate not from the top but from the centre of the circle (Helgeson and Fritz, 1998). However, identical leader behaviours may be viewed with disfavour when displayed by a woman and in a positive light when by a man. As Wajcman (1998) persuasively points out that, "the belief that women in work organizations are naturally more consensual, but that could be the expression of a relative lack of power rather than a characteristic of womanhood per se." Thus, women had to counter such prejudices also. After getting registered as a cadet in the academy, she encounters different set of attitudes and expectations. Instructors expect her to be at equal footing with men in all her endeavours, while she has certain prejudices regarding self-concept, efficacy and her conduct that the society has fed her since birth. During training, certain verbal and non-verbal gestures are perceived by her as a notion of indecency and instil moral turpitude in her. Also, the identity crisis with initial setbacks in her performance deflates her morale to achieve a purpose in life. Rosener (1990) stated that special abilities and characteristics most often associated with women are of particular importance in contemporary work settings because women are more likely than men to feel important, included and energized.

Notwithstanding the same, she makes her way through and leaves no stone unturned to conform to the desired standards of behaviour. Resultantly, women officers have proved to have the spirit, the courage and the will to carry on. They have excelled in training academies with a deep sense of purpose to serve the nation in broader perspective. They have not only enhanced their personal effectiveness by having openness to feedback but also resolved to improve upon their limitations through painstaking efforts. Most importantly, this is not only because of their commitment towards the decision to join the forces, but also because they find a deeper sense in serving the humanity. They have transcended themselves beyond the ideas of 'I, me, and myself'; and have reached the zone of 'Universal Goodness' in service to the nation.

Bridging the Attitudinal Distance

Schein (2001) proposed that men view successful managers as masculine. And women managers were characterized as less competent, less active, less emotionally stable, less independent, and less rational than male managers. Similarly, in armed forces, it is evident that the prevalent prejudices towards females, masculine environment and regimented lifestyle posed a great deal of hazards in their adjustment to the environment. Their emergence into totally male dominated arena did initially create embarrassing moments for both, but greater problem for men.

Wrapped in their tradition of graciousness and respect to women, most gentlemen officers could not treat their female counterparts at par with themselves. Senior officers pampered them as their daughters and felt any assignment given as a burden on the soft shoulders. Moreover, their subordinates were also men who belong to conservative families where they see women only in traditional roles as mothers, sisters or daughters. Consequently, men hushed their talks and behaved differently while the woman officer was around. Eagly, Makhijani and Klonsky (1992) found that when women assume male-dominated leadership roles, in which autocratic styles are the norm, and men are the evaluators, women face considerable bias in the evaluation of what constitutes effective leader behaviour. And, thus, women leaders are seen as more threatening by male subordinates especially when their leadership style is stereotypically masculine.

Over the years and having come a long way now, men have realized that these women in uniform are their efficient and able co-workers. The time is not far when we may use the term 'sisters-in-arms' as equivalent to 'brothers-in-arms'. Equally, women have learned to behave more assertively as well as compassionately after understanding the psyche of their colleagues and men.

Role Stress—An Officer and a Lady

In the era of modern warfare and low-intensity conflicts, overcoming psychological stress is more important than physical combat. As commissioned officers in crisp uniform with stars/stripes at the age of 22 to 23 years, they may often have subordinates almost of the age of their father. Hence, from day one, it is a challenge and leadership qualities are under test. Women are graced with a double-edged weapon having feelings of commitment and precision at one-edge and nurturance, perceptiveness and expressivity at the other; either facet enables them to handle persistent stress with immense resilience. One edge equips them to be an effective officer and manage the professional life; while the other edge is used to empathize with the subordinates, counsel and direct their pent-up feelings along with channelling their energies. A balance is struck by the women officers between their twin roles of a lady and an officer while maintaining dignity of either role. Many officers are married to gentlemen officers in the armed forces or in civil where they have added duties of a wife and a daughter-in-law. Thus, role switching is inevitable and they manage it well.

Gender-Role Spillover

Gender-role spillover is the carryover of gender-based expectations into the workplace and it has different consequences for women than for men (Gutek and Morasch, 1990). For instance, by meeting people's expectations of what makes a good leader, women may forsake their expectations of what constitutes appropriate female behaviour. Looking to the same, women officers have to be cautious of such a spillover during their service in defence forces.

Moral and Ethical Perspective

Armed forces as a vocation require the exercise of crudest forms of behaviour, which may be brutal and unethical at times but are essential for safeguarding the nation. The behaviours may include spying, concealing identities, deceiving informers, breach of trust and killing militants or plan to blast off enemies. Initially, females perceived such behaviours as unethical and immoral, but gradually they have aligned their ethics to the commitment towards the nation and tried to come out of the pertinent jeopardy. Also, they have proved themselves to be maintaining the highest standards of loyalty and integrity during the service.

After glancing through the various perspectives associated to the females' entry into the services, following are the various recommendations for making the defence services more approachable and compatible for females:

Recommendations at Societal and Organizational Levels

Role of Society: Professing and Practising a Psychologically Androgynous Culture

It is high time for Indian society to realize that biological sex should not be the only determinant to allocate jobs to individuals. Society, including parents, owes a great responsibility to this budding human capital for unfolding the creative talent of either sex. With the diversity of jobs and work-setting, the art-of-living lies in possessing both masculine and feminine attributes by an individual and situation appropriate usage of the either attributes. Both males and females should be promoted to be psychologically androgynous so that the nation does not miss out the services of a worthy human capital. Moreover, society should provide an appropriate platform to females for joining the services.

Role of Parents

Parents are key gatekeepers to their daughters' career and generally remain dubious of the armed forces as a career for their children. Usually, they prefer their daughters to pursue college education or at least learn a trade rather than enlist to the services. But, if their daughter has a strong aptitude and interest towards the services then they must facilitate her choice rather than being an inhibitor to the chosen goal.

Role of Educational Institutions

NCC and NSS schemes in the schools are perhaps the first interface of the student with the disciplined and arduous life, like that of armed forces. However, with the greater burden of studies in the senior classes, the ignited flame for an adventurous life is gradually doused, especially in females. Along with, a word of caution floats in context to the medical problems the female might face, if she further ventures into the area. In such a scenario, educational institutions can play a significant role in keeping the flame vibrant by promoting the adventurous females with due reinforcement in terms of their marks or extra time with the teachers. However, it in no way mean that they should totally undermine their scholastic performance, rather, they should facilitate these zestful students in striking a balance between their outdoors and academics.

Role of Vocational Guidance Councillors

Armed forces as a career should not be in the secondary list of jobs with the councillors. Neither, the career should be posed as a forbidden choice. Rather, they should promote women aspirants to join the magnificent services, which will enhance their latent skills and cherish their dream in most unique fashion. Also, the future prospects should also be adequately highlighted.

Role of Armed Forces as an Organization

- A "life-less ordinary" campaign should be proliferated at mass level not only in urban schools but at the *rural level also* by the representatives of armed forces. This will be a revelation for the much naïve students to choose on their role-models to emulate. Also, it will help in getting the best talent of the country, especially females, to the armed forces which have yet not been captivated due to the lack of awareness about the Services.

- Enthralling stands and stalls at careers fairs (e.g., Higher Options, Cork Careers Open Day, etc.) should be promoted for rapid transmission of information about the services and participation of women.
- School tours of military installations should be conducted after due permission from the relevant authorities. It will enable the students to have first-hand information about the work-setting and job demands of the enchanting career. It will weed out the prevalent stigma about the hardships that women face during the services and will project the reality in its true colours. Also, it will bridge the unobvious differences between the outside charm and the inner realities during the services. Resultantly, for those who choose the career thereafter, will be more committed, confident and better prepared for rendering their services to the nation.
- Online websites and blogs can be created for enhanced information search and retrieval about the armed forces. Certain online queries, if, answered by the active serving women officers will catalyze the process.

Role of Service Officers

- *For Women Officers*: Versatility in women officers will only flourish when they will eschew their perception of self as a 'lady'. They have to assertively accept that they are an officer first and a lady next. Resultantly, in case of adversities, they will never throw their face in the towel and will stand upright to face the music with all vigour and strength and without seeking support from anybody else.
- *For Senior Officers*: They must perceive female officers at par with male officers in best of their capabilities and should assign them tasks in the similar manner, except the roles that are prohibited for them. This will reduce the impression of female officers as 'secondary citizens' in the unit.It will also result in balancing the either ends without any frustration amongst both female and male officers who otherwise may feel that the other group is being unduly benefited because of the greater attention of their seniors towards them.
- *For Colleagues/Brother Officers*: True professionalism is a mark of the success for any organization, and armed forces are not an

exception to it. Task completion should be carried out with precision and without any compassion towards the sex of an individual. Camaraderie should flourish to an extent of professionalism but should not cross the laid out limits.

Role of Mass Media in Image Projection

- There are certain threats associated to the image of the armed forces as a profession, viz., arduous nature of the job: aggressive and masculine environment; doubts over career prospects and transferability of skills; and social stigma attached to the job, i.e., women are perceived to be in minority in the defence forces. Media should not only highlight the daring aspects but also the consequences of those daring aspects involved in the services which earn supreme respect to self and renders the brave hearts, males as well as females, a purpose in life.
- Also, post-retirement avenues should be extensively highlighted. The increasing demand of well-groomed versatile female officers is increasing day by day. Female officers after retiring have a wonderful launch pad to the corporate world, which welcomes their sharpened skills with open arms and where sky is the limit for them.
- Most importantly, *eulogizing suicide cases* to make a spicy treat for its viewers is a notion of extreme irresponsibility on the part of the media. Such cases are not because of the service environment alone but are accountable to certain personal and contextual reasons also, which in no way outnumbers the cases in the civil world. Moreover, such an act by the mass media, only multiplies the hardships for females to join the services.

Conclusion

Yes, women have it in them!! They have proved their mettle time and again at various fronts of this arduous profession. Combating the sex-role stereotype, they have been androgynous enough to realize their potentials and have successfully sailed through the 'life-less ordinary'. However, for less undulating sailing through the tempest of rough sea, there is an urgent call for the society to navigate the ship in the right direction at the right time.

It will not only help in accomplishing the task but also bring valour to the nation in terms of effective performance using the best of the capabilities of a momentous human capital.

References

Bem, S.L. "The Measurement of Psychological Androgyny." *Journal of Consulting and Clinical Psychology* 47 (1974): 783.

Cline, J. "Stress Fractures in Female Army Recruits: Implications of Bone Density, Calcium Intake, and Exercise." *Journal of the American College of Nutrition* 17, No. 2 (2004): 128.

Eagly, A.H. and Karau, S.J. "Role Congruity Theory of Prejudice toward Female Leaders." *Psychological Review* 109 (2002): 573–98.

Eagly, A.H., Makhijani, M.G. and Klonsky, B.G. "Gender and the Evaluation of Leaders: A Meta-Analysis." *Psychological Bulletin* 111 (1992): 3–22.

Gutek, B.A. and Morasch, B. "Sex-Ratios and Sex Role Spillover." *Business Communication Quarterly* 53, No. 3 (1990): 68–77.

Heilman, M.E. "Description and Prescription: How Gender Stereotypes Prevent Women's Ascent Up the Organizational Ladder." *Journal of Social Issues* 57 (2001): 657–74.

Heilman, M.E., Wallen, A.S., Fuchs, D. and Tamkins, M.M. "Penalties for Success: Reactions to Women Who Succeed at Male Gender-Typed Tasks." *Journal of Applied Psychology* 89 (2004): 416–27.

Helgeson, V.S. and Fritz, H.L. "A Theory of Unmitigated Communion." *Personality and Social Psychology Review* 2, No. 3 (1998): 173–183.

Jamieson, K.H. *Beyond the Double Bind: Women and Leadership*. New York: Oxford University Press, 1995.

Kessler, R.C., Chiu, W.T., Demler, O., Merikangas, K.R. and Walters, E.E. "Prevalence, Severity, and Comorbidity of 12-Month DSM-IV Disorders in the National Comorbidity Survey Replication." *Archives of General Psychiatry* 62, No. 6 (2005): 617–27.

Morrison, A.M. and Glinow, M.A.V. "Women and Minorities in Management." *American Psychologist* 45 (1990): 200–208.

Morrison, A.M., White, R.P. and Velsor, E.V. *Breaking the Glass Ceiling: Can Women Reach the Top of America's Largest Corporations?* Reading, MA: Addison-Wesley, 1992.

Nelson, D.L. and Burke, R.J. *Gender, Work Stress and Health*. Washington, DC: APA Books, 2002.

Post-Traumatic Stress Disorder, *National Institute of Mental Health* (June 11, 2008), <http://www.nimh.nih.gov/health/publications/anxiety-disorders/post-traumatic-stress-disorder.shtml>, retrieved on 2009-06-05.

Rosener, S. "Definition and Conceptualizations of Stress in Organizations." *Organizational Behaviour and Human Performance* 25 (1990): 184–21.

Schein, V.E. "A Global look at Psychological Barriers to Women's Progress in Management." *Journal of Social Issues* 57 (2001): 675–88.

Taylor, S.E., Klein, L.C., Lewis, B.P., Gruenewald, T.L., Gurung, A.R. and Updegraff, J.A. "Bio-Behavioural Responses to Stress in Females: Tend-and-Befriend, not Fight-or-Flight." *Psychological Review* 107, No. 3 (2000): 411–29.

The Double-Bind Dilemma for Women in Leadership: Damned if You Do, Doomed if You Don't, *Catalyst* (June 23, 2007), <https://www.catalyst.org/file/45/theper cent20double-bindper cent20dilemmaper cent20forper cent20womenper cent20inper cent20leadershipper cent20damnedper cent20if per cent20youper cent20do,per cent20doomedper cent20ifper cent20youper cent20don't.pdf>, retrieved on 25 May 2008.

Wajcman, J. *Managing like a man: Women and men in corporate management.* University Park, PA: The Pennsylvania State University, 1998.

Women in Combat: Frequently Asked Questions, *Center for Military Readiness* (November 22, 2004), <http://www.cmrlink.org/WomenInCombat.asp?DocID= 237>, retrieved on 2009-06-21.

Women in Military, *Wikipedia* (Jan 17, 2009), <http://en.wikipedia.org/wiki/Women_in_the_military> retrieved on 2009-04-17.

Ziegler, M. *Bella: Ms. Abzug Goes to Washington.* New York: Saturday Review Press, 1972, p. 73.

8

Status of Women Hawkers in New Economic Environment: A Case of Navi Mumbai

Manjari Srivastava and Sumita Sarkar

Women in Microentrepreneurship

Feminization of poverty is emerging as a typical trend in developing nations as an offshoot of globalization and open market economy. Fostering the entrepreneurship of women and the development of microenterprises can be viewed within this entitlement-capability framework, as an appropriate strategy for expanding entitlements and mitigating the feminisation of poverty. Sen (1983: 754) and feminist economists like Lucas (1999) and Agarwal (1990) have opined that the deficiency of traditional development economics was its failure to focus on "entitlements of people and the 'capabilities' these entitlements generate". Economic development is a process of expanding people's capabilities and derivatively economic development can also be viewed in terms of an expansion of entitlements. Entitlements are the alternative bundles of commodities a person can command within society and also through using one's full rights and opportunities. Overall, entitlement is influenced by ownership or 'endowment' and exchange possibilities ('exchange entitlement'). Ownership of or access to factors of production, such as land if one is a farmer, or education and training if labour is the chief factor one owns, will thus impact on one's overall level of entitlement.

For most people the income they earn through selling their labour, or the utilization of their entrepreneurial talents, and the prices of the commodities they wish to buy (the latter being related to 'exchange entitlement') will determine their entitlements. Usually, the entitlements of women are much less than that of men. Yet, entitlements in turn determine acquisition of capabilities, i.e., the ability to do this or that (e.g., be well nourished) or the failure to procure some other capabilities, such as securing a reasonable standard of well-being for household (Sen, 1983: 755).

Political power and institutional structures, cultural and social constraints also have an important impact on aggregate entitlements. Gender discrimination within these structures and constraints faced by women, therefore, provides further justification for gender-specific measures to correct imbalance and remove impediments to improvements in entitlements. This necessitates scholarly interest to understand microentrepreneurship and the women engagement very closely in relation with the changing economy and market environment.

There is no general yardstick to define microenterprise as it varies from country to country. In the US, for example, microenterprises are those with five employees and less, while a small business is categorized as one with more than five and up to 500 employees. In New Zealand, 99.5 per cent of businesses are 'small', have less than 100 employees and account for 60.3 per cent of employment. Of these small businesses, the majority are microenterprises, according to the US categorization, with fewer than five employees. They account for 85.7 per cent of enterprises and 23.3 per cent of employment (Statistics: New Zealand, 1998). A significant number of these entrepreneurs belong to women population.

In the context of developing nations, since 1990s, the participation of women in microentrepreneurship has been multiplying in numbers. However, studies on women in microentrepreneurship are not much heeded by the scholars, and no precise yardstick exists to define women microentrepreneurs as one of the major part of country's labour statistics. A significant section of microentrepreneurs are the vendors. The uncounted women labour force in microentrepreneurship, particularly women vendors, remains economically unrecognized, as they are more likely to be working in the informal rather than in the formal sector. According to Bhowmik (1997), Mumbai has the largest number of street vendors around 250,000, Kolkata 150,000, Ahmedabad and Patna 80,000, and

Indore, Bangalore and Bhubaneshwar 30,000. In another study by Bhowmik (2001) it was found street-vending profession is mainly male oriented (around 60 to 85 %), whereas it is primarily a women's domain in Imphal, about 3 per cent.

In case of women street vendors, a census conducted in Patna by an NGO, 'Nidan' in 1997 showed that 21.56 per cent of the vendors are women and 78.44 per cent are male vendors. In Mumbai, the women vendors can also be considered as 'marginalized' as statistics shows that the men outnumber female workforce, more so in the case of mobile street vendors. A random sample survey conducted by SNDT University Mumbai (2000) found that only 11 per cent women vendors operated in the established market (vendors having a fixed place for vending). Extent of female participation in hawking/vending is thus very less compared to the males.

Though the present paper brings up the issue of women vendors, it would be equally important to note that whether it is a male or female vendor, their presence has impacted the economy though their contribution is hardly felt. Street vendors also contribute to the city's growth and commerce. Their sheer numbers result in contribution in hundreds of crores of rupees. According to Sharma (1998), who headed the Brihan Mumbai Municipal Corporation commissioned TISS-YUVA study of street vendors. Mumbai annually consumes only vegetables and fruits worth Rs 750 crore in the wholesale market. The retail price is 25 to 40 per cent higher than the wholesale price. Most of these are sold to the consumer by hawkers and vendors. The total annual contribution of 2,00,000 vendors and hawkers taken together in Mumbai comes to a whopping Rs 6000 crores. In Kolkata, it is estimated that the total annual turnover of all the hawkers put together is Rs 3,000 crores. However despite these, vendors are subjected to enormous harassment by the authorities.

The population of street vendors in urban area is steadily growing and a host of factors responsible has been identified from various studies (Bhowmik, 2001; Tiwari, 2000) for the growth of street vendors in India. One of the important factors of increasing street vendors is the closer of factories and shrinkage of employment of the formal sector (Bhowmik and More, 2001). After closing down of some textile mills in Mumbai, Ahmedabad and Kolkata (Bhowmik, 2001; Breman, 2001) formal sector workers in Ahmedabad and Mumbai and 50 per cent in Kolkata, have been chosen this street vending profession for livelihood (Bhowmik, 2001).

Bhowmik (2001) pointed out a very interesting factor responsible behind the growing number of street vendors that is the increase of small and petty producers, including in manufacturing, small-scale, home-based industries. Street vendors sell different kinds of goods such as clothes and hosiery, leather moulded plastic goods and different kinds of household necessary goods, which are manufactured in small scale or home-based industries where large numbers of workers are employed. Apart from non-agricultural product, street vendors sell vegetable and fruits also. Thus, they help to sustain other group of workers by providing the market for home-based manufacturing product and as well as agricultural products (Bhownik, 2001).

Another factor behind the increase in street vendors is the demand from the urban rich. Street vendors support urban rich to provide daily requirements as available on their doorsteps because some street vendors built up their profession in front of housing complexes (Tiwari, 2000). On the contrary, lower income group of people are also benefitted and spend a higher portion of their income on purchase from street vendors because their goods are cheap and affordable. It is estimated that around 30 per cent of Mumbai workforce have at least one meal a day from vendors. It is noted that the urban poor survive themselves by working in the informal sector (Bhowmik, 2001).

Focus of Present Study

The present study explores the status of a section of women engaged in microentrepreneurship, working as vendors/hawkers in order to earn the livelihood for family, in the area of Navi Mumbai. It aims to explore their working status, social networking, linkages with market, their socio-economic background and such other factors related to the street vending and hawking.

Areas of Study

Navi Mumbai, a satellite city of Mumbai, was chosen as the place for taking up the present study on women hawkers. The city, at present, is having the population of about 0.80 million. With developing infrastructure and all the modern facilities and services available and industries ready to participate in its growth, this city is poised to be among the finest cities of India. Being the satellite city of Mumbai, it also shares features similar to the main city, especially in terms of earning livelihood by the poor males/females occupying public places especially for hawking, street vending and even begging by the poor sections of local community. The present paper focuses on the women workforce working as vendors/hawkers in Vashi and Belapur nodes of Navi Mumbai. It explores their socio-economic background and their struggle for livelihood in the era of economic boom. According to the municipal officials, there are more than 1,500 women street vendors/hawkers in the identified areas of these two nodes.

Methodology

The present paper is based on a sample survey of 108 women vendors on the roads/footpaths in Vashi and Belapur nodes of Navi Mumbai. The sample survey was supported by qualitative analysis based on a few case studies and also the focus group discussions. Interviews were used as the major tool for collecting information, along with indirect observations spread over six weeks of data collection. The main attempt was to explore their status as hawkers, their role in this informal sector, and understanding their life situations. The variables, like socio-economic background, educational level, causes of migration, support at home and support (or threat) from concerned government, nature of hawking activity, health status etc., are highlighted. Sample data is supported and enriched by case studies and a few focused group discussions.

Data Analysis and Interpretations

It was observed that a large number of rural people migrate from nearby villages in search of employment. Among this migrated rural population, a significant number of women are engaged in vegetable hawking in these two nodes (Vashi and CBD Belapur areas) of Navi Mumbai and can be easily seen working at construction sites or as street vendors. The low cost of entry into the hawking trade as well as involved flexibility are the attractive factors for these women taking to hawking and vending. The latter is more applicable to a few women vendors.

The main concern of the study was to explore the socio-economic status of women vendors/hawkers, their organizing and social networking to find a support in the society and their health status. These issues are discussed here on the basis of research finding.

Socio-economic Status of Women Hawkers

In the study, out of the 108 women vendors/hawkers, average age of women is found to be 26 years, ranging from 18 years to 65 years. A majority of them are married (86.4 %), having minimum one child. The size of the family ranges from four to seven members. Most of the women interviewed originate from poor families and are married off to the males who are also engaged in casual and informal jobs, including some of them also being vegetable vendors and hawkers. Majority of the women vendors/hawkers under focus earn less than Rs 3,000 per month, their average monthly income is Rs 2,750. These vendors in Navi Mumbai are engaged in this activity only for the sake of sustaining or supplementing the family income.

These women are from diverse communities and mostly belong to the backward classes of Maharashtrian community (82 %). More than 80 per cent of them are illiterate. Even a few literate ones (17 %) have hardly studied beyond the primary level of education.

Bhowmik (2001) in his study found that around 25 to 35 per cent street vendors are illiterate in most of the major cities while around 20 to 40 per cent street vendors have primary education. The men's daily average income is around Rs 70 in almost all major cities except Patna where it is slightly low, around Rs 50. Women earn considerably low in between Rs 40 to Rs 50 but in Patna, it is quite low like men's daily wage rate, around Rs 30 generally (Bhowmik, 2001).

Sarkar (2006) in her study of women workers engaged in the construction industry found that certain social tensions like family disputes and lack of ownership of agriculture lands or unviable land holdings often compelled such workers to move from their native villages towards city where they perceive better bargain for livelihood. Similar reasons are also cited by Bhowmik (2001), where he states that most of street vendors have migrated from rural areas to search better paid jobs in urban areas because poverty as well as lack of opportunities for gainful employment in the rural areas. It is one of the most important and easiest means of earning for rural poor as it requires less financial input and relatively low skills as comparing other occupations.

A brief profile of family background and income levels of the women hawkers under present focus is provided in Table 1:

Table 1 *Socio-economic Profile of Women Hawkers in Navi Mumbai*

(N=108)

Average age	26 years
Percentage of married women	86.4%
Average household size	5 members
Percentage belonging to the backward classes	82%
Percentage of non-Maharashtrians	8%
Percentage of literates	17%
Average monthly income of female hawkers	Rs 2,750

Observations from the information on socio-economic profile reflect that these self-employed women belong to the families which mainly live below the poverty line or just barely manage to live. In most cases (more than 90 %), their contribution towards household income ranges between Rs 2,500 to Rs 3,000 per month, with a monthly average of Rs 2,750. Almost 86 per cent of them are married and with average age of 26 years. Majority is coming from backward strata of society with no education. They have entered in this livelihood to support their families. However, their husbands or male members in the family are mostly engaged in other kind of jobs in the informal and service sector, informal economy, requiring these women to opt for hawking for supplementing the family income. There were a very few who owned land or had farming business at the place of their origin. Some of them, despite owning a land which was not fertile had to look beyond their villages for livelihood. With hardly any education, poor family background and total ignorance about any kind of governmental or NGO support, they had no other choice than to work as a vendors/hawkers, selling fruits and vegetables. Studies have shown that socio-economic background of women entrepreneurs has a relationship to the type of informal sector activity they engage in. And success of those women who venture into informal sector depends upon enabling business environment and socio-economic factors that are critical to the success of self-employed person such as age, level of education, training and access to the means of production.

Organization and Social Networking

On the issues related to organized vending, social support and networking women vendors opined that earning money is crucial for them and gender difference does not matter as long as they earn money for the family. About 70 per cent of them had the consent and support of their family for this work. There were cases where women faced harassment from their family members. In this context, Hill (1969), viewed that women's economic activity may be adopted or rejected depending upon the availability of assistance of children and family.

A further probe of these entrepreneurial women brings out the fact that they have not formed any collective group as hawkers. Also, they have not joined any formal organization. They instead have preferred to work at the individual level. Hence, there is absence of any kind of union, which can voice their rights and issues. They have also informed about the absence of any support from government officials or politicians. Street vending is not officially permitted even in the main city of Mumbai, though there are licensed street vendors (15,000 in number as reported in *Hindustan Times*, 12 June, 2008) in certain restricted areas of Mumbai. They always fear eviction from local police. Section 34 of the Police Act empowers the police to remove any obstructions on the streets. Therefore, even the presence of any kind of small union of street vendors brings no help. The case is all the more worse for women street vendors. They are highly unorganized and more vulnerable compared to their male counterparts. Ninty-one per cent of the women hawkers have chosen a particular place in these two nodes of Navi Mumbai for their daily vegetable hawking. Only a few of them (9 %) go for door-to-door vending (Table 2). Interestingly, those women hawkers or vendors who sell the fish are not disturbed by the police or municipal officials. It is assumed that they might be the original settlers of the area (fishermen families).

Table 2 *Information on Organization and Economic Activity (N=108)*

Women having family support	70%
Support from government	Nil
Presence of formal body	Nil
Women working on a fixed place as vendors	91%
Women vending door to door	9%
Women selling perishable items(fruits, vegetables, fish)	80%
Women selling non-perishable items	20%

Discussions with them also highlighted the fact that 80 per cent of them are involved in selling perishable items like fruits, vegetables, and fish. Only 20 per cent of them are selling other items like clothes, artefacts, etc. Capital investment into their trade is very low and so is the income generation. This is because they sell goods in small quantity (low capital) and women hawkers unlike their male counterparts have to give time to other activities like, take care of daily needs of the family. Such dual status makes them overburdened and vulnerable economically as well as socially.

The family support they get is not enough to wade through the precarious life. Moreover, the absence of organized union and neglect from government clearly reflect the discrimination towards the female street vendors. In general, it is found that the rate of unionization in the informal sector is low. The different studies conducted on street vendors in Mumbai, Delhi and Ahmedabad show that less than 20 per cent of them are members of union. Most of these vendors/hawkers who are members of some union are males, as the female vendors constitute a small section of the profession. In most cases, they are marginalized. Ahmedabad is an exception as the female vendors constitute a sizeable section (40%) and they are also unionized mainly due to sustained efforts of Self-Employed Women's Association (SEWA). The existence of SEWA as a union of women in the informal sector has encouraged females from the urban poor to take to street vending. Interestingly, Ahmedabad is the only city where the male vendors have the lowest level of unionization.

The non-official/illegal status of street vending along with low level of unionization has given rise to an alarming rate of illegal rent seeking by local officials, police and goons. These are also legal rent, penalty or redemption charges levied by some local self-bodies, like the Mumbai Municipal Corporation. Incidentally, no such official charges are levied by the Municipal Corporation of Navi Mumbai. NASVI's (National Alliances of Street Vendors) study of street vendors found that they pay between 10 per cent and 20 per cent of their earnings as rent. In Mumbai the total rent collected amounts Rs 4 billion annually. In Delhi, Manushi Trust, a women's organization, conducted a public hearing on problems of street vendors and cycle rickshaw pullers in the city in 2000. It was found that Rs 500 million is collected as rents daily from these people. These findings were later endorsed by the Central Vigilance Commission. However, in Ahmedabad where female vendors are unionized, rent seeking is much less. Hence legalizing the profession and encouraging trade unions would be means through which rent seeking could be reduced. But these are also the precise reasons why the authorities may resist such moves.

Health and Hygiene

Present study reveals that women vendors suffer from various kinds of ailments mainly due to hard labour, ignorance and malnutrition. There are about 82 per cent of the respondents who suffer gynaecological problems (like miscarriage, infections, excessive bleeding, irregular menstruation, etc.). About a half of them complained about joint pains and body aches. It was more common among the door-to-door vendors and women vendors in local trains of Navi Mumbai. About 77 per cent of these hawker women had a complaint of gastritis, ulcer, etc. A study of street vendors in Mumbai conducted by SNDT Women's University and ILO (2000) showed that an overwhelming majority of them suffered from ailments related to stress—hyperacidity, migraine, hypertension, loss of sleep, etc. (Table 3).

Though these women hawkers sell fruits and vegetables, the irony is that these vendors themselves were not getting nutritious meals. They

Table 3 *Incidences of Physical Ailment*

Gynaecological problems	82%
Body pain/joint pain	50%
Gastro/abdominal problems	77%

were more concerned towards feeding their children and husbands than themselves. Their priority was to be able to sell most of the items till late evening to make money. Some respondents shared their views on suffering from anxiety of not being able to take proper care of their younger ones, insecurities of the future and also harassment from the local goons who collect money from them illegally. It was further found out that these vendors were living in shanties in unhygienic conditions. They do not have proper sanitation facilities. Incidents of sexual exploitation were also told by a few female vendors.

Suggestions to Improve Status of Marginalized Street Vendors

Following are some of the suggestions which may benefit women entrepreneurs who struggle to make a living as vendors/hawkers:

Self-regulation and Organization

Street vendors are an asset to the urban system and should be given opportunity to contribute to their own in development. The fact is no plan for improving the city can be successful without the participation of urban poor. They need to be integrated in the planning process and in the campaigns for better environment. The experience of another marginalized section of the urban workforce, namely the rag-pickers, has shown this. Rag pickers are regarded as a nuisance and they are blamed for spreading garbage. They are harassed by civic authorities and middle class residents associations. In fact, these people are engaged in activities that are very positive for cleaning environment as they collect recyclable material from the garbage. Instead of victimizing them, civic authorities should co-opt them in keeping the city clean. There are instances where this has happened and their results have been positive.

There are two well-known and reputed membership based organizations namely Self-Employed Women's Association (SEWA) and National Alliance of Street Vendors (NASVI) in India. SEWA, formed in 1972, is a trade union of women who earn their livelihoods by running small business. It is the first and the largest trade union of the informal entrepreneurs in India. SEWA is working with over 9,59,698 members in 2006. In

Ahmedabad, SEWA has been able to include rag pickers in the 'clean city' campaign.

In Mumbai, the 'Stree Mukti Sangathana', a women's organization has involved rag-pickers in beautification campaign in some parts of the suburbs. Such move not only benefits the urban environment but also restore the citizenship of marginalized. An example of community networking is evident from the street vendors' association, mainly NASVI (National Association of Street Vendors of India), initiated by SEWA in September 1998, to bring together the street vendor organizations all over India, so as to collectively struggle for macro-level changes. These had become imminent to support the livelihood of around 10 million vendors who stood severely threatened due to the outdated laws and changing policies, practices and attitudes of the powers that be.

In a study conducted by NASVI, it was found that, street vendors help the poor section of society, as lower income groups (and even middle class people) spend a higher proportion of their income in making purchases from the street vendors mainly because their goods are cheap and thus affordable. Had there been no street vendors in the cities, the plight of the urban poor would be worse than what it is at present. In this way, one section of the urban poor, namely, the street vendors help similar groups to survive. Though street vendors are viewed as a problem for urban governance, they are in fact the solution to some of the problems of the urban poor. By providing cheaper commodities, street vendors are in effect providing subsidy to the urban poor, something that the government should have done.

Providing Social Security

Vending is full of insecurity and uncertainty since vendors occupy road side and accidents occur at any time (Anjaria, 2006). In addition, the social security is the major problem for all workers who are engaged in the informal sector. Street vendors, being a part of the informal sector, are not eligible for getting these benefits though they work all the 365 days in a year. Most of the street vendors do not even know the term 'social security'.

A collective effort through forming union or organization can help improve vendors' condition by empowering them through providing strong social dialogue. The main role of these organizations is to negotiate with local authorities such as municipal corporations, police stations when they are threatened by local police or municipal authorities for occupying public space (Bhowmik, 2007). Study (NASVI, 2001) on street vendors in Ahmedabad, Bangalore, Delhi, Imphal, Kolkata, Mumbai, and Patna shows that less than 20 per cent street vendors are unionized in almost major cities but interestingly it is noted that in Ahmedabad 40 per cent street vendors are unionized under SEWA. This study (NASVI, 2001) also explored that street vendors pay their 10 to 20 per cent earning as bribes to local authorities. Thus, this is one of the reasons behind the poor income condition of street vendors. Competition among street vendors has appeared in India due to inadequate number of unions/associations for street vendors or inactive performances of unions or associations (Bhowmik, 2006). As the importance of street vendors in the urban informal sector is being realized different NGOs, SHGs, co-operatives through SEWA and NASVI are coming forward and now providing social security and credit arrangement but the numbers are very few.

NASVI has organized social security schemes for its members. NASVI, pressurized government to prescribe policy for street vendors. Recently, in 2005, NASVI has adopted a scheme that gives multiple benefits to its members. The scheme includes insurance coverage on health, house and property, accidental and natural death, and coverage for permanent and partial disability. According to this scheme, members give annual premium. This annual premium varies between Rs 70 to Rs 100, which is very affordable even for poorer street vendors (Bhowmik, 2006).

Self-Employment Women's Association (SEWA), started health care schemes for their members. Some schemes are in the form of group insurance. Union has also organized the healthcare scheme for members' children. SEWA has promoted NGOs and co-operatives is to take care health related activities. The co-operatives regularly conduct different programme regarding health, nutrition, and childcare (Bhowmik, 2006). Thus, SEWA's objectives are not only to enhance the self-reliance but also to improve their economic condition and to cover social security of its members.

NIDAN (NIDAN is the name of an NGO) in Patna, which is formed by NASVI, has come forward to provide support to street vendors in towns of Bihar. NIDAN offers group insurance scheme. It is one of the successful schemes of NIDAN. It has been organized for street vendors for their health care services such as hospitalization costs and life insurance. Initially, NIDAN organized programmes for street vendors to make them familiar with different schemes regarding Life Insurance Corporation of India (LIC) and General Insurance Corporation of India (GIC). Afterwards, it helped its members to get involved with several insurance groups among street vendors in Patna and other towns (Bhowmik, 2006).

Legalizing Street Vending

The basic problem of street vendors is that of the right to existence in urban informal sector. Vending is considered as illegal although it is estimated that around 2.5 per cent of the total urban poor survive and succeed by working in this occupation in India (GoI, 2004).

As per Article 19(1)(g) of the Constitution, the street vendors are recognized as workers. The right to carry on trade or business mentioned in Article 19(1)(g) of the Constitution, on street pavements, if properly regulated cannot be denied on the ground that the streets are meant exclusively for passing or re-passing and no other use. But still they are typically treated as encroachers of public space and very marginal of them are allowed to use particular location for their activities.

Legalization of street vendors can resolve the problem to some extent. This can be done by issuing a licence to street vendors. Street vendors are not trying only to earn a livelihood but also provide valuable services to the urban population. Thus, it is the duty of the State to protect the right of this segment of population to earn their livelihood since Article 39(a) of Constitution stated that "any citizens, men and women, have equal right to an adequate means of livelihood". Thus, the 'decent work' is the fundamental rights of any workers or citizens. But ground reality is different. They are considered as unlawful and eyesore entities. In the present situation, the unlicensed street vendor is vulnerable to all sorts of extortions from various quarters. The police, municipal authorities and other local goons exploit them and extract rents for allowing them to operate in specific areas.

Poor working condition, no safety at workplace and most important that unhygienic condition at workplace, especially for women have affected them.

Initiatives from government, NGOs and civic society can help in rehabilitating them in hawking zones, and thus allow them a safer and sustainable way of earning their livelihoods. A few NGOs, like the SEWA in Ahmedabad, NASVI have mobilized the hawkers/vendors for a better treatment from the government.

Micro-lending

Street vendors have scarce resources, namely, credit, for their trade. They have no access to credit from the formal financial institutions particularly for their economic activities being a part of the informal sector. Interestingly, it is noted that this vending process works on a turnover basis and they are surviving successfully. They solve this problem depending on private moneylenders and any other sources at an exorbitant rate of interest for running their small business enterprises. For instance, in Bhubaneswar, the credit is obtained from wholesaler to be paid back at the end of the day at high rate of interest, up to 110 per cent (Bhowmik, 2001) and sometimes it exceeds to 100 to 125 per cent per day (Jhabvala, 2000).

Micro-credit for the poor has emerged as an idea that appeals to several sections of vulnerable people. The famed "Grameen Bank" of Bangladesh initiated an experiment on micro-lending, more for women, supported by economist Muhammed Yunus in 1976. It expanded to several rural areas and empowered the villagers. It is a relevant example of women empowerment from marginalized section of society (a Muslim country with strong patriarchal traditions). In India, micro-credit is not a new concept. Leading national financial institutions like Small Industries Development Bank of India (SIDBI), National Bank for Agricultural and Rural Development (NABARD) and Rashtria Mahila Kosh (RMK) have played an important role in the micro-credit. Poor have been benefited by micro-credit system, at the same time; there has been a flip side of micro-credit as well. There is a great difficulty in actually turning a profit on small loans, because of lack of expertise from borrower's side. Secondly, in reality, loan does not reach to the poorest of the poor. Poorest have low income, worse health and education and it prevents them from investing the loan in high return activity. It has also been found that poorest get tiny loans which are not cost effective even for micro-credit programmes. Still, with training and skill upgradation, this lacuna can be overcome. NABARD has been running micro-lending activity with the Self-Help Groups (SHGs).

Another example is SEWA Bank, which was set up in 1974. It was started with an initial share capital Rs 60,000 collected from 5,000 women: most of them were street vendors. Now, at present it is running with 2,00,000 depositors and a working capital of Rs 850 million. SEWA helps to promote to form SHGs for micro-credit and other activities. SEWA's micro-credit programmes have been quite successful. Earlier, street vendors have used the standard loan from SEWA Bank as investment capital to upgrade their mode of selling but recently, SEWA Bank has introduced a special working capital loan for street vendors, which is called 'Daily Loan', where vendors can borrow and they repay back at the end of the day. SEWA has promoted NGOs and Co-operatives run exclusively by women and catering only to women through which street vendors' have access to institutional credit (Chen et al., 2003: 14).

On the other hand, National Alliance of Street Vendors of India (NASVI), an independent federation, a founding member of the international alliance of street vendor organizations called StreetNet, was set up 1998. NASVI is one common federation of street vendors' unions in the country. The main aim of NASVI is to bring together trade unions, co-operatives on behalf of street vendors to carry out their trade or occupations without hindrance.

NASVI has initiated to provide credit accessibility for street vendors through promotion of SHGs, co-operative trusts, federations and different micro-finance institutions, etc. NASVI has started to make direct link with institutional financial organization to street vendors to provide business loans. In case of credit accessibility, women can access more facilities than men from different organizations, like SHGs, NGOs, Co-operatives because these organizations rely more on women than men. As in almost all major cities, daily wage rate of women is quite low than men (Bhowmik, 2001). But, in case of credit accessibility, this is reverse.

It is apparent that women vendors, as an association can be benefitted through the micro-credit.

Concluding Remarks

The present study of women microentrepreneurs (hawkers/vendors) in Navi Mumbai, in relation to their demography, socio-economic status, and working conditions highlights significant information. The study reflects that these small scale women vendors are untouched by high tidal waves of developing economy, where the rich and the mighty are reaping utmost benefits and hardly leaving anything for the poor sections of Indian society. It is observed that compared to their male counterparts; females are more likely to have lower levels of education, lack of work experience, and relevant skills. This complicates the situation if they are heads of households and main income earners. Women hawkers/vendors have much more pressure on their time compared to men and had less time to learn new skills, for leisure and for sleep. They operate from an open rather than a covered space; they operate from the street rather than a cart or stall. Their place of work is also 'illegal'. The kind of trading in which they are involved is perishable goods which generate a lower volume of trade. The investment is very low, so are the profits. These women trader are working on individual basis, and do not employ other people. They are mostly illiterate and ignorant about the kind of helps available in terms of microfinance or skill upgradation. They are reluctant to take initiatives, and street vending is one of the few options they have for earning a living (or supplementing their family income), as this does not require high skill and high capital. Unfortunately, the government more or less remains indifferent towards the street vending as a legal activity, and views these vendors as irritants to the city's development. No need to mention that street vendors perform an important role in providing services to the urban population, especially the poor. Instead of recognizing their contribution, government is often hostile towards them. The goods sold by street vendors are usually consumed by those in the informal sector as they are cheap. In fact, we have situations where one section of the urban poor (street vendors) helps the other section of the urban poor by providing low priced goods. They need to be encouraged and helped to make a dignified living.

There are other important related issues concerning their health and unhygienic conditions of living, ignorance and illiteracy and other domestic duties which are simultaneously performed by these women hawkers/vendors.

There are some organizations and unions who have taken up the issues in a very serious manner. These organizations have made their contribution in providing support to street vendors and especially women vendor to some extent. Still looking at the magnitude of the problem and the growing population of urban poor in informal economy these efforts are less.

Though there exists a National Policy on Urban Street Vendors (2004), which has highlighted the important problems and provided very specific recommendations and suggested associations to come forward to organize vendors. The policy recommendation has remained on paper only.

The present study has again portrayed the sheer discrepancies existing in social system in India, and vulnerability of women workforce as microentrepreneurs. Research results should be used to take corrective measures for this marginalized section of developing economy.

References

Anjaria, S.J. "Street Hawkers and Public Space in Mumbai", *Economic and Political Weekly* (27 May 2006), pp. 2140–46.

Bhowmik, S.K. *Urban Response to Street Trading, India.* 1997. Available at <http://www.nasvinet.org> Census of Vendors by NIDAN, 1997.

———. "Hawkers in the Urban Informal Sector: A Study of Street Vendors in Seven Cities." National Alliance of Street Vendors in India (NASVI). 2001. <www.streetnet.org.za/English/page10.htm>

———. "Social Security for Street Vendors." *Seminar* 568 (December 2006), pp. 49–57.

———. "Street Vendors in Urban India: The Struggle for Recognition." In *Street Entrepreneurs: People, Place and Politics,* edited by A. Morales and J. Cross. New York, Routledge, 2007, pp. 92–107.

———. and More, N. "Coping with Urban Poverty: Ex-Textile Mill-Workers in Central Mumbai." *Economic and Political Weekly* (29 December 2001), pp. 4822–27.

Berman, J. "An Informal Labour System: End of Labour Market Dualism", *Economic and Political Weekly* (29 December 2001), pp. 4804–21.

Chen, Martha, Joabvala, Renana and Nanavati Reema. "Investment Climate for Female Informal Business: A Case Study from Urban and Rural India." World Development Report 2005, Background paper, 2003.

Hill, P. "Hidden Trade in Hausaland." *Man* 4, No. 3 (1969): 392–409.

Hindustan Times (12 June 2008).

Human Development Report, 2004.

ILO/SNDT/SEWA/EFI. *Round Table on Street Vendors.* 2000. Available at <http://www.karmayog.com/hawkers/sndtrtsv.htm>

Jhabvala, R. "The Role if Street Vendors in the Growing Urban Economies: SEWA Academy." Ahemdabad, India: Self-Employed Women's Association, 2000.

Joshi, S. "How Development Modernized Patriarchy." *Info Change News and Feature,* 2005.

National Policy on Urban Street Vendors (2004). Also available at nceus.gov.in/Street per cent20Vendors520policy.pdf

Sarkar, S. "Women Labour-Force in Unorganised Sector: A Study on Construction Workers in Navi Mumbai." *Personnel Today* (2006): 20–27.

Sen, A. "Development Which Way to Go?" *The Economic Journal*, no. 93 (December 1983): 745–62.

Sharma, R.N. "The Politics of Urban Space." Lecture series, 491, Tata Institute of Social Sciences and YUVA, Census Survey of Hawkers on BMC Lands, 1998.

Tiwari, G. "Encroachers or Services Providers?" *Seminar* 491 (June 2000). Available at: www.seminarindia.org

Web-links

http://www.nasvinet.org/about.htm

http://nceus.gov.in/street per cent20Vendors per cent20policy.pdf

http://necus.gov.in/street per cent20Vendors per cent20policy.pdf (pp. 3–4)

http://nceus.gov.in/Street per cent20Vendors per cent20policy.pdf (p10)

www.seminarindia.org

9

Women Labour Force in Unorganized Sector: A Study on Construction Workers in Navi Mumbai

Sumita Sarkar

Development of human resources is usually determined by the size and the characteristic (in terms of size, educational standard, quality of life, income, etc.) of labour force which determines the pace and level of development of a society. Thus, it is the labour force, which plays a crucial role in development of a society. But, the nature of labour force in a developed economy differs significantly from a developing economy. In developed societies, it is more organized labour that constitutes the workforce of their nation economy. The labour is comparatively well protected and covered by an effective social security net, stretching from 'cradle to grave' service protection. However, in recent years, with the tide of 'globalization' and open market economy, the changing nature of labour force has become extremely flexible especially in the form of 'casualization' of work, i.e., part-time work, contractual labour, or sub-contracting, etc., across the globe. Developed or economically advanced countries are also no exception to such a trend. But it is important to note that flexible nature of labour force has not deprived workers from their basic social protection in these countries, unlike their counterparts (the developing ones) of world economy.

In the case of developing countries, there is a general characteristic of dualistic nature of labour market. Such dualism prevails in the forms of unorganized labour force with no standardized wages or social security benefits, on one hand, and a small proportion of organized workforce which usually enjoys standardized wages and social security, on the other.

India is one of such developing countries where about 92 per cent of the workforce is employed either in the primary sector (mainly agriculture) or in the unorganized or informal sector. As a result of liberalization and its new displacing labour technology, unorganized sector in our country is fast expanding. According to National Sample Survey Organization (NSSO), 1999–2000 data, the total employment in both the unorganized and the organized sectors in this country is about 39.7 crore, where only 2.8 crore are employed in the organized sector and the rest 36.9 crore (about 93%) in the unorganized sector. Among these 23.7 crore are those workers who are engaged in agriculture, 4.1 crore work in the manufacturing, 3.7 crore each in the services and trade, and around 1.7 crore work in the construction. Among these, about 21 per cent workforce is the females working in the unorganized sector.

The construction sector is the largest employer in India after the agricultural labour. In 1995 to 1996, 14.6 million persons were employed in the construction (approximately four per cent of the total labour force), and of these, 12.9 million were the skilled and unskilled workers. Of the estimated 12.9 million construction workers, 10.7 million (or 83%) are the "job contract" casual wage-workers. Employment within the construction industry grew at a rapid rate of 7 per cent per year, during the 15-year period (1981–1995), during which time the national growth rate of employment was only 2.3 per cent. There were 8.5 million construction workers in 1987 to 1989, 14.6 million in 1995 to 1996 and their number is estimated to reach 32.6 million in 2004–05. Of this, approximately 30 per cent were the women, that is, over 4.4 million, in 1995 to 1996 (NICMAR, 1995; Hirway, 1997).

Though several legislations, like the Minimum Wages Act, Maternity Benefit Act, Equal Remuneration Act, "Beedi" and Cigar Workers (Conditions of Employment) Act, Building and Other Construction Workers (RE&CS) Act, Workmen's Compensation Act, and Contract Labour Act, etc., are fully or partially applicable to the workers in the unorganized sector, none of these is being properly implemented. They do not have any job protection or social welfare benefits. Most of the workers in the unorganized sector, like home-based workers, daily-wage workers, domestic workers, vendors, etc., are not covered by any protective legislation.

In India, the construction industry is the second largest economic activity, next to agriculture. It also absorbs the largest number of unorganized labour force. It has also been observed that around 50 per cent of our total capital outlay in the successive Five-Year Plans has been on the construction itself, as the infrastructure development is considered to be the basic and necessary step for development (Economic Survey, 2000). The construction industry in urban areas covers a wide range of activities. It not only involves constructing good infrastructure like bridges, roads, malls, industrial structures, but also the industrial plants, cables and ropeways, reconstruction of old housing, construction of new housings stock and commercial structures. Construction industry is also the single largest employer of migrant labourers, the poorest of the poor, in Indian cities particularly in metropolises like Kolkata, Delhi and Mumbai. Official data (ILO, 2005) on India indicates that women workers in construction industry often work as part of a family unit, in which case they are not on the payroll of the contractor and may not receive any payment at all for their work—wages being paid instead to the husband. In this situation, women are to all intents and purposes 'invisible'. It is therefore not surprising to find that there are no separate facilities provided for them or for their children. In certain cases, where women work as contract labourers and under certain payroll, are discriminated with their unequal wages and longer working hours.

Construction jobs are highly labour intensive and also highly mechanized. The entire activities are mobile, seasonal, intermittent and mostly interconnected. Construction labourers are generally unskilled and therefore mostly migrants (the agricultural labourers). The workers are illiterate and only able to speak their own language. Therefore, they also lack bargaining power. Their lives are characterized by insecurity of wages, dangerous working conditions, casualization and lack of access to any kind of welfare. The daily wages of a female construction worker are about Rs 60 (or $1.20), significantly lower than a male worker (with daily wage of Rs100–120 approximately).

Mumbai being one of the major commercial cities in India, it has significant working population especially in the unorganized sector. The origin of unorganized labour market in Mumbai can be traced back to the early 19th century, with the initiation of growth and development of the city itself. Since early phase of 19th century (1854), Mumbai entered into the industrial era, mainly with the expansion of textile and later other manufacturing industries like petrochemical, automobile etc. Industrial expansion and development during the early 1960s not only pulled millions of educated and highly skilled labour force from all the states of the country, it also gained its millions of unskilled labour force in the unorganized sector. Marginal labourers mainly from primary sector, like agriculture, came from several districts of Maharashtra (with a sharp fall in agricultural productivity since early 1970s) and also from outer states to toil their labour and to secure basic source of livelihood. Furthermore, since early 1990s, the labour in unorganized sector has multiplied in number particularly due to the open economy and capitalist invasion into the retail and housing industry. Uneven development, increasing unemployment among the agricultural labourers, and poverty have created severe 'pull' factors towards metropolitan cities like Mumbai for these migrant labourers to secure a better or a minimum basic source of livelihood.

Focus of the Study

Navi Mumbai, being known as a satellite or twin city of Mumbai, caters to a large number of workforce in the unorganized sector, especially in the construction industry. The city started developing in early 1970s and presently it is the largest planned new city in the country, with an area of 344 km. The present population of Navi Mumbai is 0.75 million and is estimated to grow to 2 million in another two decades. Having a development plan for 20 nodes in Navi Mumbai region, presently, Navi Mumbai is a highly developing city and on continuous expansion of housing, roads, and other related infrastructure.

In this context, the present paper makes a modest attempt to explore life situation of female workers engaged in the construction industry of Navi Mumbai region. The paper focuses on female workers active in three specific nodes, i.e., Belapur, Nerul and Khargargh. The total population of construction workers was about 1,500 in the above nodes (both males and females). Out of these, 100 female workers were chosen as the sample for the study. The present paper mainly focuses on socio-economic condition of these female workers in terms of their prevailing wages, continuity (or casualization) and struggle with daily chores. Effort is also made to highlight gender discrimination in terms of wages or long working hours or any other benefits. Performing their dual role—preparing food, rearing children, and also doing outdoor (construction) work may bring heavy toll on their physical and psychological health. The study focuses on such aspects of their work and life situations.

Method

As stated before, the present paper is focused on a sample survey of 100 female workers in the construction industry of Navi Mumbai (viz., Belapur, Khargargh and Nerul nodes). The sample survey was supported by qualitative data through conducting a few case studies and focus group discussions. In addition, the effort was also made to interview the supervisors or mangers of the construction-units. Interviews were also held with a few NGOs which had taken up the issues of female workers in the region. The main attempt was to explore and understand subjective meaning of their work experience, and to record their life situation through interpretative approach. In-depth conversation interviews to document their experience of work, economy and life have been considered as useful information to provide a richer and deeper understanding of the issue. The major variables like place of origin, socio-economic background, education level, wage level, causes of migration, source of income when not employed in the construction work, nature of jobs, family pattern, etc. have been considered for the main part of analysis. In the case of in-depth interviews and group discussion, only guide-schedule was developed keeping main focus on the major variables as the theme of conversation.

Origin of Migrant Female Workers

Labour migration is one of the crucial factors affecting the course of socio-economic development in India. In India, unorganized sector constitutes majority of the workforce who are migrants. These unskilled labourers come from rural and backward areas of the country in search of livelihood. The data (Tables 1 and 2) show that in the construction industry, in Navi Mumbai region, almost all the female workers came from several other states, with a lead from East Zone (45%), especially from Bihar, Orissa and West Bengal followed by North Zone, especially remote villages of Uttar Pradesh (27%), and the central part of the country. As stated by ILO (2002) Annual Report, about 5 lakh migrants were reported as seasonal migrants who migrated in less than one year. Among these, 41.4 per cent alone constitute seasonal migrant workers from UP and Bihar who came to be employed in the unorganized sector. It is commonly observed that these workers bring their families along with them.

Table 1 *Origin of Female Migrant Workers*

Origin Zone	*No. of Female Workers*
North Zone	27
East Zone	45
West Zone	8
Central Zone	12
South Zone	6
North-East Zone	2
Total (N)	100

According to the present study, female workers were mostly married (92 per cent) and accompanied their husbands while moving out of their places of origin. The main "pull factor", as stated by them, was to seek gainful employment for a better living. Most women have joined their husbands little later from their home place and since then have been mobile with the change of location of their contract work. However, studies have also shown (Sidhu, 2005) that certain social tensions like family disputes and lack of ownership of agricultural lands (or unviable land holdings), often compelled such workers to move towards the city where they perceived better bargain for livelihood.

These women are mostly having children ranging from two to six in number, and sometimes also joined by a few members of their natal or in-laws family. Moving out for these workers has become a routine where about 85 per cent of these workers are in continuous search of daily or contractual job from one contractor or another. The location of jobs decides their presence in a particular place in squatter settlement and shanties. When the work is over, these females move along with their male members for another destination. Like several studies have shown (Dasgupta and Lashley, 1975; Gill, 1998; Kundu, 1998), the present data supports the extent of vulnerability that these social groups confront due to contractual and varying employers even within a city where they take up the work. The destination to workplace is usually routed through the brokers, who are their own fellowmen with seniority of their being in the sector.

Nature of Migration

As stated by these women (Table 2), they are engaged in three kinds of tenures of job, viz., permanent (43%), seasonal (41%) and day-to-day jobs, mostly unskilled (16%). In the case of permanent migrant female workers, they came to the city with their male members few years back and have stayed back in the city. They consider themselves lucky to adhere to a single employer long and wish to continue to be 'permanent' in that sense.

Table 2 *Construction Workers by the Nature of Migration*

Nature of Migration	*No. of Workers*
Permanent	43
Seasonal	41
Dependent on jobs	16
Total (N)	100

As they claimed, the permanent settlement of their family members has also helped them to be in good books of a few builders' groups. This has also created a friendly circle among the workers who provide them information about more stable jobs. These female workers have been staying in the city of Mumbai for several years now. In initial phase of their migration, like other migrants, they used to work for different employer- contractors, but are now stabilized and feel better secured than many other temporary co-workers in the construction work.

Economic Vulnerability and Dependent Family Members

When probed about the plausible reasons for which these female construction workers are compelled to work and make a living, it is observed that in a majority of these households (54%), there are about six to eight dependent family members followed by 20 per cent of them having four to six dependants in the family. Such families mostly include children and old parents or unmarried women in the family. In their own words, "it is mandatory for us to work as it provides crucial financial support to our family". A study by Nirmala Niketan (2000) observed that having little or no land in their villages, recurring draught, unemployment, and large size family create economic vulnerably to such migrant workers. In such a situation, especially for women, it comes as a compulsory additional duty to earn money along with household chores of living.

Table 3 *Number of Dependent Family Members*

Group Interval	*Dependent (no. and percentage)*
0–4	2
4–6	20
6–8	54
10+–	24
Total (N)	100

Average Family Size: 7

Other Sources of Income

While probing into their other sources of income when not employed in construction work, data (Table 4) reveals that there are 43 per cent of the female labourers whose main source of livelihood is only the construction work related jobs. The jobs are manual and unskilled and mostly to assist their male counterparts in construction work, like bringing water, collecting stone and breaking them into small pieces, carry hand load of bricks, etc. However, there are a few women who are equally skilled as male workers in the construction work. A study by the Nirmala Niketan (2000) shows that women engaged in construction activity develop skills—like their counterparts—in skilled activities, like flooring, fixing tiles, water-proofing, etc.

Table 4 *Other Sources of Income*

Source of Income	*No. of Workers*
Construction	43
Agriculture	41
Labour	16
Total(N)	100

There is a significant percentage (41 per cent) of the workforce who perform seasonal works. These female workers are agricultural labourers who move towards the city when their harvesting season at the native place is over. About 16 per cent women also engage themselves in other manual jobs, mostly the domestic work in city neighbourhoods.

Work, Wages and Living Conditions

There are mainly three types of contractual labour which bring differential wages to these female workers (Table 5). Over one-third of the female workers earn Rs 50 to 100 on daily work basis. Mostly the standardized rate is 80 to 100. In the wage range of Rs 100 to 120, there are 16 per cent female workers. These females are better experienced in the work and therefore receive higher wages. Thus, over a half of the female workers are engaged in the wage work.

About one-third of the female workers are engaged on contractual work, which means being in a 'construction project' (mainly in housing project) and toil their labour till the work is finished. A majority of them though earn low wages (Rs 50 to 100). The remaining 16 per cent workers mainly are more floating and work on daily hour basis, with a range

Table 5 *Types of Work and the Variation of Wage*

	Wages (Rs)	*Types*			*Total*
		Daily Wage Earner	*Contract (till finishing of the project)*	*Hourly Basis*	
	50–100	34	20	14	
	100–120	16	12	2	
	120+	02	0	0	
Total	100 (N)	52	32	16	

varying from Rs. 50 to 120. However, the standardized wage rate for such work usually is in range of Rs 80 to 100. Overall, their wages are lower as compared to the male workers in the sector.

Table 6 *Working Hours*

Working Hours	*No. of Workers*
Less than 8	0
8 hours	2
8–10 hours	74
10 hours +	24
Total (N)	100

For male workers, the minimum wages are of the range Rs 120 to 180. Females are thus discriminated though they also put equal amount of working hours every day as male workers. The standardized working hours are usually stretched beyond 8 to 10 hours every day (Table 6). It is relevant to mention here that under the Equal Remuneration Act, it is obligatory for the contractor to pay equal wages to his labourers independent of "gender". But, unfortunately, in this sector workers are not unionized, and employer usually takes advantage of the vulnerability of easily available "needy" female labour force.

In addition to this exploitation at the workforce, their 'dual role' further establishes the gender discrepancy in more subtle and traditional mould of housework. Most women (84%) stated that before they began their on-site work, they had to finish their compulsory housework, like cooking, cleaning, washing and feeding their children and other family members. They catch only about 5 to 6 hours of sleep everyday, after their daily routine. If there is an elderly person or a grown-up girl in the family, who would stay back, it becomes easier to look after their children. But most women (73%) prefer to carry their children to the work site. In the case of a growing boy or a girl of 10 years or more of age, they usually come along with the mother to help her in daily labour. Usually these children are not considered as a part of the contract and remain unpaid.

Health and Hygiene

According to the Census Report, 1993 women employed in construction industry mostly as unskilled labourers to carry concrete and bricks. Due to lower levels of mechanization in India, such workers endure great physical stress including numbness of hands and fingers and back injuries. These workers suffer from hearing loss, intestinal problems, respiratory diseases, and skin allergies. As a result of the heavy labour, women are prone to menstrual disorders, spontaneous miscarriage, and there is a high rate of infant mortality among their children

The present study further reveals that most of the women have been suffering from several diseases mainly due to malnourishment and excess labour. There are about 87 per cent women who stated of having gynaecological problems (like miscarriage, irregular menstruation, excessive bleeding, etc.). About 89 per cent complained that they suffered due to stomach related diseases, like gastritis, ulcer etc. (Table 7). About 67 per cent women (mostly 30+ of age) have complained about body ache and joint pain. The study by Nirmala Niketan (2000) also found that long stipulated working hours indirectly affected the health of these workers. They frequently complained of headache, allergy, chest pain, and stomach related problems. Especially for female workers, it is more joint pain and gynaecological problems (irregular menstruation, excessive bleeding, miscarriage, etc.) which affect them often.

Furthermore, psychological problems related to jobs, insecurity, economic pressure and temporary living conditions make severe effect on these women and worsen their health condition.

Table 7 *Workers Suffered from Physical Ailments*

Symptoms	*No. and Percentage*
Severe body ache/joint pain	67
Gynaecological problem	87
Dermatological problem	48
Gastro/abdominal	89

The present respondents observed that they were used to one full meal, especially at night, after they were back from work. Their lunch and breakfast were small and they usually did not have knowledge of 'adequate' food intake. For these female workers, priority was to get work as much as they could at the construction site. Health was a non-significant part unless it resulted in severe pain and sufferings. As further noticed, there were no medications or health check-up facilities available at the construction sites. It was also reported by the workers that there were not even enough security measures for these workers (like helmet, gloves etc.), and it was applicable to both the females and the males. The welfare facilities like crèches, canteen, and first aid were beyond comprehension in such kind of working conditions.

The study further brought out the fact that almost all female workers were living in shanties and squatter settlements and were on move once the work was over. It was rare that the builders would provide space for these their families to stay. Usually these workers lived at near by barren and open areas in an extremely unhygienic environment, with no toileting or water facilities.

Role of Voluntary Organizations

The growing realization about vulnerability of workers engaged in the informal sector, has drawn attention of trade unions, voluntary organizations, international funding organizations, government based organizations and even the academics. However, the fact remains that these workers (wage or self-employed) confront poor working conditions, insecurity of job and low incomes—from wages or otherwise. Efforts to organize them for improving their life situations have made a little dent.

The same applies to the construction workers. A few NGOs active in the area are: the PRIA, NIRMAN, OHSC, and Nirmala Niketan, particularly in the city of Mumbai. They have tried to organize these workers for better job conditions, and also petitioned to the courts and concerned governments, to look into the basic issues of their working conditions.

Social Networks and Social Capital

The forgoing discussion amply proves that if any dignity is expected to these construction workers, there existed none in their life. The survival proved to be the key factor that brought them, with their husbands, to the city of Mumbai, and compelled them to work in a most difficult area—the construction work. Women construction workers faced difficult task—to perform household work and also earn wages through hard work for 8 to 10 hours. During group discussions, it became quite evident that social networks (Mitchell, 1969) and social capital (Bourdieu and Wacquant, 1992) played key role both in their migration from native villages to Mumbai metropolis and their survival strategies in the city. Almost absence of social security in job and its casual nature kept the husband-wife pair hard pitched and sticking to their difficult jobs in construction industry. However, their kinship networks, friendly and community ties acted as shock absorbers and resources in difficult times. These networks provide them adequate information about various job opportunities and prospective employers in the construction industry. Day-to-day needs and setbacks like borrowings for health treatment or even daily provisions during the period of intermittent unemployment, were mobilized through such mutual support systems.

Concluding Remarks

The study on women construction workers in Navi Mumbai in relation to their wage and work conditions, origin and socio-economic background provide useful data about their life situations. The study amply demonstrates the financial compulsions which bring them from villages to work in a mega city, like Mumbai. Lack of entitlements to lands and growing competition in rural areas forces them to seek better sources of livelihood in urban areas. For decades, certain regions of the country have been prone to out-migration of nuclear families, seeking jobs in construction industry. The boom in real estate facilitates such a migration, where brokers (mainly from among the migrants) arrange jobs—both for husband and wife—in the construction sector. The jobs for the new entrants are mostly temporary and on daily wage basis. The advantage of the construction industry is that it is still labour intensive and accommodates both males and females in various kinds of manual, semi-skilled and skilled works. Those workers who stabilize in the work and develop skills of masonry, carpentry, etc., get better wages and are retained on a long-term basis by the same employers. Intra-sector mobility is also high in this trade. As compared to their counterparts, the male workers in construction industry, the females are lesser in number and also perform manual work at low wages. Usually, they work under the same project, along with their husbands or close relatives (like brother, father, uncle, etc.). Their work conditions are much strenuous, as they perform dual role—performing domestic chores, rearing children, and also acting as wage earners.

It is observed that though a few trade unions and voluntary organizations have been active in improving the lot of these workers, and have agitated to bring adequate legislation for protecting their jobs, improving their earnings and work conditions, these efforts are too small compared to the gigantic number of people seeking better and secured jobs. Frequent change of employers and their very large number also go against any hope of organizing these workers all across the regions. A social work organization in Mumbai, the Nirmala Niketan, has spearheaded their cause for several years but the end result is not very different.

Then, there are related issues like adverse effects on health of female construction workers, almost nil facilities of daytime crèches for their children, and exposure to strenuous and dangerous work conditions.

A few urgent and important needs are:

- More intensive research to focus on the working conditions of female construction workers, in the context of their dual roles at house and at the job site.
- Government initiatives to implement laws both at local and national levels which secure and improve work conditions and provide other benefits, like medication and safe work environment.

- Need of day-care centres for children at the construction sites.
- To do away with discrimination in wages and related work conditions, against male construction workers.
- To invite more and more NGOs to help and organize these workers for their better job conditions.
- To evolve a national policy for the workers in construction industry.

■ References

Agnihotri, Indu. "Globalization and the State." Paper presented at DAWN Asia-Pacific Workshop on Political Restructuring and Social Transformation, Thailand, 8–11 October 1999.

All Women's Action Society (AWAM). Draft Report on Rape Research, 2000.

Blanchard, Eric. "Gender, International Relations, and the Development of Feminist Security Theory." *Signs: Journal of Women in Culture and Society* 28, no.4 (2003): 1289–1313.

Bourdieu, P. and Wacquant, L. *Invitation to Reflexive Sociology*. Cambridge: Polity Press, 1992.

Cecilia, N.G. ASED Home page, "Globalization and Women." www.ased.org; 12: 53, 2000.

Christa, Wichterich. *The Globalized Woman: Reports from a Future of Inequality*. New York: Zed Books, 2000.

Crime in India Report. Ministry of Home Affairs, New Delhi, 2000.

Dasgupta, B. and Lashley, R., 1975, "Migration from Villages: An Indian Case Study", *Economic and Political Weekly*, Annual Number.

Dex, S. *The Sexual Division of Work*, Harvester, 1985.

Drèze J. and Amartya Sen. "Public Action for Social Security: Foundation and Strategy." In *Social Security in Developing Countries*, edited by E. Ahmed, J. Drèze, J. Hills, and A. Sen. Oxford: Clarendon Press, 1991.

Ghosh, J. "Globalization and Economic Liberalization." *ISIS Women in Action*, 1999.

Gill, H.S. Housing the Poor: An Analysis with Special Reference to Slum Colonies in Delhi, Unpublished Thesis, Jawaharlal Nehru University, New Delhi, 1992.

Gosh, J. "Gender and Microeconomics." Paper Presented in the UN committee on Status of Women, New York, 2005.

Hensmen, R. *Women in Black* 2: 2000, www.acme.journal (online).

Hirway, I. *Statistics on Informal Sector: The Case of India*. National Account Statistics (NAS), Central Statistics Organization, 1997.

International Labour Report. Report on the Organization of Unorganized Labour, ILO, Geneva, 2000.

Jain, D. "Feminization and Globalization." Synopsis Series: NCRW, Cuny and Japan Preparatory Committee Economic Dimension of Globalization panel, 2000.

Jamieson, Lynn. Lecture Series organized by the Gender Studies Unit, University of Malaya, 2000.

Kishwar, M. and Vanita, R., eds. *In Search of Answers: Indian Women's Voices from Manushi.* London: Zed Books, 1984.

Kishwar, M. and Vanita, R. "Pro-Woman or Anti-Muslim? The Shabhano Controversy." *Manushi* 32 (1987).

———. "The Burning of Roop Kanwar." *Manushi* (1987): 42–43.

Krishnaraj, M. "Globalization and Women in India." *Development in Practice* 9, No. 5 (1989).

Kumar, R. "Identity Politics and the Contemporary Indian Feminist Movement." In *Identity Politics and Women: Cultural Reassertions and Feminisms in International Perspective,* edited by Moghadam, V. M. Boulder, CO, USA: Westview Press, 1994, pp. 274–92.

Kundu, A., 1998, "Informal Manufacturing Sector in Urban Areas: An Analysis of Recent Trends", *Manpower Journal,* Vol.34 (1), April-June.

Maznah Mohamad, Cecilia N. G., and Tan Beng Hui. "Globalization, Industrialization and Crisis: The Coming of Age of Malaysian Women Workers?" United Nations Human Development Report, 1996–1999.

Mitchell, J.C. (ed.) *Social Networks in Urban Situations.* Manchester: Manchester University Press, 1969.

Mitter, Wiswa. *Growth of Urban Informal Sector in an Economy.* New Delhi: Deep and Deep Publisher, 1988.

NICMAR. Construction Statistics, 1995.

Nirmala Niketan. *Study on Occupational Health Problems of Constructions Workers in New Bombay.* Mumbai: College of Nirmala Niketan, 2000.

Peterson, V.S. and Runyan, A. *Global Gender Issues.* USA: Westview Press Inc., 1993.

Sanderson, K. and Crompton, R. *Gendered Jobs and Social Change.* London: Unwin Hyman, 1990.

Sen, K. and Malia, S. *Gender and Power in Afflient Asia.* UK: Routledge, 1998.

Shah, V. "Women Building Workers: An Area Study in Bombay" (for the ILO), NICMAR Research Documents, Mumbai, National Institute of Construction Management and Research, 1996.

Shiva Vandana. "The Effects of WTO on Women's Rights." TWN, Third World Network, Online Bookstore, 2005.

Sidhu, H.S. " Production Conditions in Contemporary Panjab Agriculture", *Journal of Panjab Studies*, Vol. 12 , No. 2, 2005, as cited in "Relations of Production and Modes of Surplus Extraction in India: An Aggregate Study" by Amit Basole and Deepankar Basu, Sanhati (www.sanhati.com), May 11, 2009, p.10.

Sundaram, S.K.G. "Organizations Working for Unorganized Labour." *The Case of Mumbai*. Mumbai: SNDT University, 2000.

Tiwari, S.G. *Data Base on Organized and Secondary Sector*. New Delhi: Global Business Press, 1993.

Walby, S. *Theorising Patriarchy*. Oxford: Blackwell Publishers, 1990.

Wong, Diana. "Globalization Reconsidered: Social and Cultural Aspects from an Asian Perspective." Unpublished manuscript, 1999.

10

Women Workers in Unorganized Sector and Brick Kiln Industry: A Case of Navi Mumbai

Sumita Sarkar

The term 'unorganized labour' means those workers who have not been able to organize themselves in pursuit of their common interest due to certain constraints like casual nature of employment, ignorance and illiteracy, small and scattered size of establishments, and so on.

As per the 2001 Census, out of the total workforce of 402.24 (77.8 per cent) million, 313 millions are the main workers and 28 (22.2 per cent) million are the marginal workers. Among these, about 8 per cent are in the organized sector and the rest that are 92 per cent in unorganized sector account for the total labour force. Unorganized workers may be categorized in terms of occupation or employment, in terms of especially distressed categories or in terms of service categories. Small and marginal farmers, landless agricultural labourers, sharecroppers, fisherman, those engaged in animal husbandry, in beedi rolling, beedi labelling and beedi packing, building and other construction workers, leather workers, weavers, artisan, salt workers, stone quarry workers, workers in saw mill, oil mills and brick kiln workers may come into the informal sector working category. The tappers, scavengers, carrier of head loads, drivers of animal driven vehicles, loaders and unloaders, belong to the especially distressed category, while midwives, domestic workers, fishermen and women, barbers, vegetables and fruit vendors, and newspaper vendors come under the service categories.

A characteristic feature of the employment situation in our country is that the percentage of workers employed on regular salaried employment is very small (16 per cent). The bulk of the workforce is either self-employed (53 per cent) or employed in casual wage employment (31 per cent). The unorganized sector is vast and varied. Over 90 per cent of the labour force works in this sector. This sector, with its overwhelming number, range and complexity of problems, has not been amenable to any statistical accuracy and precision in the same sense as the organized sector. The unorganized sector suffers from cycles of excessive seasonality of employment. Majority of the rural workers do not have stable and durable avenues of employment. Those who appear to be visibly employed are not gainfully and substantially employed, a phenomenon known as the disguised unemployment (NSSO, 2002; TeriVision, 2006, www.http://teri.res.in/teriin/news/terivision/issue18).

Female Workforce in Unorganized Sector

Women in the unorganized sector, may be married or unmarried members of the household, usually take participation in earning as a part of their family labour force. In the last one decade with the opening up of economy and casualization of labour force, women headed households have been increasing in numbers. Women are predominantly found in informal economy securing livelihood. The total workforce in our country is about 314 million, of which women constitute 90 million and the men about 224 million. The male and female work participation rates are 51.56 per cent and 22.73 per cent respectively. A majority of women workers are employed in the rural areas. Amongst the rural women workers, 87 per cent are employed in agriculture as labourers and cultivators. Amongst the women workers in urban areas, about 80 per cent are employed in the unorganized sector, like household industries, petty trades and services and building construction. The employment of women in the organized sector (both public and private sectors, as on 31, March 1999) was about 4.8 million. This constitutes 17.2 per cent of the total organized sector employment in the country. The major problems that affect them spring from the unorganized nature of industries in which they are employed. They are outside the reach of most of the protective labour laws and trade union organization (National Labour Commission Report, 2002; ILO, 2002).

Brick Kiln Industry: A Segment in Unorganized Sector in India

In India, clay bricks have been extensively used for centuries. The 'khumbhar' is a part of traditional rural community in India and has its roots in the age old history of Indian civilization. Brick kiln is at present the predominant construction material of modern India. Current demand in this activity is over 100 billion bricks a year. The fuel costs alone account for almost 30 to 40 per cent of the production cost. According to All India Brick Kilns and Tiles Manufacturer's Federation (2002) there are about 50,000 brick kilns in the country which employ average 100 employees per unit.

Bricks remain one of the most important building materials in the country. Brick making is a traditional industry in India, generally confined to rural areas. The states like Chhattisgarh, Madhya Pradesh, Rajasthan, Orissa, Jharkhand, Uttar Pradesh, and West Bengal lead in Indian brick production.

Notably, the Indian brick industry with more than one lakh production units producing about 100 billion bricks annually is the second largest brick producer in the world after China. Brick making is a traditional, unorganized industry, generally confined to rural and semi-urban areas. This industry has an annual turnover of more than Rs 10,000 crore and, very importantly, it is one of the largest employment generating industry, employing millions of workers with a significant percentage of women workforce.

The brick kilns are classified into three categories according to the production capacity as per Gazette notification on 'Emission Standards for Brick Kiln' under the Environment (Protection) Act, 1986. Small brick kiln which has the capacity to produce 10,000 to 15,000 bricks per day, the medium which has the capacity of 25,000 bricks per day and the large one which has the capacity of more than 45,000 to 60, 000 bricks per day (Singh and Asgher, 2002).

Focus of Present Study

The present study focuses on the women brick kiln workers employed in the area of Navi Mumbai, a twin city of Greater Mumbai. Outer area of Panvel city, mostly rural has been considered for the study. A total of four medium and small size 'bhattis' (kilns) were considered for the present study. This paper looks into the demographic profile, socio-economic status and working conditions of these women workers in the brick industry, and tries to unfold the facts about their livelihood issues, their responsibility towards children and family, their valuable role in economy of the household for survival (thus playing roles in both production and reproduction), their working conditions, wage structure, sanitation and hygiene, social security aspect, and above all the gender exploitation by their employers and the middleman (the broker).

The study is explorative in nature. The data was collected using semi-structured schedule, with a few in-depth case studies which are documented for detailed narration of their work life situations. Total 64 women workers were taken as the sample size, from the four brick kilns under the present focus.

Key Observations

Migrant Women Workers in Brick Kiln and Social Networking

Seasonal casual labour migration in India has conventionally been understood as the result of extreme poverty, whereby villagers are forced to become migrants for the dry six months to subsist or merely survive. The present study draws on the fieldwork from all these four brick kilns in Panvel taluka. It is observed that these migrants do not understand their movement in economic terms alone. Many see the brick kilns work as a temporary space of freedom to escape problems back at home, explore a new place and gain independence financially. In the present study, it has been observed that more than 89 per cent women workers are migrants, predominantly from nearby area of Karjat-Kasara, the rural Maharashtra of Vidharva region, and the rest 11 per cent are from nearby local areas of Raigad district. The popular notion of thousands of construction workers coming in Mumbai out of Maharashtra, therefore, is not found to be the case among these workers. Women have simply followed their husbands and family, more as a mandatory part of a woman's duty to be with husband. They stated that their men (husbands) could not get good job opportunities and therefore left homes looking for better means to secure a livelihood. A significant number of them (more than 40 per cent) stated that the seasonal agricultural work has largely been affected in their villages due to unfavourable weather conditions, lack of money and very small holdings, which do not fetch a profitable return from the agriculture to secure their lives.

More than 80 per cent workers have migrated to the kilns located in Mumbai region with the help of their earlier networking with village friends or relatives. The work they get is mobilized generally through an agent from their village, known through friends or relatives. The family members are always counted on the list as an additional and supplement labour force which will enhance the productivity of the brick kilns. Women accompanying could be mother, wife, daughter and sisters, if married, along with their children. In some cases, the contact person is given some advance amount to secure jobs in the probable brick kiln that they are going to be employed.

The social networking appears to be a strong thread to pull these migrant workers at times of their need. Women are mere followers and help their husbands in earning additional money for a comparative food security for coming months.

Social Security, Health and Hygiene

In India, people working in the unorganized sector are characterized by low earnings, poor working conditions and lack of social security. Furthermore, the workers in brick kiln belong to the lowest economic strata of labour force, and more than 60 per cent of them are landless labourers and with rural origin. When it comes to working conditions of the women workforce, the situation is precarious as there is hardly any support or sympathy to their reproductive health, with no provisions of maternity benefit, sanitation and hygiene. Protective social security measures at national and state levels exist but hardly availed to provide a financial cushion against contingent poverty that seriously affects the poor, such as sickness, accidents and old age. The implication of such measures and follow up at informal level of the unorganized sector is extremely obscure and highly manipulated. In the present study, it is observed that more than 85 per cent women workers do not feel safe while working in the kilns and perceive risks to their health while working. Most disturbing sight is the dust and heat that they are exposed to while closely working in the 'bhattis'. Also, there is no special attire given to the workers who are exposed to collect and take out the hot bricks. No medical kit is available for an emergency, and no formal sanitation at the site of all brick kilns. It is therefore not surprising that more than 44 per cent of the women workers stated that during severe or minor accidents, their health issues are ignored by the employers, and sometimes they are simply forced to look for another site for work. Even at the present brick kilns, several women (about 43 per cent) stated that their health concern was not perceived seriously by the employers. Another important factor, next to the sanitation and safety, was the lack of availability of water. Shockingly, the employers do not consider it necessary to provide water at the workplace for all the workers. When enquired, it was told by many workers, especially the women, that the basic minimum need of proper drinking water is not met by the employers. Several times, they have to fetch water for their needs during the working hours. Furthermore, crèches, maternity benefit and toilets, which are perceived of equal importance by all women workers, are simply not available. It is further mentioned that carrying bricks for long duration of hours and working in such brick kilns is very harmful to women and childrens' health; it is unsafe and unhygienic. These workers' sufferings are often worsened due to malnourishment and gynaecological diseases, along with other physical ailments (like asthma, frequent coughing and fever, backache, etc.). It is important to note that the brick kiln sector is absent of any technological equipments and mostly the nature of production is manual. The principle burden of such a hard labour falls on workers, where women play a significant role, along with their male counterparts. Even child labour is visible in the brick kilns.

Work, Working Hours and Wage Structure

With the liberalization policies, casualization is one of the trend or pattern that has been used by the entrepreneurs of informal economy against the labour force. These owners/businessman/entrepreneurs prefer to employ flexible labour force to avoid the burden of job security benefits to the employees. The labour practice stands further misused by the feminization of labour force in various sectors including the brick kilns. Such trend has substantially led to the increase of cheap, unskilled and female labour. During the present study, researcher found the incidence of higher proportion (i.e., 52 per cent) of women workforce as compared to their male counter-parts (48 per cent). This is mainly due to labour intensive manual work where the loading and unloading of brick raw material (the clay), the loading of baked bricks and even carrying the moulded bricks is frequently done by women. The baking (by heat treatment) through coal/coke is exclusively done by the males. The wages paid are proportional to a fixed output per day under various processes. Thus, preparing clay and supplying it to the person for moulding the bricks, the payment is Rs 250 per person, subject to each handling about two tons of the clay. For brick moulding the workers are paid between Rs 300 to 350 a day, subject to their moulding minimum 1000 bricks. In contrast to these kinds of workers, those who feed the coke for baking the clay and maintain proper heat treatment under various parts of the kiln, the minimum payment is Rs 350 a day.

As regards the payment of wages to the females, as such there is no discrimination except that they are more engaged in the loading or unloading of the clay or bricks. However, they are allowed to work for around six hours (minimum), and proportionately, due to the (lesser) two hours, they get lesser wages after a week or a month. Lesser hours of work for women are permitted so that they can prepare the night food and feed the children.

Another important fact which keeps the groups of workers tied to a specific kiln/contractor is the advance payment for taking up the work. This could vary from Rs 5,000 to 15,000. This helps the workers to clear their borrowings and related expenses before they migrate to the kilns. This custom obviously creates a bondage/patronage towards the kiln owner, and also the cycle of poverty which reassures the supply of labour.

For these workers, work in the kilns is not a permanent source of earning, and most of them do seasonal agricultural labour (more than 58 per cent) or work on their small farm holdings, when there is no work available for them in the kilns. Thus, brick kilns provide seasonal employment for these migrant workers, who usually come with their family, when there are no other casual labour or agricultural activities at the home place. Usually, in the kiln work, the duration of their employment varies from six to eight months, predominantly from October to June, every year.

Demographic Profile and Human Capital

As regards the ethnic background, most of these workers belong to the scheduled tribes and other backward classes. There is a very high incidence of illiteracy among them (68 per cent). Most of the women workers are married (83 per cent), rest are either a widow or single. The terms of the trade of receiving payments for work are basically contractual, to be decided by the supervisor or the employing agent. The age group of these workers range from 25 to 45 years. Certain regions of Vidharva and Raigarh districts of Maharashtra are migration prone for such work.

Gender Issues and Work Environment

With a view to further understanding the situation of women workers in the brick making industry, there is a need to do further probing. This area remains scanty of research work even though informal economy and gender issues in the unorganized sector are now under extensive focus, under the human rights approach to livelihood and dignified life options. Construction workers are now under special focus. It is expected that more studies on the kiln-workers shall emerge.

According to the National Commission of Self-Employed Women (1987), "... despite the existence of various constitutional and legal provisions safe-guarding women employment, a large number of women workers particularly in the unorganized sector, suffers from various disadvantages relating to their working lives as well as in their homes. The coverage of labour laws has not benefited these women workers in many crucial areas especially health, maternity and social security. With the changing social and economic conditions, women's productive roles have assumed new significance, but without back up support and service, a healthy combination of women's productive and reproductive role can not be sustained". These observations so aptly apply to the workers under present focus.

Being women, the negotiation for their wages is usually done by their male members in the family. They have no say in the matter. The work women workers provide is also physically strenuous like mixing of clay, processing, loading, unloading, stacking etc. The kiln work therefore is not environment friendly and for women labourers specifically. No physical abuse or violence from the owners or managers has been reported by these women workers but there are incidents of frequent fights and physical violence by their spouse. The two major lacunas in the 'bhatti' (kiln) area are the lack of proper sanitation and water, and no crèches for the children. Several women are having a significant number of small children with them. No concept of maternity benefit is introduced by these managers/owners of the brick kilns. When there is a severe illness, it is up to the benevolent attitude of the managers or the owners if they would like to meet their medical expenses or not. It is not perceived as a compulsory part of the labour welfare. Respondents have perceived that their productivity would be better if their work environment is women friendly. In terms of aspirations, more than 95 per cent of the women do not want their children to be in this job in future. They themselves have aspiration to earn more by increasing their work experience.

An Overview and Concluding Observations

Brick making as discussed in the paper is a part of the unorganized sector. There are three types of issues of unorganized sector workers that need to be addressed. These issues are to a large extent significant for the women workers in brick kiln as well. First, the regulation of their working conditions; the second is the provisioning for conditions under which they are unable to continue to work, such as poor health and disability; and the third is the measures to help them overcome situations of insecurity, such as major illnesses and the liability of losing employment or being laid off at the will of the employer, for which they have no legal remedy.

Unorganized sector work is characterized by low wages that are often insufficient to meet minimum living standards including nutrition, long working hours, hazardous working conditions, lack of basic services such as first aid, drinking water and sanitation at the work site, etc. Even a cursory glance will identify several such occupations, including agricultural labourers, construction workers on building sites, brick-kiln workers, workers in various service industries ranging from transport and courier services to the hospitality industry.

Workers often take the help of children to supplement their own earnings, and this is a major reason for the widespread prevalence of child labour in the unorganized sector. Women are given low and unequal wages. Sexual harassment is common but unarticulated due to fear of loss of employment. In such a situation, there is no question of paid leave and maternity benefits. The use of cheap labour in the unorganized sector is the major source of profit for employers and contractors who exploit the workers' lack of collective bargaining power and state regulation.

Living in abject poverty, most workers in the unorganized sector barely manage a subsistence existence. There is no question of savings, particularly for times when they are unable to work. Hazardous work conditions often cause accidents, loss of limbs, etc. Such disability is disastrous because there are no other sources of income for these households. The lack of savings and support systems also mean that there is no fall-back in other emergencies, especially major illnesses or the death of an earning member in the family. The rising costs of private health care and the systematic dismantling of the public health system in these times of liberalization are a major reason for the huge indebtedness of households in the unorganized sector. There is a pressing need to provide insurance, especially health insurance cover to the workers.

The assurance of the UPA government in its Common Minimum Programme (CMP), announced in May 2004, that it would ensure 'comprehensive protective legislation' for agricultural workers and workers in the unorganized sector, raised hopes within this section and the unions that have worked hard in the last few years to organize them. There have been several drafts of the proposed legislation, including one formulated by the Arjun Sengupta Committee. They propose the setting up of tripartite boards with representation of workers, employers and the government that will register the workers, regulate their working conditions and implement social security welfare schemes. Several campaigns, nationally and locally, and struggles launched by the workers themselves have attempted to ensure that the legislation is implemented.

The recent draft approved by the Cabinet therefore comes as a shock to all those looking forward to the passage of the Bill. For one, it lumps together the agricultural sector and the rest of the unorganized sector, when the CMP itself makes a commitment for separate laws. Most importantly, it makes absolutely no mention of the regulation of service conditions, which is the most crucial aspect of the legislation. On welfare aspects, it contains only pious declarations with no specific schemes. It introduces the concept of a Worker Facilitation Centre to be run by NGOs, thereby negating the important role played by trade unions in articulating and taking up the demands of this poorest section of workers. Worse, it makes absolutely no mention of the government's budgetary commitment to the process of providing social security. The draft therefore reveals the huge gap between the political rhetoric of the ruling sections in this country and their actual intentions.

However, failure in implementation of promises and assurances is not typical to government strategies and planning. The first draft of the National Rural Employment Guarantee Act was similarly flawed, but sustained efforts by various organizations have ultimately resulted in a piece of legislation that has the potential to bring about social and economic change in rural India. There is no doubt that the vast unorganized working sections in the country will launch yet another sustained struggle to ensure that their fundamental Constitutional rights are legally actualized.

In particular, as it is observed in the aforesaid sections, women workers in the brick kilns are not fairly treated and have been the victims of gender discrepancy. Life of these women workers in brick kilns appears to be strenuous and overburdened due to their productive and reproductive roles. While bearing and rearing children remains their primary responsibility, they are also involved in the remunerative activities. These women are unprotected and suffer from economic exploitation. Their ignorance, illiteracy, and poverty have added to their woes all the more. A great majority of them have not benefited by the protective legislation in the critical areas of wages, maternity benefits, childcare, and social security.

A few things can be stated here which should be taken into consideration especially when it comes to women labour force. Opportunities for employment and equal treatment should be the mandatory criteria which must be regulated by the labour laws and followed by entrepreneurs. These two areas should be the critical concerns for the employers and the policy makers. Casual nature of work and surplus labour have, however, given an upper hand to the entrepreneurs in informal sector to exploit workers to the fullest. Female labour force confronts more vulnerability in this sector as this section of population has been considered comparatively weak to form organized unions and flexible to be manipulated. Wage exploitation and unfavourable work environment are two common criteria in the unorganized sector for women labour force. Even the division of labour is also highly 'sex-based'. Furthermore, the conventional labour definition and classification of labour also reduce the scope for women labour force to assert themselves in the national economy and are considered of secondary importance to almost all sections of the industry. The divergent views of policy makers also lead to further complicate the issues of 'gender' and equal rights in the labour market.

Various options are expressed by the role makers and even academics regarding the role of informal economy. These range from preserving the income generating potential of this segment of micro-economy to bringing into the fold of formal sector to providing protection to workers in this sector. These divergent views pose a dilemma at the policy level; whether to promote the informal sector as the provider of employment and income or to seek to extend regulation and social protection thereby reducing its capacity to provide jobs and income (ILO, 2002). The general approach of the ILO towards such a policy has been to find an 'optimal trade off' between these two alternatives. This implies that the policy adapted should generate more jobs and higher incomes and simultaneously provide protection and better condition for work to those employed in this sector.

Given the wider heterogeneity of socio-political environment in the country and varying complexity of the nature of running informal economy, no single strategy can be suggested. Rather micro-studies in various unorganized sectors can be useful as tools for strategy formulation to that particular sector.

Brick kilns being one of the major part of construction sector have the similar nature of labour issues and gender debate. The major initiative can be taken by regulating wages, working hours, and fringe benefits. Integrated community development programmes by several NGOs can be initiated for the workers. Social security, reproductive health and work environment though have been addressed by ILO in this sector; labour organizations and civil society have to come forward to formulate an unified agenda to fight for the gender issues in the vast informal labour market.

In addition, the state and territorial authorities can take initiative to form groups or associations of consultants to government to provide vigilance and regulation to curb down arbitration in the wage discrimination and enhancing social security and better work conditions for the women, as an integral part of labour welfare programme.

The Labour Department can also provide fresh opportunity for the women workers in this unorganized sector. Favourable labour legislation needs to be formulated which provides job security and old-age pension. For example, Tamil Nadu government has already formed 14 Welfare Boards for various categories of the unorganized sector workers, and has been implementing welfare schemes through its Labour Department. Pension of Rs 300 per month is sanctioned to each aged woman from September 1, 2006. Similar strategies can be adopted across all the states in the brick making sector.

■ References

Footlose Labour. *Working in India's Informal Sector.* Breman: Cambridge University Press, 1996.

ILO Report. Delhi Section, 2002.

Moghe, Kiran. *Infochange News and Features*, September edition, 2007. <http://www.infochangeindia.org/agenda9_02.jsp>

National Labour Commission Report, 2002.

National Sample Survey Organization, 2002, 58th Round.

Rajalakshmi, T. K. *Frontline* 21, No. 5 (28 February–March 2004).

Singh, A. and Asgher, S., 2002, Impact of Brick Kilns on Land Use/Landcover Changes around Aligarh City, India, a Project Submitted to Dept. of Geography, Aligarh University, published in *Science Direct*, Habitat International, Vol. 29, Issue 3, pp. 591-602.

Singh, D.P. "Women Workers in Brick Kiln Industry in Haryana, India." *Indian Journal of Gender Studies* 12, No. 1 (2005): 83–97, Sage Publications.

——. "Living Condition of Women in Brick Kiln Industry of India: Reflecting the Agenda for Social Work Intervention." Paper proposed to be submitted in 17th Asia Pacific Social Work Conference, 7–12 July 2003, by Singh, D. P., Department of Social Work, Punjab University, Patiala, 2003.

Sunder, S., "Organizing the Unorganized." A symposium on Footlose Labour, conducted by Seminar, November 13 2003.

Tom, Miles. The Hindu News Update Service, 18 August 2006, pp. 22–49, New Delhi (July 28th UNI edition), <http://www.bioenergylists.org/en/cdmbrickindia>.

Tyagi, Harish. "Building a Bleak Future", *The Hindu*, online edition, 14 October 2007.

World Bank Report. New Delhi, 27 July 2006 (with collaboration of Community Development Carbon Fund).

11

Exploitation and Harassment of Migrant Women and Girl Children Working as Domestic Assistant

Sibnath Deb

Indian Constitution promises democracy and confers the right of equality to people of all strata, irrespective of caste, religion, and culture. But, in reality, the fundamental rights are denied to the people of lower social strata especially the people who are socially and economically backward and they experience discrimination and remain vulnerable to exploitation and maltreatment decades after decade. The factors, which are responsible for the same include illiteracy, poverty, lack of representation of people of their community in the policy making body of the nation, and low social network. In reality, in India, it is the people who struggle that are impoverished, alienated, and concerned with basics for survival. The continued struggle for equality and survival by domestic workers is a relevant example of the fact that despite the guaranteed constitutional rights their sufferings continue.

There are many evidences to indicate that over a period of time domestic work has become more 'feminized' in some sectors. Gender-based occupational segregation has been a global phenomenon. That is why in the past few years gender-based segregation has been a most commonly shared concern among researchers and social activists. As far as Indian scenario is concerned, data indicates that women workers constitute only one-third of the total workforce in India. The census of 1991 shows that number of women workers in India is 91 million out of a total workforce of about 315 million. Most of them are involved in the unorganized sectors such as agriculture, cotton and tea plucking, pottery, handloom, construction, and domestic services.

In the urban areas, especially in all metropolitan cities, domestic assistant has become a bare necessity where both the husband and wife work. This demand for an employment in the unorganized sector calls for assistance from a large number of poor rural women. On the other hand, non-availability of work/job in rural or tribal areas facilitates continuous migration of women workers to the urban cities. A major reason for this being a sharp increase of middle class women in employment. These middle class working women consider it to be below their dignity to continue with their household chores and have shifted their household workload to these poor working women preferably called them as 'maids'.

Nowadays, in almost all the families in the urban areas, there is at least one domestic assistant either as a whole-timer or part-time with variable remuneration. Remuneration varies from area to area. In an area where there is a slum, the possibility of getting a domestic assistant at a cheaper rate is higher, whereas in a area where domestic assistants come from distant places their rate is little higher. However, it varies from Rs 400 to Rs 800 per month in majority of the cases, which is undoubtedly much lower than the minimum wage of a person in an international and national standard.

Extensive literature review was carried out to find out the problems faced by the working women in general and women working as domestic assistant in particular. Findings of some of the international studies and national studies have been presented in the following section for better understanding of the existing knowledge about the subject.

International Study Findings

Denton et al. (2002) examined the effects of working in clients' homes on the mental health and well-being of visiting home care workers. The results of the study was based on a survey of 674 visiting staff from three non-profit home care agencies in a medium-sized city in Ontario, Canada. Survey results were also complimented by data from nine focus groups with 50 employees. The category of home care workers covered in the study included visiting therapists, nurses, and home support workers. Mental health and well-being were measured by three dependent variables: stress; job stress; and intrinsic job satisfaction. Multiple least squared regression analyses showed several structural, emotional, physical, and organizational working conditions associated with the health and well-being of visiting home care workers. Overall, results showed that workload, difficult clients, clients who take advantage of workers, sexual harassment, safety hazards, a repetitious job, and work-related injuries were associated with poor health. Being fairly paid, having good benefits, emotional labour, organizational support, control over work, and peer support were associated with better health. Results suggested that policy change is needed to encourage healthier work environments for employees who work in clients' homes. In another study Richman et al. (1999) hypothesized that interpersonal workplace stressors involving sexual harassment and generalized workplace abuse were highly prevalent and significantly correlated with mental health outcomes including symptomatic distress, the use and abuse of alcohol, and other drug use. Employees in four university occupational groups (faculty, student, clerical, and service workers; n=2,492) were surveyed by means of a mailed self-report instrument. Cross-tabular and ordinary least squares and logistic regression analyses examined the prevalence of harassment and abuse and their association with mental health status. The data showed high rates of harassment and abuse. Male and female clerical and service workers experienced higher levels of particularly severe mistreatment. Generalized abuse was more prevalent than harassment for all groups. Both harassment and abuse were significantly linked to most mental health outcomes for men and women. Finally, authors concluded that interpersonally abusive workplace dynamics constitute a significant public health problem that merits increased intervention and prevention strategies. Lipscomb et al. (2007) reported on the prevalence of self-reported depressive symptoms and associated factors among women employed in a poultry processing plant and a community comparison group of other employed women in north-eastern North Carolina in the southern United States. The rural area was poor and sparsely populated with an African-American majority. The largest employer of women in the area was a poultry processing plant. Findings revealed that the prevalence of depressive symptoms, based on a CES-D measure of 16 or more, was 47.8 per cent among the poultry workers and 19.7 per cent among the other working women (prevalence ratio = 2.3). After adjusting for socio-economic variables, health-related quality of life and coping style, the prevalence of depressive symptoms remained 80 per cent higher among the poultry workers. Further, the prevalence of symptoms was also higher among those who perceived low social support at work, hazardous work conditions, job insecurity, and high levels of isometric load.

Hayashi et al. (1994) stated that home care services make it possible for millions of older Americans to continue living in the community. Such services may enhance the recipients' quality of life while providing essential respite to family caregivers. But, while there had been increasing recognition of the burden borne by the predominantly female family caregivers, there had been less attention to the plight of the home care workforce. With the growth of the home care industry, the burden of care had to some extent shifted from one category of female caregivers to another. The findings revealed a pattern of harsh working conditions, low wages, and few benefits. The findings raised questions about the ethics and efficacy of government policies that are based on the exploitation of home care workers.

The exploratory and descriptive study of Musayon and Caufield (2007) explored the relationship between workplace violence and drug use in women. It also explored the perception of women workers on the relationship between workplace violence and drug use. The World Health Organization (WHO) and the United Nations have recognized violence against women and have adopted a definition of it. The Centres for Disease Control and Prevention reported that violence in the workplace has increased 300 per cent over the last decade. Alcohol misuse, occupation, and gender are associated with aggression in the workplace. Estimations of the incidence of non-fatal injuries sustained because of workplace violence and evaluations of the associated risk factors have rarely been documented. The authors covered 125 women workers between the ages of 18 and 60 years in four suburbs of Zapallal, Lima. Of the 125 women, 28.8 per cent experienced violence in the workplace. Of the 36 women who had experienced violence in the workplace, 16 agreed to participate in interviews to explore their perceptions. The data were saturated with the 16 interviews. Of the 125 workers surveyed 17.6 per cent experienced verbal violence, 9.6 per cent experienced physical violence, and 1.6 per cent were sexually harassed in their workplace. Women who were verbally abused demonstrated eight times greater risk of drug use than those who did not experience this type of violence in their workplace.

Swanberg et al. (2007) investigated whether there is an association between workplace disclosure of victimization and current employment status; and whether there is an association between receiving workplace support and current employment status among women who disclosed victimization circumstances to someone at work. Results indicated that disclosure and workplace support are associated with employment. Implications for clinical practice, workplace policies, and future research are discussed. In another study Swanberg et al. (2006) found that violent partners used a wide range of work interference tactics that women were more likely to tell someone at work about the victimization than they were to hide the information, and that co-workers and supervisors provided a range of supports to women who did disclose their situation.

Research suggests partner violence has a negative impact on women's employment. However, there has been limited examination of partner stalking and consequences for employment. In this regard Logan et al. (2007) examined partner stalking and employment consequences among two samples of women. One sample was women who had obtained a protective order against a violent partner and had worked in the prior year (n = 482), about one half of these women were stalked by their violent partner and one half were not. The second study examined qualitative information from women recently stalked (n = 62) by a violent partner. Results from both studies suggested that women who were stalked by a violent partner were significantly more susceptible to on-the-job harassment and problems. Also, women reported that stalking by a partner interfered in their work through on-the-job harassment, work disruption, and job performance problems. Sims and Napholz (1996) explored and described the experiences of African-American working women who attended a six-week intervention group to decrease role conflict and enhance psychological well-being. Authors concluded that African-American working women experienced an additional element of role conflict that is related to their ascribed role rather than their achieved role. Messias et al. (1996) carried out a qualitative study based on individual interviews with 75 Brazilian women in an impoverished peri-urban squatter community (*favela*) in south-eastern Brazil with a view to understanding women's involvement in domestic and employment contexts; identify stresses and satisfactions of maternal, spousal, and employment roles; and assess personal and environmental role constraints and resources from the perspective of women's health. Authors concluded that the confluence of role constraints affecting the participants' lives included poverty, marginalization, abuse, and lack of support and recognition by partners and society. In order to overcome great adversity and meet heavy role demands, these women relied on self, faith in God, family, and health resources.

Research has linked workplace harassment and abuse with distress and drinking. However, increasing societal attention to sexual harassment (SH) has been accompanied by pressures on work organizations to censure harassing behaviours. Richman et al. (2004) addressed altered perceptions of the organizational tolerance (OT) for SH and generalized workplace abuse (GWA), changes in the prevalence and incidence of these experiences, and their impact on distress and drinking behaviours. A cohort of workers completed a mail survey at three points in time. Questionnaires assessed perceptions of OT for SH and GWA, experiences of SH and GWA, coping, and distress and drinking behaviours. Both sexes perceived that tolerance of SH and GWA has decreased over time. Changes in reported prevalence of these experiences differed by gender, and incidence for both genders decreased more strongly than prevalence. The linkages between SH/GWA and distress and drinking changed over time, but in different ways for women and men. SH and GWA still have deleterious consequences, and replications of this research and greater efforts at prevention are needed (ibid.).

National Study Findings

In India very few studies on domestic workers have been reported. Status of girl child in rural India is associated with their involvement in domestic work as assistant at an early age. Regarding status of girl child, Devendra (1995) stated that rural children lack the advantages of modern amenities and facilities, such as transportation, electricity, media, hygiene, health care, and access to education. A young girl's status is related to her mother's status. Women are valued the most when a son is born. Girl children are considered an economic liability in childcare costs, dowry costs, and marriage support. Since the 1970s, dowry demands have increased. Daughters must meet the demands of prospective in-laws for education and dowry even after marriage. The attitudes of parents, families, and society encourage sex-selective abortion, infanticide, abuse in childhood, and domestic violence in adulthood. Rural girl children spend their time cooking, cleaning, fetching wood and water, caring for children, and working in the fields sowing, transplanting, and weeding. Girl children contribute over 20 per cent of total work at home. The only advantage a girl child has in rural areas is visibility. The greatest disadvantage is that her mother, who faced neglect herself, discriminates against her. Increasingly girl children contribute income to their household from beedi-making, gem polishing, embroidering, or paper bag making. Sometimes girls and boys work in hazardous occupations. Gender disparity is evident in school enrolment, dropout rates, literacy, and employment. In 1994, India passed a universal female education bill that offers parents incentives for access and punishment for keeping a girl out of school. Communities need to create a demand for rural girl children's education.

Deb (1997) found that most of the girls working as domestic assistants in Kolkata experienced different problems in the working place like mental torture, physical abuse in case of minor mistakes and/or not being able to follow the instruction of the landlady immediately and a small number of them also experience sexual abuse. In another research Deb (2005) studied a group of 120 migrant child labourers working in households, tea stalls, garages and shops in South Kolkata reveals that an overwhelming number of the children are abused, in some way or the other—physically, mentally, or sexually. Of those with health problems, a good number of them remain untreated. In some cases, abuse and neglect become fatal. Deb suggested that law enforcement agencies should be very strict against the perpetrators, who badly abuse and maltreat helpless children. Simultaneously, the community should be sensitized to this issue. In this regard, Non-Governmental Organizations (NGO) should take initiative for creating social awareness. Deb (2004) stated that child abuse and neglect are reflected in a variety of deeply rooted social and cultural problems in India and are directly linked to the economic condition of the country. India, a multilingual country, is presently the home for one-sixth of the total global population of which about 35 per cent is children. Although, children across the country are abused, maltreated and commercially exploited, the nature and types of abuse and neglect vary from culture to culture and from state to state.

Study of Save the Children, Kolkata revealed that most child domestic workers were girls in the age group of 11 years and above. They were either illiterate or studied up to Standard V and most of them started working between 8 to 12 years of age. Most child domestic workers used to get less than Rs 200 per month as remuneration, which was sent home to contribute to family income (Source: Report of Save the Children on Children Working as Domestic Worker, Kolkata Office, 2005). Most child domestic workers used to get less than 2 hours of rest everyday, and a very substantial slice of the child domestic workers population was made to work everyday without any rest during the daytime. Even by conservative estimates, the average working day of most child domestic workers was 15 hours long. More than one-third of the children were not satisfied with the food, clothes, and stay arrangements provided to them by their employers, and 41 per cent find the workplace unsafe. Neglectful conditions at the workplace were clearly visible through this information. The duration of work timings for these children was far longer than even that prescribed for adults working in the formal sector. Children's articulation of their feelings about their conditions at the workplace presents their unhappiness towards their current life circumstances. Most child domestic workers were allowed to visit their families only once every six months. More than one-fourth of the child domestics had been stopped from meeting their family members at least once. Child domestic workers faced all types of abuse, physical, emotional, and sexual. Within each category of abuse also, these children were made to experience a wide variety of abusive situations. Some of the important observations of SCF study are as follows:

- 68.3 per cent of total child participants in the research did face physical abuse.
- Nearly 86.0 per cent of total child domestic workers participants did face some form of emotional abuse.
- 32.2 per cent of the participants have had their private parts touched by someone.
- 22.4 per cent of the respondents compelled to touch the abusers private parts.
- 20.3 per cent of the participants were forced to have sexual intercourse with the abuser.
- 19.5 per cent of the child participants compelled to watch pornography.
- 46.6 per cent of the children did face severe physical abuse, which resulted in an injury to the body. In case of injury, children did not receive proper medical care.
- Almost 25.0 per cent of the children said that they are presently facing physical abuse.
- Perpetrators were usually someone known to the child and were in a position of power and authority over the child.
- Most incidents of abuse happened a number of times as reported.

Findings of the above studies indicate the areas which former researchers explored. The areas included effects of working in clients' homes on the mental health and well-being of visiting home care workers, interpersonal workplace stressors involving sexual harassment and generalized workplace abuse, self-reported depressive symptoms and associated factors among women employed in a poultry processing plant, relationship between workplace violence and drug use in women and so on. At the same time, it is very clear from the literature review that very little research was carried out on women working as domestic assistants internationally and locally. Four Kolkata-based studies covered some dimensions of the problems of women and/or children working as domestic assistant leaving sufficient scope to investigate the issue in depth from holistic point of view.

Objectives

- Understanding the profile of the domestic assistants.
- Understanding the factors which pushed women the unorganized sector for livelihood.
- Understanding the perceived behaviour, benefits and nature of medical care and support services received by the domestic assistants.
- Understanding the nature of exploitation and harassment experienced by women working as domestic assistant.
- Understanding the utilization of earning of the domestic assistants.
- Understanding the status of the women in their own family.
- Suggesting need-based measures.

Methodology

For a sensitive issue like this it is very difficult to proceed using quantitative approach only and thereby we proposed to unearth the issue following qualitative study approach. The present study was confined to Kolkata city only.

Sample and Sampling: A group of 85 children and women working as domestic assistants within the age range of 11 to 25 was covered in the study and they were selected following snowball technique.

Study Tools: The qualitative methods which were followed for collection of data include case study and in-depth interview in addition to a semi-structured questionnaire and data were collected following face-to-face interview method by the female investigators as per convenience of the subject. In a number of cases help from some of the senior working women was taken for collection of quality data. In-depth interview was carried out with 60 children and women while case study was done in case of rest 25 subjects.

This apart, four Focus Group Discussions (FGDs) were carried out, two each with children and women separately so that children do not feel hesitant to share their views about different issues. In each Focus Group Discussion 7 to 8 subjects were present.

A Brief Description about Data Collection Approaches

Semi-Structured Questionnaire: This is a tool to gather both qualitative and quantitative information from the subject about an issue. It allows the subject to share their exact feelings about views on an issue and justify the quantitative data through qualitative verbatim responses.

Focus Group Discussions (FGDs): These technique best suites to identify the issues not explored earlier. The general aim of this method was to use social dynamics of the group to encourage people to reveal more of their opinions, emotions, and behaviour. The issues, which were explored in the FGDs, include literacy status of women and attitude towards adult literacy programme, activity pattern of women, role of women in decision-making process, and their knowledge about the outer world and media habit.

In-depth Interviews: This technique was applied to collect in depth and more detailed information about some sensitive issues like atrocities against women and issues, which require thorough probing like daily inside and outside activities of women. It was administered personally, which allowed a degree of flexibility like the FGDs in the interviewer-respondent interaction.

Case Study: This is one of the most powerful qualitative methods to present entire picture about a situation in a comprehensive manner. It improves the quality of readability of the write up of any report.

Ethical Issues Followed

Objectives of the study were explained and verbal consent was obtained.

Subjects were ensured about confidentiality of information and under no circumstances the information shared by them will be communicated to the employer.

Subjects were informed that during the study if they wished they could withdraw from the study.

It was made clear that their cooperation was necessary only to extend help to children like them who were in distress, no special privileges or compensation or help would be given to them for agreeing to be part of the study.

Problems Encountered

Initially it was very difficult to contact the target group for data collection since they remained busy in household activities and hardly found time to talk to the researchers. Afterwards report was established with few elderly women serving as domestic assistant and asked for their cooperation for success of the study, which further facilitated the process of data collection following snowball technique.

It was very difficult at times to interview the subject because of inquisitiveness of the employer. Hence, in a number of cases more than two visits were needed to collect intended information. It was very clear that although most of them were eager to share their problem with the researchers, they were afraid of the employer.

The study was carried out with a small sample because of their engagement in the work for longer period. Another study with large sample is suggested in other part of India to check whether the situation is similar in nature.

Results

Data collected through various methods like a semi-structured questionnaire, in-depth interview, case study, and focus group discussions have been processed and presented in the following sections under different headings.

Demographic and Socio-economic Profile of the Domestic Assistants

Data with regard to demographic and socio-economic profile of the domestic assistants have been provided in Table 1 and 2. Table 1 shows that more than half (54/85) of the domestic assistants were teenagers; i.e., up to 19 years of age, illiterate; i.e., never been to school and working as full-timer; i.e., live with the family of employer. Remuneration varied from below Rs 400 to Rs 1,001 and above. However, further analysis of data with regard to remuneration revealed that teenagers who work as full-timers mostly receives up to Rs 800 per month while the women above 20 years of age who worked as part-timer and do a specific job of a house, i.e., only cleaning or washing or cooking, earn more money in a month since they work in a number of houses.

Majority of the domestic assistants hailed from the rural areas of West Bengal. The married women who work as part-time workers mostly

Table 1 *Profile of the Domestic Assistants (N=85)*

Enquiry Area	Mode of Response	Frequency	Percentage
Age	Below 12	7	8.2
13 – 16	26	30.6	
17 – 19	21	24.7	
20 – 22	13	15.3	
23 – 25	10	11.8	
26 and above	8	9.4	
Education	Never been to school	44	51.8
	Studied up to Class V	33	38.8
	Class VI and above	8	9.4
Working hours	Full-timer	53	62.4
	Work-specific i.e., part-time	22	25.9
Remuneration Per month	Below Rs 400	6	7.1
	Rs 401 – Rs 600	16	18.8
	Rs 601 – Rs 800	45	52.9
	Rs 801 – Rs 1000	15	17.7
	Rs 1001 and above	22	25.9

live in the slum areas with their husbands. More than half were unmarried (46/85) while in case of married women a good number of them were separated (15/85) and had lost husbands or did not know the whereabouts of husbands. A good number of the husbands of married domestic assistants were not doing any work while rest were involved in casual work, in office and/or running a small business (Table 2).

Table 2 *Information about Place of Origin and Family*

Enquiry Area	Mode of Response	Frequency	Percentage
Place of origin	Rural	65	76.5
	Semi-urban	15	17.7
	Urban	5	5.9
Marital status	Unmarried	46	54.1
	Married and living together	18	21.2
	Divorced/separated	15	17.7
	Husband died/no trace	6	7.1
No of children in case of married (N=39)	No child	11	28.1
	One	14	35.9
	Two	9	23.1
	More than two	5	12.8
Occupation of Husband, if married and living together (N=18)	Casual worker	4	22.2
	Working in office	3	16.7
	Running small business	3	16.7
	Doing nothing	8	44.4
Any addiction of husband (N=18)	Yes	14	77.8
	No	4	22.2
Contribution of husband in family (N=18)	Yes	7	38.9
	No	11	61.1
Any violence (N=18)	Yes	7	61.1
	No	11	38.9

Factors Which Pushed Women in Unorganized Sector for Livelihood

Although poverty was the prime reason behind joining as domestic assistants in most of the cases, a number of other factors play an important role in combination with the above for forcing a girl child or women into the unorganized sector. Among the factors which mostly forced children into unorganized sectors included illiteracy, sudden crisis in the family, ill-treatment of step mother or father and family culture to engage children in casual work. In case of women above 20 years and especially who were married some additional variables were found to be responsible for involvement of women in domestic work. These included unemployment status of husband, insistence by the husband and/or husband disappeared or sudden death (Table 3).

Table 3 *Causal Factors for Involvement in Domestic Work (N=85) (Multiple Response)*

Causal Factors	*Frequency*	*Percentage*
Poverty	65	76.5
Illiteracy	15	17.7
Sudden crisis in the family	23	27.1
Influence of step mother/father	12	14.1
Husband does not work	8	9.4
Husband forced/insisted	15	17.7
Husband left/deserted	15	17.7
Others like family culture	4	4.7

Perceived Behaviour, Nature of Medical Care and Support Services Received by the Domestic Assistants

The study has thrown a light on the behaviour of employers towards the domestic assistants. In a number of cases women and children did express agony for being ill-treated by their employers especially by landladies. Domestic assistants were not allowed to sit in the chair and/or view the television in presence of landlord and landlady. In case of leave for visiting the family, most of them did not get leave for more than twice a year that too for four/five days in each visit. Even in some cases their wage was deducted when some of them could not come back as committed on account of genuine ground. In general, there were very few examples of increment of remuneration every year. Domestic assistants work with the same remuneration year after years. According to some of the domestic assistants:

> "I also feel like to view the TV. But I am not allowed. When 'dada' and 'boudi' (landlord and landlady) go out I switch on the TV. One day I was caught and scolded"—a working girl.
>
> "This year my landlord did not allow me visit my parents for the second time"—a girl child working as domestic assistant.
>
> "My employer deducted four days remuneration from my salary since I returned four days late"—a working women.
>
> "For the last four years I have been working in a house. But they did not increase the remuneration"—a working woman.

They were often expected to wake up early but had their meals unnaturally late. Employers specially treated children inhumanly. In a number of cases when the employer went out for two or three days they locked the child indoor without access to the basic amenities (as reported by few children during in-depth interviews). Similar incidents had been reported by the newspaper in the recent past in Kolkata. The following case study is a relevant example of maltreatment in normal course received by the working children.

Case 1

Tumpa Mondol, a child of 13 years, never been to school, eldest daughter out of three siblings has been working in Kolkata to help her family. She was supposed to wake up at 5 a.m. in the morning as a response to the alarm. She was given her meals at unnatural late hours and given medicines on the other hand to prevent any health problems that may arise out of having food late. Further she was given to wear clothes that would deliberately make her look unattractive and discriminate her as a maid (a case of neglect and unkind behaviour of employer).

When the issue of medical care and support services in case of emergency was probed during the in-depth interviews and FGDs, it was observed that in most of the cases of illness self-prescribed medicine by the employer was found to be a common practice and they hardly followed up the same. Even in some cases of illness domestic assistants were shown the route to their own houses and asked to take rest. Views of some of the children and women which emerged during the in-depth interview have been provided below:

> "I told my 'babu' (employer) about my fever and he asked me to wait for two/three days and thereafter it will disappear automatically"—a girl child working as domestic assistant.
>
> "Once I had serious pain in my stomach for two/three days. I drew the attention of 'boudi' (landlady). Boudi had given me liquid medicine available at home in the second day"—a women working as domestic assistant.
>
> "Four months back the thumb of my right hand was cut by a sharp weapon while cutting the vegetables. Afterwards it was paining for seven days. Landlady did not give me any medicine"—a girl child working as domestic assistant.
>
> "Last year I was suffering from chronic diarrhoea for seven days. Dada asked me to take water with salt and sugar"—a girl child working as domestic assistant.

However, in case of some fortunate children and working women, employer consulted a qualified doctor and extended the necessary medical aid along with medicine as prescribed by the qualified doctor.

In case of emergency situations like illness of the family members, accidents and/or marriage of younger siblings, very few of them got financial support from the employer. According to some of the domestic assistants:

> "Once I asked for two months advance salary for a marriage occasion of my younger brother. My employer did give one month advance"—a women working as domestic assistant.
>
> "Three months back I got the message from my family that my father was ill. I wanted leave and some advance money from my employer. Although they allowed me to visit my family, they did not give me advance salary of one month"—a girl child working as domestic assistant.

On the contrary, few domestic assistants are lucky enough who got good support from the employer in case of emergency situation.

"My landlord in the slum area asked me to leave the house. For taking a new rent house in the same area I needed to pay advance money for which I approached my employer and they had given me Rs 2000"—a woman working as domestic assistant.

"My employer is kind enough. During any festival they give me new clothes and also for my children"—a women working as domestic assistant.

Nature of Exploitation and Harassment Experienced by Women Working as Domestic Assistants

Apart from financial exploitation, the domestic assistant is also vulnerable to physical, mental and sexual exploitation as revealed from the focus group discussions and in-depth interviews. Children are more vulnerable in all forms as stated above while the women above 20 years are more vulnerable to metal torture. Following are some of the verbatim quotations of the children which will clearly narrate the incidents of harassment experienced by the children:

"My landlady is always after me and scolding me. It is very difficult to satisfy her through my work. It seems to me that she has some mental health problems"

"My babu (employer) has a tendency to touch my private parts when 'boudi' (landlady) is out of home"—a girl child working as domestic assistant.

"She (landlady) always beat me in case of minor mistakes and/or for not being able to deliver prompt services as desired"—a girl child working as domestic assistant.

"It is very difficult to share the problems openly which we face in our working place"—a girl child working as domestic assistant.

Some of the women stated that they face typical problems. At times they feel like leaving the work. But hard reality in terms of lack of social and/or family support forces them to cope with the situation. Few of them were of the opinion that:

"We do not have any liberty. All the time I need to remain seated in the house as desired by my landlady"—a woman working as domestic assistant.

"My employer do not want to give me leave for more them three/four days at a time to visit my family members back at home in Sundarban Area"—a woman working as domestic assistant.

"It is very difficult to tolerate abusive words used by the landlady for maximum output. At times I feel like to say something. Again I think of my children"—a woman working as domestic assistant.

"My employer does not give me clothes twice a year in case of need. On the other hand, I do double the work of our verbal agreement"—a women working as domestic assistant.

In order to understand the nature of harassment experienced by the domestic assistants a detailed case study of 25 individuals was prepared. Four case studies of different nature have been provided below:

Case 1

Madhumita Kar, female, aged 11 years, got two siblings, never been to school, lost her mother at an early age. Afterwards her father got remarried and her stepmother forced Madhumita to leave house and look for work. Father had sent her to Kolkata with a neighbour who was working in a house as domestic assistant. Initially he engaged Madhumita in her work and afterwards she placed her in another house for taking care of a small child as full-timer against Rs 300 per month. But in reality Madhumita was asked to do other household chores along with childcare. One day one cup was broken while washing the same for which she was denied of dinner one night. Another day while carrying a glass it fell down and broken and she was subjected to two slaps by landlady who also deducted the price of the glass from her monthly remuneration. She was not given minimum clothes, deprived from medical care in case of minor fever and also from nutrition. She had shown her interest for basic literacy but the employer did not encourage her for the same. She used to sleep in the kitchen which was not clean and hygienic (a case of mental, physical torture, and deduction of price of a glass).

Case 2

Shipra Das, female, 16 years, studied up to class 11, second position out of five sisters, illiterate parents with almost no source of earning except a small cultivable and came from interior rural areas to Kolkata city with a neighbour in search of employment. When she came to Kolkata she was 10 years old and started working as domestic assistant against Rs 400 per month. Meanwhile she worked in two more houses. Finally, she came to a house and had been working there for four years against Rs 800 per month. But there she had been working for long hours every day, i.e., from 6 a.m. to midnight until everybody goes to bed. In other words, it may be stated that Shipra was taking care of all household chores in addition to caring of two children. Although she did not face any discrimination in terms of food and medical care, she experienced humiliation and mental torture for minor mistakes and/or for not being able to deliver prompt services at times as desired by a number of family members, which was humanly impossible. As a result, Shipra was upset a number of times. Since she came from a poor economic background she had to digest all the agonies silently. Her mother used to visit her once in two/three months to collect her remuneration for running the family (a case of mental harassment).

Case 3

Jayanti Kar, female, aged 18 years, illiterate, hailed from Sundarban area had been working in a house as domestic assistant for eight years. She had two sisters and one younger brother. Mother was alive while father died about 9 years back. Jayanti's employer was in business and dependent on alcohol. Although the landlady was not abusive but her husband used Jayanti sexually a number of times and threatened her not to disclose to anybody. Finally, she became pregnant once and undertook abortion under the initiative of the landlord. Since family was in need of support, she could not leave the place and remained vulnerable to sexual abuse (a case of sexual abuse).

Case 4

Archana Sharma, female, 17 years, studied up to class III came to Kolkata city along with her relatives for work in a house of higher government official with a hope of getting an opportunity in government service as class four staff as promised by the employer through her relative. She had one younger brother. Father was no more while mother was working as casual worker. Employer, i.e., the government higher official had two pampered children who used to order every moment for different things and in case of slightest delay in delivering the materials as desired by them they used to scold Archana badly and used abusive words. In a number of occasions Archana was beaten up by the pampered children of the employer. Instead of correcting the behaviour of the short-tempered and ill-mannered children landlady, i.e., the mother of the children the blamed Archana for the unhappy incidents at home. Unfortunately, the employer knowing fully well that his children are at fault preferred to remain silent since he was aware of short temperament and violent behaviour of his wife. Archana digested all humiliation, mental torture, and even physical abuse in the little hope of getting a permanent government job as class four staff (a case of physical torture along with mental torture).

Utilization of Earning of the Domestic Assistants

Replying to the question in what manner do domestic assistants spend their monthly salary, children mostly stated that money is sent back to home for running the family keeping one-tenth to little more of the same with them for their personal use or for fulfilling their basic needs. In case of married women they complement the family income to run the system as some of their husbands do not do any work.

"In the first week of every month my mother comes to collect the money from my employer"—a girl child working as domestic assistant.

"I send three-fourths of my salary to my family every month since I have got two sisters and one younger brother with my parents back at home"—a girl child working as domestic assistant.

"I mostly use my monthly income to run my family since my husband earns very little"—a woman working as domestic assistant.

"My husband does not do any work. More so, he is an alcoholic and remains drunk all the time. I have got two children. I am worried about the future. I work in three houses as part-time worker and earns about Rs 2,000 per month. After running the family I try to save some money every month"—a women working as domestic assistant.

Status of the Women in Their Own Family

A brighter side was revealed in some instances when asked about the status the women enjoyed in their own families. Working children and children enjoy better status at their home than that of their counterparts, i.e., non-working women in the family. When they go back to their homes they receive better attention from the parents and other family members as revealed from the in-depth interviews and focus group discussions. Few of them stated that:

> "When I go home my other siblings and parents welcome me"—a girl child working as domestic assistant.
>
> "My mother makes special food for me when I visit them back at home"—a girl child working as domestic assistant.
>
> "My in-laws give me importance since I earn money and also they expect some gift like clothes and financial support from me"—a women working as domestic assistant.
>
> "My husband looks after the children when I come for work"—a women working as domestic assistant.

Unfortunately, the negative side remains. Even after contributing to the family they did not enjoy a similar status as compared to the fortunate others. This was seen mostly in case of husbands who are addicted to alcohol and gambling. These husbands are not only indifferent in running the family and/or discharging their duties, they expect some money from the wife for alcohol and gambling.

Discussion and Conclusion

Migration from rural areas to urban areas is not a new problem but this problem has increased over a period of time in Indian society. Generally people migrate to urban areas when there is scarcity of sources of earning in the rural areas and they come to urban areas in search of means for living. The main reasons for increasing migration in the urban areas in the recent times include population explosion, division of family cultivable land among the next generation, social alienation, and poor industrial growth in the rural areas. The above situation forces a large number of people to come to urban areas. Often the women and children accompany the male members.

Discrimination, exploitation, and harassment of socially and economically deprived people in any society are a dominant feature of the 21st century. In the developing countries like India this problem is more acute and severe. Children and women working as migrant labour in the form of domestic assistants are treated badly by the employer. They hardly enjoy any freedom and get minimum leave in a year for visiting the family members. In case of any organized sector, everybody gets at least 30 days leave in a year while most of the domestic assistants do not get even one-third of this leave in a year, i.e., 10 days. In addition to low wage, i.e., commercial exploitation, they also become victims of mental, physical, and sexual harassment (Musayon and Caufield, 2007; Deb, 2006; Richman et al., 1999; Deb, 1997; Report of Save the Children, Kolkata, 2006). Children remain more vulnerable to all the above mentioned problems since most of them are afraid to raise voice against abuse and exploitation. In case of mental and physical torture of domestic assistants, landlady mostly housewives are found to be more abusive. Women above 20 years do mostly experience mental harassment and economic exploitation.

In any institution whether government or non-government there is a specific working hours, which varies from 7 to 9 hours. However, working hours for the people working in unorganized sectors is unlimited and it could be between 14 to 16 hours a day and even more, while the remuneration ranges from Rs 200 to 1,000 per month in most of the cases and without any other facilities which are offered in an organized sector. The findings of the study with regard to salary, work condition, and other benefits are corroborated by another study carried out in US (Hayashi et al., 1994). At the same time, the study of Hayashi et al. (1994) raised questions about the ethics and efficacy of government policies that are based on the exploitation of home care workers. Interestingly, working children and women do not feel exploited if their earning is utilized for the cause of own family. Rather they think it is their responsibility to support the family and in turn they also enjoy better status in the family.

ILO and the Ministry of Labour, Government of India should think over this issue and should come up with some policy for giving justice to people working in the unorganized sectors like the domestic assistants. A large number of children are working as domestic assistants against minimum wages. They are preferred since it is easier to exploit them by paying low wages for maximum output. Although child labour has been banned by the Government of India, i.e., a child below 14 years of age cannot work, in reality it is very difficult to implement such a law in a country like India because of magnitude of the problem and complications involved in proving the age. Since government declared the legal measure, now the government cannot talk about social measures like:

- Defining the working hours for the children
- Defining the minimum wage
- Ensuring safety and hygienic working condition and safe custody of the wage of the children
- Ensuring basic education for the children by the employer
- Providing medical care in case of necessity
- Not abusing the children physically and/or mentally.

These social measures would have been the right steps to be enforced in the Indian scenario to ensure protection of rights of the children working as domestic assistants and for their safety.

On the other hand, the Ministry of Women and Child Development and National Commission for Protection of Child Rights have undertaken various measures for child protection and also formulated law for framing Juvenile Welfare Board and Juvenile Justice System in every state; it will take time to implement the same in reality. However, these are good steps taken by the government.

Ironically, in India, much study has not been conducted on domestic assistants and therefore, it is very difficult to compare the picture of Kolkata city with other cities in India. Although a number of organizations have been working for the welfare of domestic assistants, most of them do not document their activities systematically and have not published the same and therefore it remains an area unknown to other social activities and researchers. However, it may be stated that most of the findings, especially those concerning the conditions of work of domestic workers, are consistent with findings of other organizations from across the country working on the same issue (Deb, 1997, 2004).

Recommensdation

The following steps are recommended for improving the situation of domestic assistants in India:

Prevention

Sensitization of larger society about the factors which force people for domestic work and to behave with them humanly and show empathy to them. This could be done through tele films and/or small TV programmes and telecasted in popular TV channels to reach the message to mass people.

Since most child domestic assistants start working while they are in the age group of 8 to 12 years, special attention should be given to this particular group while planning intervention programmes in the rural areas for prevention of child involvement in domestic work.

Government should bring effective legislation to ensure rights of the domestic assistants and for prevention of violence and harassment against them.

Intervention

Domestic assistants should be given basic information about personal safety and information about child helpline so that they can contact them if necessary.

Peer network should be strengthened so that working children and women can seek support from them in case of necessity. In this regard, NGOs should take the initiative to create a platform with like minded NGOs to enable the domestic workers to join the network.

The findings of the present study have led the researchers to raise certain questions for the valued and learned readers to think about and analyse.

How to bring justice for the socio-economically deprived people in the present Indian society and ensure their rights?

Who should take the lead role to ensure socio-economic rights for the domestic assistants so that they can also lead a life like people of larger society?

■ References

Alonso Castillo, M.M., Musayon Oblitas, F.Y., David, H.M., Gómez Meza, M.V. "Drug Consumption and Occupational Violence in Working Women, A Multicentre Study: Mexico, Peru, Brazil." *Rev Lat Am Enfermagem* 14, No. 2 (March–April 2006): 155–62.

Deb, Sibnath. *Children in Agony.* New Delhi: Concept Publishing Company, 2006.

———. "Child Abuse and Neglect in a Metropolitan City: A Qualitative Study of Migrant Child Labour in South Kolkata." *Social Change* 35, No. 3 (2005): 56–67.

———. *Defining Child Maltreatment in India.* USA: ISPCAN, 2004. Published in the World Perspective on Child Abuse and Neglect (Sixth Edition).

———. "Harassment of Urban Girl Children Engaged in Domestic Work." Presented in an International-Interdisciplinary Conference on the Urban Childhood, organized by the Institute of Child Research, Trondheim, Norway between 9–12 June, 1997.

Denton, M.A., Zeytino lu, I.U., and Davies, S. "Working in Clients' Homes: The Impact on the Mental Health and Well-Being of Visiting Home Care Workers." *Home Health Care Serv Q.* 21, No. 1: (2002): 1–27.

Devendra, K. "Girl Child in Rural India." *Soc Change* 25, No. 2–3 (June–September 1995): 189–96.

Hayashi, R., Gibson, J.W. and Weatherley, R.A. "Working Conditions in Home Care: A Survey of Washington State's Home Care Workers." *Home Health Care Serv Q.* 14, No. 4 (1994): 37–48.

Le Franc, E., Wyatt, G. E., Chambers, C., Eldemire, D., Bain, B., Ricketts, H. "Working Women's Sexual Risk Taking in Jamaica. *Soc Sci Med.* 42, No. 10: (May 1996): 1411–17.

Lipscomb, H.J., Dement, J.M., Epling, C.A., Gaynes, B.N., McDonald, M.A., Schoenfisch, A.L. "Depressive Symptoms among Working Women in Rural North Carolina: A Comparison of Women in Poultry Processing and Other Low-Wage Jobs." *Int J Law Psychiatry* 30, No. 4–5 (July–October 2007): 284–98.

Logan, T.K., Shannon, L., Cole, J., Swanberg, J. "Partner Stalking and Implications for Women's Employment." *J Interpers Violence* 22, No. 3 (March 2007): 268–91.

Messias, D.K., Hall, J.M. and Meleis, A.I. "Voices of Impoverished Brazilian Women: Health Implications of Roles and Resources." *Women Health* 24, No. 1 (1996): 1–20.

Musayon Oblitas, F.Y. and Caufield, C. "Workplace Violence and Drug Use in Women Workers in a Peruvian Barrio." *Int Nurs Rev.* 54, No. 4 (December 2007): 339–45.

Report of Save the Children on Children Working as Domestic Worker, Kolkata Office, 2005.

Richman, J.A., Rospenda, K.M., Nawyn, S.J., Flaherty, J.A., Fendrich, M., Drum, M.L., Johnson, T.P. "Sexual Harassment and Generalized Workplace Abuse among University Employees: Prevalence and Mental Health Correlates." *Am J Public Health* 89, No. 3 (March 1999): 358–63.

Richman, J.A., Rospenda, K.M., Flaherty, J.A., Freels, S., Zlatoper, K. "Perceived Organizational Tolerance for Workplace Harassment and Distress and Drinking Over Time [Harassment and Mental Health]." *Women Health* 40, No. 4 (2004): 1–23.

Sims, O.V. and Napholz, L. What are Some African American Working Women's Expressed Experiences of Role Conflict?" *J Cult Divers* 3, No. 4 (Winter 1996): 116–22.

Swanberg, J., Macke, C. and Logan, T.K. "Working Women Making it Work: Intimate Partner Violence, Employment, and Workplace Support." *J Interpers Violence* 22, No. 3 (March 2007): 292–311.

———. "Intimate Partner Violence, Women, and Work: Coping on the Job." *Violence Vict.* 21, No. 5: (October 2006): 561–78.

III
Women and Education

12

Globalization, Higher Education and Gender: An Appraisal of the Process of Reaching Out to Indian Women

Anjali Dewan

The process of globalization has transformed world trade, communications, educational activities, and economic relations since the latter part of the 20th century. Student's option for higher education is no longer constrained by national boundaries. For the first time in history in the era of globalization, world's student population truly have access to a 'global market place' of higher education. With the dramatic rise of a new Indian middle class and increased wealth of the Indian upper class, the number of students who are able to pursue education in other countries has really increased.

There is a direct nexus between the industry, corporate world and higher education, which has brought a transformation in the skills needed for jobs. There has been a corresponding change in the boundaries between arts and science subjects. Pure sciences are relegated than the applied sciences and professional skills. In the hierarchy of disciplines, new disciplines such as management, media and mass communication, and fashion technology have also risen up the ladder. Women used to take admission in general education or in arts, humanities and social sciences till the early 1990s—a trend which is still continuing. However, they are also entering the professional subjects offered in the public and private institutions in the traditionally labelled 'masculine disciplines'. The impact of these changes requires attention if the goal of social change and gender equity has to be achieved.

Feminist sociological perspectives on women's educational experience have highlighted several dimensions like their under-participation, under-achievement and under-representation; sex role socialization and stereotyping of the feminine role and its impact upon the girl's education. The segregation of girls into streams of arts and humanities and boys into science at the school level is well known. Sociologists were of the opinion that this imbalance in subjects had to be redressed to remove inequality. In India, the decision to make science compulsory up to 10th class ensured that all girls will also study science. Much has been written on the patriarchal imprint on the subject choices of women in higher education and on the feminine and masculine dichotomy of subjects.

Changing Context

There are several dimensions of changes that have taken place since 1991, the most important being the entry of private institutions, the increase in the individual cost of higher education, the entry of foreign institutions, the large number of Indian students who go abroad on self-financing basis, change in academic environment of higher educational institutions. There is a perceptible change in the choices of women especially in the metropolitan cities where they are enrolling in the new 'professional' courses such as fashion designing, computers, human resource management etc.

This paper seeks to find out the latest trends in the enrolment of women in different faculties and subjects. In addition, the data on the marginal groups such as the Dalits and tribals is also analysed. Women fiom these groups suffer the multiple handicaps of gender and tribe. The regional disparities are also as crucial as those of general population and the marginal groups.

Access and Equality

Policy Framework

Higher education was entrusted with the responsibility of protecting the constitutional provisions for positive discrimination. The commitment to broaden the student base was reflected in the financial incentives provided to Dalit and Adivasi students. Higher education has occupied a dominant position in independent India since it was perceived as a promoter of economic growth, technological development, and a tool of equal opportunity and upward social mobility. This helped in giving importance to social justice around the issues of caste, tribe, class, and gender. There has been a careful articulation of education for equality for women which is reflected in the educational policy in post-independence India. Since 1991, the policies of government have dramatically changed the otherwise privileged position of higher education. The government began to talk of setting aside public support to higher education and to make it self-financing while privatizing it. Higher education has also become a non-merit good. Private institutions have been permitted to be set up on a liberal scale without a clearly defined policy to regulate them (Anandkrishnan, 2004). The link of universities with private sector is not new in India nor is the nexus between the higher education and economy. What is disheartening is the nature and the speed of change, the motives of those who are establishing the private institutions, the lack of response from the Indian government.

Women in Higher Education

This section of the paper deals with the data on enrolment of women and men in higher education, of women across faculties/disciplines or subjects and their presence across various levels. It also lays emphasis on the difference in their enrolment in general and professional education. Starting from 1950–51 when the proportion of women was 10.9 per cent to 40.04 per cent in 2002–03, the increase has been significant. In other words, there were 14 women per 100 men in 1950–51 which increased to 67 in 2002–03. Thus, the proportion of women entering higher education has increased rapidly from 16,85,926 (32 per cent) in 1991–92 to 40 per cent (36,95,964) of all students in 2002–03. There have been also shifts in women's choice of disciplines in higher education. There are also wide disparities in enrolment by region, caste, tribe, and gender. The differences have an impact on women from the disadvantaged groups.

The programmes in higher education are divided into those of general subjects such as arts which include social sciences and humanities; pure sciences, professional courses such as engineering, medical science, teacher education, agriculture, law etc. They are also divided into masculine and feminine disciplines. Arts, social sciences, humanities, and teacher education have been viewed as feminine discipliners. On the other hand, commerce, law, engineering are masculine subjects. Medical science has not been a masculine discipline in India unlike in the western countries. In India like in the rest of South Asia, the practice of female seclusion enjoined the treatment of women patients by women doctors. This required training women doctors, thereby enabling them to enter the medical profession (Chanana, 1988). The proportion of women in some of the masculine disciplines was very less soon after independence and remained so till the 1980s with the exception of commerce. Science, a masculine discipline provides an interesting insight on disciplinary choices of young men and women. The proportion of men in science subjects was 80 to 90 per cent in 1980–81 which has come down to 59.8 per cent in 2002–03. The differential importance of general science for women and men over time has to be understood as a background to shifts in disciplinary choices in the recent past. The proportion of women in science decreased from 33.3 per cent in 1950–51 to 28.8 per cent in 1980–81. Science has never been the first preference for young women whose parents considered marriage much more important than higher education. A science degree required a longer investment of time and other resources and thus was not desirable.

Prior to 1990s, education and its linkage to the job market, early on in life was only for those men who needed jobs and was certainly not for women. These days, young women and men like to earn as soon as they can, even while in school. The revolution in values cuts across upper and middle strata, who want to begin earning as soon as possible. The daughters of city based professional parents, especially if they do not have brothers, have really undergone a great change. The parents are giving the best education to their daughters and expect them to be independent and follow careers. In this changed scenario, the priorities of women have also changed. They too want professional education and are therefore entering into masculine disciplines. The two simultaneous trends of clustering/concentration and dispersal can be seen in the enrolment of men and women in higher education. During the first three decades, while women tended to be clustered in the general disciplines of arts and sciences (nearly 90 per cent), men's participation was characterized by both clustering in arts and sciences disciplines but also significantly dispersed in others such as commerce, engineering/technical and law. Lately, the women's participation too is marked by clustering as well as dispersal. Once women enter higher education at the undergraduate level, their chances of going up to the next level increases. This may also have to do with the master's programme in management, computers and IT, media, advertising, fashion technology etc., which are popular in the metropolitan cities.

Regional Disparities

The gendered impact of social, cultural and economic disparities across states has been referred to time and again by the official committees and commissions as well as by the social scientists. These trends are continuing while the enrolment of women varies from province to province. Kerala has had the highest enrolment and even now it is 60 per cent. Thus, there are more women than men in higher education. The other states where they are more than half the proportion are Goa (58.5), Punjab (52.68), Andaman and Nicobar Islands (57.77), Chandigarh (55.5) and Pondicherry (52.6). Those with lower proportion are also the most backward namely Bihar (23.81), Jharkhand (30.40), Chattisgarh (36.70), Rajasthan (32.33), Uttar Pradesh (38.40), and Madhya Pradesh (37.20). In these provinces, the proportion is less than the all-India average of 40.05 per cent. The link between the state and professional education is very close. The variations can be seen in the growth of engineering and technology courses in the four southern states. A majority of women students were from the southern and western regions. The number of women students is highest in the states of Maharashtra, Karnataka, Andhra Pradesh, and Tamil Nadu. The regional disparities are due to several reasons. One of them is the early starting of formal education in the southern as compared to the northern regions during the colonial period. Many private engineering colleges have been established there. The socio-cultural practices and positive attitudes of parents towards the higher education of their daughters also have an impact on the women's access to professional education. This difference is to a large extent due to the practice of female seclusion in the north and its absence in the south (Chanana, 1988).

Caste, Class, Gender and Region

It is a known fact that in spite of a very well formulated policy of positive discrimination, the representation of Dalit and Adivasi students is not adequate and the proportion of women from among them is negligible. They generally join general education courses and are denied access to elite courses and institutions. In 2001–02, the proportions of SC/ST students were much less as compared to students of general categories. There were 824 SC women and 344 ST women, i.e., 4.3 per cent and 1.8 per cent respectively of all women research students. They are also better represented in states in which women have better representation and in which higher education facilities have expanded in recent years.

Gender, Subject Choices and Career Aspirations

The relationship between availability of disciplinary choices and women's ability to access them are not directly related nor are they dependent on women's academic achievement. In India, girl's academic performance is generally better or at par with the boys when they finish school. Every year, newspaper headlines highlight the better performance of girls at the school board examinations in different states. Yet when they pursue higher studies, it is not necessarily the subject of their choice. The fact is that a large majority of women may be deprived of exercising free options at the school like being discouraged by family to take up science subjects or not being sent to expensive private good quality schools. After schooling, they may not be provided the financial investment in coaching/tuition for entrance tests as they are expensive and women are not socially to work and earn before marriage.

Discipline boundaries not only limit choices, they are also dependent on the future options of life chances of women. Education still in women is an investment to fall back upon in case of the daughter becoming a widow or being deserted. Social role expectations affect the aspirations of women in other ways too. For example, in the patriarchal social structure, parents are not expected to use the income of their daughters. Therefore, even educated daughters are not encouraged to work and if they do so, it is for a short period before marriage. It is the right of the groom's family to decide whether she will work or not.

The poor parents have another problem even though they perceive the significance of education. They expect and need immediate returns from education—something which is possible through professional degrees. General education, although inexpensive, does not assure a job. So general education is useless and professional education is unaffordable. There is a lack of role models and socialization support at home. Women from these social categories are most affected by the stratification of disciplines, programmes and institutions. For a majority of young women in the academia, higher education is not linked to careers. This is the reason why women, even from well-off homes, join arts, humanities because they are cheaper, softer and shorter than the professional subjects is growing. In fact, the trends, identified in 2001, of moving away from the general courses to the professional courses which lead to jobs and careers are being reinforced. The period of post-1991 phase set forth a change which increased the social demand for a specific kind of professional education, especially skill-oriented undergraduate degrees which lead to a career and a job. Earlier an undergraduate degree, except in engineering and medicine, was a step to further higher education and was not a finishing degree. It was like an investment in their social status as well as an additional criteria for marriage.

Parental expectations and young women's aspirations have undergone a great change since mid-1990s. More women are enrolling in engineering and law but the preference for management degrees and computer related degrees and skills are higher. These subjects are available in the fast expanding private sector which responds quickly to the unmet demand for specific skills. Informal discussions with key persons reveal that computer applications and computer software engineering as compared to other specializations are popular among women. In the last few years, women have become visible in the call centres, telemarketing, front desk jobs in the multinational/private banks, hospitals, hotels etc. Most of these jobs are short-term and contractual and suit the social role expectations of women. It is also anticipated that the public and private institutions which offer contractual, low paid, short-term jobs may have in the long run, substantial number of women faculty leading to the feminization of teaching in the private higher education (Chanana, 2003).

A study of women scientists in biological sciences in the central universities and national laboratories also concludes that there are few permanent women faculty members compared to those who obtain research degrees. More women than men are holding junior faculty positions. There are fewer women students in the elite institutions such as IITs, and regional college of engineering. Modern education and skills seem to reinforce tradition for majority of women students. The new disciplines which are offered in the public and private sectors of higher education seem to meet the aspirations of only a minority of young women and their parents in the metropolitan cities to be professionally qualified, to have a career, to earn to be independent. In their case, gender and class overlap in overcoming the traditional barriers to women's education.

Conclusion

Higher education was almost free during the first four decades since it was publicly funded, but women have not achieved an equal access. It has also been denied to or made almost impossible for the women from disadvantaged groups to access because of social and economic reasons. There is a need to deconstruct the inequitable impact of globalization. Pure sciences, social sciences, arts and humanities, and the disciplines preferred by women remain confined to the public institutions. Though women are doing professional courses, many of them are not even working especially after marriage. It is important to create a broad-based database on higher education which is gender sensitive. Information about students namely about their enrolment, discipline they have joined, discipline, specialization, and institution are imperative for understanding of any system. Research on higher education deserves support so that a quantitative database can be supported by qualitative inputs. It would help in making plans for the future course of action and the research policy. It is high time that the government evolved a framework on the role and function of higher education, public, and private. This needs a visionary leader who would encompass the issues of access and equity with a focus on the education of girls and women.

References

Anandkrishnan, M. *Power Initiatives in Higher Education.* New Delhi: Sneh Prakashan and Amity Foundation for Learning, 2004: pp. 202–25.

Bachhi, Caroll. In *Managing Equity: Mainstreaming and Diversity in Australian Universities*, edited by A. Brooks and A. McInnon. 2001, pp. 119–35.

Bal, Vineeta. "Women Scientists in India: Nowhere Near the Glass Ceiling." *Economic and Political Weekly* (7 August 2004): 3647–53.

Chanana, K. "Social Change or Social Reform: The Education of Women in Pre-independence India." In *Socialisation, Education and Women: Explorations in Gender Identity*, edited by K. Chanana,1988, 2000.

———. "Visibility, Gender and the Careers of Women Faculty in an Indian University." *McGill Journal of Education* 38, no. 3 (2003): 381–90.

Economic and Political Weekly 42, No. 7 (February 2007): 17–23. A Sameeksha Trust Publication, Mumbai.

Marginson, S. "Research as a Managed Economy." *Why Universities Matter: A Conversation about Values, Means and Directions*. Sydney: Allen and Unwin, 2000.

Sassen, S. *Globalisation and its Discontents: Essays on the New Mobility of People and Money*. New York: The New Press, 1998.

Sharpe, Rachel. *Just Like a Girl*. London: Pelican, 1976.

University Grants Commission. *Annual Report 2002-03*. New Delhi: University Grants Commission, 2003.

Yeatman, A. *Bureaucrats, Technocrats, Democrats*. Sydney, Allen and Unwin, 1990.

13

Reading Motivation in Primary School Girls: A Problem of Cognitive Mapping

Debdulal Dutta Roy

With rapid changes in globalization, India is now moving towards knowledge-based society. It is important to confront with all challenges of globalization through development of reading motivation among the girls. This will reduce gradual increase in the alarming male-female literacy gap (Figure 1). Desire to put more effort on reading activity is called reading motivation. Reading motivation researchers studied it from two perspectives—self-efficacy (Wigfield and Guthrie, 1992, 1997) and desires to read (Dutta Roy, 2004).

Self-efficacy

Wigfield and Guthrie (1992, 1997) identified seven variables for assessing reading motivation based on self-efficacy theory (Bandura, 1977) and sense of self-efficacy and task values (Schunk 1991; Schunk and Zimmerman, 1997). The seven variables are: (i) reading curiosity (desire to learn about a particular topic of interest to the child); (ii) reading challenge (the satisfaction of mastering or assimilating complex ideas in text); (iii) reading importance; (iv) reading involvement (the enjoyment of experiencing different kinds of literary and informational text); (v) competition in reading (the desire to outperform others in

Figure 1 *Male-female Literacy Gap from 1951 to 2001*

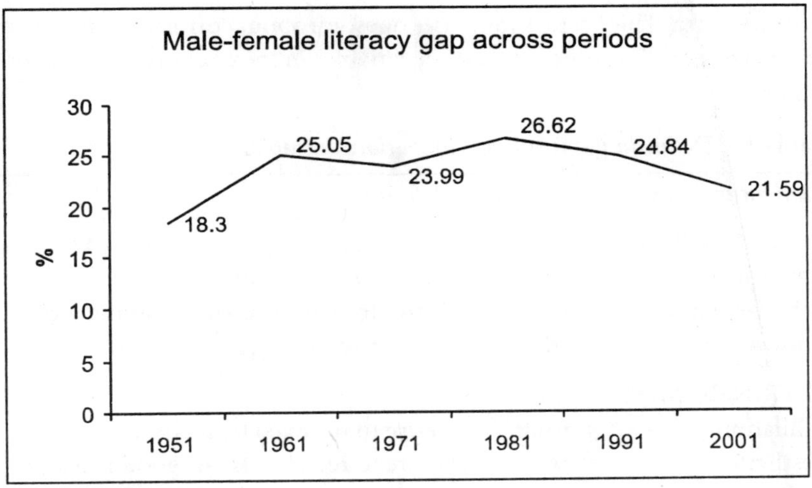

Source: National Literacy Mission; Ref: http://www.nlm.nic.in/literacy01_nlm.htm

reading); (vi) recognition for reading (the gratification in receiving a tangible form of recognition for success in reading); and (vii) reading for grades (the desire to be evaluated favourably by the teacher). Motivation for reading questionnaire (MRQ) is useful to assess all the variables.

Desire to Read

Since motivation for reading varies with culture, attempt was made to find out reading motivation of Indian students by open ended interview (Dutta Roy and Paul, 2002). They, based on content analysis of several interviews with school children noted that students desired to read for intrinsic and extrinsic motivation. Reading for application (rApp), achievement (rAch) and knowledge (rKn) are intrinsic motivation and reading for affiliation (rAff), recognition (rRecog), aesthetic (rAes) and harm-avoidance (rHarm) are extrinsic motivation. Former is coming from within and latter is coming from outer world. Table 1 shows definition of each variable.

In another study (Dutta Roy, 2004), it was noted that high achievers of primary school possessed high score on intrinsic reading motivation and vice versa. This correlation raises question about correlative structure or abstraction of reading motivation variables in the cognitive map of the children.

Table 1 *Definition of Reading Motivation Variables*

Motivation Variables	*Symbol*	*Definition*
INTRINSIC MOTIVATION		
Application	rApp	Desire to apply information
Achievement	rAch	Desire to master reading competency
Knowledge	rKn	Desire to acquire information
EXTRINSIC MOTIVATION		
Affiliation	rAaff	Desire to be loved by reading
Aesthetic	rAes	Desire to read books for good pictures
Recognition	rRecog	Desire to be recognized by others through reading
Harm-Avoidance	rHarm	Desire to avoid punishment for not reading

Abstraction

Abstraction (from the Latin *abs*, meaning away from and *trahere*, meaning to draw) is the process of taking away or removing characteristics from something in order to reduce it to a set of essential characteristics. Removing depends upon similarities and dissimilarities of the object. During schooling, girl observes several sequences and consequences of reading behaviour and tends to group them based upon their effect on her mental frame. Finally, it shapes her cognitive map. Cognitive map refers to mental representation of a set of similar and dissimilar objects, events, or ideas. Child possesses own cognitive map of reading motivation that guides his reading behaviour. It is assumed that cognitive map possesses clusters of similar and dissimilar reading motivation variables. This is developed through self-experiencing or through different social dialogues about reading. Child labels them in considering their communalities. This process is continuing within the mental frame of child constantly through private speech. Here private speech refers not to Piagetian egocentric speech (1962) rather Vygotskian's speech to self (1978, 1986). How the reading motivation variables are clustered in the cognitive map of the girls in primary schools is of current interest in this study. Current study examined this issue with girls of grades III and IV through taxonomic approach.

Taxonomic Approach

The word 'taxonomy' is derived from two Greek words—*taxis* meaning arrangement or division and *nomos* meaning law. So, taxonomy is the science of classification of related variables following set of rules. Taxonomy results catalogue used to provide conceptual framework for discussion, analysis, or information retrieval. In theory, good taxonomy takes into account the importance of separating elements of a group (taxon) into subgroups (taxa) that are mutually exclusive, unambiguous, and taken together, include all possibilities. Good taxonomy should be simple, easy to remember and easy to use. Several multivariate statistical models like principal component analysis (Dutta Roy, 2007), cluster analysis, correspondence analysis (Dutta Roy, 2002) are useful in taxonomy. In this study, cluster analysis was followed.

Methods

Sample

Sampling was done in two stages: (a) selection of sample schools from government, government aided, corporation and missionary schools under the West Bengal Board of Primary Education, and (b) selection of sample students. For selection of sample schools lists of government, government aided, Kolkata corporation, and missionary schools were collected from different sources—Calcutta District Primary School Council, Calcutta Municipal Corporation, and Police Stations of different areas. Data was collected from three government schools, five government-aided, seven schools of Kolkata corporation, and three missionary schools under the West Bengal Board of Primary Education. Government-aided schools are financially aided by the government of West Bengal. In sampling, attention was paid to equal representation of schools across north, south, east, west, and central Kolkata. In the study, 346 girls of grade III and 350 girls of grade IV participated.

Measures

Reading motivation was assessed using reading motivation questionnaire (Dutta Roy, 2004). The questionnaire consisted 42 items measuring one's desire to read for intrinsic (application, knowledge, and achievement) and extrinsic motivation (aesthetic, affiliation, recognition, and harm-avoidance). There were six items for assessing each motivation variable in a paired manner (6 items × 7 reading motives = total 42 items). Subject was asked to choose one answer out of two alternatives that she thought more appropriate if the given situation would be true for her. Scoring was based on subjects' preference to number of alternative answers for each category of variable. For each variable, the maximum possible score was six and the minimum possible score was zero. Some items of the questionnaire are given below:

1. Suppose, after promotion to a new class you are offered to read two books with two different titles. Which one will you like to read first?
   (a) Learning of mathematics through daily activities.
   (b) Study of animals of different countries.
2. Suppose, on one day you were absent in school. Next day you ask your friends to give their copy. You get two copies. Which one will you like to read first?
   (a) A newly covered copy with good handwriting.
   (b) The copy of your best friend.

The test-retest reliability and internal consistency among the items of questionnaire were high. The average correlation coefficients between time 1 and time 2 for 72 students within eight months interval ranged from 0.70 to 0.97. (Dutta Roy, 2004). Cronbach's alpha ranged from 0.61 to 0.68 (application, $\alpha = 0.65$, knowledge, $\alpha = 0.63$, affiliation, $\alpha = 0.63$, recognition, $\alpha = 0.61$, achievement, $\alpha = 0.68$, aesthetic, $\alpha = 0.65$, harm avoidance, $\alpha = 0.61$).

Analysis of Data

Cluster analysis is a useful statistical tool to understand classification of variables based on similarity and dissimilarity in properties. It provides tree diagram to understand neighbour of each variable. The distance in neighbouring provides useful information about subject's cognitive map. In the current study, single linkage cluster analysis with Euclidean distance was used.

Results and Discussion

Both tree diagrams (Figures 2 and 3) of reading motivation variables for grades III and IV extracted two broad clusters.

Intrinsic and Extrinsic Reading Motivation: Tree diagrams were based on distance matrices of Tables 2 and 3. Cognitive structuring and restructuring by the students across changes in grades were noted in the formation of clusters.

Figure 2 *Tree diagram: Single linkage with Euclidean distances of reading motivation variables for 3rd grade girls (n = 346)*

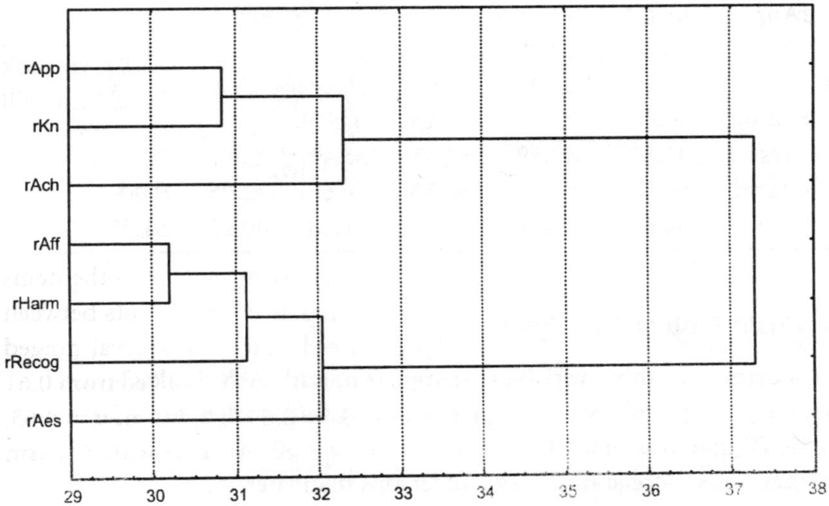

Figure 3 *Tree diagram: Single linkage with Euclidean distances of reading motivation variables for 4th grade girls (n = 350)*

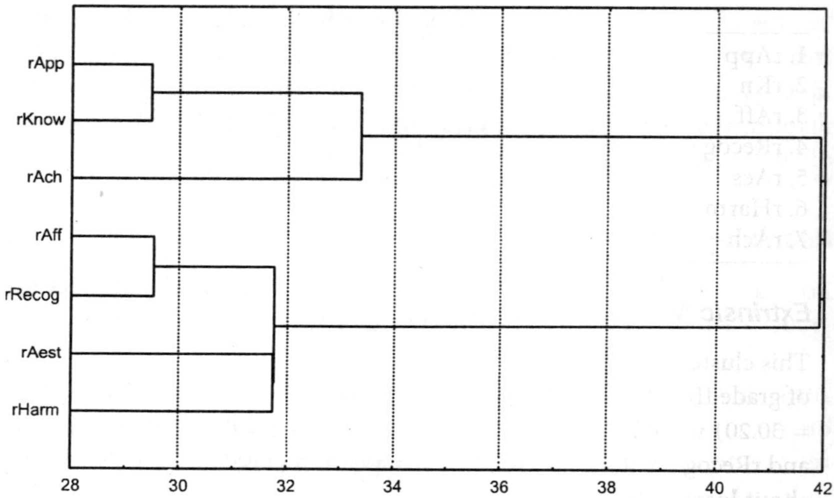

Table 2 *Single linkage with Euclidean distances of reading motivation variables for girls in class III (n = 346)*

	1	2	3	4	5	6	7
1. rApp	0.00						
2. rKn	30.84	0.00					
3. rAff	50.99	47.47	0.00				
4. rRecog	41.68	39.90	31.13	0.00			
5. rAes	45.86	42.99	32.33	35.41	0.00		
6. rHarm	58.58	57.00	30.20	39.66	32.05	0.00	
7. rAch	34.63	32.31	43.30	37.28	40.22	51.33	0.00

Intrinsic Motivation Cluster

This comprises three variables—rApp, rKn, and rAch. Linkage distance between rApp and rKn (Distance = 29.48) was smaller for students of grade IV than the same of grade III (Distance = 30.84). This suggests that former finds more applied value of lessons than later.

Table 3 *Single linkage with Euclidean distances of reading motivation variables for girls in grade IV (n = 350)*

	1	2	3	4	5	6	7
1. rApp							
2. rKn	29.48	0.00					
3. rAff	52.71	51.93	0.00				
4. rRecog	47.35	47.57	29.53	0.00			
5. rAes	50.86	48.93	34.34	34.13	0.00		
6. rHarm	62.31	62.31	31.76	35.06	31.75	0.00	
7. rAch	33.60	33.38	45.27	41.92	44.00	53.01	0.00

Extrinsic Motivation Cluster

This cluster includes four variables—rAff, rRecog, rAes, and rHarm. Girls of grade III assumed strong association between rAff and rHarm (Distance = 30.20) whereas girls of grade IV found strong association between rAff and rRecog (Distance = 29.53). This suggests that younger girls' conjecture about loss of love is almost similar to punishment. But elder girls assume that reading for others love is almost similar to reading for recognition.

Findings are important to understand development of reading motivation taxonomy across the grades. Education plays key role in forming the taxonomy, which occurs through different cognitive structuring and restructuring process. With education, this process is strengthened. Intrinsic reading motivation is well structured in both grades suggesting role of self-experiencing phenomena in grouping three reading motives. On the other hand, extrinsic reading motivation gradually takes shape suggesting role of external forces in forming structure. Younger girls find little difficulty in establishing identical properties of two extrinsic reading motivation variables namely reading for others' love and reading for recognition.

As intrinsic reading motivation is sustainable, attention should be paid to different strategies for shaping intrinsic reading motivation.

Strategies to Shape Intrinsic Reading Motivation

Enhancing Knowledge Motivation

Motivation to read for exploring information about surroundings develops through one's intention to perceive the environment as a whole. Motivation to acquire knowledge varies with age.

For younger children, play, drawing, and story telling develop intention to know. Play provides children opportunity to actively explore, manipulate, and interact with their environment. Playing with nature like plants, birds, and animals develop motivation to understand their parts of body and functions. Another way to develop knowledge motive among young children is drawing. Drawing opens a gateway to understand the surroundings. More independence in drawing helps children to develop curiosity to know. Story telling is another strategy to develop knowledge motive as by listening to story, children develop own imagination, incomplete event of story haunts them and develop curiosity to know. Story telling is a viable method for stimulating children's imaginations, ultimately leading to a higher cognitive level in student responses.

Besides above, during teaching teenaged children or adolescents in the classroom, teachers may use some cognitive strategies—(a) conceptual conflict, (b) creating climate for questioning, and (c) curiosity arousing elements. In conceptual conflict strategy, teachers will introduce conceptual conflict when possible. Learners will feel compelled to explore the conflict until it is resolved. Another strategy is to create atmosphere for questioning wherein students can test their own hypotheses through discussion or brainstorming. Curiosity arousing elements are incongruity, contradictions, novelty, surprise, complexity, and uncertainty. In the class-room, teachers may use those elements in order to develop one's intention to read for exploring information about surroundings.

Enhancing Application Motivation

Learning concepts and best practices in the classroom and then actually applying them in regular life is an invaluable experience. Modelling, drilling, and generalization are the components of application motivation. Modelling helps students in defining the task operationally, in identification of resources or materials and in planning workflows with specific time limits to design representations of lessons. Total process energizes students to drill different components of tasks, workflows. Finally, it helps to make generalization about the lesson. For example, teacher during teaching about river assigns students to develop model of river. Student in designing the model may think of different changes in depth, length, width, and movement of river or may think of some additions on the riverside of the model. In future, student can relate different issues (e.g., role of river in development of civilization) of river during study. To make this motivation sustainable, attention should be paid to influence the three layers (Figure 4) of students' consciousness (Dutta Roy, 2006). Modelling is the journey from outer layer to inner core layer of consciousness.

Figure 4 *Layers of Consciousness in Designing Model.*

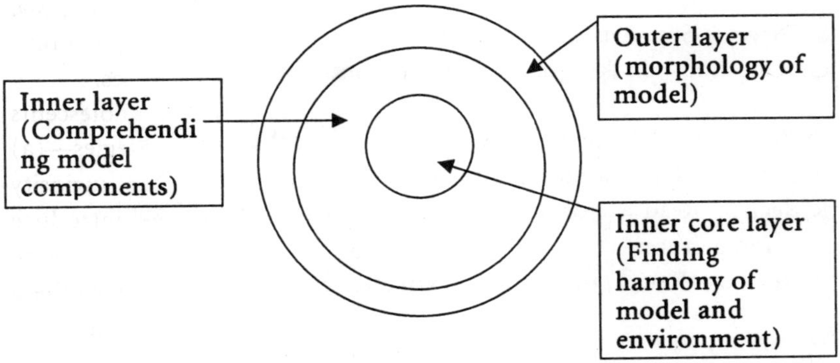

Mere reading the text and following formal rules influence outer layer of consciousness. Inner layer is affected by understanding the lesson or the components of model. And inner core layer of consciousness is influenced by finding out inner harmony between model and its application in real life.

Enhancing Achievement Motivation

In the current study, achievement motivation refers to desire to read for developing mastery over reading. Mastery over reading helps students to develop phonological awareness or the ability to identify and manipulate sub-lexical units of speech such as phonemes or rimes. It helps students to make correspondence between morphological structure of letter and sound. There is growing evidence that phonological awareness plays important role in reading and spelling acquisition in alphabetic and non-alphabetic languages (Ziegler and Goswami, 2005). Fowler (1991) argued that children who have poorly defined or degraded phonological representations will experience significant difficulties in encoding, rehearsing, storing, and retrieving speech stimuli from memory. Reading aloud, monitoring speech, and speech feedback help in phonological awareness. In classroom learning, teacher should encourage students to read the sentences of given lesson one by one and other students should follow his pronunciation. Other students will be advised to raise hands if there is any error of pronunciation. In this way, phonological awareness can be developed. After phonological awareness, teacher may pay more attention to "SQ4R" strategies in reading the text.

*S: Survey—Survey the outlines.
*Q: Question—Make question out of outlines without going in too deeply.
*R: Read—Read the material in order to answer the question.
*R: Reflect—Relate what is read to real life.
*R: Recite—Read section and take notes. Associate text with spoken words and gestures.
*R: Review—Review the material soon after reading and on a schedule.

To sum up, current study discussed three important sustainable reading motivations and illuminated various instructional strategies to nurture them.

■ References

Bandura. "Self-Efficacy: Toward a Unifying Theory of Behavioural Change." *Psychological Review* 84 (1977): 191–215.

Dutta Roy, D. "Taxonomic Appr", edited by Dr. S. Subramony and S.B. Raj. Delhi: Defence Institute of Psychological Research, 2007.

—— "Development of Picture Drawing Test to Assess Consciousness Layers of Tribal Children of Tripura." *Journal of the Indian Academy of Applied Psychology* 32, No. 1 (2006): 20–25.

——. "Development of the Questionnaire for Assessment of Reading and Writing Motivation of Boys and Girls of Grades III and IV." Unpublished Project report submitted to the Indian Statistical Institute, Kolkata, 2004.

——. "Correspondence between Item and Rating on the Checklist of Relative Importance of Computer Programming Tasks." *Journal of Psychometry* 16, No. 2 (2002): 67–76.

Dutta Roy, D. and Paul, M. "Reading Motivation of Children in Grades III and IV." *Indian Educational Review* 38, No. 1 (2002): 43–51.

Fowler, A.E. "How Early Phonological Development Might Set the Stage for Phonemic Awareness." pp. 97–117 in *Phonological Process in Literacy. A Tribute to Isabelle Y. Liberman*, edited by S. Brady and D. Shankweiler. Hillsdale, NJ: Erlbaum, 1991.

Piaget, J. *The Language and Thought of the Child* (translated by M. Gabain). Cleveland, OH: Meridian, 1962. (Original work published in 1923).

Schunk, D.H. "Self-Efficacy and Academic Motivation." *Educational Psychologist* 26 (1991), 233–262.

Schunk, D.H. and Zimmerman, B.J. "Developing Self-Efficacious Readers and Writers: The Role of Social and Self-Regulatory Processes." pp. 34–50 in *Reading Engagement: Motivating Readers through Integrated Instruction*, edited by J.T. Guthrie and A. Wigfield. Newark, DE: International Reading Association, 1997.

Vygotsky, L. *Mind in Society: The Development of Higher Psychological Processes* (M. Cole, V. John-Steiner, S. Scribner, and E. Soubermann, Eds.). Cambridge, MA: Harvard University Press, 1978. (Original work published in 1930, 1933, and 1935).

——. *Thought and Language* (translated by Alex Kozulin). Cambridge, MA: The MIT Press, 1986. (Original work published in 1934).

Wigfield, A. and Guthrie, J.T. "The Development of Achievement Task Values: A Theoretical Analysis." *Developmental Review* 12 (1992): 265–310.

——"Relations of Children's Motivation for Reading to the Amount and Breadth of their Reading." *Journal of Educational Psychology* 89, No. 3 (1997): 420–32.

Ziegler, J. C. and Goswami, U. "Reading Acquistion, Developmental Dyslexia, and Skilled Reading across Languages: A Psycholinguistic Grain Size Theory." *Psychological Bulletin* 31 (2005): 3–29.

IV
Women and Identity

14

Discerning Whispers: Reflections on Self and Identity

Sujata Sharma

Aspects of human existence that are seldom captured through mere behaviour, intrigue those who are interested in the study of human beings. The abstract richness of these human aspects makes them appear vague and sometimes even questionable.

One such domain concerns issues around self and identity. Is there a relevance of queastions like "Who am I?" Is there a core to our "self" which binds together the different "selves" that exist simultaneously? What makes for continuity and sameness along with the change? What processes are responsible for the coherence that one experiences? All these are questions, which are easier posed than answered and have often been left as areas of philosophical thought.

Ontology and Epistemology

First hurdle in taking up an area so complex is the confusion surrounding various terms. At the outset itself there seems to be ambiguity in the meaning of and relationship between the concepts self and identity; can these be used synonymously to mean the same thing? Are the same processes involved in the formation of identity as are in the construction of self?

According to Kohut, (1971), there is a difference between self (analytic) and identity (interpersonal). He sees identity as a social phenomenon that is not a focus in analytic treatment, while self of psychoanalysis reveals itself only in the analytic experience. In order to clarify the present position vis-à-vis self and identity, a review of literature is warranted. However, in this regard, theories may be seen only to be providing a structure to aid the exploration and not as the basis for it; not as a measuring stick but only as a reference point from where the exploration begins rather than ends.

From this vantage, reviewing the concepts, theorists interested in identity seem to universally agree that it has some relation to the 'self' (Ashmore and Jussim, 1997; Harre, 1989). Blassi and Glodis (1995), have further argued that any defensible definition of identity must acknowledge the subjective awareness of the self and that "central to the description of identity is a special experience of self characterized by . . . a direct focus on one's own person, aimed at capturing what is basic about it . . . (along with) the realization of what is true, real, genuine about oneself . . . (and) finally, the subjective experience of unity produced by such a realization" (pp. 406–7).

Self

Not only is there ambiguity surrounding the usage of and meaning attributed to the term self, but there are also various (at times diverse) views to explain the concept. It is important to acknowledge that the very conceptualization of the term (self) is likely to be influenced by the socio-cultural-historical factors; the theorists of self themselves had selves, and the history and experiences of those selves would not be without relevance to the conceptualization of self, as would their cultural and historical situations. Hence, we find a collection of perspectives ranging from the existential ontology by Heidegger and the early Sartre, to the eclectic positions of social constructionists, post-structuralists and postmodernists (many of who refer to self as a "hypothetical construct").

As a theoretical or hypothetical construct, the self seems closely related to our personal identity or to our belief about our personhood. However, of late there seems a new trend in the application of the term that has become an almost sublime object of cultural, individual and academic focus and utility. When used in this sense, the term self seems to have little connection with the existential/ phenomenological intuition(s), descriptions and understandings we have of our own personal identities.

Coming to the question of what self is, there is little convergence on the definition of the term, except for one notable consistency among several definitions with respect to the notion that there are two separate and distinct selves (similar to James's conception). Wylie (1968) drew a distinction between self as the "doer" and self as a passive entity. De` Charms (1968) discussed the aspects in which self appears as an origin, and the aspects in which self appears as a pawn manipulated by external forces. The origin or the controller is active and has a sense of control of the environment but as a pawn is controlled by the environment. Thorpe (1966) maintained that there are three significant characteristics of self: a feeling of unity; an awareness of internal sensibility; and an awareness of one's individual existence in the world. These characteristics of unity and internal sensibility seem to correspond closely to "I", the doer, origin, or egocentric self (Piaget, 1968) and knowledge of one's individual existence to the "me", passive self, pawn, or non egocentric self.

On the other hand, according to other theorists, while the self may appear to be of dual nature under different circumstances, there is just one self, which may be called "Causal agent self" (Duval and Wicklund, 1972). This self is a psychological structure with observable manifestations, and its functions are simply the usual functions of any organism: Perception, Thinking and Action. This self is seen as indigenous to the organism, existing from the moment the child lives and not arising from social interaction or biological development. Further the states of subjective and objective self-awareness have secondary characteristics which produce the effect of a dual self.

Some salient issues relating to the concept of the self include the theoretical considerations of the self-concept: the self as fact vs construct; subject vs object; structure vs process; and self as single vs multiple. First, the self-concept cannot be postulated as a "fact" in the sense that it can be located in space and time and has substance like properties. It must be regarded as a theoretical construct, an abstraction that is designed to describe or explain the relations among observable phenomena. The second issue refers to the distinction between experiencing self, the subject and the self-reflectivity seen as an object (like any other non-self object). This duality is often referred to as the "I" and the "Me" as suggested by

James, and also by Mead (1913), who has drawn a similar distinction in which the "I" is an actor in the present whereas the "Me" is the "I" reflected upon. I has consciousness in the sense of awareness of sensations or feelings of self and the external field but does not have the true self-consciousness associated exclusively with "Me". Many theorists regard the split between "I" and the "Me" as a superficial and artificial one. Sarbin (1943) pointed out that the distinction between the "I" and the "Me" is usually equated with the private and the public aspects of selfhood and further suggested that this distinction may not be valid in so far as a person's fantasies may be treated as an object. Such arguments made a subject-object distinction unnecessary. Alternatively one may suggest that self has both, a subjective or private aspect, and a public, objective aspect. Self cannot be a structure in the sense of being physical or substantively definable since it is not a "thing". The structure vs process dichotomy arises from following a typically mechanical metaphor, where the psychological system is viewed as having a series of component parts; and process is viewed as an outcome of the interaction of the components. We may see the cognitive mechanisms that help the individual to shift her response pattern appropriately from one situation to another situation, that is from one role to another role as "processes". The hierarchical ordering of loyalties to social roles may then be referred to as the structural aspect of the self. In this manner, self can be seen as having both structure as well as process aspects. The fourth issue relates to (the concept of ego) self as single vs multiple. According to James (1890), one would have as many social selves as there are individuals who recognize him and carry an image of him in their mind. The psychologist viewing the individual as a whole must account for ways in which the many distinct selves, each associated with a different social role, are integrated into one personality, when they are not, it results in disassociation at one end and diffusion at the other.

Identity

It remains an important question as to how people make sense of their lives and how balance is brought about between the intra-individual experiences and the external social reality. As individual progresses from infancy to old age and experiences complex and large-scale life changes, personality shapes itself into an organized form. For some, the central principle which is responsible for the organization of personality is known as the concept of identity. In this sense, the term accounts for the unity, self-sameness and continuity of the personality for the persistence of the patterns throughout the life history of the individual and for the shared sameness and solidarity of the individual within her community.

Identity addresses the paradoxical statement that humans change yet remain same. Etymologically the word identity is derived form the Latin root *Idem*, meaning the same. The Oxford English Dictionary gives the following two definitions as among the various shades of the meaning of the word 'identity': (a) the quality or condition of being same in substance, composition, nature, properties or in particular qualities under consideration; absolute essential sameness; and (b) the condition or fact that a person or a thing is itself and not something else. It is necessary to consider the identity of a person in both these senses of the term. In the former sense, identity of a person refers to certain essential qualities, and not to sameness of substance. The specific physical materials constituting our bodies do not account for our "essential" sameness, nor does the shape and size of body. The second connotation of the term identity refers to the condition that a person is the same and not someone else. In this sense it is important that a person recognizes him or herself as the same and not someone else across time and space, and the others recognize him or her likewise too.

Moshman (1998), in attempting to state what identity is, puts it as an explicit theory of oneself as a person. As he described, there are two relevant characteristics of such theories: that these are coherent and organized, not just a collection of beliefs regarding oneself; secondly, these theories are explanatory and not just a description of oneself.

Theorists have also characterized identity in terms of unity and continuity. There is no simple resolution to the issue of unity vs. multiplicity (as noted earlier), however, as many theorists have pointed out, identity formation need not be just a discovery of a pre-existing unity, rather it may involve an effort to identify/have a degree of consistency. The construction of identity does not begin or end with a unitary self but does take unity as guiding ideal. However, a sense of continuity is important in identity. Grotevant (1993) and Sarbin (1997) have pointed out that one's theory of oneself as a person consists, in part, of a narrative of a continuous self that extends across time. However, to be seen as one's identity, the narrative must have some degree of theoretical coherence and must provide a sense of oneself as a person.

The term 'identity' is used by many theorists to denote an image of the self, as Robbins (1973) surveyed the use of identity concept in anthropology and isolated three basic approaches or models: (a) identity-health model, stressing the process of adjustment and maladjustment, mostly from a clinical perspective; (b) identity-interaction model, in which identity is seen as a bridge connecting the psycho-biological drives of man's inner nature with those influences on the self, originating from society and culture; and (c) identity-world view model, emphasizing on culturally situated meanings and values.

Most theorists have further divided the concept into various aspects, components or dimensions. Erikson (1968) separated ego identity from the more generic concept of identity and distinguished positive from negative identity. Miller (1963) differentiates public identity from self-identity, which can also be broken down into components that refer to self-appraisal functions for which he proposed distinctions between actual identity, potential identity and ideal identity.

Wallace and Fogelson (1965) developed an elaborate model to examine encounters that are termed identity struggles. In this scheme, total identity is divided into four components: real identity, indicating a self-report about where the individual "really" stands with regard to particular dimensions of identity; ideal identity referring to the kind of positive identity the individual would like to emulate ; a feared identity, a negative valued identity that the individual desires to avoid; and a claimed identity, a set of images that the individual presents to others in order to influence their evaluation of his/her identity.

Perspectives on Self and Identity

The metatheories that have a bearing upon the various specific views in the understanding of the constructs include the Empericists, the Modernists, the Post-modernists, Structuralists, Post-structuralists with the Constructivists, Feminists, Phenomenologists and Developmentalists itinerant between these. The boundaries between these metatheories sometimes overlap and may not always stand for alternate and exclusive views as often indicated in the literature.

Durkheim and Comte have been some of the main influences on structuralism with later contributions from Piaget, Levi Strauss and Lacan. The main demarcation between the humanistic critical theorists and the antihumanist structuralists" accounts is in terms of a sharp distinction between science and philosophy. Structuralists view social reality as not static, and according to them society is a unique reality that is not reducible to individual psychology. It is a system governed by structural properties. As Lacan (1949) proposed that people can continually create themselves without giving themselves a fixed unity, thereby rejecting the idea of a unified self. Structuralists negated the notion of agency, they focused on the role of language in defining and charting a sense of self and identity.

Taking further from the traditional structuralist position is the socio-cultural approach to identity which asserts that in any society self-construction is too important to be left as merely a personal project. This position in study of seif reflects that although making a self appears to be an individual and individualizing pursuit, it is also a collective and collectivizing one (Gergen, 1973, 1985; Giorgi 1970; Harre 1984, 1986). Foucault (1980) and Levin (1987) have further argued that each era produces a particular configuration of self and corresponding kinds of psychopathology.

From this orientation, contexts involve significant relationships wherein language and actions serve as the primary media for the formation of self/identity. Every cultural and social group provides a vision of the "good" or appropriate; its shared ideas about "how to be" are reflected in culturally significant stories, sacred texts, proverbs, icons and institutions, as well as lived out in everyday practices of social life. In this sense, the self (as an artifact) has different configurations and different functions depending on the culture, the historical era and the socio-economic class in which it exists. In stressing on self as a necessary social construction, Erez and Earley (1993) have claimed "the self is a universal aspect of humanity and its definition is shaped differentially according to various cultural values and perspectives" (p. vii). Neisser (1988) points out that sense of self develops as people assign meaning or significance to themselves as people. This self-making process is an interpersonal and collective achievement (Baldwin 1986 ; Sullivan 1940) and depends in large part on shared ideas of those in the most significant socio-cultural niches.

The specific psychological consequences of these contrasting views of the self for behaviour are emerging as a focus of systematic analysis. Ethnographic studies have revealed marked difference in practices of self and identity (Marsella, De Vos, Hsu 1985; Choi and Choi 1990; Parish, 1991; Derne", 1992; Kondo, 1992; Rosenberg, 1992). Sharp value differences have been established and studies also have outlined how self-relevant cognition, emotion and motivation are markedly divergent depending on the view of self that anchors them. Though this view describes a cultural level of reality, one created and maintained by social representation and their supporting practices, at individual level, there may be resistance or failure to incorporate these public and mutually constructed ideas of selfhood into their meaning-making systems. Theorists working in this framework argue that as one changes context or receives differing messages from new people in same setting, one's identity is likely to undergo change. Cultural frame switching brings with it a fundamental change in what is viewed as relevant to the self, and in what should be taken into account, resulting in a far-reaching re-evaluation of who "one" is. The type of conflict in frames of personhood may vary from an extreme form as seen in case of native people migrating from small towns into larger cities or east to west, to the milder forms as experienced by people as they move across the life course.

A stable sense of identity emerges when social contexts remain unaltered and one continues to receive non-conflicting messages from significant others about who one is or should be in the is world. This implies, as Oyserman and Markus (1993) have pointed out, that the extent to which one's social representations are contradictory and grounded in different assumptions would result in his/her facing a more complex and effortful self-construction and maintenance task.

Theorists have further highlighted the creative nature of constructive processes. Gergen (1988) and Riessman (1993) have proposed an understanding of identity as a narrative, one that can be defined as the unity of a person's life as it is experienced and articulated in their own life stories. According to these theorists, each society has its own set of stories and construction rules. The storytellers therefore, are not completely free in their story telling but only receive acceptance of their stories if they adapt to these patterns and if they get the consent of other actors in their stories for their version.

Even though self is influenced and (in part) created by social and cultural factors, in present developing nations such as the Indian context, it seems to be (both at social and individual levels) a period of transition. The challenge facing these developing societies such as India is that they are neither the traditional societies as they used to be nor a duplication of the developed nations. They have their own unique situation and context which has its own dynamics. In such distinctive context, the implications for the notions of self and identity are liable to be complex.

Socio-cultural approaches provide important contribution to understand identity; however, it "must be viewed as more than a product of social messages alone in order again to explain individual variation within any given social context" Kroger (1985: 21). Smith (1994) further, proposes an adoption of a constructivist socio-cultural position which does not view the self as empty, drifting in the dizzying and disorienting cultural chaos.

Post-structuralist views grew as a gradual response (read "reaction") to and in continuation of the polar oppositional and hierarchical dualisms through which the selves are constructed in literature. These views draw on the nature of subjectivity and relation of that subjectivity to the lived and told stories. It contends that things do not exist independent of their representation in social texts and further, how they are seen is itself determined by the agendas that presume "real" worlds out there. Post-structuralist theory hence goes a step further than structuralism and opens up the possibility of seeing the Self as continually constituted through multiple and contradictory discourses that one takes up as one's own in becoming a speaking subject. This view asserts that we become that which various discourses in which we participate define as a self. It contains that things do not exist independent in their representations in social texts. Post-structuralism, in one way, tries to answer some of the issues raised by structuralists around the contradictions in the self, arising from multiple and often contradictory discourses. As Davies (1990) suggested, "... dealing with contradictions within the model can enable one to make a decision to act within the terms of one discourse rather than another at any point in time, depending on relevance, values of its product etc., or it can facilitate a decision to refuse a discourse or to refuse the positioning made available within that discourse." (p.58).

Post-structuralist accounts clarify women's position vis-à-vis identity by confirming for them their sense of self as embodied and offering a critique of the celebration of masculinity and its equation with rationality. In this sense, post-structuralism may not be seen as the death of the subject but as a means of claiming the right to subject status for those who have never been recognized as having such status in the mainstream.

The ego-psychological perspectives place the agency/ego at the heart of the issues of identity and are concerned with specific periods of crisis in an individual's life. In this context, as proposed by Marcia (1980), identity would involve establishing the commitments of work, occupation and political orientation. Among some of the earlier works, Blos (1967) emphasized the centrality of separation-individuation as precursor to identity formation, "individuality implies that the growing person takes increasing responsibility for what he does . . . rather . . . (than) on shoulders of those under whose influence . . . he has grown up" (p.168). Erich Fromm (1976) approached socialization from point of view of the individual's struggle for autonomy.

Ego-psychological theories, particularly as articulated by Erikson (1968, 1975) include, as a central feature, a special experience of self, namely the experience of a unified psychological "essence" from which superficial characteristics of the person are differentiated. Simply put, he used the construct to refer to attempts made by individuals to answer the question "who am I?"

Erikson preferred to let the concept speak for itself rather than have it lose its richness through any explicit definition. The closest it comes to is in terms of construction of a stable sense of who one is and where one is headed with one ' s life. He made the subject matter of identity more explicit by approaching it from a variety of angles—biographic, pathogenic and theoretical. In Erikson's definition three elements emerge as necessary for a sense of identity: (a) experience of inner sameness or integrity, (b) sense of inner sameness as continuous over time, and (c) experience within a community of important others. The term 'identity' refers to both, a persistent sameness within oneself and a persistent sharing of some kind of essential character with others, thereby expressing a mutual relation.

Erikson believed that development throughout life is influenced by an underlying genetic plan common to all members of our species, operating within the social context. He termed this phenomenon the epigenetic principle, or Epigenesis. In Erikson's depiction of life cycle, identity resolution is a stage specific normative crisis which normally takes place at adolescence. He sees the formation of identity as a gradual process, having its genesis right from infancy. In Eriksonian ego psychology identity consists of several interrelated elements. Many other theorists have taken these concepts further, it has been proposed that "two important processes which are involved in identity formation are exploration of alternatives and commitment to choices" (Marcia, 1980).

Marcia (1966) operationalized the construct identity in description of distinct identity statuses. He identified four styles or processes by which individuals go about the task of establishing and maintaining their sense of personal identity. He argued that the progress through, and outcome of the identity stage as depicted by Erikson can be represented in terms of these four modes of reacting to the identity crisis. Each of these identity statuses has characteristic features of its own. Diffusion is characterized by a state of uncertainty about life choices, and difficulty in taking responsibility along with difficulty with resolving vocational and ideological issues. Moratorium is characterized by relatively high self-esteem and autonomy but lack of initiative to commit to responsibility. It may include trying with various roles but non-commitment to any. These people seem indecisive about commitments because of equal and opposite commitments, although they appear quite intelligent and seem somewhat utopian in their ideological outlook.

Moratorium and diffusion, both are uncommitted to social rules and values ; however, the moratorium is in the process of searching among possibilities to match the interests and endowments, while the diffusion is not. The later identity position encompasses a diversity of uncommitted individuals from the "happy go lucky" drifter to those with severe psychopathology.

Achievement is characterized by resolution of crisis, individual makes judgments about personal beliefs and goals. High-level of self-responsibility and commitment are main aspects of this status. In foreclosure, no crisis is experienced, one simply takes on the views about themselves through others. Low self-directness and pressure to adopt family and social values is the main feature here. The individual responds to this pressure and succumbs to it. Achievements and foreclosures have both formed commitments to the above values, however, the achievement has done to strengthen a process of exploration and self-examination, while the foreclosure has primarily relied upon childhood identifications figures in adopting commitments without exploration. Another point of difference is the presence of certain rigidity in the latter, they give an impression that if they found themselves in a situation whose parental values were non-functional, they would be greatly at a loss. The individuals with an achieved identity, on the contrary do not appear as if they would be overwhelmed by sudden shifts in their environment or by unexpected burdens of responsibility.

Grotevant (1987) took concepts from Marcia's status paradigm to propose a model of identity process. He proposed that consideration of multiple possibilities and consequences ideally leads to choices that represent self-conscious long term commitments. He pointed out various factors (individual and contextual) that affect identity formation: (a) personality factors (flexibility, self-esteem, tendency to monitor one's behaviour and openness to experience); (b) cognitive competence (to consider possibilities, drain inference, coordinate multiple perspectives); (c) characteristics of one's social context (cultural support for making personal choices, family communication, patterns, educational, career opportunities and exposure to options and viewpoints); and (d) individual's general orientation, at a given point in his/her life to engage in or avoid identity exploration and commitment.

Berzonsky (1993) extended this model further to highlight the internal dynamics of constructing an identity. He conceived of identity process as a theory of self, suggested that the individual be viewed as a self-theorist engaged in a process of theorizing about self. He further argues that this theorizing is not simply a matter of gathering and summarizing data and testing prediction but involves an active process of interpreting one's experiences and generating new ones. He has distinguished three types of self-theorists marked by different styles of theorising: (a) scientific self-theorists—who "tend to be self-reflective, skeptical about self-constructions and open to self-relevant information . . . such information oriented individuals deal with personal decisions and identity concerns by deliberately seeking out, processing and evaluating self-relevant information" (p.173); (b) dogmatic self-theorists—who, in contrast, conform to "the values and expectations of significant others" these include "efforts . . . to defend against potential threats to their self-constructions. Such individuals who utilize . . . (such) approach to self-theorising have been found to . . . possess rigid self-construct systems and to be closed to novel information relevant to hard core values and beliefs" (p.174); (c) ad hoc self-theorists—who "(R)eact continually to situational demands. A poorly organized, fragmented self-theory leads them to procrastinate and avoid dealing with personal conflicts and decisions . . . situational demands and consequences will eventually determine behavioural reactions . . . situation specific accommodations are likely to be short term, ephermal acts of behavioural or verbal compliance, rather than long term, stable revisions in identity structure" (p.174).

These groups of theorists see identity formation more as a process of discovery rather than creation. According to another such view as pointed by Waterman (1992), "a person's search for identity is an effort to identify those potentials that correspond to the 'true self' for each person these are already present, unrecognized potentials, and need to become manifest and acted upon if the person is to live a fulfilled life" (p.59). In similar attempts, Blassi and Glodis (1995) have proposed that identity formation consists of "the 'discovery' that one is, inevitably and necessarily, a certain kind of person" (p.412). However, the discovery can not be taken literally and "(we) do not 'discover' our 'true selves' in the same way as a child might find a ball that has been hidden under a couch" (Moshman, 1998).

Clarity is yet to be reached on this issue as there seems to be a reality within us bearing a complex relation to the reality outside; it is important to construct our understanding of who we are. To the extent that we focus on identification of alternatives and on independent choices and commitments, it looks like a process of creation. On the other hand, to the extent that there is recognition of (howsoever faintly) already existing aspects of self, such construction looks like a process of discovery. Hence, as Moshman (1988) affirmed, although the actual construction of identity may sometimes involve more of creation and sometimes more of discovery, in general, it involves both.

Identity and Women

An increasing sense of identity is said to be experienced pre-consciously as a sense of psychosocial well-being. Its most obvious concomitants are inferred as a feeling of being at home in one's body, a sense of "knowing where one is going", and an inner assuredness of anticipated recognition from those who count. Unlike men, for women, the "inner space" or womb is seen as the basis of a positive potential for their identity. Erikson (1968) believed that interpersonal issues form the core of women's identities while vocational and ideological were of peripheral importance. According to him, a woman's resolution of issues around identity was expected to be left partially open and flexible at adolescence in order to accommodate her partner after marriage and her future families. He further suggested that much of a women's identity presides in her choice of the man she wants to be sought by, "womanhood arises when her attractiveness and experience succeed in selecting what is to be admitted to the . . . inner space for keeps" (Erikson, 1968: 283).

Feminist researchers pose criticisms to these mainstream interpretations of the concept of identity and its operationalization. As an example, a major criticism of Erikson's work in this area is that it portrays a primarily Eurocentric, male model of normality; feminists see the suggestion that women can only define who they are in relation to their mate, to be objectionable. The mainstream, traditional views are seen to have little place for subjectivity with "the sense of personal, anecdotal and individual . . . thought to detract from the certainty, reliability and usefulness of knowledge" (Elliott, 2000: 56). With respect to issues and lives of women, a review of research literature further reveals that most work has focused on clinical data and the current psychological literature has little about normal development in women (Josselson, 1988). Though a lot has been written about women, not much has gone into the phenomenological aspects or how they define themselves (their self-definition), this is so partly because often in psychological research the individual is either portrayed only as a clinical case or is a lost subject in statistical analysis. Moreover, in context of issues around identity and self, although the enquiry into the process has been relatively straightforward for men, for women, it has been quite ambiguous. Developmental psychologists and theorists seem to find the existing models inadequate to illuminate women's life (Rossi, 1980; Unger, 1983; Lerman, 1986; Peck, 1986). These theorists have stressed on need for a theory, flexible enough to encompass the multiplicity of roles, beings and circumstances in women's lives.

Research literature reveals that except for the radical shift in views of the critical theorists and feminists, various theories of human development have been based on the conception of male developmental patterns, with that for their counterparts mostly ignored or treated as an afterthought or fitted into forced overlaps. Historically, the dominant issues in female development, those of interpersonal relatedness such as affiliation and nurturance have been mostly overlooked in research. Feminist researchers have been critical of the traditional approaches to theory and methodology in social science discipline (Archer 1992; Harding 1987; Keller 1989). In particular, they have argued about the invisibility of women (just as class, race and culture) in development of any theory of a 'normal' or healthy development. According to Gilligan (1982) theorists have fallen into an observational bias, implicitly adopting male life as the norm. Other feminist researchers contend that identity has been portrayed in very narrow terms that convey a negative connotation—a rugged individualism, isolation, separateness, selfishness, maleness (Chodorow, 1974; Gilligan, 1982; Lykes 1985; Sampson, 1985). They strongly recommend theories which are attuned to the women's own voices and recognize the subjective spaces which exist for women within the particular discourse.

Attempts to understand how and why men and women differ have lead to various generalizations. Following Erikson, researchers have concluded that intimacy seems to precede or at least go along with issues of identity for women (Douvan and Adelson, 1966 ; Orlafsky, 1977; Josselson, Greenberg and McConochic, 1977; Marcia, 1980). The current theories of development seem to be focusing on separation and autonomy rather than on connection and relationship (Miller, 1976; Surrey 1984). The initial research on gender and content domains of identity indicated a neat split between predominantly male identity issues and predominantly female issues with resolution of interpersonal issues (sexuality and sex role) and ideology (religion and politics) being predictive of identity formation in females and males respectively. Further investigations however, looked at such gender differences in a different and more complex manner.

Hopkins (1982) found that interpersonal issues have no predictive advantage over occupational, religion and politics issues with respect to identity development in women. Also, it is indicated that both men and women claimed that the interpersonal area was most important to them (Bilsker, Schiedel and Marcia 1988). Gilligan (1982) concluded that men and women operate within different internal models as a result of which experiences such as achievement and affiliation are different for them even though behavioural manifestations may look similar. Hence, unlike men, for whom occupation and interpersonal concerns can be negotiated as separate and independent concerns, in case of women not merely an analysis of the content areas but an understanding of process of integration of various dimensions into a meaningful whole is necessary for an understanding of the richness of their inner lives.

An important point of departure in investigations with women is with regards to the timing and phase of occurrence of developmental processes. Whereas most studies (with men) have focused on college years (18–22 years), research with women suggested that they did not progress on the available measures of identity development during this period (Constantinople, 1969). It has been suggested that either they reach a ceiling on development before men do or they have a disphasic developmental pattern with one group achieving an initial identity before 20 years and other forming a self-constructed identity after fulfilling the socially prescribed roles.

Researches based on Marcia's status paradigm indicate that males and females negotiate different pathways to identity formation. It has been pointed out that for women different statuses hold different experiences and meanings. The experience of a moratorium, for instance, may hold a different type of threat and promise in comparison to men. Earlier studies in this respect showed that women in identity foreclosure looked more similar to those in identity achievement than did moratorium women, who appear similar to those in identity diffusion category. Marcia, (1980) explained this adaptiveness of foreclosure status on the basis that women may not be supported in the process of exploration necessary to form self-chosen commitments. Later studies however, indicated a change in direction of resemblance of moratorium to achievement and foreclosure towards diffusion. The dimension of exploration was now linked with favourable psychological characteristics. These trends in findings seem to suggest that when society encourages choices and non-traditional roles for women, they appear to negotiate moratorium without the negative consequences. Whether the moratorium stage appears advantageous or disadvantageous to women is likely to be a function of the historical period and social context within which a particular construct (dimension) is being measured. In similar sense, foreclosure would seem to exhibit an advantage over moratorium in resisting peer pressure and maintaining sense of self-esteem. If social contexts provide support for women having their own opinion, valuing themselves and pursuing high academic and professional goals, then the position would reverse.

The process of finding oneself (read Self) for women is a complicated one, for there are mental structures embedded, affecting and operating along side the concrete social structures. These mental structures can be oppressive and in women may take the form of lack of self-confidence, devaluing of own needs and desires, valuing and giving priority to others. Feminist thought approaches the concept of identity with the issues around finding (a position for) oneself—a real self/self acceptable to itself. Here the challenge lies in making the subjective experiences of the self intelligible, in this surfaces the difficulty in dealing with experiences of a fragmented and changing self that is inherent in the life stories and case histories of women. In this context, Grimshaw (1988) points that perhaps more women are in touch with the coherent parts in themselves than a unified active core self. Flax (1993) has further elaborated on the subjective and fragmented nature of self, experienced by women as against the unitary self which is an effect of many kinds of relations of domination; it can sustain unity by splitting off/ repressing other parts of its own and others' subjectivity (p.109).

A resolution of the issue of complexity and ambiguity of diverse views is not an easy one. Although there has been a lot of research inputs across theorists as well as perspectives, on issues around self and identity, the questions around relevance of these in individual lives, have received attention only recently. An understanding of human development perhaps "demands an integrated perspective involving at least some account of the organic, personality, social as well as cultural systems" (Paranjpe, 1998: 34). Whichever approach one takes, one needs to be alert for the glimpses of the subjective amidst the broader generalizable themes.

Methodology

Rationale for Methodology in the Present Study

While exploring the complex and operationally elusive constructs such as self and identity, different perspectives and orientations could lead to differences in outcomes and understanding. The differences between perspectives often culminate into contrasting approaches and subsequent problems surrounding the study of these processes and phenomena. The problem of uniqueness has been one such critical issue which has been dealt with in this study to some extent.

The apparent defying of general laws by uniqueness in individuals poses a dilemma for any research on human development. A response to this dilemma has led to two distinct branches of science: one, for dealing with the general (nomothetic) and the other for dealing with the unique (ideographic), both with their distinct methodologies regarding uniqueness. Since an important aspect in the construct of identity deals with self-sameness and uniqueness of individuals, the problems of uniqueness has a special place in the study of identity. General principles and processes seem to take unique meaning and form with regards to tapping identity elements in each individual within different cultures. Some of the ways to use ideographic approach has been through the use of life histories, biographies and personal diaries (Murray, 1938; White, 1966; Erkison, 1968). As one of the pioneering contributions in the area of identity research Erik Erikson, (1956) based his work partly on the psychoanalytical procedure, in that his "account of the syndrome of identity confusion is a 'composite sketch' of case histories of adolescent patients" (pp. 76–77). However, part of Erikson's work is also psycho-historical and based on non-clinical data such as biographies and autobiographies.

As a follow-up, Marcia (1966) proposed techniques to identify and measure four identity statuses or different modes of reacting to identity crisis: identity diffusion, foreclosure, moratorium and identity achievement. Although the status paradigm helps in operationalizing the term identity, thereby making it more accessible, the role and impact of cultural differences while using such approach remains to be investigated.

Recent researches have found more and more takers of alternative methodologies to investigate development of identity and self. One such approach to obtain an extraordinary rich corpus of material is to use aspects of ethno-psychology; this is different from the (general) ethnographic ways where the major effort is seen on applying western concepts and theories of psychological processes to understand and translate beliefs and behaviour from non-western people. According to Strauss (1976,

1977), western theories and models need to be kept at arm's length and attempts need to be made to gain anaemic reading of local psychology and personality. Only once a basic insight is gained, can the formal western psychological theories be brought into closer proximity for comparisons. Hence, in investigating culture specific aspects of issues and concepts, the proper study of ethnopsychology and ethnopersonality requires more than fragments of ethnographic observation, a consideration of the connotative meanings of the terms or the usage of language in specific societies and cultures.

Hermeneutic studies through autobiographies also provide the basis for illuminating broader issues concerning the construction of self and identity (Freeman, 1993). As to the relevance of narratives and their validity in capturing the process of construction of identity and self, Freeman(1993) takes a position as a mediator between the 'extreme reactivistic skepticism' of social constructionists and more traditional humanistic and scientific positions, "(to) speak of . . . the narratives used to represent the self is not to claim that we are prisoners of history . . . nor is it to claim that we are endowed with the magical ability to stand wholly apart from history . . . (this) suggests that there exists a margin of freedom within which to think, act and be" (p.217). There is further a need for creative imaginations if one aspires to say anything meaningful and truthful about human selfhood and identity, "(O)nly if we are ready and willing to take a leap of the imagination, a leap indeed, of faith—we will find inquiry into the elusive being (that) we call the 'self', worthwhile" (p. 232).

More radical trends have been seen in methods for identity research. A recent development originates from the work of feminist researchers. Collaborative Enquiry, as it is termed, is an extension of narrative exploration with a focus on how people 'construct' themselves in accordance with dominate narratives (Brooks and Edwards, 1997). It provides a context for articulating knowledge that does not seem consistent with the dominant discourses; basic to collaborative enquiry is that all participants hold approximately the same positional power in relationship to each other and the topic being addressed. The topic of enquiry is jointly agreed upon, and data are gathered from and belong to all participants, all members participate in interpretation and dissemination of enquiry results. The method of collaborative inquiry seems to provide a context for developing the language to tell the 'unstoried' experience of participants. There is a sharing and witnessing of the unspoken and "silent' narratives and the research context provides a safe space to venture into these aspects of experience.

The Present Study

The broad orientation for the present study is eclectic, in that, it is postmodern in spirit, giving provisions for psycho-social, social constructivist, feminist, post-structuralist views; further it is informed by the existentialist principles, with the inclusion of post-Freudian psychodynamic concepts. There is an attempt to explore the constructs and developmental processes vis-à-vis the lived experiences by seeking and allowing a space for dialogue between the existing perspectives and theories.

Further, the aim is to not to draw generalized inferences or the universals, but to create potential for accurate understanding, explanation and implications for populations with overlapping characteristics as the participants. Hence, although the focus is not to generalize the themes and elements gathered from the narratives (for all Indians and/or women), to the extent of the overlap in social-historical-cultural factors with others, these would likely give sufficient insight into the processes and issues at a macro level.

There are no hypotheses at the outset, rather, the study focuses on exploration and analysis of the subjective accounts of the lived experiences of women with the theme of change and continuity; consistency, commitment and crisis; frailty and well-being.

Research Agenda

The aim of this research paper is to appreciate and acknowledge developmental crises peculiar to the urban middle-class women in developing countries like India. More specifically:

(a) To clarify the notions of self and identity vis-à-vis sample of middle class urban Indian women; how do these constructs traverse and translate through subjective experiences of these women.

(b) To have a close look at the developmental processes from intrapersonal-social-cultural-historical perspectives; the focus is on understanding, exploring and validating these processes through and in the individual experiences using the available perspectives that may supplement and compliment the investigation.

(c) To explore dimensions of identity that hold relevance to the participants' lives, specifically with respect to gender.

Participants

Women were chosen for enquiry into the processes associated with identity in order to include the unaccounted for experiences of such groups in identity literature. Further sampling specifications have been outlined more on the basis of logicalities. More technically, incidental and convenience sampling has been employed to select the narratives and capture the elements of identity in the middle class urban Indian women. Age of the participants was considered while deciding on the study sample in order to maintain certain degree of uniformity. The narratives included in the study belong to women in their mid-20's. This phase of life has been chosen for exploration due to its potential in tapping the issues around identity and self.

Tools

Detailed unstructured interviews were used in order to capture the 'depth' and also be able to cover considerable 'breadth' of participants' lives. At the outset, participants were told about the nature and focus of the study, for a basic orientation it was emphasized that it would not be a formal interview and that they are free to talk about what they consider as important with respect to themselves and their life. To avoid awkwardness and for a better understanding, certain pointed questions were asked in the beginning of the interview, apart from that, the participants were encouraged to talk without interruptions. Apart from these detailed interviews during multiple sessions (4–9 months), short interviews were also held with the colleagues and family members of the participants.

Narratives and Analysis

The very aspect that makes these narratives interesting and useful also seems to produce narrative difficulties; such difficulty arises from focusing on the distinct cultural and discursive aspects of each narrative apart from the psychological facet therein.

From an ontological standpoint, women's identity has never been as important a category in the life cycle as issues such as intimacy and generativity have been. Issues around identity with respect to women seem ambiguous, hence they have either not been taken up or abandoned or dealt with attempts to fit into the already existing frameworks. The attempts at understanding specifically the nuances (and differences) of women's experiences are complicated further by a perception of a collective image of humanity which is one-sided, incomplete and emerging from the fact that human experience in the past has been synonymous with masculine experience.

Another challenge comes in terms of diversity in the meta-narratives on themes of self and identity; there has varying emerging voices, in terms of a conception of the processes involving these constructs. At the very least, the narratives could mean that identity is still not as important an issue for all groups of individuals. For some, having an identity could mean just aping the dominant lifestyle (the norm), while in others it could mean an actual shift or transition in life, in which case identity issues would become genuinely important to deserve attention.

This study attempts to be empathetic to the research process, at the same time, pay attention to what the narratives unveil about the participants' lives vis-à-vis the themes around self and identity. In this regard, the discussion traverses through theories that help in comprehending the narratives and probes through the different levels of intellectual enquiry—social, psychological, existential, philosophical—in an attempt to understand the complex phenomena at hand which by no means involve a linear process.

The commonality between the participants is that they are women, in their mid-late 20's, from urban India, with minimum graduation level education; although the intentional matching ends there and there are different themes emerging in each narrative, yet there seems to be a common thread connecting them all to the issues of self and identity, one that is akin to search for a sense of integrity at the core.

Narrative 1, SB

SB is a 27-year-old middle-school teacher. She has been in this profession for past three years and has a pre-Ph.D (M.Phil) in English with a degree in Education (B.Ed.). SB was born and brought up in Delhi, and had been staying with her parents till the time of the interviews; the other members in her family include her elder brother, sister-in-law and a niece. Her father is a retired government employee and her mother is a housewife. She also has an elder sister who is married and stays with her husband in the same city. Acquaintances describe her as a *sweet girl . . . soft spoken and usually smiling.* She is seen as "intelligent", hard working and sincere by her colleagues.

Interviews with SB took place during a span of four months. In the first meeting itself, SB readily divulged her concerns for physical appearance and anxiety about marriage with little probing.

In SB's narrative, signs of a polarized self appear from the outset, along with evidence of internalized disjointedness in more than one aspect of her life. There are two main themes emerging clearly in her narrative, one of a near diffusion that runs through most of the narrative and dominates different domains in her life, and the other indicating a foreclosure that emerges towards the latter part of the narrative.

SB's encounters with confusions seem to be scattered bits of crises and conflicts in different areas of life. Her decisions hardly seem to be outcomes of (pro)active choices; some of them (such as regarding studies) *just . . . happened* by default and others (such as marriage) seem to have resulted from her desperate attempts to cope with the anxiety provoking immediate situations.

In terms of specific themes in SB's narrative, her life seems to be assortment of different fragments. Cohesion seems to be missing and what come across in conversations with her are broken aspects of her self. Nevertheless, her narrative seems to throw light on some of the current crises in her life.

At the outset, SB's conflicts are evident in both, her complexes about her appearance as well as her apprehensions about initiating intimate (romantic) relationship. A random interpersonal encounter seems to have impacted SB to the extent of triggering series of precarious crises.

> It started about 4 years back, , the lady sitting next to me in a bus . . . pointed out(my) facial hair . . . I have gone through (so many times) in my mind, I don't look much into the mirror anymore . . . I can not think of meeting anyone (for dating), I keep looking at all the girls around,

> even the very young ones. I think everyone is pretty but me . . . Some one's hair, another one's complexion (but) nothing in me . . .

Although the role of intra-psychic factors in such a profound impact on the further development of individual needs to be probed, yet, the role of this incident symbolizes and significantly points out at the role of the social in construction of the individual trajectories.

SB's acute anxiety and ambivalence towards all interpersonal encounters seems to impede on both, a resolution of crisis of intimacy as well as arriving at a sense of cohesive identity.

More than once during the interviews, SB pointed to contradictions at various levels of her experiences, perhaps as an acknowledgement of a failure to integrate the diverse aspects of herself and to see them only as polar contradictions, *(A)t one level I think(that) all this doesn't matter, doesn't count at all, what matters is inner beauty . . . but then I am so very conscious of my looks . . . don't you see a contradiction there?!* Similar contradictions are visible in her views around matrimony and intimacy,

> (There is) no scene (of marriage) at the moment . . . I am happy as I am . . . (But) sometimes I feel there should be some company like others (have) . . . If I ever go (on a date) and meet any one for (the purpose of) marriage, first thing I'll do is tell him about these (facial hair). I'll say that . . . (my eyebrows are) otherwise messy . . . (now)I have stopped getting my arms waxed, (eye)brows done, (facial hair) bleached . . . why should I dress up and do all that for others . . . (but when) my father tells me that I should meet (the prospective suitors) like what I am (without removing facial hair), I cannot do that! that would be (an) insult (to me).

SB's pain and anxiety seems to intensify as she oscillates between such boundaries, not being able to come to terms with either. Certain amount of confusion in SB may reflect an incoherence of reason and desire (Griffith, 1995). She represents the struggles and dilemmas of those women who are caught in between different kinds of relations of domination which give rise to the painfully contradictory feelings that they experience. SB's oscillations between rejection and acceptance of her own needs seem to typify the oppressive mental structures that hinder the active core of being (Grimshaw, 1988).

Amidst these conflicts and contradictions, a noticeable aspect of SB's narrative is that it comes across as missing readiness for those questions that in answer generally define the core of any individual's self. Such questions often warrant a conscious quest regarding answers like "who am I' and in answering this in turn, one is likely to become more comfortable and at ease with who he/she is. Such continual growth would be inherent in the process of arriving at a sense of identity, connected to a genuine self-respect and self-acceptance, and eventually leading to an ability to be joyful even with a realization of being far from perfect (Erikson, 1968). For SB however, the situations that provide potential for explorations seem to put her in distressing conundrum; there seems to be an internal upheaval every time the circumstances demand her to integrate parts of her with each other and with the external world.

SB's overwhelming and incapacitating discomforts with indistinctness are evident in her agonized narrations through most part of the interviews. Continuity seems to be missing in her narrative as she touches on the apparent gaps she feels in her self; a split of this kind can pervade time and space as brought out in her perception and acknowledgement of a schism: *I never did anything (meaningful) . . . don't know where the time went . . . !*

Work emerges as yet another critical area of developmental crisis in this narrative. Although SB indicated having some clarity vis-à-vis her professional choice as, *(having) loved teaching from always . . . (and being) happy with . . . work . . .*, there seems to be little integration of vocation with the other themes in her life. Work remains for SB something routine, *like we get up, eat . . . do things which have to be done*, her despondence is evident in her claims that I *have done what I had to (do) . . . could have (done better) but . . . (its okay);* work helps her to "kill time" and she likes her current job for *(the school) is near home.*

With ambivalence towards her profession, SB seems to fall short of wholly identifying and exploring the potentials that could help her in defining her self and in turn, her professional identity seems to fail in giving her any sense of continuity and integrity that could potentially be at the core of her psycho-social identity. However, on the other hand, vocation if at all, only seems to provide a sense of relief in her conflicts around the domains of intimacy. Hence, given her ambivalence, what makes her see her "job" as inescapable is a question worth exploring further.

Though her job "keeps (her) going", it seems to acts only as a refuge to the "What next?" question that seems to surround many contemporary urban, middle-class Indian women. SB's dilemma could easily speak for many single, educated women in urban India who have to face the increasingly common demand from their male counterparts in favour of a "modern working wife". Hence, work seems to be a key to finding a suitable partner rather than a potential for self-exploration and extension of a coherent self; for these women, an opportunity for a clear and comfortable sense of self is snipped by foreclosing on the presently, readily available role of a "working woman",

> It's not easy (to get married) if you are not working, I've seen how difficult it was to get my sister married . . . (but I often wonder why) is it necessary to work . . . can one not just be a housewife?

With vocation as merely a means to work through the issues of connectivity, a phase which could have had a potential for meaningful bonding with fellow professionals, seems to leave her with a sense of alienation and worthlessness. Conflicts seem to pervade through SB's interpersonal relationships at work, her reactions towards authority figures reflect feelings of injustice and a sense of powerlessness coupled with an acute sense of low self-esteem.

> (An incident with a senior colleague) . . . still makes me confused . . . whether she was right or I am . . . for myself . . . I am right, I know it, but she is the boss, I'll (have to) do what she likes . . . all(others) butter her so she lets them off . . . so I'll just do as she says . . . (I feel) terrible, I used to cry and cry over it. My family said I am right and if I know that, the rest (of the people) shouldn't matter, but . . . I used to feel that she can't be wrong either she's so religious . . . but I know now that people are diplomat, so they need to be "handled' but I don't know how . . . I can not trust them. (A few days later, again I felt) completely at a loss to deal with (another) situation . . . (involving another colleague) . . . every one blamed me . . . (but) I don't think I had any choice.

There seems to be a pattern of resistance and difficulty in adapting to the contextual demands. "*I can't change . . . that's just the way I am. Every one has . . . (their) individuality . . . and (those characteristics), one can not change . . . (I think) I am very sensitive . . . (I know) it is an imbalance . . . but I can't help it . . . can't change myself now . . .*". Such acute negation of change that comes across as rigidity and insufferable conformity seems like attempts to cope with the ambiguities and insecurities. The imbalance between the outer and inner can be threatening for a not so strong and resilient sense of self and some degree of balance may be provided by the uncompromising structures that one creates as means to cope with the anxieties. Looking at it from another direction, what is clearly missing in SB's narrative, is an acceptance of all (wanted as well as unwanted) aspects of herself, which is also a prerequisite of an ability to remain independent, along with an openness and flexibility which allows for an acceptance of and adjustment with the differing world-views (Maslow, 1987).

> (I)t's not fair (that I have been asked to give a talk in the morning assembly) . . . it's just because . . . (a senior colleague) wants to corner me . . . I do not know why they do this (to me) . . . I went to (the school) Principal . . . he said it (should) not matter(to me) . . . (but) it's not easy for me . . . I get anxious . . . I need to prepare . . . last time (when I had to do something similar), I could not take my classes for a week, . . . I don't want to make them think I'm not prepared. If I refuse . . . what would Principal Sir think . . . I respect him . . . but (even) he does not understand . . . (but) he is important no matter what he said to me or did . . . (but I think) I am also important . . . (but) that is selfish . . .

Such confusions and contradictions spread through a major part of SB's narrative and seem to culminate into a state of bewilderment followed by an abrupt foreclosure into marriage (with a long-time acquaintance whose proposal she had declined on an earlier occasion on account of his "not so great looks"). She partly held her colleague responsible for making her leave the city and get married.

> (Marriage) . . . was not at all on my mind. Oh God! I would have to leave Delhi . . . I just hope and pray he's not . . . cunning, hypocrite . . . I don't mean just with me even with his juniors . . . he should be fair and just, I would hate him otherwise. . . after all this episode (at

school), I just abruptly said yes (to his proposal) this time . . . I don't know him at all.

Later, SB shared her doubts about her fiancé more clearly,

I have been feeling quite odd . . . very uncomfortable . . . I don't know how to put it . . . I think there is something wrong some where my fiancé is so effeminate . . . he would use his hands while talking . . . you know hand movements . . . like girls, I feel so awkward . . . I don't know how to clarify do you think I should ask . . . how does one clarify such things.?

Consolidation of Main Themes

In one sense, SB's narrative questions the categories used in identity literature as they fail to fully account for her subjective experiences. More specifically, the status paradigm often used to operationalize the construct seems to be of little value in understanding the complexity of her life; to label SB's turmoil, howsoever incapacitating, merely in terms of diffusion status seems reductionist. On the other hand, an appreciation of her early patterns of emotional growth and stages of development in light of the socio-cultural-historical factors may help to understand the basis for the seemingly diffusional phase and the accompanying anxiety.

Identity for SB is not meeting with her self but of ascertaining herself; her narrative conveys desperate struggles in coming to terms with dissociated parts of herself. There seems to be a futile tussle of herself with her self, regressing to a point where a sense of self-alignment and validity needs to be essentially re-established as a precursor to establishing a balanced position vis-à-vis the social context. SB's current crisis seems to bring up issues around trust that permeates her private and social experiences; more than once, she finds herself in situations where the only way she is able to validate her experiences is through the others; at the same time seeing them as biased, malicious, unreliable and in contradiction to her own experience . . . *(they) find me ugly (so) I must be!* . . . This makes the ever so complicated task of making meaning and integrating the aspects of Self as confusing, chaotic and even painful. It is not surprising that in case of differences with those in authority and her colleagues, she finds herself *confused* . . .

SB seems to be restrained in exploration; alienation is a word that repeatedly comes to mind while examining her narrative which comes as combined feelings of powerlessness, meaninglessness and frustration. As pointed out by Baumeister (1986), such sense of alienation hampers the individual's potential to find fulfilment in the options available within society, or to bring about a change in his/her condition; further, it is difficult to console them for these failures with sense of personal worth and dignity or value in struggle itself.

Her conflicts seem to be more than just around issues of identity or even intimacy, but appear to include her gender identity. At a physical level, she does not seem "comfortable" with her self, her looks, and her body; her concerns with her "shabby (looks)" seem more than just concerns for appearance but to be indicative of an intense need to feel at ease with the cultural and social norms vis-à-vis her sense of being a woman. The extent of her anxiety around sexual and gender identity and criticalness of its possible resolution for her development is reflected again in her concerns and doubts about her fiancé's sexuality which come across as projections of her discomfort around her own feminineness. Such aspects of her narrative make the oft latent complications in interaction between the social, cultural and intra-individual forces more than apparent.

SB seems to readily accept the female stereotype for herself and sees any deviation from it as a threat of exclusion; she seems to be attempting to negotiate identity issues by inclusion into the female category, and by giving in to the dominant female beliefs and stereotypes. In this light, there could perhaps be a (simpler) developmental explanation for the current crisis, where the confusions and pain could be seen as stemming from a comment made at a critical, impressionable stage in life which laid the foundations for her crisis and questioned the most basic, pertinent and socially conspicuous aspect of her self—her gender identity which led to a foreclosure of gender roles instead of explorations of holistic and integrated aspects of her self.

As regards to the important issues (vis-a-vis integration) there seems to be a pattern of chronic splitting of self/other emotions and demands so that one set of interests obliterate the other pathologically. In this respect, (an integrated) sense of self can be said to emanate only from an intermediary area of experience to which both, inner reality and external life contribute (during the early interactions of the infant with the caregivers).

Although this transitional space usually leads to an emergence of selfhood, however if seized too early by the environment, it may lead to the formation of a false self – a structure that conforms rather than lives. Perhaps similar to women in similar positions, she finds herself surrendering totally to others' expectations and demands which in turn makes her seem like . . . living through an identity of being a victim and martyr without resilient spirit in search of creating a wholesome space . . . (Parikh and Garg, 1989: 26).

Towards the latter part of the narrative, structure of foreclosure seems to provide her with well defined boundaries to cope with the confusion of the developmental processes and complexities of her socio-historical context. The first few signs of vicarious explorations appeared in SB's narrative after her accepting the marriage proposal. She seemed willing to question the roles she would be expected to take on as a wife, these signs of exploration in turn, seem to be indications of a renewed confidence in her; in this sense, marriage seemed to be a source of self-preservation; establishing for her, a sense of continuity for her.

Narrative 2, SH

SH is 29 years old, working as a dance teacher. She has been married for four years and has a son (1 year old); she stays in a joint family with her parents-in-law who are both retired. Before marriage, SH had been doing stage performances in Indian classical dance which decreased after marriage and completely stopped since her pregnancy. She misses dancing on stage and has been planning and practising for a comeback on the stage but finds it *difficult to (put in) required time.* SH is seen by her colleagues as a dedicated teacher and a very creative person; her contributions in training the students are acknowledged by her colleagues as well as the school management.

SH had an arranged marriage, she described her marriage as being "balanced" and her husband as a *reasonable man* (but) *chauvinist sometimes.* SH shared having regular "tiffs" with her mother-in-law and her inability to find a solution resulting in persistent "headaches" and depressive symptoms.

Looking at SH's narrative from a psycho-social perspective, we find in her issues of work and vocation relatively clarified. The most conspicuous theme in SH's narrative is one around her professional identity. Work for SH is a "passion"; it is her forte and "defines her". Although there seem to be simultaneous and ongoing negotiations in interpersonal and connectivity issues, she sees dance as her "calling"; her passion about dance is reflected in her zest and expressions when talking about her work.

SH's narrative seems to highlight the process of arriving at a sense of identity that incorporates the psycho-social aspects of development in terms of extending the personal into the social. Her ambition to realize her potential and capabilities is an extension of her self into the social. As for resolving the occupational/vocational crisis, she seems to "have found" herself through the creative field that helps her merge the idiosyncrasies with talent. *In dance, I can see (me) just losing myself and just Being . . . I am music . . . that is the essence of me.*

She seems to have arrived at her current identity only after a phase of exploration in order to locate her groove, *I was terrible at everything . . . the 'bad child', unlike my sister who was the goody-goody one, be it studies, discipline, everything! . . . I was the one who used to throw tantrums, be stubborn . . . I was just about an average student.*

There seems to be a kind of sincerity and integrity in SH that differentiates and makes up for her stubbornness and arrogance, for not only does she acknowledge and accept these parts of herself but also hints at a sense of dignity in proclaiming these aspects which define her. This stubbornness does not come across as an expression of a totalitarian character that one would resort to in the process of negotiating with the rejected aspects of themselves, rather seems to be a link with such a sense of self which provides her with an undefined sense of pride. For she is able to make her mark by extending these very characteristics into her life, carving out a niche for herself, being visible despite her ordinariness "*none of my tantrums or rebellion was for my own sake, but (stemmed from an inner requirement) to know the (larger) 'whys' . . . (It was never a selfish exercise but) to find and seek justification for general rules*". The pride that is reflective of a basic faith seems to have guided her towards resolving the different crises of her life. It is these very aspects which give her a strong sense of being herself. SH seems to be living on certain self-identified ideologies (Paranjpe, 1998),[1] howsoever loosely defined.

SH's narrative, helps to an extent, in understanding the ingredients of the process of arriving at a sense of identity. At the simplest, the narrative seems to convey the theme that people can make up for disappointments in life, thereby highlighting the links between health and expression of self. She seems to be driven by the need to make a place for herself in a context and such circumstances where her existence by itself carries little meaning or recognition by others. To begin with, dance provides that tool which steers her entity and identity making her "visible". In her narrative, the processes of individuation—differentiation also come to the fore; unlike women who carve their identity through relationships, she seems to be searching for a unique position for herself outside the interpersonal relationship/connectivity domain through her vocation.

Although SH appears consistently focusing on the expression of her unique personal identity, her investment is not only into the themes of ideology and vocation that are oft outlined as the main elements of psycho-social identity, but also in interpersonal connectivity domain. A closer examination of her crisis reveals her attempts at resolving the interpersonal issues (of connecting with others, communal living, and family roles) while arriving at the intrapersonal (individuation, vocation, ideology). Hence, for SH, issues around intimacy come out as important area for resolution, along with a negotiation of her psycho-social identity; in this sense, as pointed out by Erikson (1968) adequate resolution of connectivity issues and the exploration of elements of a personal identity come simultaneously such that the boundaries/dichotomies between them seem to get blurred. SH seems to personify a fusion of issues around identity, intimacy and generativity.

Even though clarity is visible in vocational and occupational areas, there is considerable experimentation and some extent of *"trying out"* visible in the interpersonal domain. In fact, SH seems to be going through a crisis of interpersonal turmoil characterized by confusion with respect to many of her close relationships, accompanied by emphatic questioning and emotionality. Hence, despite having arrived at clarity and position vis-à-vis occupational identity, the question of "who am I?', self-worth, integrity seems still very much alive and burning.

> I used to ask my mother . . . do you love me because I am your daughter or because I am SH . . . I do the same with my husband . . . (I know) she used to love me for I was her daughter . . . for my husband (I am) a wife.

SH seems to keep returning to the basic existential questions around parts of her self which is reflective of a void that she experiences. In her questioning of her roles as a wife and a daughter-in-law, she meets the disappointment of her wish to be free of the captivity of bio-social, bio-psychological symbols of society so as to be able to touch her existential qualities and Being.

Marriage for SH seems to have been a conscious decision, even though at that point in her life partly seeming like foreclosure in favour of submission to the social through interpersonal obligations, *I wanted to continue with my dance performances and was not really interested in marriage . . . (when) my parents were keen on having me get married.*

SH's decision to marry seems like a "deliberate foreclosure", yet a use of status categories seems reductionist as her decision reflects a negotiation between assertion and submission; self-interest and others' interest. Although she had *never been (romantically) involved with anyone (before marriage)*, once having decided to get married, she made sure that she "had a say" in who she would marry.

More noticeable, SH's narrative gives a glimpse into the socio-cultural dynamics that dictate the interpersonal relationships across gender and development of intimate behaviour. What is considered as the acceptable aspects of male-female relationships in a given social-historical period lays the foundations for the explorations and provide a platform for a moratorium in this domain.

> I never got into any relationships . . . (as in) affairs, I did have a lot of male friends but never went around with any body. Some (men) proposed but I was not interested . . . had seen the stormy interactions between my mother and sister on such issues, moreover, my sister went through a lot because of one relationship that she had . . . (T)he boy . . . did not have enough courage to face his parent's resistance for my sister and ditched her . . . (she) went through a lot and I thought its not worth it . . . marriage (is okay) but no affairs. In our society men are not courageous enough . . . its the girl who suffers in the end . . .

Unlike dimensions where explorations and commitment enable one to arrive at a sense of personal identity, we find that like many others in similar socio-historical context, for SH, there has been little encouragement or facilitation for exploration in interpersonal relationships. Although there does not appear a desperate foreclosure into marriage, there seems to be a kind of resignation in the discourse, which persuades her into marriage.

> My mother would say that she did not want any tension in my coming late from (dance) practice . . . she'd tell me to do whatever I wanted to once I got married . . . moreover I had started to feel the financial pressures . . . it takes quite a bit to organize stage performances . . . ironically just when my marriage got finalized, I got this job.

In SH's narrative, issues of peace-justice-equality take precedence, reflecting a negotiation of ideological preferences and putting her at crossroads with the demands of society and permissibility. At the base of the crisis is the conflict representing on one hand, a willingness to defy the constraints and categorizations imposed by the social and family structures, and on the other hand, a reluctance in expressing or committing to explorations underlined by a fear of rejection.

Such dilemmas are evident in the narrative with high stakes of losing herself on one hand and on the other, losing the world as she knows it. In SH's attempts "to understand" and empathize with her mother-in-law, she consciously endeavours to challenge the stereotype of a contemptuous daughter-in-law, although such efforts seem to be leading to exhaustion and lassitude in her which may make her vulnerable.

Although she seems to have successfully resolved elements of a stable identity, yet there is (re)emergence of crisis with a struggle around the questions of being separate from others yet enjoined with them. The domain of connectivity seems to pose for her a threat of being (di)fused with dyadic bonds and relationships instead of arriving at a sense of mutuality be it with her mother, husband, or mother-in-law; more than once during the interviews, she shared concerns about her *voice (being) nullified in their presence.*

Her disagreements with her mother-in-law and differences with the school administration seem to be sides of the same crisis, tied to an acute need to safeguard all that she has come to represent and represented by. In that, her tumultuous relationship with her mother-in-law provides expression to her fear of losing her self in the dominating presence of the latter, . . . *(A)s if I don't have any presence or existence* . . . , and reflects her anxieties of threat to all her sense of continuity and integrity that she has come to gather.

Another overriding theme in SH's narrative concerns particular experiential chasms reported by her, throughout the interviews. These interruptions seem accompanied by conflicting restlessness around categories of right-wrong, good-bad which seems to result in guilt and anxiety for her which reflect the moral proclivities on one hand and her own ego strength on the other. However, simultaneously along with these conflicts, there seems to be emergence of something describable as an ethical sense reflected in "moral restrain and ideal vision while insisting on concrete commitment to those intimate relationships and work associations by which one may hope to share a life time of productivity and competence" (Erikson, 1968: 413–28). During the interviews and discussions with SH, what comes across clearly as interplay of flexibility (in her attempts at groping with an understanding of the dynamics and pressures operating on her) and rigidity (in her categorizations of good-bad, just-unjust) makes for the finer shades of human experience.

In one way, SH seems to be caught in the battles of everyday living; whereas she seems clear in her intentions and direction of her choices, achievements, and ambition in her profession; there seems to be simultaneous reluctance, doubts and confusions stemming from the internalized conflicting social expectations on the basis of roles and gender.

SH shows a resistance to let her gender or the structural aspects of relationship act as demarcating criteria for distribution of power and privileges. In this regard, we find SH indicating her inability to . . . *understand in what way I am any less than any other person in the family, be it my husband, father in law or my son*; she refuses to be defined only on the basis of her role and hierarchical position in the family, questioning the "meaningless hierarchies" in the social/familial structure. Unlike women who foreclose on such structures, thereby accepting and taking on the implications of their position in the family hierarchy, SH seems to challenge them which perhaps also signals an associated turmoil,

> (T)here is this feeling more than once . . . that the school (administration is) not giving me (enough) space (and opportunity) . . . I get so angry, on the other hand (then) I cannot justify my salary. . . Even (at home) it's the same (struggle) . . . I had to go to watch a (dance)recording at my sister's place (and)my husband pulled a face . . . He does not understand (that) my field is different (from his) . . .

> he wants (and appreciates) these differences but also wants me to be a usual daughter-in-law (to his parents).

Such turmoil seems to unfold a normative crisis which could bring with it certain degree of role confusion wherein the individual may find it difficult to deal with a self-arrived self-definition, further resulting in counter-pointing rather than synthesizing the available options.

Having difficulty in coping with contradictory, women like SH seem to find it difficult to divide the public and private "I", thereby finding the "contradictory moral imperatives much more personally troubling as they try to integrate the un-integrable . . . struggling at the same time with the overriding imperative that links being a woman with being (G)ood", (Davies 1992: 56).

> (P)erhaps I should be a better mother, wife, daughter-in-law . . . they all make a face when I say anything (about) dance or give time (to rehearsals at home). I (don't understand that when I) have given 20 years to this field (and) am earning from it . . . why should I not give time to it? . . . (my husband) practices at home to be able to teach math to his students . . . he tells me I should give more time to (our) son but (I don't understand) . . . if I were working full time (instead of being a teacher) I would stay out (of home) for much (longer) time . . . (he fails to understand that) I need sometime for myself also.

SH seems conscious of being labelled as a deviant (female) by the "norm", *(M)y husband said to me "you are not a female . . . (you) don't even know (that) you're supposed to get water while laying the table"*. SH's dilemmas around her role and selfhood point towards the double edged sword faced by many a professional, urban women in India; they are expected to have a sense of vocational identity within the confines of familial roles, anything short or more from these parameters may be seen as aberrant. On similar lines, SH is prone to be labelled as a stubborn "*(daughter-in-law who is) eager to separate the son from his parents*"; another stereotype she sees being subjected to is of a "(head strong) working woman". Her discomfort and struggles against such stereotypes are evident in her *chatpatahat (uneasy desperation)* sometimes turning into an acute reaction, *I just want to give it all up* and at times bordering on resignation, *(I)t has tired me enough . . . (and) does not bother me any more . . . (I) guess it's a part of life . . . .*

Such restrictive explorations are likely to make the nuances of development all the more intricate and ambiguous. The extent of strain on SH is visible in the symptomatic evasiveness and avoidance both, at home and school, . . . *(I) don't feel like going home or (coming to) school . . . at times feel unwanted even at my mother's.* In absence of a platform for adequate self-expression and opportunities for integration of her experiences, SH seems to be left with little motivation to reach out to either; her energies appear to oscillate between compromise and enterprise; compliance and break-through; conforming and reforming.

However, it may be presumptuous to see these patterns as completely maladaptive, and as for many contemporary middle-class working women, it is important to look into the underlying mechanisms of such symptoms. In fact, the distressing disillusionment that is evident in SH's narrative makes the effects of foreclosure seem less unbearable than arriving at a sense of identity which entails having to undergo an unsettling phase of moratorium and unrest in a context where the social structures constrict spaces for sufficient exploration and distinctive expression of personal identity.

Despite the exhaustion and confusion in SH's narrative, something distinctive seems to be emerging along the trajectory; amidst all the instability and chaos, she seems to gather strength and satisfaction from the stability provided by time and space with her students, *(students) . . . are the best thing in my life . . . .* SH seems to be drawing an essence of herself from her work; she seems to be connected to her profession not through the givens and bounding of any roles, but by what she has managed to make of herself through her work and which is how she wishes to be defined . . . *I am not going to be respected or appreciated . . . by (students) if I were not good at my work, if I had nothing to give them.*

It is interesting that throughout the narrative, SH's self-expectations and those by others seem overwhelming but do not paralyse her, which seems owing to her conscious willingness to challenge the dominant discourses. A noticeable aspect of SH's narrative is the fact that in case of conflict situations at home and work she seems to "*make sense*" of her interface with the world, furthermore, such attempts appear very live and seem consciously taken up by her. A major aspect in her negotiations is her realization, motivation to recognize and speak about "her (collective) subjective condition and . . . (search for) the ways in which the patterns that hold the subjection in place can be subverted and turned to other ends" (Davies, 1992: 59), and in this, her conscious exploration and insight seem empowering.

SH's narrative seems to reiterate themes relevant in the lives of majority of urban, educated women; further, it echoes the assertion that one "can not separate . . . identity crisis in individual life and contemporary crisis in historical development because the two help to define each other . . . in fact the whole interplay between the psychological and the social, the developmental and historical . . . would be conceptualized only as a psycho-social reality" (Erikson, 1968: 23).

Narrative 3, MK

MK is 23 years old and is a "student of psychology", pursuing her doctorate in the subject. She has been married for the last two years. MK's husband is a researcher in economics; she is 10 years younger than him and knew him for "quite a few years" before their marriage.

MK comes across as a "serious" person with a "no nonsense attitude". In fact, for her age she comes across as much older not only in her demeanour and interaction, but even in her appearance. She is the eldest among three siblings and quite a contrast to her "bubbly and energetic" sister; her brother is the youngest of the three. Maturity and astuteness came to mind during initial contact with MK, gradually followed by recognition of much that is traded off in the process. There seemed a considerable degree of placidness in her with conspicuous absence of buoyancy.

MK is well informed about the terminologies and nuances in the research process and in acknowledgment of the nature and process of interviews with her, this narrative fits more within the collaborative research framework.

At the outset, MK expressed her "uneasiness" around the very notion of identity; during the first interview meeting with her, that began with the sharing of research theme, she expressed her dilemma (*with the construct*) *identity*, in terms of a difficulty in binding the themes of her life together and an inability to draw out any consistent theme.

One of the most conspicuous aspect of conversations with MK was a constant negotiation between the abstract (self) and the concrete (identity).

> I feel . . . (identity) is (a) very vexed issue for me, even theoretically . . . (it) is a discourse of selfhood, though just more concrete and it's this concreteness of "identity" as a term that i am opposed to . . . (I)dentity concerns where self eludes us and falls behind the "ego" to come forward to take charge . . . (it) adapts to the givens and mores . . . As a patient, I would imagine myself to have self-distortions and not identity distortions. I feel I do have a clear conception of how am developing as a person. I would tend to believe that my identity is not only my "psychic-socialization" but also emanates from my intrapsychic culture . . . then it is the suspension of ambiguity between healthiness and unhealthiness which makes life tolerable. If one process unbinds it also partially binds, like sexuality unbinds as well as binds . . . trauma binds as well as unbinds . . . drives bind as well as unbind . . . memories bind as well as unbind . . . actually there's no real polarities . . . identity is also a social construction and that . . . (one may be able to) deconstruct (in terms of) all of that which is built up through the socio-political.

MK pointed out her dilemma with questions regarding the operational relevance of the notions of identity while at the same time seemingly perplexed with the complexity that her life offers. It provides for a clarity on role of psycho-social identity as a tangible aspect of self; one that is helpful in bringing one's self to a more concrete level, through which one may be better able to derive the essence of self just as an index of contents does for a book.

Another noticeable aspect of MK's narrative is that in relation to other two narratives, where the task has been to draw out complex themes from the seemingly mundane life experiences, here it is a reversal, in terms of delineating unadorned themes from the complexity and apparent chaos. Hence, whereas at one level, identity is "continuity" which represents itself through simple themes in one's life; at another, it is "change" that is represented through transformations and pandemonium. To tap on the processes of identity, perhaps it is most convenient to trace the periods of crisis which witness both trends.

While on the one hand, MK's analysis and deconstruction of (the notions of) personal identity gives insight into her self, yet, at the same time it brings contextual gaps in current themes in her life. Such ambiguities notwithstanding, there have been glimpses throughout the narrative, of the ordinary amidst the extraordinary and vice versa.

> Parts of my life are coming, in some brief flashes . . . (I am aware of) the complexity that I might be almost offering . . . (am) just beginning with my own life as such . . . don't think (would be able to say) anything about identity as a process. (I) might (only) offer you a bundle of chaotic things . . . many things . . . and themes have been drastically changing.

Emerging Themes

In MK's narrative it is difficult to overlook the simultaneous emergence of two varied, yet interconnected themes. While at one level, the narrative brings to fore critical elements of MK's identity, at another level, issues pertaining to the validity of identity as a construct seem to be emerging with MK questioning its relevance (as a means) to capture and understand the richness of human self that is, *much more primal and primary a concern.*

Throughout the narrative, there seems to be a paradoxical avoidance of any active enunciation and expression, for MK seems unwilling to look into "how" and "what" self undergoes at various internal and external interfaces; *When I look at identity, (others' and my own) struggle becomes apparent . . . perhaps this is what I want to avoid.* It seems that in questioning the validity of the construct, MK chooses to convey not only her disdain of the notion of identity, but in fact, her theoretical stance on identity (as a construct) seems as derisive as her personal discomforts in sharing the tangible themes of her life.

Despite her acknowledgement of her discomfort with the thematic difficulties, articulation of variety of themes including her confusions seems to be running through the narrative as a meta-theme, bringing in a consistency and continuity despite the indistinctness and self-proclaimed ambiguity. Despite her assertion of incoherence and inconsistency in experiences, there seems to be a sense of larger, wider theme guiding her life and perhaps this is what accounts for a comfortable coexistence of interludes amidst continuity. Her greatest strength seems to be her ability to make meaning, and articulate the same. She seems to be able to draw out relationship between actions, thoughts and feelings and gather direction from their synthesis.

Another aspect of MK's uneasiness involves the tentativeness which surrounds her narrative. Such discomfort seems to accompany experience of not fitting in with the dominant discourses, *I'm sure you'd (at the end) see (me) as having little experience and exposure to world views.* Yet, there seem to be glimpses of the extraordinary amidst ordinariness; although at surface MK seems to be in a transitional phase and *still further looking for meaningful options,* there seems to be more beneath the layers and her narrative needs to be unveiled from an aspect of communication which at times might turn out to be as much a hindrance to an authentic dialogue and sharing as mask of a given role can be. It is significant that though, for her the issue of personal identity is "not important", and is a part of the mundane, *identity formation has been clear if not smooth or painless, but (more than that, there is a) desire . . . to engage with (my) self.*

In some important ways, the narrative accounts for a sense of well-being that is necessary for survival and eventually accounts for an integration of self and society; of consolidations of the outer and inner, of the kind that make for the difference between life histories and case studies. It highlights the distinction that lies in how one is able to negotiate the exceptional in the ordinary lives; the intensities of experiences in such negotiations could have the potential of either leading one to the steps of disorganization or to take one to the heights of fulfilment. It is not to undermine the complexity and sensitivity of such processes, but how one plays with (or is played by) the complexity would be critical. In fact, to say that the path (of arriving at a well integrated identity) would be an easy one, would be to undermine and reduce the process and essence of issues surrounding it. Moreover, it seems like the focus and clarity makes the struggles even more live at the affective level, adding to the intensity in finding one Self sans the external points of reference.

Further, on similar lines, the narrative highlights the role of unordinary circumstances in ordinary lives for it reinforces that it is only within the wider and immediate context that the course of individual development is chartered and that possible options are either created or deferred. The existing social-cultural milieu along with the macro and micro historical influences may provide space to particular themes and characteristics in ordinary lives to create potential of driving the person to the extent of looking for ways of effecting his/her yearnings. In this, it is significant that MK acknowledges the role of her family and parents as *(partly) their . . . extraordinariness* has helped her arrive at various positions vis-à-vis different issues in her life. However, in contexts where the given social-cultural-historical contexts impede such space, the typical individual trajectories may get pushed into the realms of despair.

Another appealing aspect of MK's narrative is the concurrence of intellectual processes within the emotional space. She associates meaning and attentions with utterances, taking very clear either/or positions. However, her clarity does not come across as "totalitarian" (Erikson, 1968), on the other hand, there seems to be certain amount of versatility visible throughout the narrative in the way she is able to negotiate various roles and circumstances to her benefit without getting stuck in the minutiae. She is able to draw on the various roles to her advantage by grasping opportunities through them. Her play with themes of trauma, death, life, past, future is noticeable, highlighting the elements of identity as meta-processes. There are, however, more specific themes that cannot be overlooked or else we may run into the folly of underestimating the role of the mundane.

From a developmental perspective, the narrative echoes well with characteristics of psycho-social development (Erikson, 1960; 1968). It provides for a comprehension of emergence of agency and resolution of prior developmental stages in order to face the crisis of young adulthood. However, there are some noticeable digressions from the same, in terms of issues of intimacy being addressed prior to taking up the identity ones rather than manifestation of either/or. In this, the narrative, to some extent, also challenges the dominant notions about identity which emphasize on the seemingly polar elements that are said to constitute a psycho-social identity. Further, none of the usual categories help in adequately understanding what constitutes her identity, in fact the term, as used in the mainstream discourse seems reductionist in scope to define her being.

However, a deeper analysis of the narrative seems to indicate integration beyond that of psycho-social elements. For one, MK does not seem to fit the "norm" within the dominant discourse that identifies and accepts (a well formed) identity only as per specified parameters of vocation and/or ideology and provides little scope for capturing the (richness of) Self in any other manner. However, in the most inclusive sense, identity would capture that sense of Being referred to as self and reflect its idiosyncratic articulations by individuals.

One of the most noticeable aspect of this narrative is that it creates, even if only to some extent, a possibility of insinuating an association between identity and intimacy; it provides a glimpse into the dialogical relation between the issues of intimacy and the crises of identity that have generally received little attention in the mainstream literature on development.

> I certainly have identity issues as a married person now . . . (I) am actively thinking as to where I fit in . . . also because I am not earning. I think financial independence is very very important although it doesn't get you much other than that, there has to be certain freedom one has to have in the way one thinks . . . (with time) . . . my marriage is one issue I would need to carefully work on . . . I don't think up till now I had a very stable identity of my own which is going to be an issue . . . I would have to actually carefully look at these issues as to where I stand as an adult.

The narrative lends support to the possibility of one's psycho-social identity not culminating into, but rather merging with interpersonal and intimacy issues. And with this, there seems to be an interesting foray into the oft overlooked prospect of including alternative trajectories in the discourse on identity. In this, the narrative challenges the mainstream literature on psycho-social development that has somehow implied identity and intimacy as sequential with the former portrayed as more fundamental and essential in the course of "normal" development for a healthy resolution of young adulthood crises.

Further, one may move closer to the task of arriving at a personal sense of identity if s/he is able to negotiate the gender boundaries and such "givens", without getting trapped within these. Unlike women, who in pursuit of finding their (real) self, move further away from it as the themes that they draw from and work upon are based on masculine norms, (be it regarding a successful professional or a rational being or the likes), MK chooses to reassess the themes before considering them. As discussed in case of other two narratives, women find themselves torn between what they think they are and what they think they rather not be, which in itself is ambiguous.

MK sees herself as having *not very many* "equal" *dealings* and being quite at ease with such unevenness in relationships. She lets herself be in "*funny power dynamics*" with respect to her relationships, yet seems to be able to maintain some level of healthy differentiation even in intimate relationships. In a subtle manner, MK challenges the "self-made" image offered to educated, urban women as a model, but one which results in much of the freedom gained by them being spent in competing with and coming up to the standards of success set within the norms of masculinity. Thus, MK seems to face up to the typologies that more often restrict, rather than enable any real advancement in (life of) women.

> . . . (I) haven't been able to get a job . . . never really think in terms of working . . . but I don't have many anxieties related to my professional future . . . there have been no categories that I've dreamt about, that I would want to be . . . there is an ease which comes along . . . financial independence is very important (but) it doesn't get you much other than that, there has to be certain freedom one has to have in the way one thinks

One of the other prominent themes in MK's narrative is of stillness with a degree of uncharacteristic versatility. *(s)tillness is very important (to me) . . . (I) haven't been able to get a job . . . never really think in terms of job . . . primarily there is a desire to be still . . . (mine) is a very extended studenthood in a way.* There is a visible integration of stability and change in the narrative; instead of bringing with it a risk of foreclosure, stability seems to provide her steadiness that has the potential for safeguard from disjointedness in face of ever-changing external reality.

MK seems to negotiate rather than getting overwhelmed by the anxiety and unrest arising from the pushes and pulls (from within and out). At the same time, she also seems open to exploration in face of unfamiliar situations, along with a willingness to take risks for creating choices. It is such elements that lend themselves to make in an individual what may appear as a sense of continuity amidst change and chaos by connecting various themes throughout life into a meaningful flow, *I have a lot of silences in my life . . . the articulation comes from some convictions that I have in life.*

MK's *'studenthood'* maybe seen as a space that provides her with stability as well as some movement, in the process, balancing out both. A general sense of moratorium and purposelessness that is likely to accompany such a space remains less frustrating and much short of alienating MK, as she actively negotiates inner as well as outer, potentially frustrating experiences in pursuit of meaning which seems to give her some sense of being situated.

Marriage also seems to have provided MK with a sense of stability in form of commitment. This is further reflected in her choice of partner, *(h)e (is) much more balanced than my own father or mother . . . (he is) more conventional than them. What I appreciate (about him) is that he does not carry any Utopias . . . in the averageness of life he comes across as a fine human being . . . (he)is bright in a very different sense.*

Throughout the narrative, there are glimpses of strivings that make MK's strengths more conspicuous and real. Acknowledgement of distresses within her trajectory lends itself to the authenticity of her experience and seems to account for certain amount of movement in her struggles.

> . . . (My) past conception of (my) childhood is very very traumatic . . . (I) come across as an angry person, it is quite a potent anger . . . though I have never been able to quite understand it. Part of my own tragedy in life comes from the tragedy that my parents met with . . . either they have projected on their grievances on me . . . or I have very vicariously taken over their sorrows . . . my life is . . . a good amount of bitterness and sense of trauma . . . (that comes) from their failure.
>
> A healthy part of me wants to make my life as un-tragic as possible as successful in the normal parlance . . . in fact replace 'success' with 'happiness' which my parents felt increasingly deprived of.
>
> It comes from the fact that I have been actively acknowledging their role and the kind of substance they have given me. (A) sense of completeness comes from the fact that I have had extra ordinary parents . . . that takes care of the dreadiest moments (and parts of me). They exposed (me) to issues that (I) would feel so veered with later on . . . politics is one instance where I clearly have my position now . . . activism is another instance.
>
> I am certainly more healthy (than my parents) I am not living in a world of Utopia . . . of course this is no more a time of ideology . . . when I get in touch with their patienthood . . . and only when I do so can I arrive at my own patienthood . . . (A) part of my healthiness comes from some sort of stability that I have tried to acquire in a relational mode . . . (healthiness) also comes from the fact that I think I have developed my own way of looking at . . . relationships . . . relating (with myself and others) . . . (of) living my own life. I am also in a very healthy mourning at the moment . . . don't see my self withering away, so that is where healthiness comes from.

MK's narrative suggests that what seems to abet people in their development is arrival at a balance that keeps them in touch with the mundane without losing track of the underlying depth. In this sense, MK's narrative alludes to the extraordinariness in the "ordinary" people, which entails the courage in coming to view utopias and disillusionments as only layers of the spectrum that seems to lie in between the idealism of the neurotic and the disillusionment of the psychotic, without getting caught in either.

Epilogue

An analysis of the three narratives reveals that the process of arriving at a well integrated identity for these women is not by default, but a live one. It is not a passive process but one that is dialogical and that which offers and involves choices with equal chances of exhausting itself at each juncture.

It also highlights that in attempting to understand the relevance of the construct and its manifestation in lives of women, one needs to accommodate the varied experiences of those whose lives are being examined. It becomes crucial then, that any commentary on identity and development of women remains attentive to how cultural influences may produce silences, gaps, disruptions, or contradictions in their narratives. Moreover, it seems that identity is shaped to a considerable extent by the support and sanctions that the culture provides to the individual for her choices.

It is only through a consolidation of her inner self with the social-political-historical context that a woman is able to arrive coherent sense of identity or vice-versa. There seems, even if only indirectly, the social (factors) getting camouflaged in the extraordinary (life and events) and thereby becoming more conspicuous in those that seem less than ordinary. This is what brings agency and context to juxtapose.

Further, it seems that it would be naïve to bank on exclusive categories (such as identity achievement) to describe the lives of women, further, richness of these lives can be captured either in the extremities of space (life stories) or extremities of time (life histories). As the narratives highlight and elaborate, each woman's struggle is unique; while in SH, it brings to fore, issues around self-assertion, in MK it is of loosing herself.

Tracing the research rationale, a detailed analysis of the narratives has revealed that the developmental crises are lived out differently based on the typical socio-cultural-psychological resources. For SB the struggle is lived out in issues around isolation emanating from infantile doubts and fears, for SH, the upsurge is with her struggles to be "seen" as an individual, whereas in MK, it seems to be pertaining to an integration of the inner and outer, of identity as identifications of the self with certain aspects of the other.

The narratives are indicative that for women, the effects of cultural definition are profound and complex; the expectation of society at large and the definition for what they "ought to be", seem to be changing for urban Indian women. There is evidence that in most developing societies, the traditional feminine roles are in a state of transition (Kumar, 1986). As a result, women are faced with two strong and conflicting role models: traditional feminine model and a modern, masculinized model. Contemporary urban young women receive double messages about the norms for their development which leads to a lack of clarity and sometimes even comes across as symptoms of acute distress. Hence, in contrast to the mainstream developmental theories, for women the developmental tasks often seem to be fused. In particular, MK's narrative for instance, seems to suggest that at least for some women the task of defining a personal sense of identity may wait for an appropriate time in order to be able to identify and pursue dimensions of their own choice (Constantinople, 1969).

In construing the various layers of the narratives, it can be appreciated that identity seems closer to a cumulative concept, a process not restricted to a particular stage but spreading beyond particular phase/stage particularly in lives of the contemporary educated urban Indian women.

■ Note

1 The term 'ideology' has been used in an inclusive sense as a system of beliefs, values and goals and a perspective/view on life. For more on ideology refer Paranjpe (1998: 245–46).

■ References

Adams, Gerald, T.P. Gullota and R. Montemayor (eds.), *Adolescent Identity Formation, Advances in Adolescent Development: Annual Book Series*, Newbury Park, CA: Sage, 1992.

Allan, George. "Tradition and Transition", *Psychoanalytic Review*, 81(1), 1994, 79–100.

Allen, Vernon L. and Karl E. Scheibe (eds.), *The Social Context of Conduct: Psychological Writings of Theodore Sarbin*, New York: Praeger, 1982.

Archer, S.L. "A Feminist's Approach to Identity Research", in G.R. Adams, T.P. Gullotta and R. Montemayor (eds.), *Adolescent Identity Formation*, California: Sage Publications, 1992.

Arendt, Hannah. *The Origins of Totalitarianism*, New York: Harcourt Brace Jovanovich, 1958.

Arnett, Jeffrey. "Adolescent Storm and Stress Reconsidered", *American Psychologist*, 54(5), 1999, 317–26.

Ashmore, Richard D. and Lee Jussim (eds.), *Self and Identity: Fundamental Issues*, New York: Oxford University Press, 1997.

Baldwin, M.W. and J.G. Holmes. "Salient Private Audiences and Awareness of the Self", *Journal of Personality and Social Psychology*, 52, 1987, 1087–98.

Balistreri, Elizabeth, Nancy A. Busch-Rossnagel and Kurt F. Geisinger. "Development and Preliminary Validation of Ego Identity Process Questionnaire", *Journal of Adolescence*, 18(2), 1995, 179–92.

Baltes, Paul (ed.), *Life Span Development and Behavior*, Vol. 1, New York: Academic Press, 1978.

Baumeister, R.F. *Identity: Cultural Change and the Struggle for Self*, New York: Oxford University Press, 1986.

Berzonsky, M.D. "A Constructivist View of Identity Development: People as Post-Positivist Self-Theorists", in J. Kroger (ed.), *Discussion on Ego Identity*, Hillsdale, NJ: Lawrence Erlbaum Associates, 1993.

Berzonsky, M.D. and Greg J. Neimeyer. "Ego Identity Status and Identity Processing Orientation: The Moderating Role of Commitment", *Journal of Research in Personality*, 28(4), 1994, 425–35.

Bilsker, D., D. Schiedel and J. Marcia. "Sex Differences in Identity Status", *Sex Roles*, 18(3–4), 1988.

Blassi, A. and K. Glodis. "The Development of Identity: A Critical Analysis from the Perspective of the Self as Subject", *Developmental Review*, 15(4), 1995, 404–33.

Blos, P. "The Second Individuation Process of Adolescence", *The Psychoanalytic Study of the Child*, 22, 1967, 162–86.

Blustein, David. "'Who Am I?': The Question of Self and Identity in Career Development", in M.L. Savickas and R.W. Lent (eds.), *Convergence in Career Development Theories: Implications for Science and Practice*, Palo Alto, California: CPP Books, 1994.

Bregman, George and Melanic Kellen. "Adolescents and Young Adults Reasoning about Career and Role of Parental Influence", *Journal of Research on Adolescence*, 9(3), 1999.

Brooks, A.K. and K.A. Edwards. Narratives of Women's Sexual Identity Development: A Collaborative Inquiry with Implications for Rewriting Transformative

Learning Theory. 38th Annual Adult Education Research Conference Proceedings, Stillwater: Oklahoma State University, 1997, 37–42.

Carson, David, A. Chowdhury, C. Perry and C. Pati. "Family, Characteristics and Competence in India: Investigation in Southern Orissa", *Journal of Youth and Adolescence*, 28(2), 1999.

Chodorow, N.J. *The Reproduction of Mothering*, Berkeley: University of California Press, 1978.

Constantinople, A. "An Eriksonian Measure of Personality Development in College Students", *Developmental Psychology*, 1, 1969, 357–72.

Cote, James and Charles Levine. "Relationship between Ego Identity Status and Erikson's Notions of Institutionalized Moratoria, Value Orientation Stage and Ego Domination", *Journal of Youth and Adolescence*, 17(1), 1988, 81–99.

Cote, James E. and Charles Levine. "A Formulation of Erikson's Theory of Ego Identity Formation", *Developmental Review*, 7(4), 1987, 273–325.

Cote, James E. "Identity Crisis Modality: A Technique for Assessing the Structure of Identity Crisis", *Journal of Adolescence*, 9(4), 1986, 321–35.

Davies, B. "Women's Subjectivity and Feminist Stories", in M. Flaherty and C. Ellis (eds.), *Investigating Subjectivity: Research on Lived Experience*, Newbury Park, CA: Sage, 1992.

Davies, B. and R. Harre. "Positioning: The Discursive Production of Selves", *Journal for the Theory of Social Behavior*, 20(1), 1990, 43–63.

DeCharms, R. *Personal Causation: The Internal Affective Determinants of Behavior*, New York: Academic Press, 1968.

Deckard, Barbara. *The Women's Movement: Political, Socioeconomic and Psychological Issues*, California: Harper Rowlett Publisher, 1979.

Douvan, E.M. and J. Adelson. *The Adolescent Experience*, New York: Wiley, 1966.

Duval, Shelley and Robert A. Wicklund. *A Theory of Objective Self Awareness*, New York: Academic Press, 1972.

Elliott, Anthony (ed.), *Freud 2000*, Cambridge: Polity Press, 1998.

Elliott, Anthony. *Subject to Ourselves: Social Theory, Psychoanalysis and Postmodernity*, Cambridge: Polity Press, 1996.

Ellis, Carolyn and Michael Flaherty (eds.), *Investigating Subjectivity: Research on Lived Experiences*, Newbury Park, CA: Sage, 1992.

Epstein, S. "The Self Concept Revisited or a Theory of a Theory", *American Psychologist*, 28, 1973, 405–16.

Erez, M. and P. Christopher Earley. *Culture, Self-identity and Work*, New York: Oxford University Press, 1993.

Erikson, E.H. "The Problem of Ego Identity", *Journal of American Psychoanalytic Association*, 4, 1956, 56–121.

——. "The Problem of Ego Identity", in M.R. Stein, A.J. Vidich and D.M. White (eds.), *Identity and Anxiety*, New York: Free Press, 1960.

Erikson, E.H. in White (ed.) 'Study of lives', 1963.
——. *Identity, Youth and Crisis*, New York: Norton, 1968.
——. *Dimensions of a New Identity: The 1973 Jefferson Lectures in the Humanities*, New Delhi: Light and Life Publishers, 1975.
Flax, Jane. "Multiples: On the Contemporary Politics of Subjectivity", *Human Studies*, 16, 1993, 33–49.
Flick, Uwe (ed.), *The Psychology of the Social*, Cambridge: Cambridge University Press, 1998.
Foucault, M. "'Body/Power' and 'Truth and Power'", in C. Gordon (ed.), *Michel Foucault: Power/Knowledge*, UK: Harvester, 1980.
Franz, Carol E. "A Quantitative Case Study of Longitudinal Charges in Identity, Intimacy and Generativity", *Journal of Personality*, 63(1), 1995, 27–46.
Freeman, M. *Rewriting the Self: History, Memory, Narrative*, New York: Routledge, 1993.
Fromm, E. *To Have or to Be?* New York: Harper and Row, 1976.
Gergen, K.J. "Social Psychology as History", *Journal of Personality and Social Psychology*, 26(2), 1973, 309–20.
——. "The Social Constructionist Movement in Modern Psychology", *American Psychologist*, 40(3), 1985, 266–75.
Gergen, K.J. and M.M. Gergen. "Narrative and the Self as Relationship", in L. Berkowitz (ed.), *Advances in Experimental Social Psychology*, New York: Academic Press, 1988, 17–56.
Gergen, Shotter and Gergen. "The Saturated Self: Texts of Identity", in Ruthellen Josselson, *Narrative Study of Lives*, Newbury Park, CA: Sage, 1995.
Gilligan, Carol. *In a Different Voice: Psychological Theory and Women's Development*, Cambridge: Harvard University Press, 1982.
Giorgi, A. *Psychology as a Human Science*, New York: Harper and Row, 1970.
Griffiths, Morwenna. *Feminism and the Self: The Web of Identity*, London and New York: Routledge, 1995.
Grimshaw, J. "Autonomy and Identity in Feminist Thinking", in M. Griffiths and M. Whitford (eds.), *Feminist Perspectives in Philosophy*, Bloomington: Indiana University Press, 1988.
Grotevant, Harold. "Assessment of Identity Development: Current Issues and Future Direction", *Journal of Adolescent Research*, 1(2), 1986, 175–81.
——. "The Integrative Nature of Identity: Bringing the Soloist to Sing in the Choir", in J. Kroger (ed.), *Discussions in Ego Identity*, Hillsdale, NJ: Erlbaum, 1993.
Gullahorn, J. *Psychology and Women: In Transitions*, Washington, DC: V.H. Winston & Sons, 1979.
Harding, S. *The Science Question in Feminism*, Ithaca, NY: Cornell University Press, 1986.
Harre, R. "The Self as a Theoretical Concept", in M. Krausz (ed.), *Relativism:*

Interpretation and Confrontation, Notre Dame: University of Notre Dame Press, 1989, 389–411.

——. *Personal Being: A Theory for Individual Psychology*, Cambridge, MA: Harvard University Press, 1984.

——. "Social Sources of Mental Content and Order", in J. Margolis, P.T. Manicas, R. Harré and P.F. Secord (eds.), *Psychology: Designing the Discipline*, Malden, MA: Blackwell, 1986, 91–127.

Harwood, I.H. "The Evolution of The Self: An Integration of Winnicott's and Kohut's Concepts", in T. Honess and K. Yardley (eds.), *Self and Identity: Psychosocial Perspectives*, New York: John Wiley & Sons, 1987.

Hollinger, Robert. *Postmodernism and the Social Sciences: A Thematic Approach*, Thousand Oaks: Sage Publications, 1994.

Hopkins, L.B. "Inner Space and Outer Space Identity in Contemporary Females", *Psychiatry*, 43(1), 1980.

——. "Assessment of Identity Status in College Women using Outer Space and Inner Space Interviews", *Sex Roles*, 8, 1982, 557–66.

Josselson, R.L., E. Greenberger and D. McConochie. "Phenomenological Aspects of Psychosocial Maturity in Adolescence", *Journal of Youth and Adolescence*, 6, 1977, 145–67.

Josselson, Ruthellen. *Finding Herself: Pathways to Identity Development in Women*, San Francisco: Jossey-Bass Ltd., 1988.

——. *Narrative Study of Lives*, Vols. 1–3, Newbury Park, CA: Sage, 1995.

Kakar, Sudhir. *Culture and Psyche*, Delhi: Oxford University Press, 1997.

Kegan, Robert. *The Evolving Self: Problems and Process in Human Development*, Cambridge, MA: Harvard University Press, 1980.

Keller, E.F. *Reflections on Gender and Science*, New Haven: Yale University Press, 1985.

Kellner, D. "Popular Culture and the Construction of Postmodern Identity", in S. Lash and J. Friedman (eds.), *Modernity and Identity*, Cambridge, MA: Basil Blackwell, 1992.

Kohut, Heinz. *The Analysis of the Self*, New York: International Universities Press, 1971.

Krishnan, P. Ananth. "Youth and Identity Crisis", *Journal of the Indian Academy of Applied Psychology*, 12(1), 1985–86, 28–32.

Kroger, J. "Separation-individuation and Ego Identity Status in New Zealand University Students", *Journal of Youth and Adolescence*, 14, 1985, 133–47.

——. "Identity and Context: How Identity Statuses Choose this Match", in R. Josselson (ed.), *Narrative Study of Lives*, Vol. 1, Newbury Park, CA: Sage, 1993.

——. *Identity Development: Adolescence through Adulthood*, New Delhi: Sage Publications, 2000.

Kumar, Usha. "Indian Women and Work: A Paradigm for Research", *Psychological Studies*, 31(2), 1986, 147–60.

——. "Indian Women's Quest for Identity", *International Journal of Group Tensions*, 1(4), 1979, 149–68.

Kvale, Steiner (ed.), *Psychology and Postmodernism*, London: Sage Publications, 1994.

Lacan, J. "The Mirror Stage as Formative of the Function of the I as Revealed in Psychoanalytic Experience", in *Écrits: A Selection*, trans. A. Sheridan, New York: Norton, 1949, 1–7.

Lee, Benjamin and Katheleen Smith (eds.), *Psychosocial Theories of Self*, New York: Plenum Press, 1982.

Lerman, H. "From Freud to Feminist Personality Theory: Getting Here from There", *Psychology of Women Quarterly*, 10(1–19), 1986.

Levin, Jerome D. *Treatment of Alcoholism and Other Addictions: A Self-Psychology Approach*, Northvale, NJ: J. Aronson, 1987.

Lykes, M.B. "Gender and Individuals vs. Collectivist Bases for Notions about the Self", *Journal of Personality*, 53, 1985, 356–83.

Marcia, J.E. "Development and Validation of Ego Identity Status", *Journal of Personality and Social Psychology*, 3, 1966, 551–58.

——. "Six Years After: A Follow up Study", *Journal of Youth and Adolescence*, 5, 1976, 145–59.

——. "Identity in Adolescence", in J. Adelson (ed.), *Handbook of Adolescent Psychology*, Toronto: John Wiley & Sons, 1980.

Marsella, A.J., G.A. De Vos and F.L.K. Hsu. *Culture and Self: Asian and Western Perspectives*, New York: Tavistock Publications, 1985.

Miller, J.B. *Toward a New Psychology of Women*, 2nd ed., Boston: Beacon Press, 1976.

Miller, D.R. "The Study of Social Relationships: Situation, Identity and Social Interaction", in S. Koch (ed.), *Psychology: A Study of Science*, 5, New York: McGraw Hill, 1963.

Mizuno, Shujiro. "Psychosocial Development and Moral Development: An Explanatory Comparison of Adolescence in Japan and America using Measures of Psychosocial Development", *Psychological Reports*, 84(1), 1999, 51–62.

Moshman, David. "Identity as a Theory of Oneself", *The Genetic Epistemologist: The Journal of the Jean Piaget Society*, 26(3), 1998.

Murray, H.A. et al. *Explorations in Personality*, New York: Oxford University Press, 1938.

Neisser, U. "Five Kinds of Self-Knowldege", *Philosophical Psychology*, 1, 1988, 35–59.

Nikolas, Rose. *Inventing Our Selves: Psychology, Power and Personhood*, Cambridge: Cambridge University Press, 1992.

Okun, Barbara F. *Working with Adults: Individual, Family and Career Development*, California: Brooks/Cole Pub. Co., 1984.

Orlofsky, J.L., J.E. Marcis and I.M. Lesser. "Ego Identity Status and the Intimacy v/s Isolation Crisis of Young Adulthood", *Journal of Personality and Social Psychology*, 27, 1973, 211–19.

Oyserman, Daphna. "The Sense of Personhood: Viewing the Self and Others in a Multicultural Society", *Journal of Personality and Social Psychology*, 65(5), 1993.

Oyserman, Daphna and R.H. Markus. "Self as Social Representation", in Flick Uwe (ed.), *The Psychology of the Social*, Cambridge: Cambridge University Press, 1998, 107–26.

Pals, Jennifer. "Identity Consolidation in Early Adulthood: Relations with Ego Resiliency: The Context of Marriage and Personality Changes", *Journal of Personality*, 67(2), 1999, 295–329.

Paranjpe, Anand. *Self and Identity in Modern Psychology and Indian Thought*, New York: Plenum Press, 1998.

——. *In Search of Identity*, Madras: Macmillan, 1975.

——. *Theoretical Psychology: The Meeting of East and West*, New York: Plenum Press, 1984.

Parikh, Indira J. and Pulin K. Garg. *Indian Women: An Inner Dialogue*, New Delhi: Sage Publications, 1989.

Peck, T.A. "Women's Self Definition in Adulthood: From a Different Model?", *Psychology of Women Quarterly*, 10, 1986, 274–84.

Piaget, J. *On the Development of Memory and Identity*, Barre, MA: Clark University Press & Barre Publishers, 1968.

Radden, Jennifer. *Divided Minds and Successive Selves: Ethical Issues in Disorders of Identity and Personality*, Cambridge: MIT Press, 1996.

Reinisch, June Machover, Leonard A. Rosenblum and Stephanie A. Sanders. *Masculinity/Feminity: Basic Perspectives*, London: Oxford University Press, 1987.

Riessman, C.K. *Narrative Analysis*, Qualitative Research Methods Series, No. 30, Newbury Park, CA: Sage, 1993.

Robbins, Richard H. "Identity, Culture and Behavior", in John J. Honigmann (ed.), *Handbook of Social and Cultural Anthropology*, Chicago: Rand McNally, 1973.

Rossi, A. "Aging and Parenthood in the Middle Years", in P. Baltes and O. Brim (eds.), *Life Span Development and Behavior*, Vol. 3, New York: Academic Press, 1980.

Sampson, E.E. "The Decentralization of Identity: Towards a Revised Concept of Personal and Social Order", *American Psychologist*, 40, 1985, 1203–11.

Sarbin, T.R. "The Poetics of Identity", *Theory and Psychology*, 7, 1997, 67–82.

Sikdar, A.K. "Identity Crisis of Adolescents across Cultures", *Bulletin of Educational and Psychological Research*, 5, 1974, 43–45.

Squire, Corinne. *Significant Differences*, New York: Routledge, 1995.

Strauss, A.S. "Northern Cheyenne Ethnopsychology", *Ethos*, 5(3), 1977, 326–57.

Suler, John. "In Search of the Self: Zen Buddhism and Psychoanalysis", *Psychoanalytic Review*, 82(3), 1995, 407–26.

Sullivan, H.S. *Conceptions of Modern Psychiatry*, New York: W.W. Norton and Co., 1940.

Surrey, J.L. "The 'Self-in-Relation': A Theory of Women's Development", in J.V. Jordan, A.G. Kaplan, J.B. Miller, I.P. Stiver and J.L. Surrey (eds.), *Women's Growth in Connection: Writings form the Stone Center*, New York: Guilford Press, 1991.

Unger, R. "Psychological, Feminist and Personal Epistemology: Transcending Contradiction", in M. Gergen (ed.), *Feminist Thought and the Structure of Knowledge*, New York: New York University Press, 1988, 124–41.

Von Hoof, Anne. "The Identity Status Field Re-reviewed: An Update of Unresolved and Neglected Issues with a View on Some Alternative Approaches", *Developmental Review*, 19(4), 1999, 497–556.

Walker, Moira. *Women in Therapy and Counselling: Out of the Shadows*, Philadelphia: Open University Press, 1990.

Wallace, A.F.C. and R. Fogelson. "The Identity Struggle", in I. Boszormenyi-Nagy and J. Framo (eds.), *Intensive Family Therapy*, New York: Harper and Row, 1965.

Wallerstein, Robert. "Erickson's Concept of Ego Identity Reconsidered", *Journal of the American Psychoanalytic Association*, 46(1), 1998.

Waterman, A.S. "Identity as an Aspect of Optimal Psychological Functioning", in G.R. Adams, T.P. Gullotta and R. Montemayor (eds.), *Adolescent Identity Formation*, Newbury Park, CA: Sage, 1992, 50–72.

White, Robert (ed.), *Study of Lives: Essays on Personality in Honor of Henry A. Murray*, London: Atherton Press, 1963.

Winnicott, D.W. *Psychoanalytic Explorations*, Cambridge: Harvard University Press, 1989.

Wylie, R.C. "The Present Status of Self Theory", in E.F. Borgatta and W.W. Lambert (eds.), *Handbook of Personality Theory and Research*, Chicago: Rand-McNally, 1968.

15

Gender Differentiation in Self-actualization and Personality Correlates of Professionals

Nishat Afroz and Ranjana Mittra

Psychological research in recent years has shown a major concern with the study of positive functioning of human beings in various spheres of life. The concept of positive psychological functioning examined in this paper is that of self-actualization. It is a state in which a person experiences life in a way that allows for optimal growth towards a better state of being. Self-actualization is a concept originally coined by Maslow (1954) to describe people who are intrinsically motivated, self-aware, altruistic, fully engaged in the process of living, and who actively create meaning in their lives.

The study of self has always fascinated human societies. Scholars from East and West have been engaged in unravelling the mysteries of self. All thinkers have raised similar questions (e.g., "who am I?"). However, their methods of enquiry and assumptions about human nature differ widely.

The intellectuals of West have provided us with incisive understanding of self and personality. Indian thinkers have largely emphasized the indestructible nature of self. Thus, while in the West, the self is seen as organizing principle of human existence, in the East the focus is on the imperishable nature of the being. It is often contended that these two world-views would never meet. However, at the present time, revolutionary advances in telecommunication and transportation are compelling the East and West to come closer to each other. Large-scale migration of people is making societies around the world part of a global village. With these diverse cultural influences shaping our lives, self and identity are becoming global concerns and integration of the Eastern and Western perspectives is being realized as a necessity. Studies reveal that there is some similarity between self-actualizing person of East and West. These studies suggest that a cross-cultural comparison of the views on developing human potential can provide a broader perspective (Daftuar and Sharma, 1997; Das, 1989; Coan, 1991; Chang and Page, 1991; Rangaswami, 1994; Wilson, 1988; McKenna, 2000).

Self-actualization is the prime motivation of a healthy person. It is a person's desire for self-improvement, or actual use of potentials, talents and capacities. Self-actualization need not take the form of creative and artistic endeavours or attempts. A parent, an athlete, a student and a teacher may be actualizing potential in doing well in respective pursuits. The individual must feel that they are an important and useful specimen of the nature and is made for the work they are doing. They have adequate potentials to do the job and can achieve success in that profession. Cook-Greuter (1999), Kegan (1994), and Torbert (1994) have argued that adults at higher stages of development are in a unique position to make valuable contributions to the field of education, organizational management, and social leadership because of their mature insight and intellectual flexibility. Farmer (1984) has discussed Maslow's theory of self-actualization as the foundation of humanistic education. In fact, self-actualization has provided a means by which each educator, regardless of his/her professional duties, can view the whole person.

Most of the research done in the field of personal growth and self-actualization focuses on the personality traits or demographic variables that define a person (Ford, 1991; Dahl, 1983; Ramanaiah, Heerboth, and Jinkerson, 1985; Barnes and Srinivas, 1993; Norlander, Bood and Archer, 2002). These studies have found that a variety of these types of factors influence a person's ability to self-actualize. Personal characteristics typically examined include ethnicity, age, gender, nationality, religiosity, religious group identity, socio-economic status, and general culture (Myers and Diener, 1995). Self-actualizers are described as having strong feelings of empathy and affection for all human beings and as being capable of greater love, deeper friendship, and more complete identification with others (Ryff, 1989).

Education and self-actualization are viewed as parallel processes. Both require personal investment and are defined by their progressive nature. Learning can, thus, be seen as a form of self-actualization as long as it contributes to psychological health (Merriam and Caffarella, 1998). Learning enhances the process of self-actualization, while education induces self-determination to get there. Many investigators (Schostac, 1989; Cangemi, 1987; Wacks, 1987; McAlindon, 1981) have put forward the view that education is a creative source which will help in attaining self-actualization.

The sense of one's identity or self is an important dimension of individual's personality giving each of us a unique individuality. Today society has given equal opportunity to both male and female. Male and female are aware and sensitive to their needs, aspirations and rights and are asserting themselves through economic route. A concern for their self-worth and identity, their individuality, their ability to self-actualize has therefore prime importance to social scientists. Afroz and Mittra (2002) have attempted to find out whether education and economic empowerment of women have helped them attain their inherent potentiality and growth and whether there are any specific personality traits that helped them in this direction. Findings indicate that most of professional women in spite of higher education and economic independence have not been able to self-actualize. They have the required traits that could lead them in the right direction only if they could somehow manage to strike a balance between their inner need to grow to their full potential and the demands of their traditional and social values. Somehow, education and economic independence have helped them to attain high self-regard but they are as yet not able to self-actualize.

Women are working outside the home, moving into the domains traditionally reserved for men, and vigorously pursuing careers and interests. Women can make contributions to their present and future environments at many levels. Some channel their creativity into raising children, homemaking, relationships with loved ones, or getting to know and love themselves well. Becoming a self-actualized individual, in the face of institutionalized sexism, is an intrapersonal achievement having to do with such qualities as self-efficacy, resilience, spirituality, and wisdom. The expression of talent through community actualization is another sphere of achievement that is unrecognized by standard definitions of achievement. The work of many women in arenas such as church, tribal councils, schools, and neighbourhood groups lead to significant achievements on behalf of local communities (Kerr, Arnold, Martinez-Thorne, and Napier, 1996).

Professional women, as the category label suggest are urban, well-educated women, employed as administrators, doctors, managers, scientists, lawyers and media person. These women did not necessarily have an easy time working in the male world but were certainly better educated and they considered work to be an expression of self. These women did not operate within the boundary and constraints of a given role situation and were more like men in testing boundaries and altering constraints. The process of understanding and accepting oneself, harmonizing and integrating one's motives achieved by self-realization leads to self-actualization. The quest for self-realization is both natural and necessary to evolve as a rational, fully functioning healthy individual, but yet only a few fortunate individuals who are gifted, talented or enlightened ever achieve it. Individuals are blind to their own inherent potentials and assets, and are trapped in their cultural network and sentimentalities or distorted attitudes towards oneself and one's life, from which neither are they able to free themselves nor understand the positivity of self-enhancement. Self-actualization as a creative potential and constructive personality variable could contribute tremendously to human development, especially in maintaining sound mental health (Barnes and Srinivas, 1993).

Today, the fundamental issue and concern for Indian society is how to help in the actualization process? Will education and economic empowerment help women achieve this self-growth and how does a working educated woman view her self and her work life? In India the growth development and inner experiences of women are tied to the socio-economic factors (Kakkar, 1978), and it will be logical to expect that gainful employment is likely to bring a change in the quality of life of these women. As such, economic independence of women is advocated and is now being encouraged and it is being increasingly felt that many of the women's problems and issues will be helped and solved, if the women are gainfully employed outside the home. That it will lead to sexual equality, autonomy and self-fulfilment. But have the employed women been able to contribute positively in this direction? Have they been able to fight and win exploitation and discrimination at the workplace, have they been able to achieve a happy and guilt free family life, have they been able to go even a few steps in the direction of fulfilling themselves, having a sense of self-worth and self-respect and develop and grow to their full potential? Have their high education and gainful employment taken them towards self-actualization?

The present paper aims to find out whether higher education and professional status of the subjects have helped them to attain self-actualization and whether professional males and females have different personality traits with regard to their self-actualization. In the light of the general findings of studies it was hypothesized that professional males would score higher on the POI (Personal Orientation Invention) and 16 PF (Personality Factors) than professional females and secondly a significant number of professional women will be able to self-actualize.

Sample

The sample of the study consisted of 64 male and 58 female professionals. For the present study professionals are operationally defined as those individuals who pursue a career that allows them to apply and observe the effects or outcomes of their knowledge and skills in creatively dealing with everyday demands and solving problems of their career. Included in this category are doctors, engineers, academicians, lawyers, architects and managers whose career involves challenges, responsibility, autonomy, decision-making, assertiveness, constant stimulation and problem solving. All these are growth enhancing concepts and these are likely to act as mediating variables for achieving self-actualization. Thus, the professionals have the requisite support provided by the very nature of their career for moving in the direction of self-actualization.

In the present study doctors, engineers, academicians, lawyers, architects and managers represented the professional group. They were selected from the city of Varanasi in Uttar Pradesh, India. The telephone directory was consulted and a total of 200 potential subjects were identified. Each was approached personally by the investigator and their participation as a subject was requested by explaining the purpose of the study. These 122 subjects who were willing and consented to participate by giving their valuable time were selected by the investigator. The age range of the sample was 24 years to 60 years, range of education from Graduation to PhD.

Tools

1. **Biographical data sheet** to provide necessary demographic details about the selected samples.
2. **Personal Orientation Inventory** (Shostrom, 1960).

Maslow had used extensive personal interviews and interactions to assess the self-actualized persons. However, due to the subjective nature of Maslow's data, operationalization of the concept of self-actualization has proved somewhat difficult. Various individuals have developed operational definitions of certain aspects of self-actualization. The POI (Shostrom, 1960) was developed to meet this need. The philosophical foundation of the POI was formulated from the ideas and writings of Perls, Maslow, May-Angel-Ellenberger, Fromm, Horney, Rogers, Reisman, Watts and Ellis (Shostrom, 1960). POI has stimulated a great deal of empirical research aimed at verification of hypotheses and has created further insights into the concept of the self-actualizing person.

This questionnaire assesses the level of self-actualization on the basis of two variables, Inner-Directed (support ratio) and Time Competence (time ratio). The inventory consists of 150 forced choice items with two options of comparative value and behaviour judgments. It has ten subscales that measures different indices of self-actualization. The items are scored twice, first for two basic scales of personal orientation, inner directed support (127 items) and time competence (23 items) and second for ten subscales each of which measures a conceptually important element of self-actualizing: (1) self-actualizing value (SAV), (2) existentiality (Ex), (3) feeling reactivity (Fr), (4) spontaneity (S), (5) self-regard (Sr), (6) self-acceptance (Sa), (7) nature of man (Nc), (8) synergy (Sy), (9) acceptance of aggression (A), (10) capacity for intimate contact (C).

3. **Sixteen Personality Factors Questionnaire** (16 PF, Cattell, 1973)
   The test measures the sixteen functionally independent primary factors of human personality. Out of a total of 187 items, ten to thirteen items are provided for each scale.

Procedure

The study was carried out with male and female professionals. Each questionnaire was administered as per instructions provided in the respective manuals. A necessary and adequate level of rapport was established with each subject by explaining the objective of the research. Then the questionnaires were given to the subjects to be self-administered at their own convenience. This mode of administration was followed because the subjects were fairly busy individuals. A date and time was fixed when the investigator personally collected the questionnaires from each subject.

Result

Overall findings indicated that out of 122 subjects 31 subjects, were found to be self-actualized while the remaining subjects were not able to reach the required level for self-actualization. The result of the study was analysed in three steps. In the first step a comparison of male and female on the POI and 16 PF was attempted. In the second step self-actualized and non self-actualized subjects were compared on the POI and 16 PF, disregarding their group status. In the third step a comparison of the self-actualized males and females were attempted on the POI and 16 PF.

Table 1 compares the mean scores of professional males and females on various subscales of POI. On the scale of Time Competence ($t = 3.71$, $p=.01$) and Inner Directedness ($t = 3.04$, $p=.01$) males and females differ significantly. Findings indicate that males with higher mean score on both the scale were more time competent and inner-directed as compared to females who had relatively lower mean scores on these scales.

Table 1 *Mean, SD and t-values for males (N =64) and females (N = 58) Professionals on the POI Scale*

POI Scales	Males		Females		
	Mean	SD	Mean	SD	t-value
1 Time Competence (Tc)	16.26	1.87	14.81	2.43	3.71**
2 Inner-Directed (I)	80.42	8.78	75.81	7.86	3.04**
3 Self-actualizing Value (SAV)	19.45	2.65	18.22	2.89	2.44**
4 Existentiality (Ex)	17.28	4.28	15.68	3.42	2.25*
5 Feeling Reactivity (Fr)	13.56	2.95	13.12	2.72	.855
6 Spontaneity (S)	11.59	2.20	10.74	2.05	2.20*
7 Self-regard (Sr)	12.70	1.66	12.00	2.04	2.09*
8 Self-acceptance (Sa)	14.50	3.59	13.77	2.33	1.30
9 Nature of Man (Nc)	12.07	1.80	11.63	1.73	1.37
10 Synergy (Sy)	6.87	1.30	6.27	1.18	2.65**
11 Acceptance of Aggression (A)	15.35	2.04	14.55	2.47	1.96*
12 Capacity for Intimate Contact (C)	16.29	3.97	15.93	2.85	.578

**P <.01, *P <.05

Male and female professionals differ significantly on the subscale of self-actualizing value (SAV) ($t = 2.44$, $p = .01$), existentiality (Ex) ($t = 2.25$, $p = .05$), spontaneity (S) ($t = 2.20$, $p = .05$), self-regard (Sr) ($t = 2.09$, $p = .05$), synergy (Sy) ($t = 2.65$, $p = .01$), and acceptance of aggression (A) ($t = 1.96$, $p = .05$). They do not differ on the subscales of feeling reactivity (Fr), self-acceptance (Sa), nature of man (Nc) and capacity for intimate contact (C). There are number of values that self-actualizers tend to hold and that non-self-actualizers reject. Professionals males were more able to hold and live by self-actualizing values than females. Males were more flexible in applications of values and were not locked into a rigid, dogmatic way of perceiving or behaving in the world than females who were rigid in application of values.

On the scale of spontaneity males scored higher, it suggests that they tend to be open and authentic in behaviourally expressing their feelings whereas females tend to cover up their feelings and not express them for fear of a loss of approval. On the scale of self-regard, males were able to score higher than females, it suggests that they have high self-regard. They value themselves and their accomplishments. They are aware of their strengths and appreciate them. While females do not have very high self-regard. They tend to degrade themselves, put themselves down and not accept their own strength. They tend to project their own self-worth onto others by seeing strength in them that they deny in themselves. As a result, they are often unable to live up to their full potential. Instead, they settle for less than are possible or optimal for them.

On the scale of synergy males scored higher than females, it suggest that this characteristic is the ability to synthesize opposites. They have the ability to see the positive parts of each, eliminate the negative and create a new whole based upon the synthesis of the positive aspects. They are able to synthesize and integrate opposing points of view. They tend to avoid labelling people. While females were not able to see opposites of life meaningfully related.

On the scale of acceptance of anger, males were again able to score higher than females, this suggest that males feel free to express their anger rather than repress it. While females deny feelings of anger or express it in a hostile manner.

Males and females did not differ on the scales of feeling reactivity, acceptance of self, nature of man and capacity for intimate contact. On the scale of feeling reactivity males and females both scored almost same, it suggests that they were sensitive, aware of their own needs and feelings and introspective. These feelings were their source of information that deepen perceptions of the world and support increasing effectiveness. On the scale of self-acceptance both have a tendency to feel they have to be perfect. They accept their warts as well as their strengths. They were concerned about improving things, but they do not define themselves as weak persons if they happen to have a weakness. On the scale of nature of man, both male and female professionals tend to see human beings as essentially good, and to notice and emphasize the positive qualities in self and others. On the scale of capacity for intimate contact, both male and female professionals have the ability to develop warm, authentic interpersonal relationships. They go beyond roles to relate to other people in this warm, caring manner.

Table 2 presents the mean, SD and t-test for male and female on the 16 PF measures. Findings indicate that males and females differ significantly

Table 2 *Mean, SD and t-value for Males (N =64) and Females Professionals (N =58) on the 16 PF measures.*

		Males		*Females*		
	16 PF Scales	*Mean*	*SD*	*Mean*	*SD*	*t-value*
1	Reserved / outgoing (A)	4.40	1.48	4.22	1.27	.723
2	Less intelligent / high intelligent (B)	7.34	1.64	6.82	1.37	1.86
3	Emotional / emotionally stable (C)	5.68	2.12	6.56	1.14	2.81**
4	Submissive / assertive (E)	5.26	1.45	5.56	1.25	1.22
5	Sober / happy-go-lucky (F)	4.10	1.96	3.60	1.92	1.65
6	Expedient / conscientious (G)	5.93	1.60	6.39	1.78	1.49
7	Shy / venturesome (H)	5.46	1.86	5.72	1.50	.825
8	Tough-minded / tender-minded (I)	5.07	1.56	5.01	1.39	.226
9	Trusting / suspicious (L)	6.59	1.66	6.41	1.18	.680
10	Practical / imaginative (M)	5.53	1.77	4.94	1.77	1.81
11	Forth right / shrewd (N)	5.90	1.90	6.65	2.12	2.05*
12	Confident / apprehensive (O)	5.35	1.63	4.89	1.30	1.71
13	Conservative / experimenting (Q1)	5.67	1.65	5.56	1.39	.370
14	Group oriented / self-sufficient (Q2)	6.18	1.70	6.44	1.04	1.00
15	Undisciplined / controlled (Q3)	5.95	1.38	5.48	1.31	1.91*
16	Relaxed / tense (Q4)	4.43	1.86	5.86	1.53	3.69**

**P <.01, *P <.05

on four personality factor i.e., emotional stability/emotional (C) (t = 2.81, p =.01), forthright/shrewd (N) (t = 2.05, p =.05), undisciplined/controlled (Q3) (t = 1.91, p =.05) and relaxed/tense (Q4) (t = 3.69, p =.01). It suggest that females were emotionally stable, were of calculated mind, and also highly ambitious than males. On factor Q3 suggest that males are controlled, socially precise and have regard for reputation and a proper self-image than females. On factor Q4 females were scored higher than males and it suggest that females were more tense, frustrated and driven.

Table3 presents the mean, SD, and t-values of self-actualized and non self-actualized professionals irrespective of males and females on POI. Self-actualized and non-self-actualized differ significantly on almost scales of POI except one that is nature of man.

The self-actualized group appeared to be time competent, inner-directed than the non-self-actualized group. Individuals of this group held on and lived with self-actualizing values and were flexible in

Table 3 *Mean, SD and t-value on the POI Scales for Self-actualized (N =31) and Non-self-actualized subjects (N=91)*

POI Scales	*Self-actualized*		*Non self-actualized*		
	Mean	*SD*	*Mean*	*SD*	*t-value*
1 Time Competence (Tc)	17.54	.675	14.90	2.23	6.84**
2 Inner-Directed (I)	88.25	4.02	74.81	6.96	10.16**
3 Self-actualizing Value (SAV)	20.54	1.60	18.29	2.93	4.06**
4 Existentiality (Ex)	19.67	3.07	15.45	3.66	5.77**
5 Feeling Reactivity (Fr)	14.87	2.55	12.83	2.76	3.60**
6 Spontaneity (S)	12.58	1.94	10.71	2.04	4.45**
7 Self-Regard (Sr)	12.96	1.88	12.16	1.84	2.08**
8 Self-Acceptance (Sa)	16.16	2.92	13.47	2.82	4.53**
9 Nature of Man (Nc)	12.38	1.28	11.69	1.88	1.90
10 Synergy (Sy)	7.19	.909	6.38	1.32	3.15**
11 Acceptance of Aggression (A)	16.45	1.87	14.47	2.20	4.46**
12 Capacity for Intimate Contact (C)	18.16	3.06	15.42	3.35	4.00**

**P <.01, *P <.05

applying such values and principles to life than those of the non-self-actualized group. Self-actualized group was more sensitive to its own needs and feelings, was spontaneous, had ability to like and accept themselves in spite of several weaknesses or deficiencies. Self-actualized subjects have ability to see opposites of life as meaningfully related, were able to accept anger or aggression within oneself as natural and ability to develop meaningful contact and relationship with other human beings as compared to the non-self-actualized. The overall picture revealed that self-actualized subjects were superior to non-self-actualized subjects on each dimension of the POI.

Table 4 presents the result obtained on 16 PF for self-actualized and non-self-actualized subjects. The findings indicate that the differences among groups to be significant only on two personality factors i.e., factor

Table 4 *Mean, SD and t-values on the 16 PF measures for Self-actualized (N=31) and Non-self-actualized (N=91)*

16 PF Scales	*Self-actualized*		*Non-self-actualized*		
	Mean	*SD*	*Mean*	*SD*	*t-value*
1 Reserved / outgoing (A)	4.35	1.42	4.30	1.38	.163
2 Less intelligent / high intelligent (B)	7.67	1.49	6.90	1.52	2.47**
3 Emotional / emotionally stable (C)	6.16	2.05	6.08	1.68	.198
4 Submissive / assertive (E)	5.38	1.40	5.41	1.35	.107
5 Sober / happy-go-lucky (F)	4.25	1.94	3.79	1.96	1.14
6 Expedient / conscientious (G)	5.93	1.54	6.23	1.75	.834
7 Shy / venturesome (H)	5.77	1.76	5.52	1.68	.695
8 Tough-minded / tender-minded (I)	4.74	1.50	5.15	1.46	1.34
9 Trusting / suspicious (L)	6.16	1.34	6.62	1.48	1.54
10 Practical / imaginative (M)	5.03	1.79	5.32	1.78	.798
11 Forthright / shrewd (N)	5.87	1.80	6.39	2.10	1.24
12 Confident / apprehensive (O)	5.09	1.46	5.15	1.51	.182
13 Conservative / experimenting (Q1)	5.61	1.52	5.62	1.53	.042
14 Group oriented / self-sufficient (Q2)	6.16	1.71	6.36	1.32	.675
15 Undisciplined / controlled (Q3)	6.38	1.14	5.50	1.36	3.21**
16 Relaxed / tense (Q4)	4.93	2.20	5.00	1.66	.171

**P <.01, *P <.05

B (t = 2.47, p =.01) and Q3 (t = 3.21, p =.01). The finding suggested that self-actualized were more intelligent and abstract thinkers and they are also socially precise and controlled. The findings indicated that self-actualized and non-self-actualized persons did not differ significantly on the remaining scales of 16 PF. This suggested that they had almost a similar personality profile irrespective of the groups to which they belonged, which helped them to move towards self-actualization. The mean scores of the self-actualized subjects ranged between 5 and 6 on most of the factors of 16 PF, except on intelligence, emotional stability, suspicious, self-sufficiency and controlled. On these scales the scores were on the higher side. This suggested that these individuals were highly intelligent, emotionally stable, suspicious, self-sufficient and controlled.

Table 5 and 6 presents the results obtained on the POI and 16 PF for self-actualized males and females. Self-actualized males and females did not differ on any of the POI and 16 PF scales except on one factor that is

Table 5 *Mean, SD and t-values on the POI scales for Self-actualized males (N=22) and females (N=9)*

	POI Scales	*Self-actualized Males*		*Non-self-actualized Females*		
		Mean	*SD*	*Mean*	*SD*	*t-value*
1	Time Competence (Tc)	17.54	.671	17.55	.726	.037
2	Inner-Directed (I)	88.59	4.52	87.44	2.45	.714
3	Self-actualizing Value (SAV)	20.31	1.55	21.11	1.69	1.25
4	Existentiality (Ex)	20.09	3.30	18.66	2.23	1.18
5	Feeling Reactivity (Fr)	14.54	2.59	15.66	2.39	1.11
6	Spontaneity (S)	12.72	1.75	12.22	2.43	.650
7	Self-Regard (Sr)	13.13	1.83	12.55	2.06	.772
8	Self-Acceptance (Sa)	16.40	3.09	15.55	2.50	.732
9	Nature of Man (Nc)	12.50	1.33	12.11	1.16	.761
10	Synergy (Sy)	7.22	.972	7.11	.781	.318
11	Acceptance of Aggression (A)	16.68	1.93	15.88	1.69	1.07
12	Capacity for Intimate Contact (C)	18.59	3.21	17.11	2.52	1.23

**P <.01, *P <.05

Table 6 *Mean, SD and t-values on the 16 PF measures for Self-actualized Males (N=22) and Self-actualized Females (N=9)*

16 PF Scales	*Self-actualized Males*		*Self-actualized Females*		
	Mean	*SD*	*Mean*	*SD*	*t-value*
1 Reserved / outgoing (A)	4.50	1.53	4.00	1.11	.882
2 Less intelligent / high intelligent (B)	7.68	1.42	7.66	1.58	.026
3 Emotional / emotionally stable (C)	6.04	2.33	6.44	1.13	.485
4 Submissive / assertive (E)	5.22	1.47	5.77	1.20	.989
5 Sober / happy-go-lucky (F)	4.45	1.81	3.77	2.27	.874
6 Expedient / conscientious (G)	5.86	1.28	6.11	2.14	.398
7 Shy / venturesome (H)	5.90	1.82	5.44	1.66	.659
8 Tough-minded / tender-minded (I)	4.81	1.68	4.55	1.01	.435
9 Trusting / suspicious (L)	6.00	1.44	6.55	1.01	1.04
10 Practical / imaginative (M)	5.27	1.83	4.44	1.66	1.17
11 Forthright / shrewd (N)	6.09	2.02	5.33	1.00	1.06
12 Confident / apprehensive (O)	5.31	1.55	4.55	1.13	1.32
13 Conservative / experimenting (Q1)	5.68	1.46	5.44	1.74	.389
14 Group oriented / self-sufficient (Q2)	6.18	1.73	6.11	1.76	.102
15 Undisciplined / controlled (Q3)	6.31	1.24	6.55	.881	.517
16 Relaxed / tense (Q4)	4.45	2.21	6.11	1.76	1.99*

**P <.01, *P <.05

Q4 (relaxed vs tense). Score indicate that females are tense as compared to males who are relaxed. On remaining factors both self-actualized males and females have scored more or less in similar manner.

Discussion

The overall results indicate that professional males and females are generally able to function effectively and have the requisite level of competence or ability to develop towards a higher level of self-actualization. The investigators believe that the professionals have the required support provided by the very nature of their career as engineers, consultant doctors, management consultants, whose career entails challenges, responsibility, autonomy, decision-making, assertiveness, constant and varied stimulation, problem solving—all growth enhancing concepts which should act as mediating variables for achieving self-actualization. Professionals were those individuals who could see the results of their endeavour and creativity. Whether male or female, they are more self-actualized than normal highly educated individuals (McClure et al., 1988; Sherrill et al., 1988; Schindler et al., 1986; Gundersheim, 1982; Rotella et al., 1980; Carlson et al., 1980). They also have some supportive personality traits that may help them develop into individuals who are healthy, creative, emotionally secure, intelligent, and who have the ability to express spontaneously their creative potentials in diverse ways.

An assumption of the present study was that higher education along with attendant learning, skill training, and highly placed careers would provide the subjects with many growth enhancing conditions that may enable them to achieve self-actualization. But in spite of this, the number of self-actualized females were less as compared to their male counterparts. Though they are highly educated and settled in respectable career, yet they are not able to self-actualize like males. They do not function on an effective level so as to move towards self-actualization. The finding of the present investigation points out that the ability to self-actualize is dependent upon the beliefs and values inculcated in the Indian women by culture and philosophy. Most of the professional women were not able to reach the required level of self-actualization. The Indian culture and philosophy teaches the values of selfless service to others, thinking of and helping others, sacrifice, care, nurturance, compromise and adjustment at ones cost to bring happiness and peace to others (Afroz et al., 2002). All these feelings and values do not seem to be conducive to the growth of self-actualization.

Some studies have pointed out that self-actualization was positively and significantly related to the degree of professionalism (Fetzer, 2003). Findings of the present study also supported this. Out of 122 subjects, 31 subjects was able to self-actualize. It shows a positive indication. Self-actualization needs have been rated as important by Indian managers, regardless of differences in their occupational levels (Venkatraman and Anantharaman, 1991). Indian managers, including officers, have been found to be more oriented towards higher level needs than non-managers and clerks (Kulkarni, 1981). Officers attach greater importance to growth needs than do clerks who in turn attach greater importance to existence needs than do officers (Rao and Kulkarni, 1998).

Findings of the present study suggested that the greater number of male professionals were able to self-actualize and they also scored higher as compared to self-actualized females on the POI, which suggests that females seem not to be functioning at an effective level to be able to self-actualize. One reason may be that balancing career and family remains a largely female issue, strongly affecting the professional choices of women more than men (Arnold, Noble and Subotnik, 1996). Afroz, et al., (2002) have also reported that the most of the professional women in spite of high education and economic independence have not been able to self-actualize. They have the required personality traits that could lead them in right direction. In one study self-actualization needs and esteem needs of employed females were compared to those of female homemakers (Betz, 1982), it was found that they were higher for the former group. Another study that compared males and females (Humphrey and Lehman, 1984), found that well-educated females were inclined to pursue domesticity and service to others as the prime source of self-fulfilment. In order to develop their talents and potentialities in the face of obstacles, women must cultivate a number of protective factors known collectively as 'resilience'. Resilience is the ability to respond to stress with competence (Garmezy and Tellegen, 1984). Some studies cite qualities such as intelligence, emotional flexibility, independence, sensitivity, curiosity, and the willingness to reach out for love and support as central components of the resilient personality (Anthony and Cohler, 1987; Garmezy and Tellegen, 1984; Dugan and Cotes, 1989). Because they were committed to living as fully as possible, they developed their talents and abilities, acquired a high degree of personal discipline, and were willing to fight to preserve their own souls.

The beliefs, attitudes, traditions, and ideals of parents, extended families, communities, and cultures shape women's ambitions. Thus, a woman must learn to see clearly the psychological and socio-cultural parameters of her life, consciously choosing those she will keep, discard, or modify. It is suggested the institutions of higher learning are supposed to give them support to increase their autonomy, creativity, effectiveness in teaching and research, development of self-regard, self-acceptance and meaningful contact in the community.

The present results could be seen in the light of Maslow's (1971) contention when he pointed out that many women have a fear about themselves. They do not utilize their intellectual abilities to the fullest because they fear social rejection. Studies support Maslow's arguments and suggest that many women will have difficulty moving towards actualization because of environmental forces restricting their options. The subjects of the present study had well-reputed careers with national and international recognition of their academic contributions, and were the recipient of various prestigious awards. Thus, all prerequisites of self-realization were present among them. In spite of all these, however, only a limited number of subjects were able to self-actualize, and those who were able to self-actualize, also did not cross the mean standard score for each scale. It is difficult to specify reasons for it, however, we may look at it in terms of differences in cultural orientation (Eastern vs Western), domain specificity of self-actualization (work vs family), and the appropriateness of the POI as a tool of measurement of self-actualization.

The review of cross-cultural studies on self suggests that there are relatively consistent cultural differences between Western and Eastern cultures (Marasella, Devos and Hsu, 1985; Shweder and Bourne, 1984; Triandis, Bontempo, Villareal, Asai and Luca, 1988). The Indian society supplies a variety of evidence in support of interdependent construal as against independent construal of self in the Western cultures. The conceptualization of a person in the Indian context generally centres around the dynamics of shared lifestyle, relationship maintenance, dependence proneness, and need for approval (Sinha, 1988). Here the control is often distributed. Self is constituted and realized only in relationship to others (Misra, 1994). This difference in orientation of Indians seems to be the reason why the subjects having ideal growth enhancing support of their careers were still not functioning effectively in their development towards the self-actualization.

Another reason may be that we have studied self-actualization here in work context. Some studies indicate that work is a mode of self-realization. But in Indian society family has occupied an important position. People pay more attention to their family than other things. Their first priority is the family. One may even say that Indians are family-oriented. This orientation sometimes facilitates and sometimes poses hindrances to the work domain. Indian cultural, social and religious values are based on love, tolerance, and sacrifice. People put others' interest before their own. Maintenance and respect for familial and other relationships, and consideration and conformity to the traditional demands are deeply rooted in Indian culture (Singh and Misra, 2000). It seems to be another reason for less effective functioning in development towards self-actualization.

Another important reason may be that as POI measures self-actualization dimension rooted in the western culture where the attainment of materialistic and individualistic goals of self-actualization are emphasized, whereas Indian notion of self-actualization is based on the realization of spirituality, this could be an important reason why less number of subjects could be identified as self-actualized, because the ultimate goal in Indian thought is self-realization and spiritual pursuit.

■ References

Afroz, N. and Mittra, R. "Do Personality Traits Define Self-actualization in Employed Women?" *Journal of the Indian Academy of Applied Psychology, 29* (1–2), (2002): 61–66.

Anthony, E.J., and Cohler, B.J. *The Invulnerable Child.* New York: The Guilford Press, 1987.

Arnold, K.D., Noble, K.D., and Subotnik, R.F. *Remarkable Women: Perspectives on Female Talent Development.* Cresskill, NJ: Hampton Press, 1996.

Barnes, B.L., and Srinivas, R. "Self-actualization in Different Sex Sub-groups". *Journal of Personality and Clinical Studies, 9,* 1–2, (1993): 19–24.

Betz, E.L. "Need Fulfillment in the Career Development of Women". *Journal of Vocational Behaviour, 20,* 1, (1982): 53–66.

Cangemi, J.P. "Education and Self-actualization". *Journal of Instructional Psychology. 14,* 4, (1987): 164–175.

Carlson, J.M., and Hyde, M.S. "Personality and Political Recruitment: Actualization or Compensation". *Journal of Psychology 106,* 1, (1980): 1117–1120.

Cattell, R.B. *Personality and Mood by Questionnaire.* San Francisco: Jossy-Bass, 1973.

Chang, R., and Page, R.C. "Characteristics of the Self-actualized Person: Visions from the East and West". *Counseling and Values, 36,* 1, (1991): 2–10.

Coan, R.W. "Self-actualization and the Quest for the Ideal Human". Special issue: Handbook of Self-actualization. *Journal of Social Behaviour and Personality, 6,* 5, (1991): 127–136.

Cook-Greuter, S. "Postautonomous Ego Development: A Study of its Nature and Measurement". Unpublished doctoral dissertation, Harvard University, Cambridge, MA., 1999.

Daftuar, C.N., and Sharma, R. "Beyond Maslow: An Indian Perspective of Need-hierarchy". *Journal of the Indian Academy of Applied Psychology, 24,* 1–2, (1997): 1–8.

Dahl, R.J. "How the Personality Dimensions of Neuroticism, Extroversion and Psychoticism Relate to Self-actualization". *Personality and Individual Differences, 4,* 6, (1983): 683–685.

Das, A.K. "Beyond Self-actualization". *International Journal for the Advancement of Counselling, 12,* 1, (1989): 13–27.

Dugan, T.F., and Cotes, R. *The Child in Our Times: Studies in the Development of Resiliency.* New York: Brunner/Mazel, 1989.

Farmer, R. "Humanistic Education and Self-actualizing Theory". *Education, 105,* 2, (1984): 162–172.

Fetzer, S.J. "Professionalism of Associate Degree Nurses: The Role of Self-actualization". *Nursing Education Perspectives, 24,* 3, (2003): 139–143.

Ford, J.G. "Inherent Potentialities of Actualization: An Initial Exploration". *Journal of Humanistic Psychology, 31,* 3, (1991): 65–68.

Garmezy, N. and Tellegen, A. "Studies of Stress-resistant Children: Methods, Variables, and Preliminary Findings". In F.J. Morrison, C. Lord, and D. P. Keating (eds.), 1984. *Applied Developmental Psychology.* Orlando, FL: Academic Press.

Gundersheim, J. "A Comparison of Male and Female Athletes and Non-Athletes on Measures of Self-actualization". *Journal of Sport Behaviour, 5,* 4, (1982): 186–201.

Humphrey, M. and Lehman, C. "Adolescent Fantasy and Self-fulfillment: The Problem of Female Passivity". *Journal of Adolescence, 7,* 3, (1984): 295–304.

Kakkar, S. *The Inner-world: A Psychoanalytic Study of Childhood and Society in India.* Delhi, Oxford University Press, 1978.

Kegan, R. *In Over Our Heads: The Mental Demands of Modern Life.* Cambridge, MA: Harvard University Press, 1994.

Kerr, B., Arnold, K., Martinez-Thorne, Y., and Napier, L.A. "Gender's Contributions to Realize Talent Over the Life Span: Old Pitfalls, New Paradigms". Panel presented at the Esther Katz Rosen Symposium on the Psychological Development of Gifted Children, Lawrence, KS, 1996.

Kulkarni, A.V. "Reward Expectancies in Relation to Cognitive Styles". Unpublished Ph. D. thesis, Nagpur University, 1981.

Marasella, A.J., Devos, G.S., and Hsu, F.I.K. *Culture and Self: Asian and Western Perspective.* New York: Tavistock, 1985.

Maslow, A. H. *Motivation and Personality.* New York: Harper, 1954.

Maslow, A. H. *The Farther Reaches of Human Nature.* New York: Viking Press, 1971.

McAlindon, H.R. "Education for SAZ". *Training and Development Journal,* 35, 10, (1981): 85–91.

McClure, B.A., Holladay, K.L., and Faster, C.D. "Effects of a Personal Growth Group on Self-actualization of Female Gymnasts". *Perceptual and Motor Skills, 66,* 1, (1988): 165–166.

McKenna, J.J. "On Being at Both Center and Circumference: The Role of Personal Discipline and Collective Wisdom in the Recovery of Soul". *Spirituality, Ethics and Relationship in Adulthood: Clinical and Theoretical Explorations.* Miller, Melvin. E and West, Alan N. (eds.). Madison CT. Psychological press/International Universities Press Inc, 2000.

Merriam, S. and Caffarella. *Learning in Adulthood: A comprehensive guide.* San Francisco: Jossey-Bass, 1998.

Meyers, D. and Diener, E. "Who Is Happy?" *Psychological Science, 6,* 1, (1995): 10–19.

Misra, G. "Psychology of Control: Cross Cultural Considerations". *Journal of Indian Psychology, 12,* (1994): 8–45.

Norlander, T., Bood, S. A., and Archer, T. "Performance During Stress: Affective Personality, Age and Regularity of Physical Exercise". *Social Behaviour and Personality, 30,* 5, (2002): 495–508.

Ramanaiah, N.V., Heerboth, J.R., and Jinkerson, D.L. "Personality and Self-actualizing Profiles of Assertive People". *Journal of Personality Assessment, 49,* 4, (1985): 440–443.

Rangaswami, K. "Self-actualization and Beyond: Union with Universal Self, the Highest Motive from Indian Perspective". *Indian Journal of Clinical Psychology, 21,* 2, (1994): 45–50.

Rao, P.U.B., and Kulkarni, A.V. "Perceived Importance of Needs in Relation to Job Level and Personality Make-up". *Journal of the Indian Academy of Applied Psychology, 24,* 1–2, (1998): 37–42.

Rotella, R.J., Gansneder, B., Ojala, D., and Billing, J. "Cognitions and Coping Strategies of Elite Skiers: An Exploratory Study of Young Developing Athletes". *Journal of Sports Psychology, 2,* (1980): 350–354.

Ryff, C.D. "Happiness is Everything, or Is It? Explorations on the Meaning of Psychological Well-being". *Journal of Personality and Social Psychology* 57, (1989): 1069–1081.

Schindler, T.M., and Waters, M. "Athletic Involvement and Aspects of Self-actualization". *Journal of Sport Behaviour, 9,* 2, (1986): 59–69.

Schostac, J. The Play of Education. Special Issue: New Directions For Educational Theory:II. Conceptualizing the Problems of Educational Change". *Cambridge Journal of Education. 19,* 2, (1989): 207–223.

Sherrill, C. and Rainbolt, W. "Self-actualization Profiles of Male Able-bodied and Elite Cerebral Palsied Athletes". Special issue: Perspective on Disables Persons. *Adopted Physical Activity Quarterly, 5,* 2, (1988): 108–119.

Sinha, D. "The Family Scenario of a Developing Country and its Implications for Mental Health: The Case of India". In P.R. Dasan, J.W. Berry, and N. Sartorius (ed.), *Health and Cross Cultural Psychology: Toward Applications.* Newbury Park, California: Sage, 1988.

Singh, J.K., and Misra, G. (2000). "Understanding Contentment in Everyday Life". Special Millennium Issue. *Indian Psychological Reviews, 55,* 4, 113–124.

Shostrom, E.L. Edits Manual for POI. *Educational Industrial Testing Services.* San Diego, California, 1960.

Shweder, R.A., and Bourne, E.J. "Does the Concept of the Person Vary Cross Culturally?" In Marashella, A J. and White, G. M. (Eds). *Cultural Conceptions of Mental Health and Therapy.* Dordrecht: A Reidel, 1984.

Torbert, W.R. "Cultivating Postformal Adult Development: Higher Stages and Contrasting Interventions". In M.E. Miller and S. Cook-Greuter (eds), *Transcendence and Mature Thought in Adulthood: The Further Reaches of Adult Development.* New York: Rowman & Littlefield, 1994.

Triandis, H.C., Bontempo, R., Villareal, M.J., Asai, M., and Luca, N. "Individualism and Collectivism: Cross-cultural Perspectives on Self–in Group Relationships". *Journal of Personality and Social Psychology, 54,* (1988): 323–338.

Venkataraman, S., and Anantharaman, R.N. Need Satisfaction and Need Importance Among Managerial Personnel. *Journal of Psychological Researches, 25,* (1991): 15–20.

Wacks, V.Q. A Case for Self-transcendent as a Purpose of Adult Education. *Adult Education Quarterly, 38,* 1, (1987): 46–55.

Wilson, S.R. "The Real-self Controversy: Toward an Integration of Humanistic and Individualistic Theory. *Journal of Humanistic Psychology, 28,* 1, (1988): 39–65.

V

Women and Family

16

Psychological Fallout of Violence Against Women in the Family

Roomana N. Siddiqui

Women in our society have been idolized, revered and worshipped in the image of a mother. They are considered as an epitome of everything that is associated with tenderness, nurturance, empathy and sensitivity. Someone who can never do anything wrong and has the arduous task of socializing her children in the right values of her culture. But the irony of the fact is, that despite having such a positive image and a positive role, this very mother just because she carries the "female tag" is often subjected to violence in various forms. As females have held positions of diminished power in our society they have been silent recipients of the abuses and physical assault inflicted on them on a regular basis.

Violence against women is a direct infringement on her psychological boundary—the invisible barriers that protect the integrity and rights of an individual. Failing to defend and to stand for herself under attack, she looses some of the most treasured part of herself, i.e., her integrity, her belief in herself, the real 'I'which is the core of her inner self and each time it is a little death.

Impact of Violence on the Battered Female

Being regularly abused and battered, victims suffer from many emotional problems, the most common affective behaviour being depression, helplessness, suicidal thoughts, withdrawal, anxiety, lack of interest and concentration in their activities, a sense of worthlessness, low self-esteem and insomnia. They may also experience panic disorder that is characterized by discrete period of unexpected intense discomfort. Attacks generally start with fear or apprehension along with symptoms of shortness of breath, dizziness, increased heart beat, sweating or fear of dying (APA, 1994).

Not surprisingly battered women frequently manifest symptoms and characteristics defined as the "battered woman syndrome" (Walker, 1979). The battered woman syndrome has three major components:

- Post-trauma symptoms associated with victimization, specifically including re-experiencing the violence through intrusive thoughts or dreams and numbing or reduced expression of affect;
- "Learned helplessness" resulting from repeated abuse. Depression and a sense of lacking control of the environment are often artifacts of the learned helplessness, but it does not necessarily result in passivity on the part of the victim; and
- Coping responses viewed as self-destructive by others, including behaviours that appear to placate the offender or numb the victim to the abusive environment.

Battered women struggle with their traumas that get further reinforced by poor self-esteem. Positive self-perception gets challenged by an experience with violence (Janoff-Billman, and Frieze, 1983). The negative self-image perpetuated by violence, forces the individual to question their views about themselves as worthy or good. Often trying to understand the situation in which they find themselves, women engage in self-stigmatizing thoughts, and end up blaming themselves for the situation. This belief that one is weak and not worthy results in increased psychological distress.

As mental health professionals have begun to intervene with battered women, distinct levels of mental health need have become apparent. Violence of the partner is a primary source of distress amongst most of the battered women. When the stressor is removed, either by separation from the partner, or by his meaningful involvement in treatment, symptoms of psychological distress are also ameliorated. These are women whose psychological injuries do not meet the criteria for clinical diagnosis, but who may be suffering with great distress.

The mental health need of a second category of victims is more profound, generally resulting from a long-standing exposure to the traumatic stress of the violence. Victims within this category frequently exhibit post-trauma related symptoms and may appear to mimic the behaviour of a hostage held captive for an extended period. Other applicable diagnostic categories include depressions and affective disorders and dissociative and anxiety disorders. A growing body of research indicates that battered women frequently present symptoms characteristic of Post-Traumatic Stress Disorder (PTSD). PTSD is a diagnostic category, which is specifically linked to the experience of a traumatic event and is characterized by a re-experiencing of the trauma; avoidance of stimuli associated with the event, and increased autonomic arousal (American Psychiatric Association, 1994). The likelihood of developing PTSD has been found to increase when stressors are experienced under conditions of perceived life threat, injury, and a great deal of force (Finkelhor, et al., 1983), all of which are characteristic of domestic abuse cases. More pronounced mental health needs are also generally found among adult spouse abuse victims who have a childhood history of physical or sexual abuse, an experience not uncommon to battered women.

The Fallout of Family Violence

In the context of the family system violence against females specifically the "mother" has wide ranging implications both for the person being victimized and for the children who are witness to these brutalities. Traditionally women have been trained since birth to be tolerant, submissive, and self-sacrificing. Such characteristics are virtues of the nurturing woman, but unless they are coupled with a healthy respect for the self, they may lead to martyrdom and victimization. When we add to this the cultural realities of submission, backgrounds of pathology, alcoholism, poverty, and patriarchy, the woman may lose all sense of identity and become vulnerable and insecure. She may even slip into the abyss of mental illness, addiction, or deviant behaviour.

Victimization has direct implications for a female's effectiveness as a parent. Having a scarred psyche, the female in the role of a mother is not able to bring up her children in the most congenial manner. Their role as caretakers is undermined because the disorganization offers little nurturance, support and supervision for children. Her child rearing strategies are fraught with self-doubt, insecurity and psychological pain. It has far-reaching social impact as in our society it is the mother's privilege and responsibility to nurture and socialize her children. On her depends the identity that her daughters and sons will assume, and through it daughters become primed to look after others and repeat the mothering they get. This forms a vicious circle. Their mothering in turn creates a new generation of females whose personality is characterized by a relatively permeable psychological boundary that has great risk of losing itself in the morass of intertwining relationships.

As parents are role models, boys and girls who witness violence quickly learn that violence is an appropriate way of resolving conflict in human relationship; interaction of family members contains violence; and that violence is sanctioned as a mode of stress management. Applying the social information-processing model (McFall, 1982) violent spouses lack the social skills necessary to generate, select or enact non-violent solutions when confronted with conflict situations (Auglin and Hollzworth-Munroe, 1997). Exposure to violence in the family of origin negatively affects social relationships later in life (Wolfe, Wekerle, Reitzel-Jaffe and Lefebre, 1998). Family violence is one of the most consistent predictors of relationship violence among adults (Smith et al., 2000, Hotaling and Sugarman, 1986; Carr and Van Deusen, 2002). Researches indicate that the vast majority of batterers had witnessed these behaviours in their families of origin and the rate of wife beating is dramatically higher for sons of batterers compared with sons of non-violent fathers (Straus, et al., 1980; O'Keefe, 1997; Magdol et al., 1998; Lackey, 2003). Learning theorists speculate that same-sex modelling (Kalmus, 1984) or differential socialization (Sugarman and Frankel, 1996) may account for such gender differences. Girls may learn that victimization is inevitable, hence suffering in silence is reinforced while boys are likely to act out, become disobedient, and behave in a defiant and destructive manner. According to Patterson (1982), it is a progression towards anarchy within such families.

Historically, children have been the "forgotten victims" of domestic violence as there has been a mistaken belief that children in the home can somehow escape direct exposure to the violence and its effects. Within the last decade, child advocates and domestic violence experts have started taking a broader view of who is victimized by domestic violence by beginning to address the negative psychological impact it has on children who witness violence between parents.

The impact of domestic violence on children is complex, as it must take into account cases where children witness adult violence, cases in which children are also targeted for abuse by the batterer, and cases where a child is injured by stepping in to protect a victimized parent. The impact is manifested in emotional, behavioural, cognitive and physical spheres of the child's life. The child who silently watches his / her mother being disgraced and demeaned in front of her in Bandura's (1960) terminology "vicariously" experiences the humiliation, abuse and assault. Thus witnessing parental violence and later expressing it as a form of behaviour is analogue to Bandura's observational learning paradigm (1977). Since mother is part of the 'extended self' (James, 1907) the perpetrator, by victimizing the mother, is indirectly and in a very subtle manner brutalizing the young psyche of the witnessing child. These leave permanent psychological scars on the developing minds.

Psychoanalyst Freud (1964) has argued that the events and experiences of early childhood determine the character and personality of the individual and form the base from which future personalities take shape. They suggest that an individual, who is a combination of both conscious and unconscious process, is the consequence of the way in which the society has influenced the child via the family. It has been argued that the unconscious mind of an individual seems to be structured by what goes on emotionally within his or her family. Since everyone depends on mother or mother substitute for survival the unconscious that one ends up with depends on the repression of events and conflicts set up in early childhood involving these people.

Davidson, in his book *Conjugal Crime* (1978), pointed out that the witnessing children are the most pathetic victims because the childhood conditioning colours their entire lives. They try to evaluate and judge the world through what they saw. According to Kakkar (1988), serious fallout, mainly for the girl child, is that she develops a heightened hostility and envy towards males. If a woman perceives that the main premises of the absolute status hierarchy between sexes are mainly gender and if she is prevented to express herself and her resentment then her unconscious destructive impulses towards the male child is bound to be strong. But in patriarchal societies it is possible that she turns the aggression against herself and thus transforms the cultural devaluation into feelings of worthlessness and inferiority. This results in self-depreciation, which is characterized by low self-esteem, depressive moodiness, extreme touchiness and morbid sensitivity in interpersonal relationship.

Children raised in an environment of wife abuse exhibit a range of problems. Wolfe, Jaffe, Wilson and Zak (1985) studied a sample of 198 children from violent and non-violent families. They reported that children of battered women were significantly higher on behavioural problems and lower in social competence than children in comparison group. Wolfe and colleagues suggested that the impact on the child witnessing family violence might be partially mediated by factors associated with maternal stress. Going a step further, Jaffe et al. (1986) compared the impact of direct and indirect exposure to family violence on school aged boys. Boys who had witnessed violence between parents were compared with children from a provincial child welfare agency who had been physically abused by their parents. The findings reveal that boys exposed to family violence had behaviour problems similar to those shown by abused children but differed from those shown by children from nonviolent families. Perez and Wisdom (1994) found that abused neglected adults scored significantly less than control group individual on IQ and reading ability even when effects of age, sex, race and social class was controlled.

Violence in the family often makes the child to withdraw and gets manifested in internalized difficulties, such as somatic disorders, insomnia, heightened anxiety, depression, guilt and damaged self-esteem, many of which result from the self-perception of helplessness in the face of violence (Jaffe et al., 1987; Hughes, 1988; Pynoos and Eth, 1984). Post-trauma symptoms are also seen in child witnesses of violence, in large part due to the over stimulation and terror to which they are routinely exposed. Children's reactions to witnessing domestic abuse may also be more aggressive in nature. A child may model the offender and act out aggressively with parents, siblings, peers or others (Straus, et al., 1980).

Most of the children live in shame and are embarrassed by the family violence. It undermines their sense of self-esteem and the confidence they have in the future. Sometimes they also experience guilt out of a sense that they could not prevent the violence or that they might have been the cause of it. They often get confused and have divided loyalty in wanting to protect their mother but still respecting their father's authority in the family. The uncertainty and the intensity of the abuses inflicted on the mother can also cause psychopathology. As the basic need of attachment to their mother gets disrupted it threatens the child's sense of security in relation to their social environment.

Conclusion

In conclusion one can say that crimes against females or would be mothers is a crime not only against the female community but it is a crime against humanity. It is a well-known statement that "the hand that rocks the cradle rules the world". But if these very hands are inadequate, unsure, lack confidence and are shaky then one can imagine the wider social implications. If the female, who is the repository of the culture and instrumental in passing on the legacy of the culture to the next generation, is victimized and traumatized it can shake the very fabric of the society. A psychologically disturbed mother cannot raise a mentally healthy child because the legacy of abuse, torture, silent suffering and psychological numbness passes from one generation to another. Breaking this viscous cycle is the greatest challenge of any society. This requires change in attitude, de-categorization of the gender schema and a change in the social structure that is severely in disfavour of women. Apart from providing her legal options the social and psychological reality also has to change because without changing the customs, values and consciousness no social transformation is possible that can liberate women from her present condition.

■ References

American Psychiatric Association. *Diagnostic and Statistical Manual of Mental Disorders* (3rd ed.). Washington DC: American Psychiatric Association, 1994.

Auglin, K. and Hollzworth-Munroe, A. Comparing the response of maritally violent and non-violent spouses to problematic marital and non-marital situations. Are the skill deficits of physically aggressive husbands and wives global? *Journal of Family Psychology*, 11, 3, (1997): 301–313.

Bandura, A.J. *Relationships of Family Patterns to Child Behavior Disorders.* Progress report USPHS Research Grant M—1734. Stanford University, Palo Alto, California, 1960.

——. *Social Learning Theory*. Englewoods Cliffs, NJ: Prentice Hall, 1977.

Carr, J.L. and Van Deusen, K.M. "The Relationship Between Family of Origin

Violence and Dating Violence in College Men." *Journal of Interpersonal Violence*, 17(6), (2002): 630–646.

Davidson, T. *Conjugal Crime: Understanding and Changing the Wife Beating Pattern*. New York: Hawthorn, 1978.

Finkelhor, D., Gelles, R.J., Hotaling, G.T., and Straus, M.A. (eds.) *The Dark Side of Families: Current Family Violence Research*. Beverly Hills, CA: Sage, 1983.

Freud, S. *An Outline of Psycho-analysis*. In Standard edition, Vol. 22. London: Hogarth Press, 1964.

Hotaling, G.T., and Sugarman, D.B. An analysis of risk markers in husband-to-wife violence: The current state of knowledge. *Violence and Victims*, 1, 101–124, 1986.

Hughes, H.M. Psychological and behavioural correlates of family violence in child witness and victims. *American Journal of Orthopsychiatry*, 18, 77–90, 1988.

Jaffe, P., Wilson, S., Cameron, S., Zajc, R. and Wolfe, D. Are children who witness wife battering in need of protection? *Journal of the Ontario Association of Children's Aid Societies*, 31, 3–7, 1987.

Jaffe, P., Wolfe, D.A., Wilson, D.A., Wilson, S., and Zak, L. "Similarities in behavioural and social maladjustment among child victims and witnesses to family violence." *American Journal of Orthopsychiatry*, 56, (1986): 142–146.

James, W. *Psychology: The Briefer Course*. New York: Holt, 1907.

Janoff-Bulman, R. and Frieze, I. "A Theoretical Perspective for Understanding Reactions to Victimization." *Journal of Social Issues*, 39(2), (1983): 1–17.

Kakkar, S. "Feminine Identity in India." In R. Ghadially (ed.), *Women in Indian Society*. New Delhi: Sage, 1988.

Kalmus, D. "The Intergenerational Transmission of Marital Aggression. *Journal of Marriage and the Family*, 31, (1984): 11–19.

Lackey, C. "Violent Family Heritage, The Transition to Adulthood and Later Partner Violence. *Journal of Family Issues*, 24, 1, (2003): 74–98.

Magdol, L., Moffitt, T.E., Caspi, A., and Silva, P.H. "Developmental Antecedents of Partner Abuse: A Prospective Longitudinal Study." *Journal of Abnormal Psychology*, 107, (1998): 375–389.

McFall, R.M. A Review and Reformulation of the Concept of Social Skills. *Behavioural Assessment*, 4, (1982): 1–33.

O'Keefe, M. "Predictors of dating violence among high school students." *Journal of Interpersonal Violence*, 12, (1997): 546–568.

Patterson, G.R. *Coercive Family Process*. Eugene, OR: Castalia, 1982.

Perez, C.M., and Wisdom, C.S. "Childhood victimization and long-term intellectual and academic outcomes." *Child Abuse and Neglect*, 18, (1994): 617–633.

Pynoos, R.S., and Eth, S. "The Child as Witness to Homicide." *Journal of Social Issues*, 40(2), (1984): 87–108.

Smith, S.M., Rosen, K.H., Middleton, K.A., Busch, A.L., Lundeberg, K., and Carlton, R.P. "The intergenerational transmission of spouse abuse. A meta-analysis." *Journal of Marriage and the Family*, 62, (2000): 640–654.

Straus, M.A., Gelles, R.J., and Steinmetz, S. *Behind Closed Doors.* Doubleday, Anchor, 1980.

Sugarman, D.B., and Frankel, S.L. Patriarchical ideology and wife assault: A meta analytic review. *Journal of Family Violence*, 11, (1996): 13–40.

Walker, L. *Battered Women.* New York: Harper and Row, 1979.

Wolfe, D.A., Jaffe, P., Wilson, S.K., and Zak, L. "Children of battered women. The relation of child behaviour to family violence and maternal stress." *Journal of Consulting and Clinical Psychology*, 53, (1985): 657–665.

Wolfe, D.A., Wekerle, C., Reitzel-Jaffe, D., and Lefebre, L. "Factors associated with abusive relationships among maltreated and non-maltreated youth." *Development and Psychopathology*, 10, (1998). 61–85.

List of Contributors

Sumita Sarkar has been involved in gender studies for the past five years and is mainly specialized in gender and labour research. At present, she is Dean of Research at IBSAR, Belapur Campus, Navi Mumbai.

Susan Hawthorne is a Research Associate at Victoria University, Melbourne (Australia) and has a Ph.D. in Women's Studies and Political Science from the University of Melbourne.

Lovely Mamta Dhulia is associated with the Department of Psychology, University of Allahabad, Allahabad.

Purnima Singh is Professor, Department of Humanities and Social Sciences, IIT, Delhi.

Debjani Mukherjee is Head of the Department of Psychology at St. Thomas College, Bhilai, Chhattisgarh.

Promila Singh is heading the School of Studies in Psychology at Pt. Ravishankar Shukla University, Raipur, Chhattisgarh.

H.L. Kaila is Professor and Head (Psychology), S.N.D.T. Women's University, Mumbai.

Jayanti Gokhale is Deputy Director, Institute of Business Studies and Research (IBSAR), Karjat.

Nidhi Maheshwari is employed with DRDO for the last four years as a psychologist serving in Selection Centre East, Allahabad for the selection of Indian Army officers.

N.P. Singh is Scientist 'F' and heads Strategic Behaviour Division, Defense Institute of Phychological Research, DRDO, New Delhi.

Manjari Srivastava is Associate Professor in Human Resources and Behavioural Sciences Department, School of Business Management at NMIMS University, Mumbai.

Sibnath Deb is faculty in the Department of Applied Psychology, University of Calcutta, Kolkata.

Anjali Dewan is faculty in Home Science, St. Bede's College, Himachal Pradesh University, Shimla.

Debdulal Dutta Roy is Reader in the Psychology Research Unit of the Indian Statistical Institute, Kolkata.

Sujata Sharma is an alumnus of University of Delhi. She has taught psychology at IBHAS, Amity University. She has been working on mental health issues with adolescents and their families and has also been associated with a number of schools in Delhi.

Nishat Afroz is faculty in psychology, Mahila Mahavidyalaya, Banaras Hindu University, Varanasi.

Ranjana Mittra is Reader, Department of Psychology, Mahila Mahavidyalaya, Banaras Hindu University, Varanasi.

Roomana N. Siddiqui is associated with Department of Psychology, Women's College, Aligarh Muslim University, Aligarh.

Index

abstraction, 238
Afroz, N. and R. Mittra, 307, 318, 319
Agnihotri, Indu, 6
Alexander, M. Jacqui, 32
Alward, R., 90
Anandkrishnan, M., 229
Aneeja, G., 117
Anjaria, S.J., 162
Anthony, E.J. and B.J. Cohler, 319
Archer, S.L., 265
Armstrong-Stassen, Marjorie, 74
Arnold, K.D., K.D. Noble and R.F. Subotnik, 319
Ashmore, R.D. and Lee Jussim, 252
Atkinson, Ti-Grace, 24
Auglin, K. and A. Hollzoworth-Munroe, 330

Bandura, A.J., 331
Barnes, B.L. and R. Srinivas, 306, 308
Batliwala, S., 41, 43
battered woman syndrome, 328
 components of, 328
Baverman and Chowers, 93
Bellear, Lisa, 35
Bem, S.L., 139
Bergeron, Suzanne, 26
Bernard, 12
Berzonsky, M.D., 262
Beteille, A., 42
Bhave, J., 89, 90
Bhowmik, S.K. and N. More, 153
Bhowmik, S.K., 152, 153, 154, 156, 163, 164, 165, 166
Biebly and Biebly, 110
Bilsker, D.D., D. Schiedel and J. Mercia, 265
Blanchard, Eric, 12
Blassi, A. and K. Glodis, 252, 263
Blos, P., 260
Boserup, E., 45
Bourdieu, P. and L. Wacquant, 182
Breman, J., 10, 153
brick klin industry
 in India, 189, women workers in, 190–95
Brooks, A.K. and K.A. Edward, 269
Brown, D., 91, 97
Bystydzienski, J., 41

Calliot, R., 90, 95
Cangemi, J.P., 307

Caputi, Jane, 26, 28
Carlson, J.M. and M.S. Hyde, 318
Carr, J.L. and K.M. van Duesen, 330
casualization, 6, 192
Cecilia, N.G., 4, 5, 7
Celina, K. Armbrust, 10, 14
Chanana, K., 232, 233
Chang, R. and R.C. Page, 306
Chen, Martha, Renana Joabwala and Nanavati Reema, 166
Chodorow, N.J., 265
Choi, Jin-Sil and Jeeng, Seon-hee, 13
Chowdhry, U., 69
Chowdhury, S. Roy, 7, 8, 9
Clarke, De, 25
Cline, J., 137
Coan, R.W., 306
commodification of women, 12
conscientization of women, 45
  aspects of, 45
Constantinople, A., 266, 297
construction industry
  in India, 172, women's participation in, 171
construction workers
  in India, 171, women among, 171
Cook-Greuter, S., 306

Daftuar, C.N. and R. Sharms, 306
Dahl, R.J., 306
Das, A.K., 306
Dasgupta, B. and R. Lashley, 176
Davidson, T., 331
Davies, B., 259, 286, 288
Davis, S., 68
Deb, Sibnath, 206, 221, 222
Denton, M.A. et al., 201
Derrida, J., 3
Deutchman, J., 42
Devendra, K., 205
Dex, S., 4
domestic assistants/maids, 201
  in Kolkata (India), socio-economic profile of, 211–12; factors responsible for, 213; exploitation and harassment of, 215–19
  problems faced by, studies on, 201–8
Douvan, E.M. and J. Adelson, 265
Dugan, T.F. and R. Coles, 319
Duncan and Perucci, 111
Dutta Roy, D. and M. Paul, 237
Dutta Roy, D., 236,238, 239, 240
Duval, Shelley and Robert A. Wicklund, 253

Eagan, J., 3
Eagly, A.H. and S.J. Karau, 140
Eagly, A.H., M.G. Makhijani and B.G. Klonsky, 143
economic development
  process of, 151
economic empowerment, 46
  of women, 46, efforts towards, 46–49
Eddy, Fanny Ann, 33
Ede, M.M., 88
education, 49
  and self-actualization, 306
  role of, in empowering women, 49–52
empowerment, 41
  concept of, 41, from gender perspective, 41–43
Erez, M. and P. Christopher Early, 257
Erikson, E.H., 256, 260, 264, 268, 275, 285, 288

Ezumah. N. and C.M. Di Domennici, 14

family structure
impact of globalization, 9–11
family violence, 329
fallout of, 329–33
impact of, on children, 331–33; on battered females, 327–29
family-friendly workplace, 90
role of employers in providing, 95–113
Farmer, R., 306
feminization of labour/employment, 6
feminization of poverty, 14, 151
in India, 14
Fetzer, S.J., 318
Finkelhor, D. et al., 329
Flax, Jane, 267
Ford, J.G., 306
Foucault, M., 257
Fowler, A.E., 245
Freeman, M., 269
Freire, P., 41
Freud, S., 331
Fromm, E., 260

Gage, Carolyn, 33
Garmezy, N. and A. Tellegen, 319
gender bias, 61
gender equality, 42
in Indian Constitution, 43
gender induction
in armed forces, 131, role of society in, 145–46
perspectives on evolutionary, 136–37; historical, 137; neuro-biological, 137–39; psychological, 139–44; moral and ethical, 145
gender inequality, 45
gender justice, 43
gender, 3
impact of globalization on, 4–6
gender-based segregation, 200
gender-egalitarian society, 55
gender-empowerment approach, 55
Gergen, K.J. and M.M. Gergen,
Gergen, K.J., 257, 258
Ghosh, J., 7, 12
Giddens, A., 42
Gill, H.S., 176
Gilligan, Carol, 265
Giorgi, A., 257
global village, 305
globalization, 3
and heteropatriarchy, 24–34
and women labour force, 5–6
process of, 3, 227
Godbois, 90
Gosh, I., 14
Griffen, V., 42
Griffiths, Morwenna, 274
Grimshaw, J., 267, 274
Grotevant, Harold, 255, 262
Gulati, L., 10
Gundersheim, J., 318
Gutek, B.A. and B. Morasch, 144

Harding, S., 265
Harre, R., 252, 257
Hawthrone, Susan, 25, 29, 30, 31
Hayashi, R., J.W. Gibson and R.A. Weatherley, 203, 221
Hebsur, R.K., 8
Heilman, M.E., 142
Heipman, M.E. et al., 140
Helgeson, V.S. and H.L. Fritz, 142
Henry, C. and F.N. Washington, 68

heteropatriarchy, 23
  and globalization, 24–34
Hill, P., 158
Hoefferth, S.L., 92
Hopkins, L.B., 265
Hotaling, G.T. and D.B. Sugaman, 330
Hughes, H.M., 332
Humphrey, M. and C. Lehman, 319

identity
  and women, 263–67
  concept of, 251, 254–56
Indian Constitution, 200

Jaffe, P. and D. Wolfe et al., 332
Jaffe, P. and S. Wilson et al., 332
Jain, D., 4, 5, 12, 14
Jain, S. and L. Krishnamurthy, 51
Jameison, K.H., 139
James, Willaim, 331
Jameson, F. and M. Miyoshi, 3
Janoff-Bulman, R. and I. Frieze, 328
Jeffreys, Sheila, 33
Jhabvala, R., 165
job involvement, 60
Josselson, R.L., E. Greenberger and D. McConochie, 265
Josselson, Ruthellen, 264

Kabeer, N., 42
Kaila, H.L., 73, 86
Kakkar, S., 308, 331
Kalmus, D., 330
Karl, M., 14, 42
Kasper, K., M. Meyer and A. Schmidt, 73
Kegan, R., 306
Keller, E.F., 265
Kerr, B. et al., 307
Kessler, R.C. et al., 138
Khallar, M., 92
Kirkcaldy, B.D. and A.F. Furnham, 72
Kishwar, M. and R. Vanita, 12
knowledge-based society, 236
Kohut, Heinz, 252
Krishnaraj. M., 12,14
Kroger, J., 259
Kulkarni, A.V., 319
Kumar, R., 12, 14
Kundu, A., 176

labour force, 170
  in a developed economy, 170
  in a developing economy, 170
  in India, 171, 187, women in, 171, 200
labour market
  in developing countries, 171
Lacan, J., 257
Lackey, C., 330
Lawler, E.E. and D.T. Hall, 60
Lerman, H., 264
Levin, Jerome D., 257
liberalization
  in agriculture, 14, impact on women's status, 14–17
  process of, 7, in India, 7
Lipscomb, H.J. et al., 202
Logan, T.K. et al., 204
Longwe, S., 42
Lykes, M.B., 265

Machida, Tina, 32
Magdol, L. et al., 330
managerial stress, 72
  in Indian women, 75–84, strategies to cope with, 85–86
  studies on, 72–74

Mannheim, B., 64
Marasella, A.J., G.S. Devos and F.I.K. Hsu, 320
Marcia, J.E., 261, 265, 266, 280
Marsella, A.J. et al., 258
masculine disciplines, 227
Maslow, A.H., 305, 320
McAlindon, H.R., 307
McClure, B.A., K.L. Holladay and C.D. Faster, 318
McFall, R.M., 330
McKenna, J.J., 306
Menon, S., 89, 91
Merriam, S. and Caffarella, 307
Messias, D.K., J.M. Hall and A.I. Meleis, 204
Meyers, D. and F. Diener, 306
micro-credit, 165
  in India, 165–66
micro-enterprises, 152
micro-entrepreneurship, 152
micro-lending, 165
Miller, D.R., 256
Miller, J.B., 265
Misra, G., 320
Mitchell, J.C., 182
Morgan, Ruth and Saskia Wieringa, 33
Morrison, A.M. and M.A.V. Glinow, 142
Morrison, A.M., R.P. White and E.V. Velsor, 141
Moser, C.O.N., 40
Moshman, David, 255, 263
Mumbai, 173
  unorganized industrial sector in, 173, labour workforce in, 173
Murray, H.A. et al., 268
Musayon Oblitas, F.Y. and C. Caufield, 203, 221
Myers, R. and C. Indriso, 91

Nausbaum, K., 89, 90, 93
Navi Mumbai, 154, 173
  women hawkers in, 155–56: socio-economic status of, 156–58; organization and social networking of, 158–60; health and hygiene of, 160–61
Neisser, V., 257
Nelson, D.L. and R.J. Burke, 142
Niessen, A. and S. Ruenzi, 70
night shift working women, 89
  employers' role in providing family-friendly workplace to, 95–113
  in India, 89–90
  studies on, 90–93
Norlander, T., S.A. Bood and T. Archer, 306
Ntombela, N., 92, 125

O'Keepfe, M., 330
of women, in industrial sector, 66–70
Oi-ling, S., L. Luo and C. Cary, 73
Oyserman, Daphna and R.H. Markus, 258

Paranjpe, Anand, 267, 281
Parikh, Indira J. and Pulin K. Garg, 280
Patterson, G.R., 330
Peck, T.A., 264
Perez, C.M. and C.S. Wisdom, 332
Piaget, J., 253
Piocos, E., 70
Pynoos, R.S. and S. Eth, 332

Ramanaiah, N.V., J.R. Heerboth and D.L. Jinkerson, 306
Rane, A.J., 92

Rangaswami, K., 306
Rao, P.U.B. and A.V. Kulkarni, 319
Raymond, Janice G., 33
reading motivation, 236
  in primary school girls, 240–43
Reese, S., 93
Richman, J.A. et al., 202, 205, 221
Riessman, C.K., 258
Rivera, C., 108
Rivera-Fuentes, Consuelo and Linda Birke, 31
Robbins, Richard H., 256
Rose, K., 46
Rosener, S., 142
Rossi, A., 264
Rotella, R.J. et al., 318
Rustamfram, N., 89
Ryff, C.D., 306

Sampson, E.E., 265
Sarbin, T.R., 255
Sarkar, S., 156
Schein, V.E., 143
Schembri, Jim, 27
Schimink, 108
Schindler, T.M. and M. Waters, 318
Schostac, J., 307
Schunk, D.H. and B. Zimmerman, 236
Schunk, D.H., 236
self
  and identity, difference between, 252; perspectives on, 256–63
  concept of, 251, 253–54
  study of, 305
self-actualization
  concept of, 305–9
  education and, 306
  gender differentiation and, 311–17
self-actualizers, 306
Self-Help Groups (SHGs), 165
Sen and Snow, 92
Sen, A., 151, 152
Seppanen, P.S. et al., 92
Sharma, Maya, 34
Sharma, R.N., 153
Sharma, S. and V.K. Kapoor, 64
Sharma, S.L., 42,52
Sherrill, C. and W. Rainbolt, 318
Shostrom, E.L., 310
Shweder, R.A. and E.J. Bourne, 320
Sidhu, H.S., 175
Sims, O.V. and I. Napholz, 204
Singh, J.K. and G. Misra, 321
Sinha, D., 320
Smith, S.M. et al., 330
Straus, M.A., R.J. Gelles and S. Steinmetz, 330, 332
Strauss, A.S., 268
street vending
  legalization of, 164
Sugerman D.B. and S.L. Frankel, 330
Sunderson, K. and R. Crompton, 4
Surrey, J.L., 257
Surrey, J.L., 265
Swaminathan, M.C., 106, 108
Swanberg, J., C. Macke and T.K. Logan, 203, 204

Taap, A.M., R. Fontaine and Chong Siong Choy, 73
Tannenbaum, A.S., 64
Tasto, D.L. et al., 90
taxonomy, 239
Taylor, S.E. et al., 138
Thadani, Giti, 28, 30, 33, 34
Thompson, Denise, 27
Thorpe, 253
Tibaijuka, A., 14

Tiripano, Tsitsi, 33
Tiwari, G., 153, 154
Torbert, W.R., 306
Triandis, H.C. et al., 320

Unger, R., 264
unorganized labour, 187
  in India, 187, 195, women among the, 171, 187, 188–89
unorganized sector, 171, 195
  in India, 171, 188, women labour force in, 171, 187

Valian, V., 69
Venkataraman, S. and R.N. Anatharaman, 318
violence against women, 327

Wacks, V.Q., 307
Wajcman, J., 142
Walby, S., 4, 107
Walker, 110
Walker, L., 328
Wallace, 89
Wallace, A.F.C. and R. Fogelson, 256
Waterman, A.S., 263
White and Keith, 88
White, Robert, 268
Wieringa, S., 42
Wigfield, A. and J.T. Guthrie, 236
Wilson, S.R., 306
Wittig, Monique, 32
Wolfe D.A., P. Jaffe et al., 332
Wolfe, D.A., C. Wekerle et al., 330
women at work, 5, 73
  impact of globalization on, 5–6, 6–9
  women construction workers in, 173–74: migration of, 174–77; socio-economic status of, 177–80; health and hygiene of, 180–81
  women in, studies on, 152–53
  women labour force, 171
    in India, 171, 200, in unorganized sector, 171, 187, 188–89, 201
women
  and development, 40, theoretical approaches to, 40–41
  in armed forces, 131–35, in India, 135–36
  in industries, 59
  in micro-entrepreneurship, 151–52, in India, 152–54; in higher education, 229–31, impact of globalization on, 231–34
women's empowerment, 42
  conceptions of: unidimensional, 42; multidimensional, 42
  in political sphere, 53–54
  initiatives towards, 43, in India, 43–45
  role of education in, 49–52
women's rights, 52
women's status
  impact of liberalization in agriculture on, 14–17
women-centric development, 39
working in night shift
  phenomenon of, 78
working population
  in India, 88, women in, 89–90, 171

Ziegler, J.C. and U. Goswami, 245
Ziegler, M., 130